THE OXFORD
ILLUSTRATED HISTORY
OF NEW ZEALAND

This double canoe built with modern materials to the traditional Hawaiian design was sailed without compass or other navigational aids from Hawaii to Tahiti and returned (twice), from Samoa via Rarotonga to Tahiti and from Tahiti via Rarotonga to New Zealand. Photograph by Will Kyselka.

THE OXFORD ILLUSTRATED HISTORY OF NEW ZEALAND

EDITED BY
KEITH SINCLAIR

Auckland

OXFORD UNIVERSITY PRESS

Oxford   New York   Melbourne

Oxford University Press

Oxford University Press, Walton Street, Oxford OX2 6DP

OXFORD   NEW YORK   TORONTO
DELHI   BOMBAY   CALCUTTA   MADRAS   KARACHI
PETALING JAYA   SINGAPORE   HONG KONG   TOKYO
NAIROBI   DAR ES SALAAM   CAPE TOWN
MELBOURNE   AUCKLAND
and associated companies in
BERLIN and IBADAN

Oxford is a trademark of Oxford University Press

First Published 1990
© Oxford University Press 1990

ISBN 0 19 558209 8

Jacket designed by Hilary Ravenscroft
Photoset in Baskerville by Rennies Illustrations Ltd,
and printed in Hong Kong
Published by Oxford University Press
1A Matai Road, Greenlane, Auckland 5, New Zealand

Contents

Preface   vii

1. IN THE BEGINNING   1
   Bruce Biggs

2. THE MĀORI PEOPLE AND THE BRITISH CROWN (1769-1840)   21
   Claudia Orange

3. THE PIONEERS (1840-1870)   49
   Jeanine Graham

4. THE GOVERNORS AND THE MĀORI (1840-1872)   75
   James Belich

5. RAILWAYS AND RELIEF CENTRES (1870-1890)   99
   Raewyn Dalziel

6. CENTRALIZATION AND NATIONALISM (1891-1912)   125
   David Hamer

7. ANCESTRAL VOICES: MĀORI PROPHET LEADERS   153
   Judith Binney

8. THE FARMERS TAKE OVER (1912-1930)   185
   Miles Fairburn

9. DEPRESSION AND WAR (1931-1949)   211
   Erik Olssen

10. NEW ZEALAND IN THE WORLD (1914-1951)   237
    Malcolm McKinnon

11. THE NATIONAL GOVERNMENTS AND SOCIAL CHANGE (1949-1972)   267
    Barry Gustafson

12. NEW ZEALAND AND THE OTHER PACIFIC
ISLANDS   295
    Mary Boyd

13. MODERN MĀORI: THE YOUNG MAORI PARTY TO
MANA MOTUHAKE   323
    M.P.K. Sorrenson

14. HARD TIMES (1972-1989)   353
    Keith Sinclair

Further Reading   373
Index   382

Preface

One of New Zealand's earliest historians, William Pember Reeves, wrote a poem in which an Englishman writes to a colonist that New Zealand was a country 'Where men but talk of gold and sheep / And think of sheep and gold'. It was, he wrote,

A land without a past; a race
Set in the rut of commonplace

The colonist denies this; and certainly Reeves did not believe it himself. He wrote an outstanding short history of New Zealand. Nor is this the view of New Zealand presented here.

New Zealand is a country extremely remote from other lands. It was settled by two sea-faring peoples, Polynesian and British, after crossing immense oceans in small vessels. It was the scene of prolonged warfare in the nineteenth century and much earlier. Late last century it was hailed as 'the social laboratory of the world'. By 1893 it was the most democratic state in the world, or that had ever existed. In the late 1930s, with the introduction of 'social security', it was one of the first examples of the welfare state. Its history has been far from commonplace.

New Zealand has had numerous general histories, since the first history was published 140 years ago. The present volume does not altogether reject the outlines of its history as they have been analysed in earlier books. For instance, as in A. S. Thomson's *Story of New Zealand* (1859), and most other New Zealand histories, there is a strong emphasis on Māori history and on race relations, one rarely found in histories of comparable British former colonies like Australia and Canada. Moreover, the Māori do not disappear from the story in the late nineteenth century, as they do in some of our histories. The discussion of race relations continues up to the modern Waitangi Tribunal.

The outlines of political and economic history, of elections, booms and slumps, can scarcely ever be altered completely. The election of the Liberal Government in 1890 and of the Labour Government in 1935 remain as major turning points; Seddon and Savage are still seen as major figures. However, emphases do alter. Much less attention is given to the New Zealand Company and other colonizing agencies than in most earlier books. There is much less detail about constitutional history. On the other hand, there is far more social history than in almost any earlier history of the country. Hence the reader will learn a great deal about the lives of ordinary people, and rather less about politicians and legislation. And where politicians remain central, they are sometimes regarded in a different light from in the past; Miles Fairburn, for instance, presents 'Bill' Massey in an original light.

The women's movement had a major influence on New Zealand society in the 1970s for the first time since the 1890s. The importance of women's history is emphasized: indeed, there is probably more discussion of that topic than in any previous general history of the country.

The Oxford Illustrated History of New Zealand summarizes, and brings to the attention of the public, recent advances in research into New Zealand history, as well as reflecting changing attitudes towards what written history should be. It also expresses, of course, the interests and views of the authors. They are all professional historians except for the linguist, Bruce Biggs, who writes the chapter on pre-European Māori society.

This book is intended for the general reader and for students, not for professional historians. Nevertheless, historians will also share with their colleagues new perspectives and insights into aspects of our past, for instance in Judith Binney's chapter on the Māori prophets.

The narrative is mainly chronological, with literary and art history woven into the story, and not discussed separately as in many national histories. However, there are specialist chapters on three topics, on the Māori prophetic tradition, on New Zealand and the Pacific islands, and on foreign policy up to 1951. External relations are also woven into the chapters on New Zealand history since then.

The illustrations contribute significantly to one's understanding of New Zealand history. It is important to *see* Seddon or Grey as well as to read about them. Photographs give us some sense of their personal presences. Jeanine Graham makes a special effort to integrate the visual historical evidence with the written. The camera came to New Zealand in about 1850, only ten years after the first planned settlement, so the country's European and modern Māori history is extremely well illustrated by photographs.

I should like to thank Ms Anne French, the Publisher, who also carried out much of the picture research, for her contributions to this book. Librarians in the Alexander Turnbull Library, the Hocken Library, the National Museum, Canterbury Museum, Otago Early Settlers Museum, Auckland Institute and Museum, Nelson Provincial Museum and other libraries were extremely helpful in finding relevant pictures.

KEITH SINCLAIR

1. In the Beginning

BRUCE BIGGS

Long after the great island chains of the western Pacific had been settled, the myriad small islands of the eastern ocean remained empty. Then, 3000 years ago, a seafaring people from the west who had already settled in Fiji, migrated against the trade winds, to settle Samoa and Tonga. They were root-crop agriculturists, fishermen, and potters who made fine, decorated pottery now called Lapita after the site in New Caledonia where it was first identified by archaeologists. But above all they were seafarers.

Their vessels, built from the great timber trees of Fiji, were capable of carrying perhaps fifty people on long voyages. Their navigators used guiding stars (*kaveinga*)[1] especially in equatorial latitudes where the fixed stars follow a straight path from east to west each night. Knowing the star that passed perpendicularly over one's island provided a homing beacon for the discoverers probing ever further to the east. When provisions ran low without a landfall being made, it was always possible to call off the beat against the prevailing trade winds and run down-wind on a reach. As long as the appropriate star rose to the zenith each night one could be sure of heading for home.

By the time of Christ, the people who may now be called the Polynesians had discovered and settled islands as distant as the Marquesas, 10,000 kilometres east of Fiji.

To strike north posed a more difficult navigational problem for the explorers. As one moves into higher latitudes the apparent star paths become parabolic and only when they are rising or setting do stars provide a reliable guide to direction. The Pole Star, which always indicates due north, would help explorers to maintain direction on an outward voyage but a real problem would arise on attempting to return from an unsuccessful probe. Although raising the appropriate star to the zenith would locate the right latitude it would not determine whether the returning voyagers were east or west of home.

A wrong guess would send them in exactly the wrong direction. A possible way of overcoming this problem, one which has been used successfully in modern

---

[1] Words in italics are reconstructions of Central Eastern Polynesian, the language immediately ancestral to Māori.

experiments in navigating without instruments, is to sail deliberately too far east (or west) and then, when the appropriate star is directly above, to sail west (or east), 'running down the parallel' of latitude until the landfall is made.

We do not know whether this technique was actually used by Polynesian explorers. We do know that by 400 A.D. Polynesians from the Marquesas islands had settled the Hawaiian islands 5000 kilometres to the north-west. Whether any of the settlers could or did return to their Marquesan homeland we cannot determine, but there is some evidence for a second settlement of Hawaii from even more distant Tahiti.

In the extreme south-west, New Zealand still lay apart and empty as it had done for more than fifty million years since the breakup of the ancient Gondwanaland continent. More isolated by the vastness of the world's greatest ocean than other lands, and occupied only by birds and coastal mammals, it was now the last habitable land mass of any size to remain unpeopled.

Ko te papa o te rangi e tū iho nei	The floor of heaven above
Poka i runga, poka i raro	Pierce it above and below;
Wāwāhia te tāuhi rangi,	Split the cover of heaven,
Patupatua te tāuhi rangi.	Destroy the cover of heaven.
Whakamoea Taihoro-nukurangi	Lay Taihoro-nukurangi to rest.
Tītoko nga pewa o Rehua i te rangi	Raise Antares' brow in the sky.
Ka marewa Atutahi, ka rere Tautoru,	Canopus rises, Orion is on high,
Ka whakamau ake ahau	And I hold fast
Ki a Pātari-kaihau.	To the Smaller Magellan Cloud.
Ka kōwhiti te marama, he pae whenua,	The moon is new on the horizon,
Ka whiti au.	When I cross.
Ko Aotea! Ko Aotea!	To Aotea! To Aotea!

(Te Karakia o Ruānui, Ruānui's Chant *JPS* 66:227, 243, trans. B.B.)

The discovery of Hawaii from the Marquesas was a remarkable achievement, but at twenty degrees north latitude Hawaii is still within the zone of the trade winds that blow steadily and predictably for half of each year. New Zealand lies far to the south of the trade winds, in the stormy waters and unpredictable weather of the Tasman Sea. The southern hemisphere, moreover, has no Pole Star to provide a constant compass point.

In spite of these difficulties, on an early summer day rather more than a thousand years ago, a well-provisioned catamaran crewed by Polynesians from either the Cook Islands or Tahiti broke through te taha atu o te rangi (the far side of the sky) and made its landfall on the north-eastern coastline of the North Island. According to a well-known tradition, the canoe was the Mata-hourua (hourua is the Māori equivalent of Polynesian *foulua* 'catamaran') and it was captained by Kupe.

An aerial photograph of Rarotonga, a small but high island about 3,000 kilometres north-east of New Zealand. Some traditions suggest that this is the island from which New Zealand was settled. *RNZAF*

The crew had, by good luck or good management, taken advantage of the favourable weather patterns that sometimes occur in the early summer months and, sailing between the atmospheric depressions that move unceasingly from the west across the Tasman, had avoided the danger of being swept too far east into the emptiness of ocean that reaches south to the Antarctic ice-pack, and raised the new land without undue difficulty.

As was their wont, the women aboard had guarded carefully a small stock of viable plant material which included coconuts (*niu*), paper mulberry (*aute*) cuttings, gourd (*fue*) seeds and yam (*ufi*), sweet potato (*kuumala*) and Colocasia (*talo*) tubers. They were planted immediately and carefully tended, for the future quality of life depended on their successful propagation.

It would be found that in spite of arriving during the appropriate planting season of early summer, several of the species were doomed by New Zealand's temperate climate. But at least the few precious seed kūmara, remembered by Te Arawa and Tainui people as te kete rukuruku a Whakaoti-rangi (the closed-up kit of Whaka-otirangi), were to survive.

An indication of the landfall is provided by the survival of the kūmara. In Polynesia the sweet potato grows all year round and is propagated by slips. Only in the north of the North Island would the first plants have survived through the New Zealand winter to provide growing slips for next year's crop. A stroke of luck had landed the voyagers in the only part of New Zealand that allowed the familiar technique of cultivation to continue for a time. Further south and inland, frosts precluded the growing of sweet potato until a way had been discovered of storing the tubers under carefully controlled conditions of temperature and humidity.

The kūmara came through, together with the paper mulberry, the taro, the gourd and, marginally, the yam. Other plants that were brought, coconuts certainly and perhaps plantains and breadfruit, failed.

The settlers were less successful in transporting livestock from home. Perhaps the exigencies of the voyage resulted in their arriving with no pigs, but at least one pregnant dog had survived and, according to tradition, smelt the new land before it could be seen. There was one stowaway, the Polynesian rat (*kiore*).

The new land, which even before they landed was seen to be incomparably larger than the islands they knew, was without quadrupeds, but it swarmed with birds, including flightless birds that stood nearly twice as high as a man. Countless sea-birds nested here, the coastal waters teemed with fish, and the inter-tidal zone held a much greater variety of succulent molluscs than any tropical island. Great seal rookeries were dotted about the coast and on outlying islands. Initially, at least, there was no shortage of protein.

As exploration proceeded, everything was found to be on an unfamiliarly large scale. The mountains were higher, and the highest were clothed in an unfamiliar whiteness that the discoverers could only call foam (*fuka*). The rivers, wider and deeper than the streams of home were likened to, and named *awa* after the deep passes into the island lagoons. There were great bodies of inland water too, which, knowing no lakes, they called lagoons (*roto*) or seas (*moana*).

In all the islands with which they were familiar the vegetation, originating as it did almost entirely from south-east Asia, consisted of virtually the same, relatively few species. But the New Zealand flora, through its ancient Gondwanaland connection, has much in common with that of both Australia and South America and its subsequent long isolation had resulted in the evolution of many endemic genera and species which were unfamiliar.

The old names were bestowed on each new plant that shared some feature of those at home. But the New Zealand bush contains such a variety of plant life that the East Polynesian botanical vocabulary was insufficient and the settlers were forced into coining new, compound names.

Perhaps the most useful plant in Polynesia, after the coconut, is the pandanus (*fara*) whose long, narrow leaves are plaited into mats and baskets. There was no pandanus here, but a number of plants had leaves or flowers which resembled it. The two species of New Zealand flax were called hara-keke (strong-pandanus) and whara-riki (small-pandanus), respectively, and the epiphytic Collospermum was called the kō-whara-whara (pseudo-pandanus), while the edible flower bract of Freycinetia was called tā-whara (pandanus fruit), *taa* being their word for a hand of bananas.

The Malay apple (*kafika*) does not grow here, but its Polynesian name is a component of at least three New Zealand tree names: the kahika, better known today as the pohutukawa, whose many-stamened flowers are similar to those of the Malay apple; the kahika-tea (white *kafika*) whose fruit, like those of its namesake, are edible; and the kahika-a-toa (warrior kahika), better known as mānuka, from whose hard, tough timber weapons were fashioned.

New Zealand as it looked to the first Polynesians. Its size dwarfs the total land mass of Polynesia. Photograph by Quentin Christie. *DSIR Division of Land and Soil Sciences*

This sort of linguistic adjustment and invention can suggest the likely homeland of the Māori. Of particular interest are new, apparently coined names, for creatures whose distribution is restricted in Polynesia. The handsome bird *Porphyrio*, for example, was common in western Polynesia, where it is called *kalae*. In New Zealand it is called pākura (red head) in eastern Māori dialects and pūkeko (the side-glancer) elsewhere. This suggests that the discoverers of New Zealand came from an island (such as Rarotonga or Tahiti or even the Marquesas) where there were no swamp-hens.

The Māori words for seal are all peculiar to New Zealand and are probably innovations referring to various characteristics of these animals: kekeno (look about), ihu-piro (smelly nose), kake-rangi (sky-climber, perhaps from the habit of rearing up). As seals were found in the Marquesas but not in Tahiti or Rarotonga, the Marquesas are counter-indicated as the Māori homeland.

A slightly different line of reasoning provides another item of evidence against a Marquesan homeland. The proto-Polynesian word for duck (*toloa*) retains that meaning in the Marquesas but was redefined as gannet in Tahiti and Rarotonga. In New Zealand the word means albatross.

Much can be inferred about the small group of 'founders' who carried the restricted gene pool which would ensure that their descendants differed in small but significant ways from the populations of Hawaiki. The voyagers were young and fit. The old and the sick do not set out on strenuous voyages of discovery and we may be sure that theirs was such a voyage, for experienced seafarers would not stray by accident so far from the familiar equatorial star paths. It has been demonstrated by computer-simulation that drifting from south-east Polynesia to New Zealand is extremely unlikely. In any case the successful importation of food plants confirms that the first canoe to touch our shore was not some disabled drifter. Quite possibly all of the voyagers were potential breeders.

From skeletal and other evidence it is known that their early New Zealand descendants were tall and muscular, the men averaging five foot seven inches, the women being noticeably shorter. Men and women shared the task of paddling canoes as is indicated by the presence of a particular groove on the lower surface of the collarbone. The life span was short, averaging perhaps thirty-five years, and the women seldom had more than four children.

Though their general nutrition was adequate they suffered from diseases of the gums, occasioned by a generally soft diet, which suggests that the fibrous fern root was not adopted as a staple food for some time after the first settlement.

Significantly, the discoverers brought none of the viruses and bacteria that cause measles, rubella, chicken-pox, scarlet fever, gonorrhea or mumps. Nor were they carriers of the more serious scourges of tuberculosis, smallpox or syphilis. Yaws, a disease related to syphilis, was common in Polynesia, but it did not reach, or did not survive in New Zealand. In spite of early statements that leprosy occurred in New Zealand, current medical opinion is sceptical. Evidence of severe, even crippling

A Māori chief drawn by the French artist de Sainson in 1827 at Bream Bay, near Whangarei. *Auckland Museum*

arthritis is widespread in the skeletal record. Infection from decaying teeth and pneumonia were probably major killers.

Everything in the new land was unfamiliar or exaggerated. Even the summer days that marked their arrival were longer than any experienced in lower latitudes, prompting the name Aotea-roa (long daylight). Higher mountains, rougher seas, marked seasonal variation, great tidal range, many different soil and rock types, more and different fish, shellfish, birds, trees and plants. A vast supermarket awaiting its first customers.

All of these differences demanded major adjustments to the old way of life, but none more than the change of climate. The cool, open-sided houses of the tropics had to be replaced by smaller, cosier, walled dwellings. The felted bark-cloth garments were neither warm nor weather-proof and were eventually replaced by hand-woven capes of durable flax fibre, but that would demand a new weaving technique which would not be invented immediately.

Among the discoverers was at least one expert in Eastern Polynesian mythology, one of the world's great oral literatures. This must be so because comparative folklore shows that the Māori retained as much of the old mythology as any Polynesian people. Passed by word of mouth for a thousand years, the essential identity of say, the Marquesan and Māori versions of the story of *Tafaki* who climbed the heavens, or *Maui* who fished up new lands, is astonishing.

Mythology explains the otherwise inexplicable and justifies the natural and social order. In the Māori creation myth Rangi the male sky mated with Papa the female earth to produce sons, each of whom personified a division of nature — Tangaroa, the ocean, fish and reptiles; Tāwhiri, winds and weather, and so on. The sons, irked by their cramped quarters between the bodies of the primal lovers finally succeeded in separating them. They then formed from earth the first female, Hine-a-tauira, the Model Maid.

Tāne, the first-born of the Sons of Heaven, was assigned to fertilize Hine. She bore a daughter who was taken to wife by her father. Her horror, on learning her husband's true identity, provides the charter for the taboo on incest. She fled to Te Po (the Night World) which had preceded Te Ao (the World of Light) in the evolution of the universe. There she remained as guardian of the realm from which children are conceived and to which all must return when te ringa kaha o Aitua (the strong arm of death) strikes.

When Tāne pursued her and begged her to return, she said succinctly, 'Haere koe ki Te Ao hei whakatupu i ā tāua tamariki; tukua au ki Te Po hei kukume mai' (Go back to the World of Light and rear our children; leave me here in the Night World to gather them in).

Later, the hero Māui, fisher of lands and discoverer of fire, was killed when he endeavoured to reverse the process of birth by creeping into Hine's body. The myth is explicit that had he succeeded people would not die. Death remains invincible, requited only by te maringi o te roimata (the shedding of tears).

The Māori ancestors modified the old Polynesian mythology somewhat to suit their new circumstances. The great forests of New Zealand played a large part in their new lives and Tāne, god of forests and bird-life became more important in the New Zealand pantheon where he alone of the Sons of Heaven was equal to the task of forcing the sky away from the earth to allow the human race to develop. The sweet potato's increased importance as a food crop and the difficulties associated with growing it here demanded special ritual protection so its care was assigned to a new god Rongo-mā-tāne, in whose name we may detect Rongo the old god of peace and prosperity in combination with Tāne.

The detailed similarity of the Polynesian and Māori myths prove that it is possible for information to be preserved orally for many centuries. The myths are obviously mythical, dealing as they do with gods and heroes. They are succeeded in the Māori historical sequence by stories of the discovery and settlement of New Zealand by canoe voyagers from Hawaiki, stories that in a broad sense must be true. New Zealand was settled from Eastern Polynesia, and they could only have come by canoe.

Uia mai koe e nga whenua	When people ask you
Ki te kauwhau whakapapa,	To recite your pedigree,
Māu e kī atu,	You must say,
Wareware ko au, he tamariki,	"I am forgetful, a child,
Tēnei anō te rangona ake nei,	But this is well-known,
Tainui, Te Arawa, Mātātua,	Tainui, Te Arawa, Mātātua,
Kura-haupō, Toko-maru,	Kura-haupō and Toko-maru,
Nga waka ēnā o ō tūpuna	Were the ancestral canoes
I hoea ai te moana nui.	That crossed the great sea.
E takoto nei.	Which lies here.

(Te Waiata a Peou moTe Tahuri, Peou's Lament *Nga Moteatea* V.2 p.266, trans. B.B.)

The canoe traditions, and most if not all tribes feature a named canoe in their traditions of origin, agree on several significant points: there were a number of canoes; they all made their landfall on the east coast of the North Island; they all came from a place named Hawaiki; they arrived (by genealogical reckoning) about five or six hundred years ago.

It is certain that the settlers came from the Eastern Polynesia, where the name Hawaiki is well-known, and arrived at a part of New Zealand where the climate was warm enough to grow at least some of the tropical plants they brought with them. The genealogical chronology raises a problem, however, since we now know that New Zealand was already occupied from North Cape to the Bluff at least nine hundred years ago.

There are several possible explanations. After the initial discovery more than a thousand years ago there may have been several later arrivals. At present it is not possible to support this with other than traditional evidence. Alternatively, the canoe traditions may refer, not to settlement direct from Polynesia, but to migration from one part of New Zealand to another. There is archaeological evidence such as the distribution of the type of fortified position called ring-ditch, that suggests an early expansion southwards from North Auckland at about the time that genealogies place the canoe traditions. But the question is by no means settled.

Aku ara ra ko Tūrongo,	My path is Tūrongo
I wawaea ki te tai rāwhiti,	Who travelled to the east
Ko Māhina-a-rangi,	And Māhina-a-rangi
Ko te rua ra i moe ai a Raukawa.	The womb where Raukawa slept
Na Raukawa ko Rereahu	Raukawa had Rereahu
Na Rereahu ko Maniapoto,	Rereahu had Maniapoto,
He ara tautika mai ki ahau.	A direct path to myself.

(Te Pātere a Ngoki, Ngoki's Chant, unpublished, trans. B.B.)

Rangi-tuke, a chief from Kawakawa who had spent some time in Sydney, was painted by Augustus Earle at Russell in 1827. *Alexander Turnbull Library*

As the population increased, possibly doubling every thirty years, and as people dispersed throughout the country, separate tribal groups developed, groups which passed on tales of their origins. These historical traditions tend to be vague about the period subsequent to the arrival of the canoe and prior to the establishment of the tribe, a point marked in the genealogies by the name of the founding ancestor, whose name it usually bore. Then the traditions and the validating genealogies become more coherent, self-consistent and detailed.

Typically, tribal tradition begins with incidents associated with the arrival of the ancestral canoe and a genealogy linking one or more of the crew with present generations. Then there is a gap of several (genealogical) centuries which is bridged sketchily, or perhaps only by a single genealogy, until the time, ten to fifteen generations before the present, of the ancestor from whom all members of the particular tribe descend. Increasing detail fills out the traditional record from this point on, but the pieces of the mosaic may be known only to the descendants of the individuals concerned.

An example is a segment of the history of the North Island tribes who claim descent, wholly or in part, from the crew of the Tainui canoe, and who, by the nineteenth century, occupied the territory from the Auckland isthmus and the Hauraki plains south to the mouth of the Mokau river and the western shores of Lake Taupo. Along their eastern boundary they impinged on the descendants of Te Arawa, another ancestral canoe. Their western boundary was the Tasman Sea.

Those who regarded themselves as being of Tainui descent were divided into many tribes, subtribes and sub-subtribes. Two of the largest divisions, the Waikato tribes of the Waikato and Lower Waipa river valleys and of the west coast north of Kawhia and Ngāti Maniapoto of the King Country, have a traditional history which is particularly well known.

It begins with the arrival of Tainui, the ancestral canoe, which made its landfall at Cape Runaway in the north-eastern Bay of Plenty at the beginning of summer when the pohutukawa trees were in bloom. One of the chiefs, remarking on the profusion of red ornaments in the new land threw his treasured red-feather head-dress into the tide where it was washed ashore and found later by another who, when asked to return it, refused with the quip 'he kura pae, whano kē' (cast away treasure is gone forever) a saying equivalent to the English expression, 'finder's keepers'.

After a quarrel with the people of Te Arawa over the ownership of a stranded whale, the chiefs Hoturoa and Raka-taura took Tainui northwards into the Tāmaki River, subsequently a northern boundary of the tribal territory, and hauled it across the narrow isthmus into the Manukau Harbour. They then sailed down the west coast of the North Island as far as the mouth of the Mokau River, later the southern boundary of the tribal territory. There they left one of the anchors, a dumb-bell shaped stone which now lies in the grave-yard at Mānia-roa marae.

Returning northwards the canoe came into Kawhia Harbour where its final resting-place is marked by the two stone pillars Hani and Puna near the marae at Maketu. Kawhia was the centre from which the Tainui tribes expanded to populate the area demarcated by the saying 'Tāmaki ki raro, Mōkau ki runga; Manga-toatoa ki waenganui; Pare-Hauraki, Pare-Waikato, te kaokao roa o Pā-te-tere' (Tāmaki in the north, Mōkau in the south with Manga-toatoa in the midst; the bastions of Hauraki and Waikato and the long rib of Pā-te-tere).

Tāwhao, a chief six or seven generations below Hoturoa the leader of the Tainui canoe, lived at Kawhia with his wives, the sisters Punui-a-te-kore and Maru-te-hiakina, both of whom conceived at about the same time and brought forth sons. Whatihua, the child of the junior wife, was born shortly before Tūrongo, the child of the senior wife, a fact which has provided grist for tribal arguments down the centuries. Let each tribe say who was senior.

The half-brothers Whatihua and Tūrongo grew up together at Kawhia. Tūrongo courted a Taranaki woman named Rua-pū-tahanga who was to join him at Kawhia. While making preparations for her arrival Tūrongo was tricked by Whatihua into

These carvings in the meeting-house on Waipapa marae at the University of Auckland depict the priest, Raka-taura and the high chief Hoturoa of the Tainui canoe. *University of Auckland*

building a guest-house that was too small to accommodate her retinue.

Whatihua then invited Rua-pū-tahanga and her party to occupy his larger guest-house and took the opportunity to alienate the lady's affections by pointing out that her intended was nothing but he tahā wairere (a leaky calabash), unable to extend appropriate hospitality to guests.

The upshot was that Whatihua married Rua-pū-tahanga. The jilted Tūrongo left, not for overseas, as would have been the case in the Polynesian homeland, but over-land to te tai-rāwhiti (the eastern coast) where, at a village within sight of today's Te Aute college, he met and married Māhina-a-rangi. When Māhina-a-rangi became pregnant Tūrongo decided to take her back to his own territory. The child, a boy named Raukawa, was born during the trek, by the warm springs at O-koroire.

Tawhao then divided the Tainui territory between his two sons, the half-brothers Whatihua and Tūrongo. From the Puniu River, just south of Te Awamutu, to Tamaki, (now Auckland) was Whatihua's. To Tūrongo went the land south of the Puniu. Thus the two half-brothers mark a main division of the Tainui people into Turongo's descendants, the Ngāti Raukawa and Ngāti Maniapoto, and the Waikato tribes, descendants of Whatihua.

Tūrongo's son Raukawa became the eponymous ancestor of the people who occupied the north-eastern portion of Turongo's domain, which borders the Waikato River and contains the great mountain Maungatautari. In the early nineteenth century many Ngāti Raukawa followed Te Rauparaha to the southern part of the North Island where they continue to occupy the area about Otaki.

Raukawa had a son, Rereahu, famous chiefly for producing with his second wife Hine-au-pounamu, eight children, of whom several became name ancestors of important tribal groups of later years. Maniapoto, oldest of Hine-au-pounamu's children is the eponymous ancestor of Ngāti Maniapoto, the tribe that includes, for some purposes at least, Ngāti Matakore, Ngāti Kinohaku, and Ngāti Rereahu, the descendants of his brother, sister and father respectively, thus contradicting the general rule that the eponymous ancestors of subtribes are descendants of the tribal eponym. That some descendants of Rereahu are currently endeavouring to re-assert their separate identity from the descendants of his son Maniapoto illustrates that history has a future as well as a past dimension.

The Māori trace ancestry and descent through both males and females, a method which greatly increases the number of genealogical lines to be remembered. As the proverb has it 'he kāwai hue, he kāwai tangata' (human pedigrees are like the runners of a gourd plant). The complexity is simplified a little by the concept of tāhuhu (ridgepoles) or aho ariki (chiefly lines) which consist ideally of first-born males. One's genealogical status is indicated, but not necessarily determined, by the number of generations one is away from the aho ariki.

Consider the tāhuhu from Maniapoto, eponymous ancestor of Ngāti Maniapoto, and first-born of the eight children of his mother Hine-au-pounamu and Turongo's grandson Rereahu, to Wētere te Rerenga, a prominent nineteenth century chief of Ngāti Maniapoto. It is an unbroken male line to which most tribal pedigrees will attach at some point.

Maniapoto = Hine-mania
|
Te Kawa-irirangi I = Mārei
|
Runga-te-rangi = Pare-raukawa
|
Mania-opetini = Pare-raumoa
|
Tai te Ngahue = Kaputuhi
|
Mania-uruahu (Te Kanawa-whero) = Oneone
|
Taikehu (Tūkehu)
|
Te Kawa-irirangi II
|
Rangi-tuataka
|
Te Kawa-irirangi III
|
Tākerei
|
Wētere te Rerenga

It has been said that much of tribal history concerns murder and revenge. This, and the role played by the tensions occasioned by inter-tribal marriages, can be illustrated from the fragment of genealogy above. Te Kawa-irirangi I was killed by his brother-in-law; his son Runga-te-rangi was killed by *his* brothers-in-law while he was seeking to avenge the murder of his half-brother Tukemata at the hands of *his* brothers-in-law. Runga-te-rangi's son Mania-opetini was drowned in the Waikato River on the way to avenge his grandfather's death.

Tūrongo's brother Whatihua, traditional lord of the northern domains, and his stolen bride Rua-pū-tahanga had two sons, each named for the Hawaikiian ancestor Uenuku. Jealous of Whatihua's other wife Apakura, Rua-pū-tahanga returned home to Taranaki, leaving her baby son Uenuku-te-rangi-hōkā behind.

On reaching adulthood the latter joined his mother's people in Taranaki and there his son Hotunui was born. Hotunui returned to Kāwhia and married there. His wife's people accused him of theft and he, despite the fact that his wife was pregnant, left Kāwhia and went off to the Hauraki district, leaving instructions about the naming of the new baby. The son, Maru-tūahu, later joined his father and became the name-ancestor of the Hauraki tribe Ngāti Maru.

Whatihua = Rua-pū-tahanga
|
Uenuku-te-rangi-hōkā
|
Hotunui
|
Maru-tūahu

Enough has been said to show how the traditions validate, in a relatively detailed and consistent way, the existing disposition and interrelationships of the tribes of Tainui. Their historical accuracy can be disputed but hardly disproved.

During the centuries after the first discovery of New Zealand the ancestors had adjusted to and coped with an environment vastly different from the tropical islands of the ancestral Hawaiki. They had increased in numbers from possibly a single canoe crew to in excess of 100,000, occupying the coasts and the shores of the country's rivers and lakes in some density and the great forested areas of the interior rather more sparsely. They were familiar with every inch of the mainland and the off-shore islands. The whole country was claimed by one tribal group or another, by long occupation and use, or by more recent conquest.

Old techniques had been adapted and new ones invented to exploit the resources of land and sea. A way of life based on villages but involving a good deal of temporary dwelling near seasonal resources was the pattern over most of the country. The density of population and the size of the group that lived and worked together varied with the nature of the environment. Groups living in fertile northern areas with a

A fortified village at the time of Cook's third voyage. Drawing by Webber. *Alexander Turnbull Library*

largely agricultural economy were larger than those more dependent on hunting and gathering.

During the centuries of exploration, settlement and population increase, the new environment had been subject to changes, none of them catastrophic and some due to their own impact on it. Two of the main protein sources of the first centuries, the giant flightless birds and the mainland seal rookeries were depleted or had disappeared entirely. In the South Island in particular great areas of forest had been destroyed by fires. New Zealand was not quite the untouched, unspoiled land their ancestors had discovered.

Nevertheless the changes had been gradual and there had been nothing like the drastic readjustment demanded of their founding ancestors. With the advent of Europeans and their culture a new equally drastic and sudden change of environment would follow without further migration on their part. Steel, potatoes, and pigs were the first major agents of change.

It would be difficult to overstate the impact of steel on a stone-age technology, especially one where bush-clearing and wood-working are important. Contemporary observations about the shift from stone to steel in New Zealand are virtually absent, probably because it took place so rapidly. In the New Guinea highlands where the change took place just fifty years ago, stone implements were totally abandoned as soon as steel was obtainable; and steel moved along traditional trade routes ahead of actual contact between whites and natives. It can be assumed that much the same thing happened in New Zealand. Greywacke and argillite adzes were simply laid

2. *Défrichement d'un Champ de Patates.*

By 1827, when this drawing was made, potatoes had replaced fern-root as the staple food throughout New Zealand. Drawing by de Sainson. *Auckland Museum*

aside, but previously treasured greenstone adzes were re-shaped into equally valuable neck pendants (hei tiki) sculpted into human images whose outlines conformed to the shape of the original adzes.

The news of the advantage of metal travelled fast. When the British explorer, Captain James Cook, arrived at one hitherto uncontacted place, the Māori requested iron, but were unable to recognize it when it was offered. Later voyagers found an insatiable demand for iron and steel in the form of large nails from which chisels could be fashioned, knives, plane irons (to be used as adze-blades), axe-heads and even hoop-iron. Such items made it infinitely easier to fell trees and to dress and carve timber.

Cook had planted potatoes at Doubtful Sound in 1773 and found them still growing two years later. Root agriculturists would not be slow to see the advantage of a hardy, quick-maturing crop that required little attention between planting and harvesting. By 1805 Māoris were growing 'immense quantities' of potatoes and some maize at the Bay of Islands. In 1813 Māori potato plantations more than forty hectares in size were seen at Bluff in the extreme south of the South Island, an indication of the enthusiasm with which the Māori received a storable carbohydrate source that would grow anywhere in New Zealand and not be confined to a few favourably warm areas. Potatoes replaced fern-root entirely, and kūmara largely, as the source of carbohydrates. The latter required careful tending, tricky storage and favourable growing conditions. Potatoes grew anywhere, easily, and were easy to store.

The European voyagers carried a surprising amount of livestock with them. In 1769 the French explorer Jean de Surville presented a pair of hogs to a Māori chief at North Cape and urged him to breed from them. In 1773, Cook's second expedition liberated pigs, geese, barnyard fowls and goats in the South Island, as well as planting various vegetables, including, most importantly, the potato. In 1805 twenty-six sows, four boars and two goats were sent to the Bay of Islands from Norfolk Island by P.G. King, governor of New South Wales. Pigs were the animals that found most favour. They were fenced out of the cultivations rather than in enclosures, being allowed to run free in the bush and uncultivated lands. In short order, pork became the main source of protein and areas of bush once valued for their fowling potential were now seen mainly as pig runs.

The earliest imports from the West were not all advantageous. In 1790, or thereabouts, an epidemic 'of a dysenteric character' called rewharewha spread from the Mercury Bay area, and about five years later a disease called tingara (sic, perhaps te ngārara) broke out at the Bay of Islands and 'spread like fire among flax'. Scrofula, a form of tuberculosis, was prevalent by the early nineteenth century and by the middle of the century, epidemics of influenza, whooping cough, mumps, measles and scarlet fever had attacked the Māori population.

Much has been made of the role of mana (power based on hereditary rank and personal achievement) and tapu (ritual prohibitions) as social controls in Māori society. Equally important was a general aggressiveness which settled disturbances of the social order by some form of conflict.

Within the group, infringements were dealt with by institutionalized plundering called muru whereby the offender was harangued, physically attacked and stripped of material possessions. Intra-group quarrelling marked not only breaches of custom (breaking the law) but social imbalances and realignments caused by such universal features of the human condition as marriage and death. There must be few other societies where guests were (and are) welcomed by such displays of hostility as the distorted features, protruding tongues and threatening shouts of the haka (war dance) provide and where the lack of disputation over the final resting-places of the deceased is seen as belittling them.

Offences committed by other groups demanded lethal retaliation. In settling both internal and external conflict the executant body was called taua (attacking party) and the aggression was termed whawhai (fighting). Utu was demanded in both cases, a word whose meaning is compensation although in appropriate contexts it can be translated as revenge.

The Māori were a fierce people, as the first arrivals from Europe found to their cost. Forty men were killed from the crews of Cook, the Dutch explorer Abel Tasman and the ill-fated French explorer Marion du Fresne. Cook in particular had ample opportunity to note and comment on evidence of hostility between Māori groups. Inter-tribal warfare was endemic and male children were dedicated at birth to

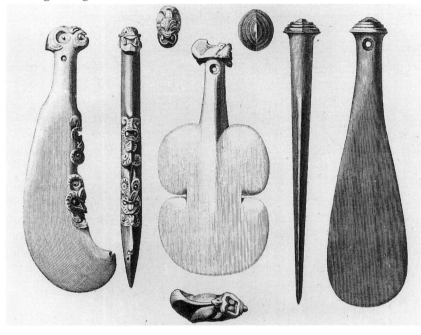

Although stones and spears were sometimes thrown, most Māori fighting was hand to hand with short clubs (patu, mere) or hand-spears (taiaha, māipi, tao). Drawing by Hawkesworth. *Alexander Turnbull Library*

'bearing the spear and the club, fighting and raging, killing war-parties and destroying forts'. Warfare was said to be he taonga tuku iho (a treasured heirloom).

Māori warfare has been seen as a response, not to shortage of land, but to shortage of cleared land, the argument being that it was easier to take another's plantations than to clear your own with firestick and stone adze. However, there is little evidence from tradition that warfare was primarily aimed at territorial expansion. Whatever the underlying causes, the stated reasons for fighting were insulting remarks or gestures (kanga) and revenge.

A death in battle or as a result of mākutu or whaiwhaiā (witchcraft) demanded retribution. An unavenged death was a mate ngaro, (a hidden death). Taking a life in return was spoken of as ranga i te mate (lifting the death), or huke i te mate (digging up the death) or ngaki i te mate (clearing the death). When accomplished the original death was said to be ea, a word often translated as 'requited' though its literal meaning refers to rising to the surface of water after immersion.

Such was the force of a mate ngaro that a male child might be raised with the prime purpose of 'lifting' it. The traditions contain stories of maidens refusing marriage, or wives denying conjugal rights until specific deaths had been avenged.

It is quite possible that the efflorescence of warfare that began in the first years of the nineteenth century, before any tribes had acquired firearms, resulted from the additional leisure time that accrued as a result of the ease with which potatoes could be grown. In the past the traditional season of war began after the kūmara crops were planted in October and November. Potatoes are planted earlier. However that might be, it was the musket that resulted in an orgy of bloodshed that began in the north where tribes were first to acquire firearms. It rapidly spread southward as, initially in self-defence, the southern tribes secured a supply of guns by actively encouraging Europeans to settle among them. Then the guns were used to settle old vendettas, to facilitate territorial expansion and to enhance the mana toa (warrior status) of those possessing them.

While it is not clear who provided the Māori with their first firearms, it is known that muskets were used in inter-tribal warfare by 1815. Speedy recognition of the power of firearms to settle old scores set a premium on them. Hongi Hika and other chiefs travelled as far as England to secure muskets, or goods which they could exchange for them. Traders and even missionaries were drawn into supplying them. Whole tribes toiled in the swamps cutting and dressing the flax that paid for them.

For twenty years the missionaries promoted their message of peace and goodwill largely unheard while the tribes settled old debts and contracted new ones in an orgy of bloodshed. Conflict, that old cultural taonga, was in over-supply. The war-parties were often away from home for many months and covered hundreds of miles. The expedition 'Amio-whenua' left the Kaipara during 1821, travelled down the east side of the north Island as far as Wellington and back up the west coast, covering at least 800 miles and being away about nine months. Other expeditions ravaged the South Island and in 1835 a Taranaki tribe dispossessed of its traditional territory commandeered a European vessel and invaded the Chatham Islands.

In the meantime te ringa kaha o Aituā (the strong hand of death) was attacking on other fronts. With epidemics occuring and some of the new diseases becoming chronic, warring expeditions became less frequent, perhaps because the manpower to mount them was lacking.

Quite suddenly, conversion to Christianity became fashionable and whole tribes converted. By 1840 inter-tribal warfare had almost ceased. It might have been hoped that with the signing of the Treaty of Waitangi by over 500 influential Māori leaders covering most of the country that peace would become permanent.

Such was not to be. Within three years, two of Maoridom's most precious taonga, land and conflict itself, resulted in the renewal of strife, this time with tauiwi (the foreigner). The Wairau incident in 1843, Heke's war in 1845, the attacks in the Upper Hutt Valley in 1846 and the war at Wanganui in 1847 were the preludes to the larger conflicts of the 1860s and early 1870s in which old tribal conflicts were often continued as 'friendly natives' were enlisted in the wars against the 'rebels'.

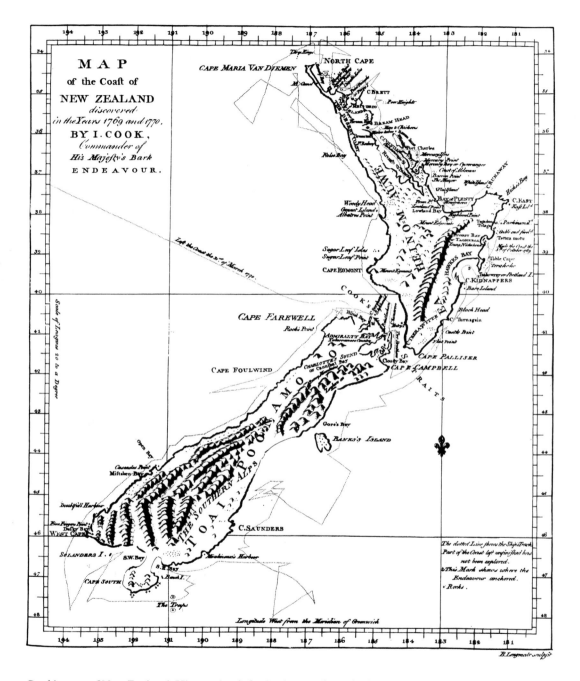

Cook's map of New Zealand. His naming left a lasting mark on the land and is repeated daily in various ways, most notably in weather forecasts, such as Bream Head to Cape Colville. *Alexander Turnbull Library*

2. *The Māori People and the British Crown* (1769-1840)

❧

CLAUDIA ORANGE

First contact between Māori and European involved Ngati Tumata-kokiri people and Abel Janszoon Tasman, a Dutch East India Company explorer. Tasman brought his ships, *Heemskerck* and *Zeehaen*, to anchor on the evening of 18 December 1642, near Wharewharangi Beach in present day Golden Bay. Two canoes approached and the rowers hailed the ships, sounding an instrument 'like a Moorish trumpet'. Tasman's crew responded and one, who could play the trumpet a little, replied with some tunes. This exchange, possibly interpreted by Ngati Tumata-kokiri as a challenge to fight, led the following day to the death of four Europeans. Tasman left without landing and named the spot Moordenaers (Murderer's) Bay.

Brief and confused as this contact was, it was from Tasman's visit that the country received the name by which Europeans would know it, New Zealand. Isolated in the South Pacific, the land had remained the fortress of independent tribes. They knew no other race and thought of themselves simply as tangata māori — 'the local people'. They were aware of the shape of the country's main islands and had their own names for them. Māori demonstrated this for the British explorer, James Cook, who, having completed a scientific voyage to Tahiti, 'rediscovered' New Zealand in 1769. At Whitianga chiefs used charcoal to draw on the deck of the *Endeavour* the earliest known map of the North Island, 'Aotea'. But Cook's expedition was creating its own maps. Although some coastal landmarks retained their Māori names, the cultural stamp of Cook's homeland bit permanently into New Zealand's geography. A quiet intrusion into the land's Māori identity, this naming was part of a global mapping that would seriously challenge Māori independence. Cook claimed parts of the country for his sovereign, George III. It was a routine procedure and Britain neither confirmed nor followed up the claims immediately, but Cook's visit opened up the possibility of further British intrusion and ultimately dominance. Indeed Cook noted suitable sites for settlement.

In the six months spent in New Zealand, Cook's expedition acquired extensive

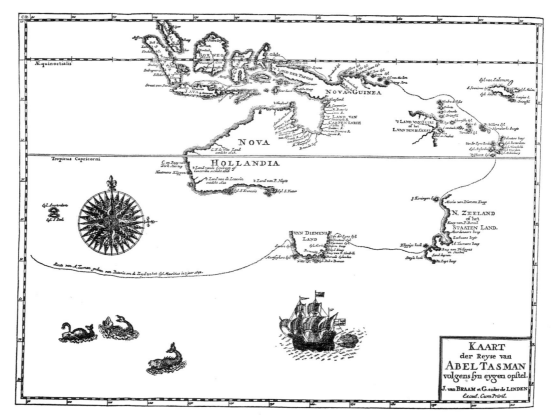

Tasman's map of Australia and New Zealand. *National Museum*

knowledge of the land, its people, and its flora and fauna. His two further visits (1773 and 1777), like the first, were recorded in detail by the artists and scientists who accompanied him. Their drawings, writings and specimens, an invaluable record, launched New Zealand into the orbit of metropolitan Europe. Few countries newly discovered by Europeans have been so richly documented and described. Cook's journals, first published in 1773, were for years the basic reference texts for any ship's captain venturing into the Pacific.

Cook had clashed with the Māori on several occasions, with deaths on both sides, but he was surprisingly reluctant to lay any blame. Despite the usual European aversion to cannibalism and other attributes considered brutal, he admired Māori ability in crafts and construction, weaponry and war, fishing and horticulture, and revealed much respect for Māori customs, habits and characteristics. His testimony established a not unfavourable reputation for the Māori people, which the accounts of subsequent European visitors supported, providing Europeans with a basis for understanding a complex and diverse people.

Cook's success in New Zealand was largely based on the relatively easy and

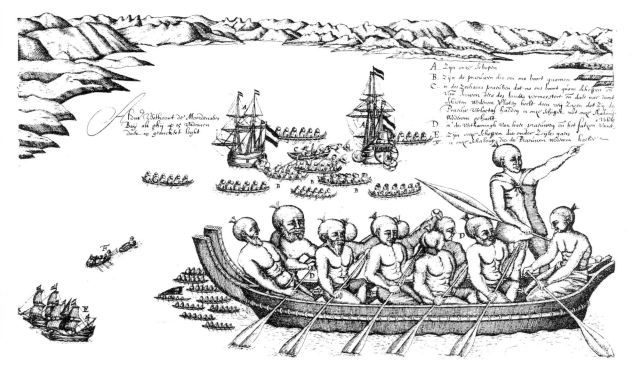

The violent encounter between Māori in a group of canoes and members of the crew from Tasman's ships, the *Heemskerck* and the *Zeehaen*, drawn by a Dutch artist. *Alexander Turnbull Library*

immediate exchange of information through the interpreting of Tupaea, a Tahitian priest who joined the first expedition, and on the rapid establishment of barter. Cook's vessels needed food and water. The Māori were attracted by tapa cloth, nails and small goods. Each side had to modify its behaviour to get what it wanted. Cook sought not to offend Māori custom (though his men inevitably trespassed), while Māori learnt that Europeans would not tolerate what they considered to be theft. Both races exploited Māori women for their own purposes. Both sides resorted to force, the Māori feeling the sting of the musket; but both also sought accord.

Cook's visits proved that with a mutual respect, often based on a show of force by both sides, Māori and European were capable of coming to terms with each other in a constructive way. When Europeans blundered, the results could be disastrous for both races. In 1772 the Frenchman Marion du Fresne, through a series of misunderstandings, was killed with fifteen of his crew at the Bay of Islands. The French vengeance — three villages were destroyed and heavy casualties inflicted — was never forgotten by Māori in northern New Zealand. Cook, on the other hand, was remembered warmly in oral tradition and the British connection was later acknowledged by Māori when they were shown their likenesses in Cook's printed journals.

The mutuality of interests established on Cook's visits suggested the pattern that race relations would follow for the next forty to fifty years. It was an uneasy racial partnership: Māori would accept Europeans only if they proved useful or harmless. At any time they possessed the power to drive Europeans out or to destroy them. Europeans, however, could withdraw from or avoid the country, which would deprive Māori of useful goods. There were, then, checks and balances. Although contact would never be altogether predictable, the interdependence of the two races would be a crucial factor in determining relationships.

By 1830 Māori New Zealand had accepted several groups of Europeans, each bringing different pressures to bear on Māori society — from the 1790s sealers, whalers and traders, and from 1814 missionaries. By 1839 there were 2000 'permanent' settlers, about 1400 in the North Island and 600 in the South. Most were dotted on riverine or harbour sites, or were part of coastal enclaves. 'Transients' who had spent short periods on shore could be numbered in thousands. Few Europeans knew inland regions until the early 1830s when Māori guides introduced missionaries to the hinterland. The exploitative nature of early European commercial activity left the land largely untouched. A few missionaries and trader-settlers purchased a little land in the 1830s. In the late 1830s, however, there was a rush of speculative 'purchases' by New South Wales buyers, most not followed up, and a small influx of genuine settlers who wanted land. Both gave forewarning of the impending European struggle to wrest the land from the Māori.

By 1840, through written and published accounts as well as by personal experience, Europeans knew a good deal about the Māori people. Their observations were often biased and limited, but they were a basis for understanding a people who had lived in New Zealand for over 1000 years. Māori society was both homogeneous and varied with a shared belief system, culture and language, but with strong tribal identity based on kinship. Authority rested in a recognized chiefly leadership, partly hereditary, partly won by prowess in battle and ability to support kin. Chiefs and common people often shared in consensus decisions; captives had few rights. There was no central government and chiefly authority was limited. Mana and tapu, central points of Māori belief and behaviour, had to be respected by Europeans to avoid conflict. The karanga of welcome — haeremai — and the hongi of greeting were often expected by newcomers to the country.

Europeans tried to estimate the size of the Māori population. From Cook's visits to 1840 their guesses ranged from 100,000 to 200,000. Since no Europeans were acquainted with the whole country, accurate figures are not possible.

With the establishment of the British penal colony in New South Wales in 1788, British interests began to exploit New Zealand's resources — seals, whales, timber, flax and agricultural products. In 1792, in the far south of the South Island, the first sealing gang was left at Dusky Sound, and in the first quarter of the nineteenth century gangs from Sydney, Hobart, Britain and America worked the shoreline from Dusky Sound round to the Otago coast. In a burst of furious activity that tapered off in the 1820s, they virtually exterminated the seals. In 1806 a single vessel entering

Whaling ships at anchor off Kororareka in the Bay of Islands. A sketch by Louis Le Breton, an artist on Dumont D'Urville's third voyage of exploration which visited New Zealand from March to May 1840. *Alexander Turnbull Library*

Sydney carried 60,000 skins destined for the making of felt hats. The gangs, left for months and even years at a time, established semi-permanent shore stations. A workable accord with local Māori was essential. Many of the sealers formed partnerships with Ngai Tahu women, founding families that later turned to whaling, trading, boat-building and subsistence farming. Their numbers were not great, but in the South Island they formed a significant union of Māori and Pākehā (as non-Māori New Zealanders were called) which led to a lasting mixing of the races.

British and American sperm whalers called irregularly after 1802 at northern harbours, mainly the Bay of Islands, to refit and refresh. Although the massacre of the *Boyd*'s crew in 1809 deterred Europeans for a time, shipping began to increase steadily from 1815. By 1830 Kororareka (later called Russell) was well established as a trade and supply port for whalers and Pacific traders. There was only a handful of resident Europeans, but, on a single day in 1830, thirty ships with a total complement of about 1000 men were at anchor, with up to 300 on shore. In the 1830s the whaling activity peaked; as the number of British and colonial vessels dropped, French and American ships increased. In 1839 an American consul, James Clendon, was appointed.

The shipping had a marked effect on Māori in the north. It began a struggle for chiefly patronage of the European. Chiefs were caught up in an exchange of European goods for provisions and services, including those of their women. An initial demand for nails, fish-hooks and metal tools gave way around 1814 to an arms race as muskets, powder and shot became the most sought-after trade items. By 1819 Bay of Islands Māori were heavily armed with muskets. Māori elsewhere were not but, as European traders observed, they would do anything to make up the deficiency. By the 1830s Māori in the north and much further afield were organized to supply the needs of the shipping. Tribes changed their patterns of settlement, organized their labour resources and cultivated crops suitable for trading — potatoes, other vegetables and fruit — and pigs, introduced first by European explorers, and later supplemented by gifts from New South Wales governors and missionaries. Some coastal tribes come close to starvation in winter and spring as supplies were reserved for trade. In the early 1830s there was a well recognized rate of exchange of provisions for guns and equipment, but by the mid-1830s the market was saturated. Māori sought a greater variety of items — blankets and woollen 'slops' in the winter, and year-round tomahawks, knives, calico, clothing of all kinds, pipes and tobacco.

From the earliest contact, the whalers and trading vessels recruited Māori as crew. Māori 'learnt the ropes' quickly and served on the ships of all nationalities in New Zealand waters. Many travelled to Australia, Asia, North America, England and Europe, and might spend up to three and four years on the ships. By the 1830s some had risen to the rank of mate and officer on British and colonial vessels, only their foreign status debarring their appointment as ship-master, as it did Chief Officer 'Baily' of the whaler, *Earl Stanhope*. In Sydney and Hobart Māori sailors were a common sight in the 1820s and 1830s. At a gala day in Hobart in 1838, a third of the oarsmen in the whaleboat races were Māori. By 1840 the Sydney harbour-master's crew was all Māori. Returning sailors and travellers, having acquired some English, often became the trade negotiators for their tribe. Sometimes they simply slipped back into the traditional mode of life and dress but, as explorers of the world beyond New Zealand, their infusion of information to their tribes was important. Relations between the Māori and the whalers, often fraught with trouble in the early years, improved as the whalers adjusted to Māori demands and Māori became more conciliatory. It was a working relationship, never entirely amicable. The whalers, usually a transient summer phenomenon, at least in the north, seldom made permanent ties.

The shore whalers were different. While the sperm whalers fished the open sea in all seasons, shore whaling operated from April to October, catching and processing the right (or black) whale for its oil and whalebone. Financed mainly by Sydney and Hobart merchants, shore stations were established from the late 1820s. By 1839 there were up to thirty stations: in the North Island at Kapiti, and in Taranaki, Hawke's Bay and Poverty Bay; in the South Island at Tory Channel, Cloudy Bay, Banks Peninsula, Waikouaiti, Otago Harbour and Preservation Inlet. French, American and occasionally ships of other nationalities also exploited the fisheries, operating usually from ships anchored in bays.

The shore establishments were often substantial settlements. The Weller station at Otago Heads had about eighty cottages and 120 men at its peak, a quarter of whom

The 'anchorage' at Otago as it appeared to the crew of Dumont D'Urville's ship *L'Astrolabe* in 1840. For some years prior to 1840 whaling settlements on the Otago coast had brought dramatic changes to Māori life. *Alexander Turnbull Library*

were Māori; and Johnny Jones, based at Waikouaiti, was said to employ 280 men in his seven stations in 1839. Out of season the men turned to general trading in pigs, potatoes, fish and flax. As shore whaling expanded in the 1830s Māori formed the core of many of the gangs, working the boats, processing the whales, and sometimes selling whalebone on their own account. Many adopted the clinker-built whaleboats in preference to canoes; they were more seaworthy and could be built to suit local weather conditions. The whaling stations were normally under the patronage of the local tribe and the whalers more often than not had Māori wives. It was a tough life, characterized by the whalemen's heavy drinking bouts; but the women kept tidy homes and raised fine families. The arrangement suited both parties: Māori acquired new skills and manufactured goods, as they were drawn into a money economy; the whalers had labour and a land base.

Shore whaling, with its limited intrusion upon the land, did not have such a marked effect on Māori life as did the flax, timber and general trading that developed in the North Island in the 1820s. From 1793 New South Wales governors made several unsuccessful attempts to foster a New Zealand flax trade. The last in 1823, much publicized, stimulated private interest and by 1830 an export trade in flax was booming. Acting for Sydney firms, usually as general traders, agents were left in coastal locations to negotiate with local Māori for cargoes of flax. Tribes committed themselves to a highly labour intensive effort to meet contracts. Usually it required

'View of the Kahukahu Hokianga River 1839.' Charles Heaphy's view of the timber-milling establishment run by George F. Russell at Kohukohu on the Hokianga Harbour. *Alexander Turnbull Library*

altering settlement and food production patterns. The women, who normally had prepared flax for weaving, were hard pressed to produce a quality dressed flax fibre in bulk. The trade peaked in 1831 and began to decline, but by then it had introduced a nucleus of semi-permanent settlers who were dependent on the Māori for labour, as the Māori were on them, for handling their produce. Some agent-traders — Phillip Tapsell at Maketu and John Rodolphus Kent at Kawhia and Ngaruawahia — ensured their success by marrying into their associated tribe. Through his musket trading, Tapsell became a significant factor in inter-tribal feuds in the Bay of Plenty.

A search for timber also attracted Europeans to New Zealand. British commercial vessels first took spars from the Thames district in the 1790s, and naval ships called in 1820 and periodically thereafter. That year the Hokianga harbour was proven navigable and local chiefs began to solicit traders. In 1826 Patuone travelled to Sydney; he was prepared to leave his son there as guarantee for the safety of any ships' crews who came to the Hokianga. Later that year an agent for a Sydney firm, Raine and Ramsay, negotiated for the purchase of Horeke to establish a timber-trading centre.

The timber trade was a joint European-Māori venture, the Horeke yard employing several dozen Māori as well as European. Chiefs took a personal interest in the enterprise, regularly supervising the felling of the trees. Some became, as did Te Taonui (patron of Horeke), expert at calculating the quantities of timber involved. Under chiefs' direction Māori labour usually loaded the vessels. Ships more often than not were expected to pay anchorage fees, a practice adopted at other harbours from the mid-1830s. In Sydney a special wharf was opened to handle the sale of the spars. Horeke also became a substantial shipbuilding yard. Between 1827 and 1831 the yard built the 40-ton schooner *Enterprise*, the 140-ton brigantine *New Zealander* and the barque *Sir George Murray*.

In the 1830s timber mills opened elsewhere — at Coromandel under William Webster and at Whitianga under Gordon Browne. The Bay of Islands traders Clendon and Mair had timber interests; and in the Waikato, the Hauraki Gulf and the Kaipara several hundred sawyers were operating by 1840. By then the trade was employing hundreds of Māori who gained skills not only in dressing timber but also in cabinetmaking and boatbuilding.

The sealers, whalers and traders had no other mission in New Zealand than to exploit the resources of land and sea. They did not actively seek to change Māori society. The missionaries did. The first Church Missionary Society (CMS) men arrived in 1814, setting up stations in the Bay of Islands, first at Rangihoua and later at Kerikeri and Paihia. They were followed in 1823 by the Wesleyans who, after an unsuccessful start at Whangaroa, selected the Hokianga as their base. They continued to work on the west coast, under an arrangement which left the east coast to the CMS. In the 1830s this accord broke down and the two groups began to expand. The CMS had ten stations by 1839 while the Wesleyans had opened eleven. A Roman Catholic mission, under the French Bishop J. B. F. Pompallier, began work in the Hokianga in 1838. Shifting his headquarters to Kororareka the following year, he and his Marists made exploratory sorties in several localities.

The first CMS mission, largely conceived by Samuel Marsden, senior chaplain to the penal colony, was to 'civilize' as a first step to conversion. Marsden, long in contact with Māori visitors to Sydney, was impressed by their qualities and characteristics:

> The natives of New Zealand are far advanced in Civilization, and apparently prepared for receiving the Knowledge of Christianity more than any Savage nations I have seen. Their Habits of Industry are very strong; and their thirst for Knowledge great, they only want the means.
>
> The more I see of these people, the more I am pleased with, and astonished at their moral Ideas, and Characters. They appear like a superior Race of men.

Marsden believed that Māori had a capacity to change, by which he meant to accept Western values and behaviour. In particular he wanted to 'excite a spirit of trade' which would lead to Māori dependence on European merchandise and open the way to Christianity. But the first missionaries — Thomas Kendall, William Hall and John King — selected for their skills and encouraged to trade, had a desperate struggle to maintain their Western values. They led a miserable existence under their patron chief Hongi Hika. Henry Williams and his wife Marianne, at Paihia from 1823, had more success. Unlike his predecessors, Williams refused to be forced into the musket trade to survive. His aim was to become self-sufficient and to pursue a policy of 'Christianization'. Emphasis was placed on preaching and teaching.

Through the 1830s other missionaries arrived. Conceiving their mission stations as enclaves of Western culture in a heathen world, the men and women (missionaries in their own right) set out to create an alternative life-style. By visitors' accounts they succeeded. The missionaries operated as a team. Both men and women engaged in domestic chores and in the men's absence the women ran the mission. The men concentrated on acquiring a good knowledge of the language and both men and women taught in the mission schools. In 1828 Jane Williams wrote of her efforts with the girls at Paihia:

> The elder ones are very useful in washing, ironing, sewing and nursing, and begin to write and read with tolerable ease; these acquirements afford us much pleasure, but we are more satisfied at perceiving that they become more orderly and obedient, and that their habits are more decorous and less dirty, though there remains much, very much to be reformed outwardly, to say nothing of the cleansing and purifying requisite for the inner man, and which nothing short of the Saviour's blood can effect.

But changes to the 'inner man' were not in evidence. Indeed pupils regularly absented themselves from the schools. Tribal needs took precedence and the 'shipping' had to be served — a constant distraction to the Māori and irritation to the missionary.

Māori initially subjected the missionaries to a good deal of bullying and intimidation. Henry Williams found his way of handling this: 'The only mode we have of punishing these people is to forbid them entrance, and to tooitooi [tuhituhi] them. That is note them down in writing . . . We can shew our displeasure by not speaking to them; which they feel very much.' Sometimes such methods were successful, but the missionaries were subjects of a Māori world. Disgusted and horrified by much of it, they did their best to insulate their families.

Māori treated the missionaries much as they did traders — they were useful for their goods and skills and for enhancing the mana of their patron chief. As James Kemp, mission blacksmith, observed in December 1824: 'Their object in letting us live amongst them, is to get all they can from us'. It was the same in the Hokianga where

Patuone protected the Wesleyans; the pattern would be repeated as the missions expanded. The Māori people had their own concerns — tribal advancement and inter-tribal relations — which inevitably led to war. Warfare was an established part of the Māori social system, but to traditional reasons for war — such as taking revenge for affronts — had been added a fiercer struggle to increase economic resources for trade. The musket made that struggle all the keener as competition for raw materials, trading outlets and Pākehā traders fuelled old antagonisms. More useful for its power to intimidate than to kill, the musket was crucial to success in the new wave of warfare that it stimulated.

Northern Māori, heavily armed with muskets, began their destructive war expeditions southwards in 1818. In 1819 Patuone, Nene and Tuwhare of Hokianga led a large force to Taranaki and as far as Cook Strait. They were joined by Te Rauparaha and Ngati Toa from Kawhia. When Hongi returned from London in July 1821, equipped with new arms financed by the sale of gifts, the scale of the expeditions increased. Northern war parties reached as far south as Cook Strait and went inland to Rotorua and Waikato.

The effects of the wars went further. Under pressure from the northern tribes, hapū in the Waikato and Taranaki began a series of migrations in the 1820s. Eventually they settled the west coast of the North Island south of Taranaki, and the Cook Strait region including Kapiti and parts of the South Island. The migrations involved hapū of Ngati Toa, Ngati Raukawa, Te Atiawa, Ngati Tama and Ngati Mutunga. The resident tribes — Ngati Apa, Muaupoko, Ngati Ira, Rangitane and Ngai Tahu — were either conquered by the newcomers or made alliances with them, and came to an accommodation — often uncertain — over sharing their lands.

In the 1830s many of the migrants and southern Māori, by then fully equipped with arms, continued the northern pattern and engaged in heavy fighting. In 1835 Ngati Tama and Ngati Mutunga, fearing further aggression, migrated to the Chatham Islands, where they slaughtered the local population. Hawke's Bay and Wairarapa Māori, also seeking to escape attack, took refuge at Mahia. Over a period of fifteen years these wars and migrations effected a major redistribution of population. They were also a major cause of population decline. At one estimate the male fighting population declined by 20% to 25% between 1800 and 1840. Figures vary widely from 20,000 to 80,000, but the decline in population was noted by Māori too.

However, it is likely that the more disastrous killers were European diseases, their effects spreading from first contact with Cook's expeditions: influenza, dysentery, whooping cough, measles, scrofula, tuberculosis, streptococcal infections and venereal disease. Some moved through the country in epidemic proportions; others, like flu, were by the late 1830s striking each year in spring and autumn. Some of the diseases were not necessarily killers, but traditional remedies were often inappropriate, and a communal life style facilitated the spread of disease and inhibited recovery. Changes in Māori economic and social habits, gaining momentum in the 1820s, contributed to the widespread ill health of the 1830s. Observers also noted child deaths through malnutrition.

It was in the context of these changes and upheavals that the first conversions to Christianity came in 1830 — in the north, where change in Māori society was most marked. By 1840 Māori who could say they were 'going mihanare' (conforming at least to the external conventions of Christianity) were counted in thousands. Although full membership of the three mission bodies was quite small before 1840, the impact of Christianity overall was very considerable. In 1845 George Clarke estimated that, out of the total of about 110,000 Māori, roughly 64,000 were nominally Christian.

The nature of the Māori 'conversion' has been much debated by historians. It has been attributed to cultural dislocation, caused by European impact in all its facets, and to the relevance of Christianity to such circumstances, to better missionary methods and particularly literacy, and to the intrinsic value of the religion itself, as Māori taught and understood it. Perhaps all have a place, in varying degrees, in different parts of the country. It has been said, probably accurately, that the missionaries have been credited with more influence than they exerted and blamed for more harm than they caused. Certainly in most areas the expansion of trade preceded or paralleled that of religion. But although the missionaries did not begin the economic and social changes affecting Māori communities in the 1820s and 1830s, they were well placed to benefit from them. They filled roles that made them useful and for a time indispensable to a rapidly changing Māori society — trader, teacher, peacemaker and healer.

From the late 1820s they began to act as peace mediators, both at Māori request and on their own initiative. Each party probably intended to use the other; certainly the mediation was not always successful. Wars continued in the 1830s, disrupting the CMS mission stations in the Rotorua-Bay of Plenty district, but there were signs of exhaustion. Chiefs found it harder to raise large war parties. Individuals found reason for evading the fight. In this context the peace of Christianity served a useful purpose. A truce could be arranged without a loss of mana. Speaking of an inter-tribal reconciliation, the missionary A. N. Brown was probably not far from the mark when he wrote that 'Pride would have prevented either party making peace, but neither were ashamed of doing so while the Missionaries were advocates for it and parties to it.' Some chiefs and hapū established new Christian settlements. The most well-known was at Matamata under Wiremu Tamihana Tarapipipi. Some chiefs were simply pleased to have more time for profitable pursuits. Within a few years Nuka Taipari at Tauranga saw the value of peace. More of his young men were reaching adulthood. A visitor saw 250 of them on a fishing expedition in 1843.

The missionaries also turned to advantage the impact of European diseases. Although the medicine of the missionaries was often just as inadequate as traditional medicine, missionary explanations gave meaning to the inexplicable. They told the Māori that the new diseases were either God's visitation or the Devil's. God was punishing the Māori for former barbarities. Whatever the explanation, Māori illness was 'turned to God's account'. Māori were more inclined to accept Christian teaching. Some were prepared to believe that the European god had superior powers that might

A missionary distributing Bibles to Taranaki Māori. *Alexander Turnbull Library*

work, as Māori gods did, to the people's advantage.

Missionaries also aimed to undermine Māori confidence in their social and religious institutions — the power of tapu and the tohunga, the sanctity of burial grounds — stressing the inferiority of Māori and the superiority of European culture. Chiefly authority was deliberately undermined by missionary attacks on warfare, slavery, and polygamy. Unwilling to set aside their wives, senior men like Te Kani-a-Takirau could sense a loss of their status as younger men acquired new mana through association with Christianity and Western ideas, skills and goods. Some chiefs decided to opt for Christianity and so combine the new with traditional leadership, the course taken by Nopera Panakareao at Kaitaia, which facilitated the conversion of his people, Te Rarawa. Others attributed their conversion to the religion itself. At Tauranga, Matiu Tahu, at one time the tohunga of Otamataha pā at Te Papa, defended the nature of Māori conversion: 'You are not satisfied with us', he told A. N. Brown, 'and you often express a fear that our religion is only lip service, that it has no root in our hearts. You forget what we were and what we have thrown away — our cannibalism, our murders, our infanticide, our Tapus, which were Gods to us. What prevents our return to these things but Religion?'

Tahu had supported the establishment of Tauranga's CMS mission from 1835 and was, by the 1840s, its most trusted teacher. He was one of numerous Māori preachers and teachers who carried knowledge of Christianity to tribes either in advance of direct missionary contact or in association with it. The Māori missionaries were sometimes, like Piripi Taumata-a-Kura on the East Coast, released captives of Ngapuhi; or, like Te Ahu of Rotorua, youths who attached themselves to missionary households. In the 1830s, in areas remote from European contact, they brought about the rapid adoption of Christian ideas and forms — 'sitting still' on Sundays, building chapels, and reciting prayers and hymns. In 1839 Henry Williams described a Paihia student, Matahau, who had returned to the Otaki area to his kinsmen, 'amongst whom he has laboured with astonishing zeal and perseverance, has taught very many to read and has instructed as far as he was able in the truths of the Gospel so that many tribes for some distance around call themselves believers, keep the Sabbath, assemble for worship, and use the liturgy of the Church of England.' Although at times diverging from orthodox Christian teaching, Māori teachers were effective, their role in Māori conversion recognized as essential by the missionaries. But equally important was the printed word.

From 1827 the missionaries produced translations of religious texts. From 1833, 3300 copies of a 170-page book of scriptural extracts and an 88-page prayer book went into circulation. By 1836 both the CMS and the Wesleyans had presses, and by 1840 William Colenso at Paihia had produced the whole of the New Testament. Although thousands of copies were printed the supply was insufficient to meet the demand created by a sudden Māori 'craze' for reading and writing, which some missionaries thought had superseded draughts as a pastime. Novel and exciting, literacy gave mana to the newly initiated. Those who learnt to read and write passed the skill to others. In the process much of the Christian message was passed on too. Missionaries with their books and their skills were now eagerly sought after by tribes as useful acquisitions, much as tribes competed at the same time for other Pākehā.

The change in Māori attitudes looked like a triumph for the missionaries. In committing the Māori language to written form they had made themselves, at least temporarily, indispensable to the Māori. Restricted to religious matter, Māori could only pursue literacy through association with the missions. It was a monopoly that gave Christianity a brief, high profile. More than any other single factor, it was the decisive one leading to conversion. The missionaries, few in number and limited in activity, had an invaluable aid in spreading not only Christian ideas but the complex web of Western cultural notions with which Christianity was surrounded. Māori curiosity, discussion and evaluation were stimulated.

There were benefits to be had by 'going mihanare' — skills, knowledge, peace and trade — but as more Māori communities were caught up in the burst of European activity in the 1840s, the limits of Māori 'conversion' would become apparent. The acceptance of Christianity was, as with other European intrusions, adopted and adapted on Māori terms. There was no total rejection of Māori beliefs and customs — the missionary aim — nor complete acceptance of the Christian ethics and mores of Victorian England. There was a great variety of belief and practice. Disconcerting to the missionaries, however, were those who rejected missionary teaching and produced their own movements — a blend of traditional Māori religion and Christian

(**10**)

Marree	A cough
Marokee	Dry
Mátta	Face
Mattou	Fish-hook

18.

Matou	Understand
Mátte	Illness
Madua	A parent
Míllo mílto	Thread
Moana	Salt water
Moongha	Bed
Moka	Flax
Moki	A marked fan
Momói	Sore
Moora	Blaze

19.

Mootoo	The lips
Moto	Fist fighting
Motoo	A low island
Mouee	The first man
Náddoo	A wave
Nammoo	A sand fly

(**11**)

Narkee	A button
Napo	Last night
Narko	Fat
Nárro	A fly
Nawkí	Whose
Náttoo	A scratch

20.

Nehoo	A tooth
Nau (or gnaw)	To bite
Ora	Life, health, &c,
Owhì	Who
Paddoo	Dirt
Páhoo	A bell, drum, &c.
Pattie	A war club
Parlo	The ball of the hand
Papa	Breech
Patua	To kill
Pekou	To get upon the back
Píppee	A cockle

21.

Peto	The navel
Pona	A knot

Thomas Kendall, one of the first CMS missionaries in New Zealand, began the task of committing the Māori language to written form. This is a section of the first book in Māori — *A Korao no New Zealand* — which he sent to Sydney for printing and publishing in 1815.

ideas — the first appearing in the north in 1833. Whatever the reasons for rejection or acceptance of Christianity, it became a major part of the Māori way of life within a few decades.

In the 1830s Māori adoption of aspects of Western culture was marked. Traditional clothing gave way to the blanket, to shirts, pants and other items, often worn in unconventional ways. European visitors noted that old customs and habits seemed to be dropping away and new ones taking their place. Hair was sometimes cut shorter. Shaking hands became an accepted greeting, the 'how do you do' and other English words entering the Māori vocabulary. Places such as the Hokianga were moving towards a money economy. Tobacco became a favoured trade item and a few Māori began trying out the taste of alcohol. Europeans thought that Māori were easier to deal with. There was less theft and Māori were less sensitive about the accidental breaking of tapu by Europeans. There was wide experimentation with European mannerisms and life-style. In the far south of the South Island, Tuhawaiki became adept at trade negotiations, built himself a weather-board house and trained a bodyguard of men whom he clothed and equipped like British soldiers. In the Bay of Islands, Taiwhanga, one of the first converts, set up as a commercial dairy farmer. He supplied the Bay with butter and with fruit and vegetables which he had learnt to cultivate in the 1820s during a lengthy visit to New South Wales. He built his own plough and a weather-board house, and defied custom by cooking inside.

Change of this sort, however, was most evident in coastal New Zealand where contact had been long and intense. Tribes inland and away from trade outlets were less affected. From one area to another there was great variation. Northern New Zealand, often regarded by contemporaries (and later by historians) as typical of the whole country, was unusual. Even among Māori who followed European ways there was a selective adoption and blending of the new with the old. Nevertheless, several decades of contact with the European world had indeed made a great impact on Māori society. Yet that contact had brought about not so much the revolutionary change sought by some Europeans as accretions on a traditional culture that retained its resilience and adaptability. Europeans saw the outward aspects of change and many believed that Māori, embracing trade and Christianity, were well along the way to 'civilization' and to that amalgamation with the British that missionaries and other Europeans had so long thought possible. They anticipated an eventual Māori acceptance of their own culture as inferior and of European supremacy. Such assumptions were dangerous.

In the 1830s the nature of European intrusion into New Zealand changed. Trade expanded steadily. Exports more than doubled between 1831 and 1839. Annual shipping in the Bay of Islands increased from 89 ships in 1833 to 151 in 1836, and 155 in 1839. Seventeen ships engaged in a regular trans-Tasman trade, and there were the visits of whalers and Pacific Islands traders. Trade brought permanent settlers. At the beginning of the 1830s the European population in the North Island was estimated at a little over two hundred. In January 1839 Henry Williams thought it was near 1300, not counting the fifty Māori-European children in the Bay of Islands (for whom a school was proposed). The entire country had roughly 2000 Europeans by 1840, all British apart from about fifty Americans and twenty French.

The Europeans were a mixed lot. Apart from the missionaries, there were retired ships' captains, traders, artisans, ships' deserters, escaped convicts, drifters and Pākehā-Māori (Europeans who had married into a tribe, adopting the tribal life-style). The numbers of respectable settlers grew markedly after 1835. Dealing in flax, timber and general goods, they often built their own trading vessels. The Māori people were partners in this trade growth, supplying pork, potatoes, maize, wheat and other foodstuffs. Traders negotiated for the use of small areas of Māori land for their commercial needs, but their livelihood depended on reaching a *modus vivendi* with local Māori. By the late 1830s a different type of settler, one seeking land, was appearing. (The CMS missionaries, too, began to purchase land for their families.) Robert Maunsell distinguished between the two types of settler, noting of the former that 'instead of their subjecting, they are subject to the natives'; whereas the latter were less likely to feel a need for accord or to allow that Māori rights had to be respected. As the historian Peter Adams rightly observes: 'The stake in such an inherently competitive situation was no less than the political control of the country.'

The basis for official British intervention in 1840 had been established by the commercial and missionary activities of the previous fifty years. As the seaward frontiers of New South Wales expanded, colonial governors took a special interest in New Zealand as a supplier of resources, for which they were keen to cultivate good relations with the Māori people. Early in the nineteenth century Governor P.G. King had invited Māori in Sydney to confer with him about the ill-treatment of Māori crewmen. Taken on in New Zealand and often stranded in New South Wales or elsewhere, they had no easy redress for mistreatment and default of wage payment. King offered them repatriation or trade-training. Although these were declined, the governor's concern pleased the Māori and established a basis for better relations. King followed this up by sending gifts — iron tools, fruit tree seedlings and livestock — to Te Pahi, a leading chief who controlled a good anchorage for European shipping in the Bay of Islands. Te Pahi and several of his sons responded by visiting New South Wales in 1805-1806, presenting King with fine cloaks and a stone mere, and staying with him at Government House for nearly three months. (One of Te Pahi's sons went on to England.) The two men engaged in a profitable exchange of knowledge. An able and shrewd character, Te Pahi convinced King that Māori and British could work together productively. The chief became the focus of government hopes for an ongoing alliance, but these came to nothing when Te Pahi was killed in 1810.

King, however, issued orders to try to curb the ill-treatment of Māori on ships operating out of Sydney; and five years later, Governor Lachlan Macquarie attempted to apply more stringent rules. A good behaviour bond was required of ships' masters, and Europeans were urged to act prudently in New Zealand. They were to pay just wages and to refrain from pressing either male or female into service. British subjects guilty of serious crimes against the Māori were threatened with severe punishment. These orders were repeated in 1814 when the missionary, Kendall, was appointed a Justice of the Peace in New Zealand. On his departure in November 1814 to establish the first mission in the Bay of Islands, he was accompanied by three Bay chiefs, Hongi, Ruatara and Korokoro, who were invested by the New South Wales government with authority to implement the orders. No Māori was to be removed by ship, nor crew discharged without the chiefs' permission, which Kendall would certify. Macquarie's moves, like King's, were of dubious legality, and had little practical effect: by one account, they were 'laughed at a good deal'. Yet they were more than gestures of goodwill. Macquarie was publicly claiming a kind of jurisdiction in New Zealand, an indication that he believed that the Crown had a responsibility for the actions of British subjects and for the protection of Māori. This interest would lead ultimately to permanent intervention.

Shipping problems involving Māori continued to engage the New South Wales governors' attention and were not remedied by imperial statutes in 1817, 1823 and 1828. New Zealand was undeniably independent territory, outside the limits of British dominion. Yet paradoxically the expansion of New South Wales trading interests in the 1830s was confirming the country as a colonial sphere of interest as well as compounding legal problems. British traders and travellers in New Zealand looked to the governors to smooth their passage. They expected the Crown's representatives to extend hospitality to Māori visitors in New South Wales. They hoped that Māori leaders well-treated in Sydney would reciprocate in New Zealand. If chiefs were slighted, traders feared for their safety and for the security of their commercial interests. The value of good relationships had been learnt from bitter experience. Because it paid to conciliate the Māori, New South Wales governors showed them the Crown's benevolent face. Māori were often received at Government House and they acquired personal experience of the colonial official establishment.

Marsden also urged Māori leaders to visit New South Wales and to stay at his establishment at Parramatta. There they learnt agricultural techniques and trade skills, were initiated into a European life-style and were introduced to government circles. Māori came to expect a personal relationship with the Crown's representative and developed unrealistic expectations of continuing special treatment. In 1828 the English artist Augustus Earle observed a Waikato chief's arrival in Sydney: The chief awaited an audience with the governor and, having adorned his person 'to the greatest advantage' and dressed his hair with oil and feathers, he sat for two days before his wish was satisfied. The notion of a personal approach to the Crown took a few Māori to England. The most notable visitors were Hongi and Waikato, Ngapuhi chiefs who were favoured with an audience with George IV.

From 1820 relations with the British Crown had also developed through the British navy's search for spars and timber. Major chiefs became involved – Te Horeta Te Taniwha of Thames, Makoare Te Taonui, Nene and Patuone of Hokianga, and Titore of the Bay of Islands. The reciprocal nature of the trade was usually confirmed by gifts. Titore, acknowledging Britain's past conflict with France, offered to reserve certain trees from which spars could be cut in any future Anglo-French engagement. The commitment was acknowledged by the gift of a suit of armour and a letter from the King. Traders took advantage of the mana ascribed by Māori to the monarchy. Joel Polack claimed that his rank rose 'full five hundred percent' when Māori knew he was from London, the kāinga (village) of King George. They concluded that he was related to the monarch 'by blood and marriage' to live so close. Marsden's long-standing involvement with New Zealand was crucial in encouraging this Māori understanding of the Crown. On his seven visits to New Zealand between 1814 and 1839, he consistently promoted the belief that the Crown had a parental interest in protecting the Māori people. By 1827 the establishment of a Māori settlement in New South Wales was contemplated as a sanctuary from inter-tribal fighting.

Despite a growing war weariness and a greater Māori interest in Christianity in the 1830s, a *pax Britannica* based on Christian precepts was not immediately likely. Continuing inter-tribal unrest seemed a predictable part of the New Zealand scene. Disappointing as this was to Europeans who saw nothing constructive in Māori warfare, it was a growing trade in preserved Māori heads that particularly dismayed Marsden and Governor Ralph Darling. Preserved initially to be subjected to tribal ridicule, the heads of enemy chiefs, quite recognizable, were later traded to Europeans and were often carried back to their home tribe. Marsden and Darling feared that the gruesome business would add new tensions to Māori-European relationships and might lead to a major breakdown of inter-tribal relations. Marsden had long appreciated the need for a more settled trade relationship with Māori New Zealand and believed that this was being set at risk by the activities of criminal elements and unscrupulous exploiters from whom the Māori needed protection. For their part colonial traders simply wanted more favourable conditions for the expansion of trade.

How to settle the dilemma of New Zealand's legal situation in relation to New South Wales remained an unresolved issue. One incident in 1830 brought the matter to a head — the participation of British subjects in the *Elizabeth* affair. An English captain and crew entered into a trade deal with the Ngati Toa chief, Te Rauparaha, to convey him and a war party to the South Island in return for a cargo of flax. Te Rauparaha's aim was to wreak vengeance on the unsuspecting Ngai Tahu for the death of a kinsman. Tamaiharanui, a senior chief, was tortured and killed, along with some of his family. The grisly details of the case appalled Europeans and perturbed other Māori. From the Bay of Islands two Māori emissaries, Ahu and Whare (probably Wharepoaka), travelled to Sydney to lodge a protest with Darling. Ahu, a relative of Tamaiharanui, sought compensation for the deaths, while Whare was concerned about the wider implications: Europeans interfering in Māori quarrels could possibly lead to more serious inter-tribal battles.

In the end the culprits went unpunished. John Stewart, the *Elizabeth*'s captain, escaped the law by jumping bail. Delays in hearing the case were partly the result of legal uncertainties regarding New South Wales jurisdiction over British subjects in New Zealand. Marsden, with some exaggeration, pressed the point that the Māori people at large were looking for British protection. Darling's response, supported by a series of memorials from merchants, missionaries and interested individuals was accepted by the Colonial Office: a British Resident was to be appointed in New Zealand.

James Busby arrived at the Bay of Islands to take up the position in May 1833. The appointment satisfied no one. Busby's salary and expenses had to be found by a reluctant, parsimonious New South Wales Treasury, and Britain declined to support the Resident with a warship stationed permanently in New Zealand. Busby could not call on military support and could not hold magisterial office in an independent territory. The powerlessness of his position irritated local British residents who were seeking effective action in a variety of disputes. Where these involved Māori, Busby could be little more than a kind of race relations conciliator. Yet among northern chiefs he laid the basis for a working relationship. Over the next six years chiefs were to appeal to him as Kaiwhakarite, a facilitator. Disputes over theft, cattle trespass and land, were brought to his notice. If his record in controlling Europeans was not as good as Māori might have expected, this weakness would be used as a telling reason for a formal British intervention in 1840.

At the suggestion of local chiefs, Busby and his family settled at Waitangi. There he attempted to carry out one part of his instructions — to encourage Māori towards a 'settled form of government'. In March 1834 he held a great gathering where chiefs were invited to choose a national flag. The flag was needed for shipping. From the late 1820s ships built in New Zealand were refused registration in New South Wales because New Zealand was not British territory. In November 1830 the Hokianga-built *Sir George Murray* had been seized in Sydney and her cargo impounded. On board were almost certainly the chiefs Patuone and Te Taonui, who had seen the action as offensive to their mana. When Busby arrived other ships were needing registration. Busby shrewdly saw a chance of settling the registration issue and at the same time creating an embryonic Māori government. Three flags, made to Henry Williams's design and brought from Sydney by HMS *Alligator*, were displayed on short poles for the chiefs to choose from. The voting was split and no time allowed for debate, but the country had a national flag. It was immediately hoisted, together with the British flag, cheered by some fifty Europeans, and accorded a 21-gun salute. Gazetted in Sydney, the flag ensured that New Zealand-registered ships (certificated by Busby on behalf of the chiefs) could freely enter Australian ports, a point of pride for trade-seasoned chiefs. Recognition of the flag became, in Māori understanding, acknowledgement of the mana of New Zealand and a special mark of Māori identity. The flag was flown at the Bay of Islands in the 1830s and remained a symbol of an independent Māori nationality.

Busby hoped the flag ceremony might lead to a governing conference of chiefs, but nothing came of it. He seized another opportunity in October 1835, when he organized a Declaration of the Independence of New Zealand. The move was sparked off by the threat of a Frenchman, Baron de Thierry, who was planning to establish a 'sovereign and independent state' in the Hokianga on a large, though disputed, land purchase. Busby's personal animosities with Thomas McDonnell, appointed Additional British Resident in 1834, were also involved. But Busby's primary purpose was to assert the independence of the country under the protection of the British Crown, a move which he believed would make the country 'a dependency of the British Empire in everything but the name'. He dispatched the Declaration with thirty-four signatures in November 1835. When the Crown acknowledged the Declaration in 1836, at one stroke it accepted both the independence of the country and the role of protector. Committed to this scheme Busby continued to collect signatures and by July 1839 had fifty-two, mostly northern chiefs who were designated the United Tribes.

The Declaration asserted the 'Rangatiratanga', the independence and chieftainship of the land. All sovereign power and authority in the land, 'Ko te Kingitanga ko te mana i te w[h]enua', resided with the chiefs 'in their collective capacity'. The signatories thanked King William IV for his acknowledgement of their flag and asked him to continue to be 'the parent' (matua) 'of their infant State . . . its Protector from all attempts upon its independence'. An annual congress at Waitangi was proposed and southern chiefs were invited to join the Confederation of United Tribes.

Contemporary European observers in New Zealand doubted if the Confederation

HE WAKAPUTANGA O TE RANGATIRATANGA O

NU TIRENE.

—

1. KO MATOU, ko nga tino Rangatira o nga iwi o NU TIRENE i raro mai o Haurake, kua oti nei te huihui i Waitangi, i Tokirau, i te ra 28 o Oketopa, 1835. Ka wakaputa i te Rangatiratanga o to matou wenua; a ka meatia ka wakaputaia e matou he Wenua Rangatira, kia huaina, "Ko te Wakaminenga o nga Hapu o Nu Tirene."

2. Ko te Kingitanga, ko te mana i te wenua o te wakaminenga o Nu Tirene, ka meatia nei kei nga tino Rangatira anake i to matou huihuinga; a ka mea hoki, e kore e tukua e matou te wakarite ture ki te tahi hunga ke atu, me te tahi Kawanatanga hoki kia meatia i te wenua o te wakaminenga o Nu Tirene, ko nga tangata anake e meatia nei e matou, e wakarite ana ki te ritenga o o matou ture e meatia nei e matou i to matou huihuinga.

3. Ko matou, ko nga tino Rangatira, ka mea nei, kia huihui ki te runanga ki Waitangi a te Ngauru i tenei tau i tenei tau, ki te wakarite ture, kia tika ai te wakawakanga, kia mau pu te rongo, kia mutu te he, kia tika te hokohoko. A ka mea hoki ki nga tau iwi o runga, kia wakarerea te wawai, kia mahara ai ki te wakaoranga o to matou wenua, a kia uru ratou ki te wakaminenga o Nu Tirene.

4. Ka mea matou, kia tuhituhia he pukapuka, ki te ritenga o tenei o to matou wakaputanga nei, ki te Kingi o Ingarani, hei kawe atu i to matou aroha; nana hoki i wakaae ki te Kara mo matou. A no te mea ka atawai matou, ka tiaki i nga Pakeha e noho nei i uta, e rere mai ana ki te hokohoko, koia ka mea ai matou ki te Kingi kia waiho hei Matua ki a matou i to matou tamarikitanga, kei wakakahoretia to matou Rangatiratanga.

Kua wakaaetia katoatia e matou i tenei ra i te 28 o Oketopa 1835, ki te aroaro o te Rehirenete o te Kingi o Ingarani.

Ko Panakata, no te Patu Koraha.	Ko Tareha, no nga te Rehia.
Ko Ururoa, no te Taha Wai.	Ko Kawiti, no nga te Hine.
Ko Hare Hongi.	Ko Pumuka, no te Roroa.
Ko Hemi Kepa Tupe, no te Uripotete.	Ko Kekeao, no nga te Matakeri.
Ko Warepoaka, no te Hikutu.	Ko te Kamara, no nga te Kawa.
Ko Titore, no nga te Nanenane.	Ko Pomare, no te Wanau Pane.
Ko Moka, no te Patu Heka.	Ko Wiwia, no te Kapo Tahi.
Ko Warerahi.	Ko te Tao, no te Kai Mata.
Ko Rewa.	Ko Marupo, no te Wanau Rongo.
Ko Wai, no Ngaitewake.	Ko Kopiri, no te Uritanewa.
Ko Reweti Atua Haere, no nga te Tau Tahi.	Ko Warau, no nga te Tokawero.
Ko Awa.	Ko Ngere, no te Urikapana.
Ko Wiremu Ieti Taunui, no te Wiu.	Ko Moetara, no nga te Korokoro.
Ko Tenana, no nga te Kuta.	Ko Hiamoe, no te Uru o Ngongo.
Ko Pi, no te Mahurehure.	Ko Pukututu, no te Uri o te Hawato.
Ko Kaua, no te Herepaka.	

Ko Eruera Pare, te Kai Tuhituhi.

—

Ko matou, ko nga Rangatira, ahakoa kihai i tae ki te huihuinga nei, i te nuinga o te Waipuke, i te aha ranei, ka wakaae katoa ki te wakaputanga Rangatiratanga o Nu Tirene, a ka uru ki roto ki te wakaminenga.

Ko Nene.	Ko Panakareao.
Ko Huhu.	Ko Kiwikiwi.
Ko Tona.	Ko te Tirarau.

He mea ta i te Perehi o nga Mihanere o te Hahi o Ingarani, i Paihia.

He W[h]akaputanga o te Rangatiratanga o Nu Tirene: A Declaration of the Independence of New Zealand. This declaration, organized by British Resident James Busby, was signed by 34 chiefs at Waitangi on 28 October 1835 and by July 1839 had a total of 52 signatures. The original was in long hand. This is one of two printings made by the mission press at Paihia in 1837. *Auckland Public Library* would ever work. There was no indigenous political structure upon which to base a united congress. The country was too large and tribal divisions too strong. Although by the 1830s Māori had a sense of 'Maoriness' gained from shared experiences with the European world, their concerns were primarily tribal and would remain so for many years. A congress committee met with Busby occasionally but a house of assembly was never built. Nevertheless, the Declaration document (in Māori) was twice printed and became for the Māori people a foundation for their assertion of autonomous rights in the nineteenth century and up to the present.

No one knew better than Busby that the Declaration was no substitute for effective government. With minimal resources and confronted by an increase in trade-related problems from 1836, Busby peppered an unsympathetic Governor Richard Bourke with appeals to support his position. Early in 1837 inter-tribal fighting in the Bay of Islands, involving European riff-raff, persuaded Bourke to send HMS *Rattlesnake*, under the command of William Hobson, to assess the situation. Bourke requested Hobson and Busby to submit reports on the state of New Zealand. Recognizing the distinct reluctance of the British government to become more involved, Hobson ruminated on a limited intervention by Britain — a selection of several sites for a 'factory' system akin to the early British trading factories in India. This solution had long since been dismissed by Busby who favoured a formal protectorate. The 'miserable condition' of the Māori, he argued, had 'some claim of justice upon the protection of the British Government', particularly in view of the humanitarian policy then being asserted in favour of native peoples in British colonies.

The two reports and a series of dispatches from Bourke and Busby, together with petitions from both New Zealand and Sydney traders, all arrived at the Colonial Office in December 1837. The dismal picture they painted — of a rapidly deteriorating colonial frontier — was somewhat exaggerated. Traders at the Bay of Islands had set up a sort of vigilante group, the Kororareka Association, in 1838, but their concern was more for property than life. There was certainly brawling and theft — typical of all frontiers — but there were few major crimes. Nevertheless, London officials were now persuaded that further intervention in New Zealand was a necessity. A burst of speculative land purchases and a seeming apathy amongst some Māori seemed to support this conclusion.

The Colonial Office was also influenced by the plans of several private colonization groups, in particular the New Zealand Association (later Company). The company aimed to establish a New Zealand colony on the principles of Edward Gibbon Wakefield. In May 1839 the company's directors sent off the *Tory* to make the first company land purchase; the first of several shiploads of emigrants followed in September. The inevitability of colonization forced the government to act.

The Colonial Office, guided by its evangelical humanitarian officials, had vacillated through 1838. But in December the Secretary of State for Colonies, Lord Glenelg, had sought Hobson's appointment as Consul. In 1839, under a new Secretary, Lord Normanby, plans for New Zealand had firmed up. Hobson was convinced by his 1837 visit that there was so much British labour and capital invested in fisheries that British intervention was inevitable and even desirable in view of a rapidly diminishing Māori population. He recommended securing sovereignty over the whole country and was given discretion to try for all or part.

Hobson left in August 1839 with instructions from Normanby for setting up a British colony. Crown authority was to be assumed initially by Letters Patent, New Zealand becoming temporarily a dependency of New South Wales. Normanby admitted that though New Zealand lacked a concerted political authority the country had been officially acknowledged as a 'sovereign and independent state'. Hobson would have to negotiate a transfer of sovereignty to the Crown by seeking the 'free and intelligent consent' of the Māori. Normanby went into a good deal of apologetic explanation for intervention: it could not be justified by the small settler group of roughly 2000; it was needed to fulfil a duty to the thousands of expected emigrants, and to uphold the rights of the Māori. Despite this statement of intent to maintain a dual obligation, the Colonial Office was not striking a balance between Māori and settler interests. By 1839 the Colonial Office was no longer contemplating, as they had previously, a Māori New Zealand in which settlers had somehow to be accommodated, but a settler New Zealand in which a place had to be kept for the Māori.

At a brief stop-over in Sydney, Hobson was sworn in as Lieutenant-Governor of any territory he might acquire and enlisted personnel for the nucleus of a civil service. He arrived at the Bay of Islands on 29 January 1840 with a proclamation, issued by Governor George Gipps, which declared that all past and future land purchases in New Zealand would be valid only if confirmed by the Crown. He announced that he was assuming his duties as Lieutenant-Governor, anticipating Māori acceptance of his mission. To treat with the Māori, especially the Confederation chiefs, for a cession of sovereignty was his first concern. He carried no draft treaty. Over several days a text was put together with the help of his secretary, James Freeman and Busby, who offered to organize a meeting of chiefs. Invitations, extended later to non-Confederation chiefs, announced a gathering at Waitangi on 5 February. By then, a draft treaty in English had been hastily translated into the Māori text that would be signed at Waitangi on 6 February and elsewhere over the following six months.

The translation, made by the missionary Henry Williams and his son Edward, diverged in meaning from the English text. The all-important transfer of sovereignty was not conveyed clearly. The treaty guaranteed 'te tino rangatiratanga', the full authority of chiefs over their lands, their dwelling places and other valued treasures ('ratou taonga katoa'). As Busby had drafted this article, it guaranteed simply 'possession'. Chiefs, on the other hand, ceded 'kawanatanga', the governorship of the country. 'Rangatiratanga' was the term used for chiefly independence in the 1835 Declaration of Independence; and Māori had long been treated to a very personal kawanatanga — the Crown's benevolent face in New South Wales. The treaty also promised Crown protection and the same rights and privileges as British subjects. Not surprisingly few Māori understood the implications of this treaty of cession.

KO WIKITORIA, te Kuini o Ingarani, i tana mahara atawai ki nga Rangatira me nga Hapu o Nu-Tirani, i tana hiahia hoki kia tohungia ki a ratou o ratou rangatiratanga, me to ratou wenua, a kia mau tonu hoki te Rongo ki a ratou me te ata noho hoki, kua wakaaro ia he mea tika kia tukua mai tetahi Rangatira hei kai wakarite ki nga Tangata Maori o Nu-Tirani. Kia wakaaetia e nga Rangatira Maori te Kawanatanga o te Kuini, ki nga wahi katoa o te wenua nei, me nga motu. Na te mea hoki he tokomaha ke nga tangata o tona iwi kua noho ki tenei wenua, a e haere mai nei.

Na, ko te Kuini e hiahia ana kia wakaritea te Kawanatanga, kia kaua ai nga kino e puta mai ki te Tangata Maori ki te Pakeha e noho ture kore ana.

Na, kua pai te Kuini kia tukua ahau, a WIREMU HOPIHONA, he Kapitana i te Roiara Nawi, hei Kawana mo nga wahi katoa o Nu-Tirani, e tukua aianei a mua atu ki te Kuini ; e mea atu ana ia ki nga Rangatira o te Wakaminenga o nga Hapu o Nu-Tirani, me era Rangatira atu, enei Ture ka korerotia nei :---

Ko te Tuatahi,

Ko nga Rangatira o te Wakaminenga, me nga Rangatira katoa hoki, kihai i uru ki taua Wakaminenga, ka tuku rawa atu ki te Kuini o Ingarani ake tonu atu te **Kawana**tanga katoa o o ratou wenua.

Ko te Tuarua,

Ko te Kuini o Ingarani ka wakarite ka wakaae ki nga Rangatira, ki nga Hapu, ki nga Tangata katoa o Nu-Tirani, te tino Rangatiratanga o o ratou wenua, o ratou kainga, me o ratou taonga katoa. Otiia ko nga Rangatira o te Wakaminenga, me nga **Rangatira** katoa atu, ka tuku ki te Kuini te hokonga o era wahi wenua e pai ai te tangata nona te wenua, ki te ritenga o te utu e wakaritea ai e ratou ko te kai hoko e meatia nei e te Kuini hei kai hoko mona.

Ko te Tuatoru,

Hei wakaritenga mai hoki tenei mo te wakaaetanga ki te Kawanatanga o te Kuini. Ka tiakina e te Kuini o Ingarani nga Tangata Maori katoa o Nu-Tirani. Ka tukua ki a ratou nga tikanga katoa rite tahi ki ana mea ki nga tangata o Ingarani.

(SIGNED)

WILLIAM HOBSON, Consul & Lieutenant-Governor.

Na, ko matou, ko nga Rangatira o te Wakaminenga o nga Hapu o Nu-Tirani, ka huihui nei ki Waitangi. Ko matou hoki ko nga Rangatira o Nu-Tirani, ka kite nei i te ritenga o enei kupu, ka tangohia, ka wakaaetia katoatia e matou. Koia ka tohungia ai o matou ingoa o matou tohu.

Ka meatia tenei ki Waitangi, i te ono o nga ra o Pepuere, i te Tau kotahi mano, ewaru rau, ewa tekau o to tatou Ariki.

The Treaty of Waitangi in Māori was first printed on 17 February 1840 at the Paihia mission press. A second printing was run off in 1844 during the war in the north. This copy is one of several treaty copies held by National Archives and is probably one of the 1840 prints. *Auckland Public Library*

On 5 February, in an enormous marquee erected on the Waitangi lawn, the treaty was presented to a gathering of hundreds of Māori. Also present were Hobson's entourage, English and French missionaries and some local Europeans. Although Williams's Māori text failed to convey the full meaning of the national sovereignty being negotiated, explanations might have clarified the ambiguous text. They were not adequate. Couched in terms designed to persuade chiefs to sign, explanations skirted the issue of a sovereignty cognizable at international law and presented an ideal picture of the workings of British authority within New Zealand. Māori authority might have to be shared, but it would be enhanced by British jurisdiction which would apply mainly to controlling troublesome Europeans. Hobson would merely be more effective than Busby.

For over five hours chiefs debated the treaty. Many experienced in dealing with Europeans were critical. Those associated with the Roman Catholic Bishop Pompallier, resident at Kororareka, made shrewd, informed observations about the likely consequences of Māori agreement to the treaty. The chief Rewa observed that though land had been sold 'this country is ours . . . we are the Governor — we, the chiefs of this our fathers' land'. If Māori accepted the governor, New Zealand would suffer the fate of other countries taken by the British. Keenly aware of the Australian experience, Māori wondered how different New Zealand would be. By the end of the day, however, supporters of the British missionaries had swung the tide of opinion in favour of the treaty. That night, camped on the flat land near Waitangi river-mouth, chiefs discussed the proposal amongst themselves, and on 6 February some forty-five chiefs gave their agreement. Before the signing William Colenso, the mission printer, expressed doubt about the extent of Māori understanding. He no doubt knew that in addition to the short-comings of translation and inadequate explanations, some chiefs had arrived late, even as the signing was in progress. Hobson impatiently brushed aside his protest. By contrast, Pompallier's request that religious tolerance be observed was accepted. The assurance included Māori custom (ritenga) too.

The Waitangi gathering set the pattern for subsequent meetings at Waimate and Hokianga in February. These and later signings were, said Hobson, merely acts that 'further ratified and confirmed' the initial signing which he regarded as the '*de facto*' treaty. Nevertheless, Hobson did his best to obtain as many signatures as possible. When he suffered a stroke on 1 March at the Waitemata Harbour, he deputed negotiations to several missionaries and to two army men. Several manuscript copies of the treaty were widely circulated. At some fifty meetings the total number of chiefs agreeing to the treaty reached over 500 by September when the last signatures were taken.

With the exception of thirty-nine chiefs who signed an English treaty text at Manukau Harbour and Waikato Heads, chiefs signed a Māori treaty text. Five women were allowed to sign, their mana acknowledged by missionary negotiators. On the Kapiti coast other women unsuccessfully protested their right to participate. They shrewdly observed that the other party to the treaty was herself a woman, Queen Victoria.

Horeke a view of the feast given by the governor to the natives at the Muarahi Hokeanga
cap¹ macdonald   *Feb 1840*

The missionary Richard Taylor made this sketch of the feast at Horeke, given by William Hobson on 13 February 1840, the day after the treaty was signed at Mangungu on the Hokianga Harbour. *Alexander Turnbull Library*

The organization of treaty signings was a haphazard affair. In the north the significance of the signings was marked with feasting and the customary gift-giving. Elsewhere Māori agreement depended a good deal on tact and patience of negotiators. Some chiefs bluntly refused to sign and this sometimes meant the absence from the treaty compact of whole tribes — Te Arawa of Rotorua and Ngati Tuwharetoa of Taupo. Ngati Ruanui of South Taranaki was not given a chance to accept or decline, and some areas — Hawke's Bay — were barely touched by negotiators. Some chiefs agreed to sign but with great reluctance. Makoare Te Taonui of Hokianga, an experienced trans-Tasman traveller, voiced his concerns:

> We are glad to see the Governor; let him come to be a Governor to the Pakehas (Europeans). As for us, we want no Governor; we will be our own Governor. How do the Pakehas behave to the black fellows of Port Jackson? They treat them like dogs! . . . The land is our father; the land is our chieftainship; we will not give it up . . . first, your Queen sends missionaries to New Zealand to put things in order, gives them £200 a year; then she sends Mr. Busby to put up a flag, gives him £500 a year, and £200 to give to us natives [in gifts]; now she sends a Governor.

But Te Taonui signed in the end. He was probably convinced, as other chiefs were, that the government wanted not the land but an insubstantial sovereignty.

Explanations given at several treaty meetings support the conclusion that, though Māori expected the treaty to initiate a new relationship with the Crown, it would be one in which Māori and Pākehā would share authority. The intervention of Britain would not diminish their chiefly mana and would even enhance their rangatiratanga (control over tribal matters). Other motives for Māori adherence to the treaty would become apparent later — expectation of increased trade and of the Crown's involvement in land sales (in some districts a wish for Crown protection from importunate Pākehā purchasers, in others a wish to sell more land); desire for various material benefits, assistance in handling the changes disturbing Māori life and, not least, the possibility of manipulating British authority in inter-tribal rivalries.

But the most decisive factor in persuading Māori was missionary advice that Maori welfare would best be served by accepting the treaty. In this respect the long cultivated, personalized image of the Crown was played upon: The treaty was the Queen's 'act of love' towards the Māori people, Henry Williams explained. Missionary explanations were also crucial in determining that the treaty would be understood, by Ngapuhi initially and later by other tribes, as a covenant between the Māori people and the Queen as head of the English Church and state. The treaty would be seen as a living bond, with all the spiritual connotations of the biblical convenants. Māori and Pākehā would be linked in both a spiritual and temporal sense, almost as one people.

For Hobson the religious understanding, if grasped at all, was only a part of the business of obtaining sovereignty; and though he was certainly aware of Colonial Office desire to deal more fairly with the Māori, to improve on the record of British settlement, his main commitment was to securing British sovereignty, as rapidly and as completely as possible. In May 1840, before all circulating copies of the treaty had returned to him, he proclaimed sovereignty — over the North Island by virtue of cession, over the South Island by right of discovery. He argued that the move had been forced upon him by New Zealand Company settlers who had established themselves in January at Port Nicholson (Wellington). In March they had introduced a form of government which claimed to derive its legality from local chiefly authority. The flag of an independent New Zealand flew above the settlement. Hobson reasoned that the settlers were illegally assuming powers of government that were the prerogative of the Crown. He dispatched Willoughby Shortland to read the proclamations and to require allegiance to the Crown. Hobson informed the Colonial Office of his proclamations which were officially published in the *London Gazette* on 2 October 1840, thereby ratifying the treaty.

Even as the treaty was still being signed round the country, Māori were beginning to doubt the wisdom of accepting the new authority. Many Pākehā were provocatively flaunting Britain's newly acquired status and telling the Māori people that they were 'slaves [subjects?] of the Queen'. Some Māori threatened to retaliate by knocking the offenders on the head. George Clarke, appointed Protector of Aborigines in April 1840, warned Hobson that the Māori people were weighing the advantages and disadvantages of their relationship with the new administration. That they might be 'enslaved' was a fear heightened by New Zealand's status as a dependency of New South Wales until May 1841, when the Charter for the new colony came into operation.

Hobson now faced the daunting task of reconciling Māori and settler interests. The treaty, much vaunted by officials as the 'Magna Carta' of Māori rights, at least laid down some guidelines for race relations, but its fish hooks rather than its benefits would soon be evident to the Māori people. Before the colony was a decade old, Hobson's words to each chief signing at Waitangi — 'He iwi tahi tatou' ('We are now one people') — would be challenged.

3. The Pioneers
(1840–1870)

JEANINE GRAHAM

Latitude, longitude, wind direction, rain, wind, sun: it is the exceptional emigrant journal or colonist's diary that does not make frequent and explicit reference to weather conditions. Tropical heat made confined shipboard quarters almost intolerable. Contrary winds forced ships to tack for days off a long-awaited New Zealand shore. Squalls and salt spray drenched treasured possessions piled high on the foreshore. The Antipodean sun scorched tender English complexions. A sudden wind change could cause a burn-off to raze uncontrollably all the settler homes, possessions and livelihoods in its path. Household and farming routines were dictated and disrupted by the weather, a wet Monday wash-day being the despair of many a colonial housewife. No single factor was as dominant an influence on a pioneer existence as the climate. Yet the visual record of the pioneers ignores this fact. There are no pre–1870 illustrations which depict the reality of everyday life in the rain. The images are of pioneer life in continuously fine weather.

A closer examination of the pictorial sources for the first three decades of official European settlement reveals many similar anomalies. Life for colonial children was dominated neither by the formality nor the footwear depicted in the family portraits of those years. The majority of married women were constantly producing children yet pregnancy is invariably hidden from the photographer's lens. Death was a common and inevitable occurrence. The visual record does not portray this normality.

The disparity between image and reality was rarely caused by deliberate distortion. The misleading engravings of the early and mid-Victorian era, when artists in London endeavoured to depict written description in visual form, convey misconceptions of a metropolitan view of life in the Antipodes. The most common distortion was the cosmetic one. Fathers suddenly looked years younger when judicious 'touching up' of a family group negative removed some of the furrows on paternal brows. Relatives at Home were never to know that the faces of their colonial

Since the deterioration of many pre-1870 portrait negatives makes it difficult to reproduce the evidence of 're-touching' clearly, this photograph of the Lammas family, 1894 has been selected to show the contrast. Note in particular the transformation of the father's furrowed brow. The grainy texture of the complexions indicates where re-touching has occurred. *Nelson Provincial Museum*

nieces, nephews or grandchildren were not quite as the photograph or portrait depicted. Freckles, spots and windburn were the hallmarks of a colonial complexion but the blemishes disappeared in the 'likenesses' sent Home. That the artist and photographer 'selected' their images (and, in the case of the photographers, viewed an inverted image through their lenses) was no more a distortion of 'reality' than the selective accounts of colonial diarists and letter writers who conveyed only something of their experiences in words. Many did not write until the worst of their difficulties seemed to be over. Others could not write at all. Through oral history some tales of such pioneers have been handed down but there are no family stories for the one in every two adult men whose colonial existence proved to be a solitary one.

The advent of official European settlement in New Zealand was followed closely by the arrival here of the camera. Just as many specimens of the country's flora and

fauna had been depicted by artists and scientists during the previous half century, so many aspects of the lives of the pioneers would be portrayed in sketchbooks, paintings, photographs and prose. Such is the richness of the visual and documentary evidence that much of what was seen, spoken and thought by the pioneers can be detected. It is the smells and sounds of pioneer life that are lost: the screeching of the flax scutching machines; the incessant thudding of the stamper batteries; the booming of the kākāpo and the shrieks of whēkau. Gradually a distinctive colonial accent emerged along with a sense of colonial identity but for the early pioneers, the voices of life were as varied in dialect as the regions from which those settlers had come. Few pioneers escaped the smell of horse manure and the stench of household refuse, the aroma of freshly-baked bread and the equally pervasive mutton stew or roast of pork.

Although the record of pioneer life is richly illustrated, there is no inherent superiority of the visual over the written evidence. For a variety of technical, physical and cultural reasons, both the painter and the photographer tended to focus on a relatively limited range of themes. The landscape is well depicted; so too are the practical accomplishments of the tauiwi (strangers). How the pioneers felt in their new environment is conveyed in oral tradition and written record but only rarely in visual form. Furniture, clothing, embroidery, books, farm equipment, camp ovens, slates and climbing roses: the artefacts of the pioneer period are as diverse as the characters of the pioneers themselves. There is no one source that embodies this variety any more than there is any one incident that typifies the pioneer experience. Incorporating the visual evidence as an integral part of the historical record, however, enables a fuller appreciation of the harsher realities of pioneer life and dispels something of the romanticism with which much of the pioneer period has often come to be imbued.

Major political, economic and social developments occurred during the decades 1840 to 1870. The European population grew from an estimated 2000 in 1839 to outnumber the Māori by 1858 (approximately 56,000 Māori to 59,000 European). By 1872 the European total had reached 256,000 while the Māori population was proportionately less than one-fifth of that number. Settlers from Great Britain and the Australian colonies erected domestic, commercial and public buildings in a number of coastal locations. Auckland and Wellington were founded in 1840, Wanganui and New Plymouth 1841, Nelson in 1842, Dunedin 1848, Christchurch in 1850. This nucleus of pioneer settlements became a permanent one though all suffered periods of erratic economic growth.

Farming and trading opportunities led the pioneers to move into and beyond the hinterland of these early towns, the nature of land settlement and development being influenced by Crown ordinance, the landscape itself, the attitude of Māori tribes in each area and, eventually, by the plethora of regulation emanating from the provincial governments established under the 1852 Constitution Act.

New Zealand was in effect six colonies, with each of the provinces — Auckland, Taranaki (New Plymouth until 1859), Wellington, Nelson, Canterbury and Otago — vying for human and economic resources. As settlers dispersed, new provincial authorities were created: Hawke's Bay in 1858, Marlborough 1859, Southland 1861. The impetus for expansion was generally pastoral and progress steady though unspectacular. In Central Otago and on the West Coast of the South Island, however, change was sudden and dramatic. With the discovery of gold at Gabriel's Gully in 1861, the 'rush' began. The colony's total European population more than doubled within the decade and thousands converged on areas where previously the only Pākehā had been explorers. While pioneers in Taranaki's war zone were living within limits circumscribed by military authorities, their gold-seeking contemporaries in the south were constantly on the move, following one rumour after another. Some of the gold towns they established would remain: others would be as ephemeral as the vision of wealth itself.

Although settlers of British origin predominated in all of the settlements established during the first decade, each community developed a distinctive identity. The physical environment, especially the climate and the natural resources of the landscape, played a significant role in shaping that character. So too did the background, the aspirations, the financial and personal resources of the pioneers, as

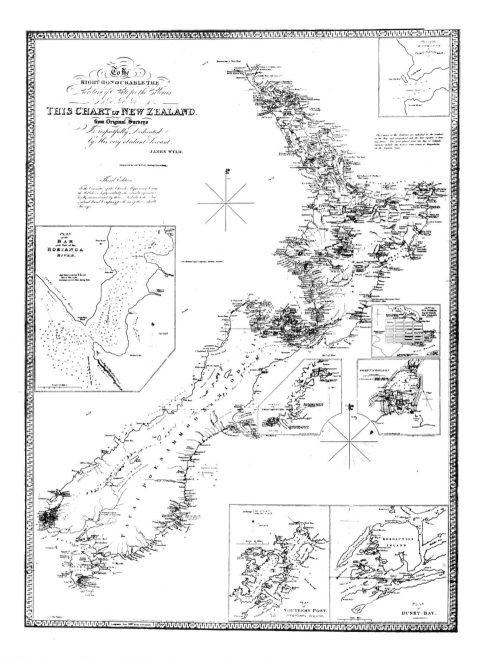

New Zealand was well served by its early map-makers, John Arrowsmith and James Wyld were the most eminent during the pioneering period. This 'Chart of New Zealand from Original Surveys' was completed by Wyld in 1858. A comparison of this map with his earlier 1843 and 1848 editions and the later 1870 version demonstrates the extent of European knowledge and settlement of Aotearoa prior to 1871. *Waikato University Library*

evidenced by the contrast between Presbyterian Dunedin and Anglican Christchurch. The differences emerged despite the philosophy of planned settlement which all but Auckland had in common. The theory espoused by English publicist, Edward Gibbon Wakefield, who sought to avoid the coarseness of frontier society by a combination of selective immigration, controlled land purchase and concentrated settlement, proved sufficiently attractive to inspire a number of founding associations. Practical application of the theory was fraught with difficulties, most of which stemmed from metropolitan ignorance of the New Zealand terrain and disregard for the nature of Māori land ownership. Colonists in Nelson, New Plymouth and Wellington were particularly disadvantaged by the New Zealand Company directors' initial tendencies to rank emigrant welfare as a concern secondary to shareholder dividend. The privation endured by the pioneers of all three communities, Nelsonians in particular, was exacerbated by a chronic shortage of capital, irregularity of supplies, and administrative ineptitude made worse by the eight or nine months or more that it took for Company officials in New Zealand to obtain policy decisions from their London superiors. Settlers in Otago and Canterbury were much better served by their founding organizations.

The regional diversity that was so striking a feature of the colonial landscape came to be expressed in political form during these early years. Although the 1852 adult male franchise was a relatively liberal one, involving a property qualification that was not difficult for Europeans to attain, involvement in political life at the General Assembly level was in effect restricted to those who possessed material resources commensurate with their political ambitions. The constant changing of politicians during 1854 to 1864 while the bicameral General Assembly met in Auckland, may have reflected the disillusionment of the idealistic but was more likely a comment on the financial and personal costs involved in holding political office. Yet while the photographs record the serious, stern, ostensibly middle-aged appearance of these bearded and formally-dressed elected representatives, the impressions conveyed are very limited ones. Several of these formal figures had served a pioneer apprenticeship dressed in fustian trousers and flannel shirt; they were adept at making damper and cooking pigeon stew; they could sail a boat, splice a rope and gut snapper. Most had their personal passions as well as their political ones but the fullness of their lives could not be captured in the visual medium. Only rarely is that richness suggested, as in the case of William Rolleston, Superintendent of Canterbury Province and reputedly a man of stuffy disposition. Because of his friendship with Dr A. C. Barker, that skilled amateur photographer who differed from many of his pre-1870 contemporaries in that he was prepared to risk including people in his photographs, there are images of Rolleston which temper the formality of the official portrait. 'The Argument', a staged discussion between Rolleston and an older founding father, J. E. FitzGerald, is a well-known Canterbury image. Less well-publicized, however, is the sequel, 'The Result of the Argument', in which FitzGerald and Rolleston are posing as if about to resort to fisticuffs.

Violence was an everyday occurrence in a hard-drinking male-dominated society and it was not unknown for politicians to revert to physical means of political point-scoring. It was, however, impossible technically for the pre-1870 photographer to capture any genuine incident since exposure times demanded that subjects be still. Barker's friendship with Rolleston provided another image unusual in the pre–1870 political collection, that of a politician in relaxed pose with his wife and children. New Zealand's early political leaders were hardly ever viewed in this fuller personal context. Not until the 1890s would politicians use the potential of the camera to appeal to electorates which from 1893 included women voters. The family scenes that were to be so much a part of Richard ("King Dick") Seddon's campaign style are totally absent from the pre-1870 visual record. Public and private lives were separate.

Although public political activity was a masculine field, concern about such matters was not. Sisters, wives and cousins also held opinions on a wide range of current issues, expressing them vigorously within household confines or in correspondence with close relatives and friends. Women were excluded only from formal involvement in the new constitutional arrangements. Where pioneering men and women were in successful working partnerships, mutual respect meant that a wide range of topics were discussed. Moreover, given the size of most colonial houses, it was simply not practicable for women to withdraw while men talked of public issues. Doubtless there were many for whom such open discussion required a social readjustment, given the conventions of their upbringing, but as the correspondence of Taranaki's Richmond/Atkinson clan suggests, only a foolhardy politician would have the temerity to disregard totally the viewpoint of his female relatives.

From some perspectives, the record of the founding years is an orderly one. The young colony moved constitutionally from the Crown Colony system which precluded direct settler representation and provided a Crown-appointed governor and his executive council, to a system of representative and then responsible government by 1856. The progress was not as rapid as some of the more politically active of the settlers wished. Many of the southern settlers, irked at what they perceived to be mishandling or neglect of their interests by a Governor resident in Auckland, campaigned vigorously for such 'natural rights' as 'no taxation without representation'. Political agitation by this somewhat select few increased when despatches revealed that Governor George Grey had successfully recommended a postponement of representative government until race relations in the colony were more settled. Political billboards and private letters during the late 1840s reveal that the Cook Strait activists were not mollified by the expedient of a lieutenant-governor in their midst. Edward Eyre's unfortunate manner and difficult relationship with his superior officer aggravated an already tense situation. Yet political rights had merely been delayed, not denied. In 1852 the British Government passed the New Zealand Constitution Act and the subsequent establishment of both provincial and central government structures by 1854 provided ample opportunity for nascent politicians to try their skill. By 1870 much of the administrative rationale for separate provincial governments had been undermined through the changes in internal transport and communications but the strength of regional loyalties would long outlive the political structure in which those feelings had been expressed most vehemently. The public buildings erected during the provincial era reflected the importance of political structures in the life of the pioneer communities. As the photographs indicate, far more resources were devoted to the building of provincial council edifices than were allocated for the comfort of representatives to the central government until the mid-1860s. In a country lacking a substantial social élite based on birth and breeding, those whose financial resources enabled them to pursue political interests soon acquired considerable social standing.

Although the colony's constitutional status was significant for all of its citizens, most settlers cared far more about every-day economic issues. The cost of living was much higher than many had anticipated, for initially all manufactured goods had to be imported from the United Kingdom or the Australian colonies. Until surveys were completed and land titles secured, the majority of early colonists eked out a subsistence existence. Auckland settlers fared best of all, situated as they were amongst Māori tribes who daily plied their fresh fish, fruit, pork and potatoes on the waterfront or in the streets. The close socio-economic relationship between Māori and Pākehā that was so essential to northern prosperity and so integral a part of the capital's developing identity was unique. Settlers in other areas benefited from Māori goodwill: Auckland residents depended upon it.

Illustrations of the 1840s give little idea of the privation endured by countless individuals and families. In Nelson, a settlement to which labourers and their dependents had been despatched with reckless disregard for their future employment prospects, the tragedy of armed conflict at the Wairau in 1843 devastated a community already struggling to survive. Many of the settlers who endured the poverty and the hardship did so simply because they had not the means of leaving. Photographs of the 1860s provide evidence of what was eventually accomplished despite this inauspicious beginning. Of the anxieties experienced by women malnourished during pregnancy; of men whose health was permanently undermined by the hours of hard physical labour in which they were engaged; of children dressed in sacking there are no contemporary illustrations. Publicist, photographer and artist alike focussed on the successful.

The subsistence economies of the early 1840s were gradually expanded as wealthier settlers followed the example of their Australian counterparts and took up pastoral farming. The subsequent dispersed settlement was anathema to Wakefieldian theorists but more practical counsels prevailed. The flax and timber that had been the mainstay of the pre-1840 export economy came to be superseded by wool, wheat and, in the 1860s, gold production. The change within thirty years was astonishing. Those who had come in the 1840s were proud of what had been accomplished. Those who arrived in the 1860s were often much more critical, noticing the limitations of services without experiencing what it was like to have no amenities at all. The visual record of this 'progress' is particularly rich when the mid-century photographs of the emerging urban landscapes are combined with the sketches and paintings of the 1840s townscapes. Photographers were also resident in

Flooding was a constant hazard for West Coast miners, disrupting the diggings and causing damage to the towns, most of which were built in close proximity to the rivers which provided access to transport. In this 1869 image of Kaniere Junction, on the banks of the Hokitika River, the shambles in the foreground appears to have been caused by minor flooding. *Canterbury Museum*

the instant towns of the sixties, the gold mining settlements full of activity and humanity, predominantly male but not exclusively so. Yet in the visual impressions of the Shotover, Nevis, Cromwell or Charleston, Dunganville, No town, Brighton or Napoleon's Hill, most men are photographed in the streets, not at the diggings.

For the pre-1870 period there is substantially more visual evidence of the hotels, shops (and occasionally the brothels) that served the mining communities than there is of the conditions under which the miners lived as well as worked on site. That remarkable exception, the famous Gabriel's Gully tentscape, depicts hundreds of men amongst the piles of tailings and poses the immediate questions of sanitation and wood supplies, since an open fire was usually the miners' only source of cooked food and warmth. For virtually every aspect of pioneer working life there is a paucity of visual information. Photography was too expensive and too cumbersome a process to be a form of social comment. Professional photographs took images that they hoped to sell, especially during the *carte-de-visite* craze of the late 1860s. The tasks of domestic

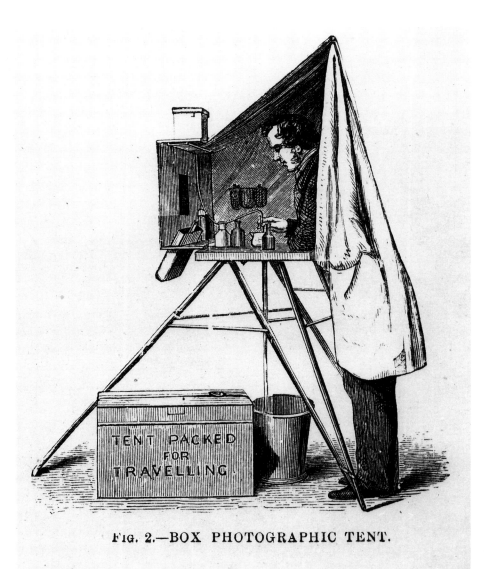

FIG. 2.—BOX PHOTOGRAPHIC TENT.

Travelling photographers had to transport the means by which their wet-plate negatives could be processed as soon as possible after exposure. Mobility was therefore restricted and many of the early photographers preferred to operate from an urban base. *William Main collection* servant, boot-maker, clerical worker or shop assistant had no commercial appeal. Of economic activity beyond the enclaves of settlement there are some pre-1870 illustrations, of tree-felling, farming and trading for example, but little that complements the graphic descriptions to be found in many of the letters and diaries of the time. There are, however, two important exceptions to this general observation: the drawings of surveyors and explorers. Despite the rain, the food shortages, the mosquitoes and the high level of personal discomfort experienced on the job, many of the early surveyors could not resist interspersing measurement with sketch in their field-books. The result is a unique portrayal of one of the most essential yet most hazardous of occupations in pioneer New Zealand.

Much of the effort which contributed to colonial economic development went unrecorded simply because it was so unremarkable. Work in the home was rarely depicted since few men shared William Bambridge and A. C. Barker's facility for sketching women in their unpretentious domestic settings. The often vital role of older children as child minder, domestic help, farm labourer and general errand boy or girl is only partly recognized in the written record and even less so in the visual. Yet despite the often restrictive and inadequate nature of the images, many of the political and economic facets of pioneer life can at least be glimpsed through pictorial evidence. Social aspects are covered less comprehensively.

The physical environment posed the greatest challenge to the pioneers. Few settlers had any idea of the landscape and the conditions to which they were coming. New Zealand Company emigration propaganda was persuasive and misleading, as were the drawings of Company employees whose images conveyed little of the reality

Bambridge was unusual in regarding daily household chores as worthy of recording. Sophia's makeshift washing arrangements in the Bambridge's Auckland home in 1846 are atypical, however since most laundering tended to be done outside, weather permitting. *Alexander Turnbull Library*

of dense bush, rugged terrain, heavy rain and gale-force winds. Contending with the elements in all their scorching or soaking intensity was difficult for new arrivals accustomed to the shelters of a civilization centuries old. Immigrants from the mid-1850s onward had no comprehension of the apparent emptiness that had confronted their predecessors of the previous ten years. The sketches, maps and plans of the 1840s reveal the rapidity with which temporary shelter was erected in the embryonic settlements. Frequently these makeshift conditions were endured by settlers for months at a time. Packing cases, tarpaulins and tents of all shapes and sizes, barely adequate as temporary homes in summer, were often all the protection that the settlers had in wet, cold and windy conditions, as in the first Otago winter when men and women struggled with open fires and cast-iron utensils in order to provide food for themselves and their families.

Settlers in the urban enclaves could normally look forward to a more permanent weatherboard dwelling within twelve months though it could be some years before the initial two-roomed colonial cottage (bedroom 12′ x 9′, living-room 14′ x 12′) gained the addition of a back kitchen (14′ x 10′ 6″) and second bedroom (10′ 6″ x 9′) For those individuals and families seeking to make a living off the land, the first rough shelter might last for years. Many pioneers, Chinese goldminers especially, demonstrated considerable ingenuity in their use of indigenous building materials. In areas of light rainfall, for example, the cob cottage was cheap to erect and adequate as a shelter — except for the dust problem when the nor'easter blew. As with most other aspects of pioneer life, accommodation conditions varied markedly. Those with substantial capital resources at their disposal had a very different experience. Pastoral homesteads in Canterbury and mercantile dwellings in Dunedin, for example, were usually large and comfortable. Household staff were employed. The owners of such properties were not ground into anonymity by the poverty and fatigue of their life-style. That the pictorial legacy of the pastoralists' existence is far more extensive than that of the neighbouring small farmers is a salutary reminder that class differences based primarily on wealth were an integral part of pioneer Pākehā society.

Despite frequent reference made in letters and, later, published pioneer reminiscence to the intermingling of all classes in colonial society, there was a widespread acceptance that class differences were part of the 'natural order' of life. Many pioneers moved upwards socially. Domestic servants especially often altered their circumstances quite dramatically through marriage and judicious property investment. More intangible, however, was the changing sense of self-worth which pioneers from all strata of society experienced. Many recognized that, in coping with the vicissitudes of colonial life, they were drawing upon personal qualities and strengths hitherto unsuspected. Some had no such resources. Others exhibited a new-found confidence as well as a range of new skills. Relatively few pioneers would have perceived themselves to be failures.

One of the most unnerving aspects of pioneer life for settlers of the first three decades was its unpredictability. This characteristic pervaded all aspects of life.

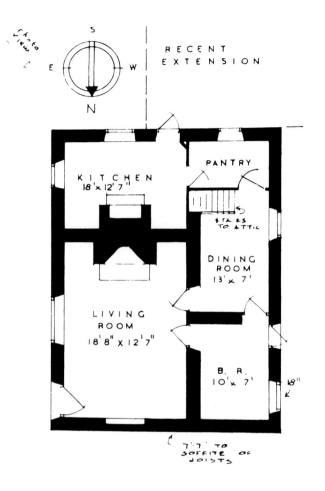

This plan of a cobhouse built in Canterbury in the 1860s represents a fairly substantial dwelling for there were two attic rooms, most probably used as bedrooms, above the main floor. Attempts to reduce the impact of prevailing northerly winds did mean, however, that a good deal of sunlight was excluded as well. *Making New Zealand*

Settlers from a stable landscape found that they had come to what was, geologically speaking, a very young country. The earthquake of 1848 was a shattering experience for the Cook Strait settlers. Quickly they adapted to building in wood rather than brick, a precaution that stood them in good stead when the more severe shocks of 1855 caused less actual damage of property though more land uplift. Farmers soon learned that the climate was a force to be reckoned with, the snowstorms of 1867 in high country Canterbury causing disastrous stock losses. Drought, gale-force winds, torrential rains, floods, frosts and landslides were all part of the pioneer experience. So too were the plagues of locusts and caterpillars that decimated crops.

Some of the environmental hazards were self-inflicted; the threat which introduced birds posed to Canterbury wheat crops was one of the most costly, and the disastrous consequences of the rabbit infestation were only beginning to appear by 1870. Few of the pioneers gave any thought to replenishing the fertility of soil exposed by burn-off to excessive leaching. It was accomplishment enough to have felled a section of native bush with axe, saw and fire, though many a burn wrought needless destruction on surrounding farms and forest.

Unfamiliarity added to the feeling of uncertainty. Pioneers adjusting from a northern to a southern hemisphere found that even night-time star-gazing was disconcertingly different. The evergreen bush provided little indication of the changing seasons. The whole rhythm of the land had first to be learned before this new environment could be understood. While farmers were the group most vulnerable to the unpredictability of weather patterns, all settlers were affected adversely when climatic conditions prevented ships from landing essential supplies. Most colonials depended upon coastal communications. The action of wind and tide saw sand-bars build up in many of the river mouths which served as harbour entrances, that of the Hokitika claiming twenty vessels in 1865 alone. Goldminers lost their possessions and sometimes their lives. The wreck of *HMS Orpheus* on the Manukau bar in 1863 and the foundering of the *City of Dunedin* in Cook Strait in May 1865, had much more tragic outcomes.

It is one of the truisms of pioneer life that the early settlers found themselves having to turn their hand to all manner of unexpected activities. Men cooked meals and washed clothes; women ran shops and pubs; husbands delivered babies; wives made bricks. Some of the role changes were relatively short-lived and for a specific purpose. Much harder for civilian pioneers of all social classes to accept was the taking up of arms. Few emigrant settlers had imagined that pioneering would involve military action.

In human terms, coping with the indigenous inhabitants of Aotearoa was probably the most disconcertingly unpredictable aspect of life for the pioneers, including those who had come to New Zealand in the decades prior to 1840. In both the North and the South Islands, many colonists had no direct contact at all with Māori people. Attitudes were shaped by hearsay, imagination and assumption. Others had constant association, a situation which reinforced presumptions of cultural superiority for some, but by no means for all, of the tauiwi. Few of the post-1840 arrivals seem to have considered what the Pākehā invasion may have meant to the Māori. In men, women and children alike, ignorance bred distrust and eventually hostility. Scarcely any Pākehā children grew up with Māori friends. Taranaki settlers whose entire life-style was disrupted by the conflicts of the 1860s, were bitter that an issue of colonial importance was being fought out at their expense. Nelson settlers coped fairly generously with the subsequent influx of women and children as refugees. Colonists throughout the country and across the Tasman contributed towards a settler relief fund. Such was the cultural gulf that none thought of compensating Māori communities for their losses.

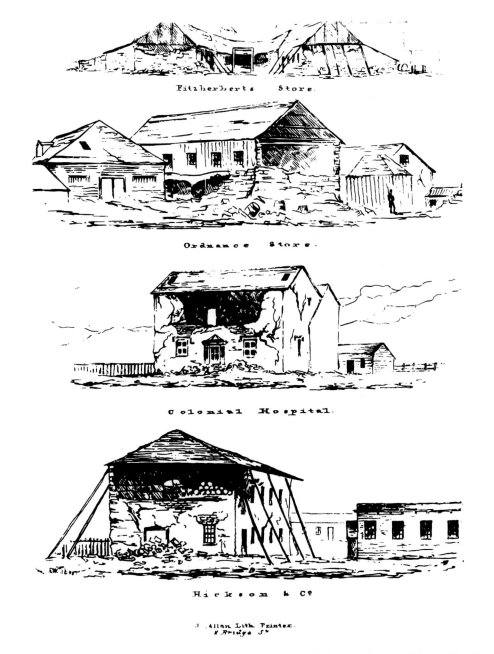

Fitzherberts Store.

Ordnance Store.

Colonial Hospital.

Hickson & Co

J. Allan Lith. Printer.
Bridge St.

While this lithograph, based on a drawing by surveyor Robert Park, reveals something of the damage to buildings in Wellington after the 1848 earthquake, the sketch also demonstrates the very functional architectural style prevalent in the early settlements where capital resources were limited. *Alexander Turnbull Library*

The visual records of cultural contact change in emphasis. Most pre-1840 illustrations are of Māori people in their own setting or in situations of peaceful contact. Incidents in the Bay of Islands, the Hutt Valley and the Wairau in the 1840s are depicted but the principal emphasis is still that of interaction in situations of trading, farming and travelling. In the 1860s, the images are of conflict. Army personnel trained to sketch the landscape also sketched battle sites. Engravers turned prose into pictures and contrasted the heroic and the heathen.

The tensions of the 1840s and 1860s brought a novel range of experience for the pioneers. Civilians took up arms, some enthusiastically, others reluctantly, some voluntarily, others only through compulsion, resentful that they should be risking their own lives and that of their families to remedy a situation which many maintained had arisen through official ineptitude. While many women believed by the 1860s that the time had come to 'teach the natives a lesson', few enjoyed the new perception of domestic gun and axe as defensive weapons. Just as it took the Cook Strait settlements years to recover from the shock and uncertainties consequent upon the Wairau disaster, so Taranaki, Bay of Plenty and Hawke's Bay pioneers found the events of the 1860s an unwelcome setback to their aspirations. Neither the paintings nor the photographs of the conflicts capture this range of emotional responses. Nor is there any real sense of the destruction for both Māori and European communities. There are paintings of military encampments, sketches of the planned engagements, maps of battle sites, diagrams of pā construction. The pre-1870 war correspondents could capture the battle scene in prose or a pen or pencil sketch, but it was Taranaki newspaper death notices that conveyed the fuller picture of the disruption and devastation in human lives. Infants and young children were the prime civilian casualties when the basic living conditions of a frontier township were strained to accommodate families forced to abandon their farms. The visual record of the Anglo-Māori wars emphasizes the preparation but not the pathos, the anticipation of victory but not the aftermath of broken limbs and broken lives. Few pioneers shared the artist's perception of war as a glorious enterprise. Even fewer supported the viewpoint of those courageous critics who dared to challenge the prevailing political standpoint that the encounters were both necessary and righteous.

Yet, as the pre–1870 pictorial evidence indicates, pioneer life was not all politics, money and war. Highdays and holidays feature significantly. Provincial anniversary day regattas, race meetings and balls are depicted in sketches, watercolours and engravings, the latter with some degree of artistic licence where ballroom furnishings are concerned. In the photographic record of pre–1870 there is also the sense of how important royal occasions were in the lives of the expatriates — weddings and visits were celebrated with public procession and gathering. The visual images emphasize the grand occasions but the pioneers early exhibited a tendency to relieve their routine with smaller scale festivities. Picnics were the most universal form of family and community recreation with adults and children alike sharing in the fun of three-legged races, cricket and the companionship which women especially may have found to be the most valuable aspect of these gatherings. In some social groups the

The marriage of the Prince of Wales, 16 June 1863, was celebrated in balmy Nelson with a mid-winter open-air banquet in Trafalgar Street, attended by adults and children alike. *Nelson Provincial Museum*

conversation doubtless turned on Home news, recent novels and philosophical dilemmas. It seems probable, however, that men and women alike made the most of the opportunity to discuss the practical problems of their pioneer existence, with economic and agricultural topics preoccupying working men just as food preparation and preservation, clothing, gardening and child care were the predominant concerns of most married women. Whatever the social standing of their husbands, pioneer women had to plan ahead for the essential provisions of their household.

Urban dwellers had more opportunity for companionable discussion than did their country counterparts for townsmen could meet regularly in the heart of their pioneer settlement, the local hotel. These buildings served a range of social purposes. Political meetings took place there as did daily discussion on the ways of righting the wrongs of the colonial world — water supply, high food prices, shipping delays, New Zealand Company malpractice, officialdom's ignorance of the real needs of the people, trouble with the Māori. Liquor was consumed in considerable quantity, much of it imported and therefore the source of substantial customs revenue, but local production increased rapidly. Alcohol was scarcely ever in short supply in pioneer society. Few publicans went bankrupt.

Yet the hotels, which were the centre of so much that was coarse and violent in pioneer society, served other purposes. On the West Coast during the gold rush heydays at least one-third of the hotels specifically advertised facilities for families. Birth notices in the *Grey River Argus* for 1870 suggest that many women may have forsaken their primitive or isolated dwellings in the last days of pregnancy to seek the relative comfort and security of town hotels where the assistance of a midwife or the support of another woman could more readily be procured.

Although there were notable exceptions, most of the first pioneers migrated as nuclear family units or as single individuals. In many instances, an extended family network was quickly established for it was common for brothers and sisters to join the original emigrants. Eventually parents and other relatives might also make the decision to uproot. The establishment of extended family support networks was, nevertheless, a process that happened over years, not months. In the meantime, many a younger man and woman embarked upon a colonial marriage without any older family member or friend to turn to for guidance. Family lore of dealing with pregnancy, childbirth, childhood ailments and 'women's problems' was rarely available in the first critical years. Traditional herbal remedies were unprocurable initially. By the 1860s new arrivals in the older settlements were able to draw upon the accumulated experience of those who had emigrated ten or twenty years before them, but in the frontiers of settlement such reassurance was scarce. Many women worked for months, even years, without enjoying the companionship of other women. Yet even in the towns, pioneer women could lead an isolated existence. The establishment of 'Main Street' did not encourage daily shopping. Neighbourhood deliveries of essential foodstuffs, the convention of formal visiting, and the day-long involvement in domestic chores meant that many women hardly ever had the opportunity to relax with friends. Anxieties were, for the most part, shared within the marriage rather than outside it.

Both the risks and the rigours of pioneer life put tremendous strain on marriage relationships, a strain not eased by the almost incessant production of children over what was often a twenty-five year period. Women bore the brunt of the daily stress but the prevailing social ethos, that a man was a failure if he could not provide adequately for his wife and family, imposed pressure on men who discovered that they were unsuited physically or temperamentally for the labour-intensive nature of pioneer life. Some had the personal or material resources to surmount the problem. Others resolved their difficulties by leaving them.

The loss of the family wage-earner or care-giver, whether by desertion, mental illness or death, placed all remaining family members in an extremely difficult position in an era where charitable aid and community help were the only means of assistance. In such circumstances colonial children grew up very quickly. In the large families of those first decades, only the last-born had time and opportunity to be a child. In the vast majority of cases pioneer children were expected to work and, both within and outside the home, their labour was essential to the functioning and economic viability of the family enterprise. Older children fetched and carried for younger siblings from an extremely young age. Such was the labour-intensive nature of pioneering life that many parents felt that they had no option but to involve their children in tasks not all of which were in keeping with a youngster's age and strength. In general terms, boys spent more time in helping their fathers and girls their mothers but there was no rigid division. If wives worked on the farm, husbands generally helped in the house. Sons and daughters followed the example. Children growing up in rural locations especially absorbed an ethic in which the character-building benefits of hard work were reiterated without question. For town children too, childhood was often brief. Girls contributed to the running of the household in a myriad of ways, with Monday wash-day, Tuesday ironing, Saturday knife-cleaning and boot-blacking, and daily emptying of the slops being amongst the routines most abhorred. Youngsters ran messages for their parents and for neighbours. In the years before compulsory elementary schooling, many entered underpaid domestic service at a very young age, often barely nine or ten. Rural children were an unpaid labour force even earlier. Yet, of the vital economic role which these children played in pioneer society, there is simply no substantial visual evidence.

For the majority of parents there was probably little reason for them to question their expectations of their children. Many of the pioneers were self-educated; others were barely literate. Working class settlers had emigrated in hopes of material improvement for themselves and their families. That the children should contribute towards the attainment of that goal was self-evident. For the most part, country children had the experience of working alongside their parents, both indoors and out, a situation in which there was some possibility that the family unit would grow to be a very closely-knit one emotionally. Children of the colonial gentry, however, were often subjected to a routine little different from what they would have experienced in Britain. Frequently they were returned there for their education and so grew up distanced physically and emotionally from the land of their birth.

Many children in the developing townships seem to have been left largely to their own devices. Whether from choice or necessity, girls tended to remain around the home. Older boys soon formed themselves into rival gangs. Orchards were raided, races contested, fights were fought. The activities may have been mischievous but were not wilfully destructive. Corporal punishment was one form of discipline, deprivation another. The visual record suggests that obedience was an integral part of children's relationships with their elders. Of the genuine affection that also pervaded family circles there is very little impression.

Love, laughter and the spontaneity of life are missing from the illustrative record. The facial images are stern, serene, enigmatic, resigned, occasionally even terrified. The children are serious, earnest, above all intent on following parental or photographer's instruction that they should keep watching the object specified. Infants and toddlers alike are uncharacteristically solemn and still. Technical

The device illustrated in this pre-1870 photograph of 'Mrs Balme's Little Girl' was widely used by portrait photographers. Usually a parent seated alongside would hide the support but any evidence of its existence would be removed when the negative was retouched. *Nelson Provincial Museum*

limitations and Victorian sensitivity are the cause. The five to six second exposure time with the whole plate camera meant that a subject's slight movement resulted in a blur. The exposure time was reduced during the 1860s with the introduction of the half-plate and quarter plate cameras but rigidity was still a requirement. A close look at many contemporary photos reveals that the ramrod-straight back and upright lift of the head was achieved with the aid of back and/or neck-supporting devices. Victorian propriety probably accounts for the absence of outward signs of affection in the photographs. Physical contact between adults is usually limited to the touch of a hand on a shoulder; that between parent and child restricted to a youngster sitting on a parental knee. Formality rather than friendship is the consequent impression. The visual image is overwhelmingly one of the pioneers as serious individuals for whom emotions were a force to be kept firmly under control.

Tears are absent also. Neither painters nor photographers captured people expressing their emotions. It is only the artist's quick sketch which conveys some sense of the spontaneity of feelings, as in William Strutt's remarkable depiction of a Taranaki bush burn about to blaze out of control. Victorian sensibilities tended to prevent any artistic intrusion at times of sorrow. Death is rarely depicted.

The most significant of the missing images then are those which deal with the emotional aspects of pioneer life. Fortunately letters and diaries do survive which, written as they were for private not public purposes, reveal that the tauiwi did care deeply for one another. The anxiety of a husband stranded with a doctor on one side of a flooded river while his wife coped virtually unaided with her first childbirth on the other; the concern pervading the correspondence of a military officer separated by the breadth of the North Island from his life partner and their young children: the image of the stern unbending *pater familias* is simply not in accord with the written evidence. Similarly, while the sheer busyness of colonial mothers meant that they spent little time relaxing with their children, maternal affection was expressed constantly, in letter and in action.

The pioneers of these first decades faced more emotional upheaval than succeeding generations could ever have imagined. Even the smells and sounds of the new land were different. Country women missed the scent of wild roses and honeysuckle. Former city dwellers could only imagine the echo of horses' hooves on cobbled streets or the clamour of the market-place. Local breweries provided ample quantities of acceptable liquor but the atmosphere of the corner pub at Home was irreplaceable. Observance of the traditional Christian festivals of comfort and promise was strange when the seasons were 'wrong'. Few pioneer women had envisaged making pounds of raspberry jam on Christmas Day. And always there was the loneliness, the pain of which intensified whenever a long-awaited letter from Home brought news of the death of a family member or a friend. For some families the separation of one generation from another was far more traumatic than is suggested by the paintings of dockside farewells. When parents and their children departed, the family unit might be incomplete. An older son or daughter was left behind to care for ageing relatives, to be a source of companionship and comfort to

Acres of bush were needlessly destroyed when burns blazed out of control, because of sudden wind change or sheer carelessness. William Strutt's 1856 Taranaki sketch protrays vividly the awe and terror which such conflagrations could arouse. *Alexander Turnbull Library*

them. Such children were not always reunited with their families in the Antipodes. For many pioneers, only their faith in a life hereafter sustained them through the anguish of farewells that they knew to be final on this earth.

The extent and variety of letters surviving from the pioneering era demonstrate the determined efforts made to maintain personal ties. For the illiterate and barely educated, the task was a formidable one. Letters could only be written or read with another person's assistance, a situation which was not conducive to the expression of more personal feelings. Moreover, as family histories reveal, for older relatives in Britain, the arrival of a letter from the colony could mean a visit to the pawnbroker before the recipient possessed the resources to have the correspondence read and answered. Under such circumstances, it was far more difficult for many labouring class emigrants to maintain anything other than the most erratic of family contacts. The more literate pioneers wrote frequently and graphically, detailing current political and economic concerns, reporting the state of both settlement and personal fortunes. Some correspondents clearly regretted their decision to come to New

Zealand: others revealed their determination to succeed despite the setbacks that they had experienced. Many relished their new lifestyles.

For adults uprooted from all that was familiar, pioneering could be a severe test of personal stamina. To make the decision to emigrate in the first place suggested a certain strength of character though not all marriage partners were equally enthusiastic about the prospects. Younger children were usually caught up with the excitement of an adventure; older siblings occasionally shared something of parental apprehensions. Adjustment to New Zealand conditions was rarely rapid or easy, whatever the marital and material status of the individuals concerned. A governor's wife could feel even more lonely than a seamstress, a lawyer just as disconcerted as a labourer. Both the shipboard experience and the proximity of early housing meant that the first arrivals in each settlement were sustained by a mutual support network. But population increase and movement undermined that co-operative spirit and left many individuals with a strong sense of personal isolation. Many found reassurance through spiritual means; some found solace in alcohol. The fatigue induced by daily labours was another palliative. Thousands of women and men alike flourished in their new environment, becoming more self-confident and adventuresome, enjoying the opportunity of self-reliance. Others felt helpless and overwhelmed. Suicides occurred as did mental illness. Not all of the problems were related to economic difficulty either, for children and wives were being neglected and deserted even in times of prosperity. Pioneer life could be a stressful experience and the men and women who coped best were those in supportive relationships and those who possessed an inner fortitude, the basis of which was, most usually, their religious belief.

Photographs dating from the 1860s give no sense of the overwhelming youthfulness of the population in the 1840s and 1850s, when at least one-quarter of the immigrants were children, and to be over forty-five was to be old. The portrait photographers of that third decade were recording individuals prematurely aged by the childbearing and hard domestic or physical labours of twenty years. Many of the women appear to be quite muscular; few are fat. The basic nature of the diet and the incessant demands of the household routine ensured that obesity was not a common problem. Adults and children alike tended to be physically fit since 'shank's pony' was the only form of conveyance to which all had ready access. Horses were soon imported but were too expensive to be a common possession until colonial-bred stock became available. Water transport was the usual means of moving goods from one settlement to another, bullock carts the slow but reliable method used on land.

The pace of pioneer life was therefore slow. Men, women and children walked — to visit friends, to obtain supplies, to seek employment, to attend such schooling or church service as might be available. Many women led very restricted lives territorially while others undertook quite epic journeys, often when in advanced stages of pregnancy. Injured bushmen or goldminers were carried by teams of workmates for miles through difficult terrain. Surveyors and explorers walked themselves beyond the limits of normal human endurance. Babies and toddlers rode in gin cases strapped to the side of packhorses while adults walked alongside in the mud or dust, the ruts and the potholes that were the characteristics of a colonial track. Pioneers who relied on coastal transport often had their patience sorely tried owing to the erratic nature of shipping services and the unpredictability of sailing conditions.

Pioneer life was hard. Kitchen equipment was heavy cast-iron, the open fire the only source of heat for cooking in summer and winter. Virtually every task both inside and outside the home was physically laborious. On Monday wash-day water had to be fetched, kindling and firewood chopped, the copper boiled and clothes rubbed on a washboard with home-made soap. Rinsing, wringing and pegging out on a prop line (the collapse of which meant a repeat of the whole process) were then followed by a Tuesday of starching and ironing with a flat iron. Outdoor work took place from dawn till dusk. Indoors the mending, knitting, sewing, child care, food preparation and preservation went on well into the hours of darkness. Sheets were turned, socks darned, baby clothes knitted, adult garments re-fashioned into children's clothes, newspapers read, letters written, floor rugs hooked and children nursed, all by the flickering light of home-made candle or slush lamp and, later, paraffin lantern. Most pioneer homes were small, bedrooms and beds were shared. Privacy was the privilege of the rich.

Everyday life had its dangers. Cemetery headstones tell of children who died from drowning — a constant colonial danger given the open drains, uncovered water wells, water races and the proximity of so many settlements to streams and rivers, the course and volume of which could change so suddenly. The open fireplaces, matches and candles that were essential to daily living also claimed young victims. Toddlers died from sulphur poisoning as a result of sucking the heads of wax vesta matches. Children playing with fire lost their lives when the smoke and flames of inflammable curtains, clothes, straw or scrub overcame them. Youngsters suffered horrendous pain from burns caused by scalding water. Some did not survive. The unhygienic conditions with which many settlers were surrounded took its toll of infants. Illegitimate babies were very much at risk, often suffocating through being 'overlain'. Starvation and neglect were alternative strategies. Yet not all unwanted children met a similar fate. The records of the Canterbury Provincial Council in 1869, for example, detail the number of children supported by charitable aid. The provincial government provided an average of seven shillings and eight shillings weekly to women who were responsible for the nursing and care of orphaned or abandoned youngsters. Often children in care still had a parent living but many widowers with young dependents were forced to resort to church or provincial government agencies. Permanent family breakup often ensued when the parent moved away, ostensibly in search of better employment.

Pioneer life was hazardous for adults too. Childbirth took a heavy toll, death as a consequence of prolonged labour or septicaemia being two frequent causes. Some women virtually worked themselves to death. Others overcame illness and enjoyed longevity. For men the most common forms of death related to the physical environment in which most of them worked. 'Fall of earth' was the usual cause of

Fires claimed lives and caused hundreds of pounds worth of damage in the highly inflammable wooden towns of pioneer society. Wet sacks and wooden buckets of water were ineffectual once a fire began to spread and residents could only flee for their lives when disaster overtook a township, as in the 'Great Fire of Lyttleton', 24 October 1870. *Canterbury Museum*

death by accident in mining areas. Drowning was a frequent occurrence. Many of the fatalities resulted from attempts to cross swollen rivers and inability to swim in an era when boats were the principal form of transport. In other instances the victims had not been sober. Men working in the bush with saw and axe sometimes miscalculated the direction of a tree fall. Usually it was a mate who was killed by a 'sailer' — a branch broken off as the tree crashed to the ground. Men and boys died from gunshot wounds since firearms were often loaded when carried or stored. Many men made heroic efforts to get their wounded mates to a doctor. Blood poisoning could render their efforts in vain. Medical attention was too expensive to be sought lightly. For more minor accidents and illness, the pioneers treated themselves. Common sense and castor oil were the usual prescriptions. Fortunately the colonial climate lived up to some of the health claims made for it but epidemics of scarlet fever and measles did occur, often resulting in multiple deaths within the families afflicted. Many pioneers suffered chronic ill-health, headaches and rheumatism being two of the conditions most frequently recorded. Toothache was common, and extraction was the solution. Bad breath and body odour were prevalent.

That the pioneers experienced a good deal of heartache and hardship cannot be disputed. Most women, single or married, felt keenly their isolation from family and friends. A majority of adult men never found the opportunity to alter their solitary lifestyle. In later years, the unmarried pioneers would often end their days in a boarding house, hospital or benevolent institution, the only place that they could call 'home'. It is also apparent that many pioneers responded to the challenges and the setbacks with extraordinary fortitude and optimism. Contemporaries noted that the atmosphere in the settlements gradually changed as political and personal competitiveness and materialism came to predominate, but initially there was manifest a sense of vitality and common purpose as the pioneers sought to create their new and better world. The visual record of their subsequent achievement is remarkably rich. As human-made artefacts, the pictures reveal a great deal about contemporary attitudes for the artists, photographers, surveyors and explorers were themselves pioneers. The illustrations capture places at one moment in their history and enable comparisons to be made over time. The rich portrait collection of adult and child pioneer may, in one sense, be too static an image of a people whose energy and application were normally arrested only on a Sunday but the evidence is there, nevertheless, of what the subjects thought important to preserve for posterity. By viewing the visual images as sources of information and insight in their own right, not as mere appendages to the written word, the remarkable diversity of pioneer life becomes apparent.

4. *The Governors and the Māori* (1840–1872)

❦

JAMES BELICH

On 25 April 1873, three Pākehā settlers were working near the Waikato town of Cambridge, on land they believed to be in the British-ruled colony of New Zealand. Suddenly, they were attacked by armed men, who believed this to be territory of the Māori King. The settlers ran, two escaped, but the third, Timothy Sullivan, was caught and killed. There was nothing surreptitious about this. The names and whereabouts of Sullivan's killers were well-known to the colonial government; his head was displayed near the Kingite-Pākehā border; and his heart was taken to the King's capital at Te Kuiti. Some Kingite leaders regretted the execution, which had followed repeated warnings, but largely because the victim was Sullivan and not his employer, E.B. Walker.

If we had to invent a simple test of real sovereignty, of who actually ruled the central North Island in 1873, the question of punishment for so blatant a deed would be a good one. As is often the case, history makes invention unnecessary. To leave Sullivan's killer unpunished, wrote Judge Frederick Maning, would be 'avowedly to give up the assertion of sovereignty of the crown over a large part of New Zealand'. But punishment would mean a war which the government was not sure it could win, and Sullivan was never avenged. The government failed the test. In 1873, one year after the end of the New Zealand Wars, nine years after the King Movement was allegedly crushed at Orakau, and thirty-three years after the Treaty of Waitangi, according to legend, made New Zealand British by the stroke of a pen, the Māori were still the real governors of perhaps half the North Island.

Between 1840 and 1872, and for a number of years thereafter, the history of Māori-Pākehā relations is the history of two independent zones or spheres. Neither zone was politically unified. Maoridom was split into numerous tribes and hapū, and these terms themselves may be too simple. Ngati Ruanui often grouped their many hapū into three major hapū or sub-tribes. Waikato had three tiers above hapū level: the Waikato-Ngati Maniapoto-Ngati Haua alliance; Waikato proper; and the various

Frederick Maning. His "Old New Zealand" persisted in places until the 1880s. *Canterbury Museum*

tribes which comprised it, such as Ngati Mahuta. Ngapuhi had three hapū-groups; Ataiwa two, plus three associated tribes; and the Arawa 'tribe' consisted of several smaller tribes. Hapū, temporary or permanent groups of hapū, tribes, and temporary or permanent groups of tribes — all could be political actors.

The Pākehā zone was hardly less complicated. Old-style settlements included whaling, mission, and trading stations and shanty ports like Kororareka, serving and exploiting their Māori hosts like tick-eating birds on a buffalo. This was the 'Old New Zealand' portrayed by Frederick Maning, and it persisted long after 1840. Even as late as 1880 the Kingite port of Kawhia had something of its flavour. The new-style settlements such as Wellington were instant townships modelled on E.G. Wakefield's plans and had less room for Māori in their scheme of things, but had to make room in practice. These were grouped in provinces, boroughs, and counties, divided into interest groups and the private empires of powerful men, and overseen by settler legislatures and cabinets, distant Imperial authorities and their semi-independent representatives, the governors. The components of both zones changed over time and context, sometimes in response to each other; a shifting mosaic, more like the Holy Roman Empire with its 300 states than the solid British pink of the old school atlas.

Until 1845, the persistence of Māori independence was hardly surprising. The coercive power of the infant Pākehā state initially consisted of a few drunken constables; they were soon joined by 150 Imperial troops — all the military might of

Sir George Grey, Governor from 1845 to 1853, and again from 1861 to 1867. *National Museum*

a large hapū. Governors Hobson and FitzRoy were not the men to make much out of little. Robert FitzRoy, another naval captain, who succeeded Hobson in 1843, was morally upright and not unintelligent, but he was also somewhat narrow and obsessive. (He later headed the British meteorological service, and was said to have committed suicide after allegations that his weather forecasts were more often wrong than right.) He was replaced in 1845 by the enigmatic George Grey, who was talented, subtle and unscrupulous. His brilliance extended to propaganda as well as practice, and historians often have difficulty in separating the two. Grey had more ability than FitzRoy, and he also had more resources, including 1000 imperial troops. Even this was no more than a large tribe, and Grey, FitzRoy and Hobson all pursued a policy intended to subject the Māori with a minimum use of force.

This policy was based on two assumptions: that the Maori were unusually intelligent (for blacks) and that intelligence translated into the desire to become British. Both humanity and tight Imperial finances therefore dictated that the Māori were to be converted to being governed as they were to Christianity: by example, gentle pressure, and wise guidance. Between 1840 and 1860, apart from a brief period of conflict in the 1840s, it seemed to Grey and others that this new evangelism, or 'moral suasion', was being remarkably successful. And it is quite true that the Māori responded eagerly to all four of its cornerstones: God and money, law and land.

Missionary activity was part of the Old New Zealand which bridged 1840. Each year, the missionaries reported a mounting score of souls until by about 1850 the great majority of Māori had been saved. These 'conversions' were not what the missionaries fondly hoped. Māori were attracted to Christianity by such things as novelty, fashion, material advantage, and access to literacy, and their commitment was seldom complete. But it would be a mistake to assume that such conversions were insincere or frivolous. They were simply not exclusive. Māori religion had always been open, able to incorporate new gods such as newly deified ancestors. Christianity was adapted and incorporated into traditional beliefs, changing them perhaps, but not replacing them. It may be that the Māori cults, or prophetic movements, such as Pai Marire and Kai Ngarara, were an integral part of this process, not a reaction to it. The prophetic movements known are already numerous — six in Taranaki alone between 1845 and 1867 — and more may remain to be discovered. Most were linked together, and their influence extended far beyond their most obvious adherents. Perhaps the prophetic movements were the basic mechanism of incorporation; making the necessary adjustments, reconciling old and new beliefs and both with their contexts.

So the Māori *were* Christian — Anglican, Methodist, Catholic, or even all three. But it was their own kind of Christianity, and they were still heathens as well — and often adherents of a particular prophet. Empathizing especially with the Old Testament, some considered themselves Jewish to boot. The Māori did convert to Christianity, but they also converted it. This was not what Pākehā evangelists, old or new, had in mind.

Another prop of the new evangelism was commerce, which some Europeans considered more effective even than God in converting savages to civilization. There is no doubt of the breadth of Māori economic engagement with the Pākehā, though more research is required into its depth. The Māori supplied food — potatoes, kūmara, wheat, maize, pigs, fish and fruit — to the Pākehā zone. According to the *New-Zealander* of 1848: 'the Maoris are our largest purveyors of foodstuffs; so large indeed as nearly to monopolise the market and to exclude Europeans from competition.' By the 1850s, the Māori milled the wheat themselves, and transported

Bugler William Allen sounds the alarm before being cut down in the attack on Boulcott's Farm, Wellington, in 1846. 'Boy' Allen was actually aged about twenty, and is unlikely to have been quite so dwarfed by his foe as this picture suggests. *Alexander Turnbull Library*

Māori retailers, selling peaches and melons. *Alexander Turnbull Library*

everything to market in carts, canoes, small coastal vessels and even quite substantial schooners. They also grew and processed flax, dug kauri gum, and had some share in the whaling and timber industries. A few worked permanently in the Pākehā zone as servants or labourers; many visited in tribally-organized groups for seasonal work, including prostitution. Pākehā travellers in the Māori zone provided more business; they needed guides, river ferries and accommodation houses, like the 'Whare-Pākehā' at Manawapou in 1851. Māori provided markets for European manufactures and imported goods, such as clothing, guns, sugar and rum. In 1850, an Auckland settler wrote that the Māori 'are estimated to consume some 25 or 30 £ worth of British manufactures yearly per head'. Economically, the Māori came to depend on the Pākehā, but the reverse was also the case. Moreover, commerce did not have the expected effect of breaking down tribal structures by increasing individualism. No doubt some Māori became genuine capitalists, using their money to make more, but normally work was organized collectively and profits used for collective ends, such as security or status. The tribes were commercialized; but commerce was also tribalized.

A further cornerstone of the new evangelism was land — Māori land sold to Pākehā. Mixing the two peoples geographically was thought to be the quickest road to 'amalgamation', and of course the Pākehā zone needed land to expand. Normally, Māori sold willingly — for many reasons, some of them short-sighted. Some sellers were duped, though the reverse was occasionally the case, with the same piece of land sold three times over to gullible Pākehā. Land purchases up to 1840 were a mess, notably those made by Wakefield's New Zealand Company, and most were subsequently overturned. Thereafter, except for a brief period under FitzRoy, the Crown did all the buying. This reduced the cash price, but increased the validity of sales by obtaining the consent of a higher proportion of owners, or at least the chiefs who represented them. The government's master land buyer was Donald McLean, a clever, almost Grey-like, Scot who did not sweat — 'I never sweat. Domett does, awfully.' McLean and his colleagues sometimes tricked, pressured, and cut corners in their purchasing, especially in the South Island, and specific 'sales' might be bitterly disputed. Often, however, land was bought from Māori who knew what they were doing and wanted to sell.

A major Māori motive was the desire for Pākehā neighbours. They wanted Pākehā markets, goods, skills, and services and sometimes handy buffers against other tribes, who dared not attack someone else's Pākehā for fear of scaring away their own. These factors were ends in themselves, but simultaneously they were means to an end: mana. 'Mana' is often defined as authority or prestige but the term 'spiritual capital' may better reflect it for Pākehā. If capitalism, the Pākehā system, is used as an analogy for the Māori system, then mana was its capital, the accumulation and use of which was in itself desirable. Pākehā were the new currency in an old game — what historian Ann Parsonson describes as 'the pursuit of mana'. Frederick Maning outlined the early denominations:

> A *pakeha* trader was . . . of a value, say about twenty times his weight in muskets . . . A book-keeper, or a second-rate pakeha, not a trader, might be valued at, say, his weight in tomahawks — an enormous sum also. The poorest labouring pakeha . . . might be estimated at, say, his weight in fish-hooks.

But inflation set in during the 1840s. A couple of Pākehā parked in the tribal garage were no longer enough, and the major players began to deal in whole towns, the ultimate status symbol. Unfortunately for the new evangelism, Māori looked upon 'their Pākehā' (a very common phrase) less as moral exemplars than as cherished possessions.

The final cornerstone of the new evangelism was law. In 1860, Governor Thomas Gore Browne, who had succeeded Grey five years earlier, wrote that: 'English law has always prevailed in the English settlements, but remains a dead letter beyond them.' This was largely true. Māori law predominated in the Māori zone, Pākehā in the Pākehā. But the new evangelism sent legal missionaries out into the Māori zone — 'Protectors of Aborigines' before 1847, 'Resident Magistrates' thereafter — and they had some effect. In some areas, at some periods, in some instances Māori voluntarily accepted their law, especially in Māori-Pākehā disputes. Occasionally, backed by police or military forays from the Pākehā zone, they were even able to coerce acceptance. More often Māori applied their own versions of Pākehā law themselves, whether as official 'assessors' or self-appointed magistrates, adding it to their own practices as they had added Christianity. Generally, Pākehā Resident Magistrates were more of a diplomatic service than a legal one. But a minority of Māori, especially when visiting the Pākehā zone or living on its fringes, were forced or persuaded to accept British law.

On the other hand, a minority of Pākehā conformed to Māori law: Pākehā under Māori control are the forgotten minority of New Zealand race relations. Scattered settlers living in Māori areas were frequently subjected to muru — legal plundering — for offences such as stock trespass. Small Pākehā communities might have Māori overlords, willing and able to impose their own law if pressed. The Ngapuhi chief Hone Heke demanded that the leader of the Whangarei settlers correct various transgressions in 1844. 'Act accordingly for the reason that I love you and your children . . . also for you belong to me . . . If the Europeans will not listen, and continue to do wrong, neither will the Maoris take heed, therefore I will place the transgressors in a very small place indeed.' Even in the large town of New Plymouth, the settlers complained, with only partial exaggeration, of being 'subjected to the domination of a savage race.'

The new evangelism did chalk up some points, but the Māori subverted it more than it subverted them. Like Dr Frankenstein, some Māori found their Pākehā dangerous servants, but others succeeded in controlling them. Consequently, the New Zealand situation between 1840 and 1860 was one of 'informal empire' — a loose overlordship which permitted some local autonomy and exerted just enough control to cheaply obtain the desired economic and strategic benefits. The question is, whose informal empire was it, Māori or Pākehā? The answer varied over time and space.

It was in the south that the legend of rapidly imposed British rule had most substance. Ngai Tahu owned most of the South Island, but had been badly damaged by Ngati Toa invasions in the 1830s, and numbered less than 2000 people. During the 1840s under the able chiefs Tuhawaiki and Taiaroa, the southern Ngai Tahu were able to cope with their old-style Pākehā fringe, the whaling stations of Foveaux Strait and the Otago coast, though the weaker northern hapū had some trouble at Banks Peninsula. Between 1844 and 1857, however, Ngai Tahu sold off almost their whole Island in a number of shady deals. On this land, the new-style settlements of Dunedin and Christchurch were founded in 1848 and 1850.

Ngai Tahu sold partly because they wanted more Pākehā, and partly because they feared that if they did not, Ngati Toa would. But there were also discrepancies between Māori and Pākehā conceptions of the land sales. Māori literacy may not have been so widespread as some historians suppose, and even if it was, as D. F. McKenzie has pointed out with regard to the Treaty of Waitangi, it was solid and solemn verbal agreements which mattered to Māori, not the scratchings on paper Pākehā chose to

Te Rauparaha and Te Rangihaeata, whose 'empire' in the Cook Strait region was taken over by Grey. *National Museum*

make as souvenirs. Ngai Tahu believed they had agreed to sell far less land, and in practice they were quite right for some years. They continued to exploit the natural resources of 'crown land' as they had always done. The vast South Island 'purchases' did not turn white in a day, but were actually occupied gradually. With continued use of traditional resources combined with intensive agriculture for the new Pākehā markets, the Ngai Tahu population and economy stabilized during the 1850s. But, from about 1860, the discovery of gold and potential for sheep meant that Dunedin and Christchurch, containable at first, burgeoned beyond all measure. Ngai Tahu were simply dwarfed, then shouldered aside, without war, but not without protest and non-violent resistance.

In the Cook Strait region (the top of the South Island and the bottom of the North) one loose informal empire was replaced by another during the 1840s. Te Rauparaha's hegemony was impressive, but it was narrowly based: on good relations with Pākehā, who supplied guns and wealth, and on the limited military power of the small Ngati Toa tribe, the rest being jealous allies and imperfectly conquered enemies. Land sales presented an opportunity for subtle utu, and Wakefield's New Zealand Company went to little trouble to ascertain the rightful owners. Disputes arose early around the settlements of Wellington and Nelson. In 1843, Ngati Toa turned back surveyors from disputed land at Wairau and fifty armed Nelson settlers set out to teach Te Rauparaha the reality of British sovereignty. Instead, they learned the reality of Māori independence. Twenty-two were killed, and armed posses of civilians never again took on the Māori though they often threatened to do so. FitzRoy did not punish Te Rauparaha, so failing the Sullivan test of real sovereignty. Some bitter Nelson and Wellington settlers claimed that they were Māori-dominated, oppressed fiefs of the Ngati Toa empire.

When renewed fighting broke out near Wellington in 1846, however, Grey was able to exploit the weaknesses of this empire. Te Rangihaeata, a close associate of Te Rauparaha, and his Wanganui ally Te Mamaku, made some successful raids into the disputed Hutt Valley. But many fellow-tribesmen and allies, including Te Rauparaha, valued Pākehā too highly to support Te Rangihaeata, and some, who also resented Ngati Toa overlordship, actually fought against him. Though unable to secure any decisive military victory, Grey drove Te Rangihaeata north of Waikanae, and, in a stunning coup, treacherously seized and imprisoned the neutral Te Rauparaha, permanently crippling his mana. Up to 1858, 'no event during the English rule ever caused so much sensation among the natives'. Caught naked and unarmed in his house, the old chief struggled desperately until a British sailor grabbed his testicles, so symbolizing the low morality and high effectiveness of Grey's tactics.

The autonomous Māori zone continued to exist in the Cook Strait region. Pākehā Wellington stopped at Waikanae and even south of this, mediator-chiefs like Wi Tako Ngatata had considerable influence. But the loose suzerainty once exercised by Ngati Toa passed to the government, and in the immediate environs of Wellington and Nelson its control soon became more or less complete. Grey had removed Te Rauparaha and slotted into his place.

So much, from the Pākehā viewpoint, for the good news. Wellington and the South Island made up 60% of New Zealand in terms of acres, but only 10% in terms of Māori. Further north, in the bulk of Maoridom, the situation was different. Ngati Kahungunu of Wairarapa and Hawke's Bay considered themselves poorly supplied with Pākehā. In 1844, numerous appeals from them for settlers appeared in the Wellington press — 'I wish for some white people as neighbours'. It was a Kahungunu chief who set out the definitive Māori position on land-price: 'Should the Pakeha wish to purchase land here, encourage him; no matter how small the amount he may offer, take it without hesitation. It is the Pakeha we want here. The Pakeha himself will be ample payment for our land, because we commonly expect to become prosperous through him.'

With Ngati Kahungunu encouragement, small-holders, pastoralists, and traders penetrated to Wairarapa in the 1840s and Hawke's Bay in the 1850s, where there was a substantial town at Napier by 1858. To achieve this, Ngati Kahungunu sold half their land, but they tended to keep the best, or lease at good rentals, and Pākehā were a compensating economic resource. 'The native leases yield £9,000 a year in Hawke's Bay,' wrote a local official in 1863. 'The three Native mills, the crops of wheat and maize, the money earned by shearing, labour and timber, amounts, I am credibly informed, to an even larger sum.'

At Wanganui, on the west coast, the situation was not dissimilar, despite some initial friction. The town of Wanganui, founded in 1841, was considered by the Lower

Wanganui hapū to be their property, and they defended it in 1847 against their upriver kin, led by Te Mamaku, who also had several indecisive skirmishes with British troops. Even Te Mamaku maintained he was opposed to the presence of soldiers in Wanganui, not to settlers. After 1848, when a widely-accepted sale of 80,000 acres was made, the town and tribe of Wanganui co-operated quite smoothly. Further north, at New Plymouth, the Atiawa survivors of the Waikato invasions were also keen to obtain Pākehā. 'Give us Pakeha,' wrote the Waitara people in 1844, 'and we will give them land.' The situation was again complicated by careless New Zealand Company land buying, and by the return of 600 Atiawa exiles from the Wellington area, under Wiremu Kingi Te Rangitake. Government investigations disallowed most company land purchases; Wiremu Kingi's people did very well economically at Waitara; and both factors created resentment among the New Plymouth Pākehā. But the settlers did not have the power to do much about it, and though the inter-racial relationship was less easy than at Napier or Wanganui, it worked for a time.

New Plymouth, Wanganui, and Napier represented the median of Māori-Pākehā relations. Tribe and town were twin communities co-operating in an often tense but more or less equal 'symbiosis'. In a vast region spanning the middle of the North Island, the heart of independent Maoridom, Māori tended to exercise more control over their Pākehā. Some isolated areas, such as the Urewera, had no Pākehā, and relied for European goods and knowledge on Māori middlemen. Throughout the region, little land was sold, but at first this was partly for want of buyers. Ngati Maniapoto, later one of the two tribes considered most hostile to the Pākehā, frequently appealed for settlers in the 1840s. The pattern tended to be one of a scattering of Pākehā inland (300 lived in the Waikato in 1855); a fringe of small port-settlements (Raglan, Kawhia, Tauranga, and Turanga); and access to large towns, especially Auckland. Founded in 1840, Auckland was initially controlled, as pioneer settler Logan Campbell admitted, by its Ngati Whatua hosts. But Ngati Whatua found their servant soon outgrew them, becoming the centre for a large trade with Waikato and the Bay of Plenty.

In Northland, Māori had been managing Pākehā for a generation before 1840, and they were quite good at it. Rarawa and two factions of Ngapuhi each had a substantial European trading settlement; at Mangonui, Hokianga, and the Bay of Islands. Ngapuhi intended to keep both their independence and their Pākehā, but there were problems with the latter. The imposition of customs dues and the removal of the capital from the Bay of Islands to Auckland led to an exodus of Pākehā. One Ngapuhi faction, represented by Hone Heke, took strong measures against such government interference, leading to the Northern War of 1845-1846, fought as much for economic collaboration as political resistance. The other faction, represented by Tamati Waka Nene, opposed this, fearing it would cost even more Pākehā. Fighting a separate war within a war, Waka Nene defeated Heke at Te Ahuahu on 12 June 1845. But prior to this, Heke and his ally Kawiti had twice defeated the British, at Kororareka and Puketutu. In late June, FitzRoy at last received reinforcements, and mounted an expedition against Kawiti's pā of Ohaeawai to reverse these defeats and complete the work of Waka Nene. For the first time, the Māori clashed in full battle with a substantial force of British troops.

The Ngapuhi had had plenty of experience of musket-armed enemies, and had adjusted the design of their pā accordingly, but they had never faced a foe so fanatically convinced of their own superiority, so ready to incur the losses involved in frontal assault, or so well equipped with artillery. The British out-numbered them 600 to 100, and had an irascible but not incompetent commander in Colonel Henry Despard. Unfortunately for Despard, the old chief Kawiti happened to be a bona fide military genius. He revolutionized the pā by inventing anti-artillery bunkers integrated into a system of firing trenches, with earth replacing wood as the major building material. Despard assaulted on 1 July, believing the garrison had been pulverized by his artillery bombardment. It had not, and he was bloodily repulsed. A drawn battle at Ruapekapeka in January 1846 failed to rectify the situation and, despite Grey's claims to the contrary, the war ended unfavourably for the British.

The fighting of the 1840s firmed up the two zones, setting the limits on their co-operation. The British won no major battles at Wanganui or Wellington, but in the latter district the strategic result favoured them. The seizure of Te Rauparaha more than compensated for the humiliation of Wairau. The Pākehā zone expanded and became quite powerful; by 1860 the European population of the North Island (about 40,000) was within sight of the Māori (about 60,000); the larger new-style settlements shook themselves free from Māori suzerainty. But the Northern War symbolized the other side of the equation, reaffirming and guaranteeing the independence of the Māori zone.

Relations between the two spheres, then, covered a wide spectrum. At the extremes, were Māori and Pākehā communities which controlled minorities of the other people. The Pākehā-controlled Māori minority has received most attention from historians. To the Pākehās' credit there was very little legislative discrimination against these Māori. But as the Speaker of the colonial House of Representatives wrote in 1863, 'no legislation will ever make a white man regard a coloured man as his equal'. Māori who accepted the invitation to become 'brown Britons' usually discovered the British did not really mean it. The treatment of Māori-controlled Pākehā, the subject of very little research, appears to have been better, largely because the Māori had no evangelical mission, no particular desire to impose their way of life on others. But it was not particularly good. 'No more mercy is shown by a Maori Runanga [Council] to a Pakeha, than by an Auckland jury to a Maori.' Further along the spectrum were Pākehā communities who exercised varying degrees of loose suzerainty over Māori communities, and vice versa.

Finally, there was a growing middle ground where towns and tribes co-operated on a basis of rough parity: economically interdependent, politically allied but autonomous, a more or less equal partnership. The partnership was often tense and uneasy; it derived partly from mutual misunderstanding; it was based more on pragmatism than principle or policy. But, on the whole, it worked well enough to make 1840–1860 the heyday of New Zealand race relations. Yet, in 1860, this remarkable symbiosis collapsed into bitter conflict.

In 1864, John Gorst, an exceptionally observant young official, reflected on a change in Māori attitudes to land sales during the 1850s.

> The land was little valued by them as soil; they cared only for the enjoyment of what we should call territorial dominion . . . . By sale to Europeans, while Europeans were few and weak, no power or territorial dominion was parted with. The purchaser became one of the most valuable possessions of the tribe: the chief called him '*my* Pakeha', and the tribe called him '*our* Pakeha'. He traded with them, procured them guns . . . promoted their importance, and was at the same time dependent on them for protection and completely at their mercy . . . all his greatness and grandeur were their possessions and redounded to their credit. But as the number of Europeans increased these relations were altered; a sale involved parting with the dominion of the soil.

Gorst underestimated Māori attachment to their land as such, but on the whole he was right. 'Land sale' was increasingly coming to mean the cession of all forms of control. The correlation was still far from perfect: large sales might not be implemented by occupation for years, pockets of Pākehā land surrounded by Māori were still governed by the latter, but in general British rule was following the surveyors. During the 1850s many Māori, even those otherwise most eager for interaction with Pākehā, therefore turned against land selling. A loose land holding movement grew up, often associated with a great conference at Manawapou in Ngati Ruanui territory in May 1854. Between 1855 and 1858, this movement merged into another: the Māori King Movement.

The first king, the great Waikato chief Potatau Te Wherowhero, acceded in 1858, selected through a lengthy process of negotiation and consensus, involving many tribes. On Potatau's death in 1860, he was succeeded by his son Tawhiao. Described as 'colourless' by the settlers, Tawhiao seems actually to have had considerable breadth of vision and spiritual depth. But he was a symbol as well as a leader, and other chiefs, notably Wiremu Tamehana, the 'King-maker', and the leading generals Rewi Maniapoto and Tawhana Tikaokao were at least equally influential. The King Movement had few of the institutions of a European-style state — it experimented with some, such as police and tax, without great success — and this deceived some contemporaries (and historians) into imagining it was ineffective and narrowly based. In fact, it mobilized in war a higher proportion of its resources than most European states were capable of at the time, though its methods were much less formal. Its support was always very widespread, and by 1863 encompassed the majority of Māori, though practical factors meant not all could fight for it. The movement was only an anti-landselling 'league' in a secondary sense; its primary purpose in opposing land sales was to protect Māori independence. It was conceived, wrote Tamehana, as a 'plan by which the Maori tribes should cleave together, and assemble together, so that the people might become one'. The South Island Māori who sent ammunition, the Ngapuhi who protected escaped Kingite prisoners of war, and the warriors who marched to distant Waikato to support traditional enemies — all did so, in the words of a Urewera chief, 'to show sympathy for the island in trouble'. Using the term 'nationalism' for this phenomenon may be somewhat deceptive and Eurocentric, but not using it is even more so.

The emergence of the King Movement and the slowing of land selling did not make war inevitable. The King was no threat to the Pākehā zone, which already contained more land than the settlers could use. Even at crowded New Plymouth, 20,000 acres of Crown land awaited private purchase. Particular groups of settlers no doubt wanted particular pieces of Māori land, but to suggest that this was enough to commit the British to a major war is to stretch conspiracy theory too far. The basic problem was one of collective Pākehā expectation. For various reasons, not all of them blameworthy, the Pākehā believed it was their destiny to rule New Zealand fully. Most agreed that the Māori were inferior to them, though they were divided on whether the inferiority was temporary or permanent. Many thought, well before 'Social Darwinism' legitimated the conviction, that the Māori would fade away before them into physical or cultural extinction by a 'law of nature', or 'progress'. While the Māori zone was gradually diminishing through land selling, it seemed that nature was indeed on course. When the King Movement put a stop to this, many Pākehā, Governor Browne among them, concluded that nature needed a little help. Browne and Grey, who returned for his second governorship in September 1861, persuaded or manipulated a half-reluctant imperial government into providing it.

Browne hoped that a single 'sharp lesson', a local show of force, would be all that was required, reversing the lesson of the Northern War. In 1859, a junior Atiawa chief 'sold' the Waitara block in Taranaki. The senior chief, Wiremu Kingi (William King) Te Rangitake, vetoed the sale, but Browne decided to enforce it. 'I must,' he wrote, 'either have purchased this land or recognised a right which would have made William King virtual sovereign of this part of New Zealand'. In practice, that was exactly what he was, as the British had tacitly accepted up until then. War broke out on 17 March 1860 and raged almost continuously for thirteen years.

But Waitara, even land as such, was only a trigger, a match which lit a fuse already laid. One of the chiefs behind the Waitara sale was said to have wanted revenge for an affair his wife had had with a supporter of Wiremu Kingi's, at the village of Karaponia (California). We may as well attribute the conflict to adultery in California, as call it the 'Land Wars', a label which lets too many Pākehā, advocates of the war with no interest in Māori land, off the hook.

King Tawhiao, a Māori leader much underestimated in the Pākehā record. *National Museum*

The Taranaki War itself lasted for one year, until 18 March 1861. The local combatants, Te Atiawa and the New Plymouth settlers, both fought well, but in keeping with the basic issues at stake, the main combatants were the King Movement and the British Empire. The Māori sought, largely successfully, to fight in Taranaki without damaging economic interaction elsewhere. Māori who had killed Pākehā outside New Plymouth in one month, traded with other Pākehā in Auckland the next. British forces grew from 900 to 3500, a medium-sized army in New Zealand terms. Māori forces grew from 200 to around 1000, occasionally more. If these numbers were converted to man-hours, the discrepancy would double, for the Māori were part-time soldiers against full-time soldiers — they had no wages to replace them in their domestic economy. The Kingites reduced this problem through a kind of informal shift-system: parties fought in Taranaki for a few weeks, then returned home to plant or harvest and gather supplies, and were replaced at the battlefront by other parties.

One thousand warriors at one time therefore represented a turnover of at least two thousand. But the British still had greatly superior resources and a clear-cut plan: to smash the main Māori warrior force in a single decisive battle, the 'sharp lesson' which would teach them who really ruled New Zealand.

The British did manage two modest successes: at Mahoetahi on 7 November 1860, when a small Ngati Haua force was caught in an unfinished pā, and at 'Number Three Redoubt' at Huirangi on 23 January 1861, when Kingite warriors unwisely attacked a strong fort and were repulsed. But the Māori scored several minor victories and on the one occasion that the British assaulted a completed pā at Puketakauere on 27 June 1860, they were heavily defeated.

Again, the British problem was the modern pā, dozens of which were mass-produced by the Maori during the Taranaki War. These formed a rough cordon around New Plymouth, penning in the British, absorbing their expensive thrusts, and acting as bases for a supplementary guerilla campaign against settler property — during which the Ngati Ruanui tribe earned the nick-name of 'the Ngati-ruin-ruin-us'. Modern pā were effective, but they were also expendable, and the Māori readily abandoned them when appropriate, as the *Taranaki Punch* bitterly recognized.

> Sing a song of sixpence
> A tale about the war
> Four and twenty niggers
> Cooped up in a Pa
> When the Pa was opened
> Not a nigger there was seen
> Is not that a jolly tale
> To tell before the Queen

Late in the war, the British general Thomas Pratt tried to pierce the pā cordon at a single point with sustained and methodical siege operations — 'sapping'. But the Māori merely dug a new pā as Pratt dug up to the old.

The war ended on 18 March 1861, when Tamehana and McLean arranged a ceasefire. Both armies were fully intact. The British kept Waitara, but the Maori seized a larger block of Pākehā land as hostage for it, and Browne's attempt to assert real sovereignty over the Māori zone had clearly failed. He saw that the King Movement was the principal obstacle, and decided to topple it by invading its Waikato heartland. Before he could do so, he was dismissed and replaced by Grey. Grey took up Browne's plan (the precise timing of his decision is a matter of debate) but with much better preparation. He built up a supply and transport system, including steamers for the Waikato River; he tricked the imperial government into supplying extra troops; and he tried, in his own words, to 'reduce the number of our enemies' by such measures as the return of Waitara. Then on 12 July 1863, his army invaded the Waikato, ushering

Cameron's storming of a pā at Katikara, Taranaki, on 4 June 1863. The Māori garrison may have been only fifty strong. *Alexander Turnbull Library*

in the largest and most important of the New Zealand Wars.

Peaking at 14,000 men, this army was by far the largest, best prepared, best equipped, and most well-led British force New Zealand had yet seen. With armoured steamships, sophisticated heavy artillery, and telegraph communications, it was quite a modern war effort. Grey's preparations allowed the able British general, Duncan Cameron, to keep up continuous pressure, in contrast to the sporadic expeditions out from base of previous wars. Against him the Kingites could muster no more than 2000 soldiers at any one time — a large army in Māori terms, representing a turn-over of 4000-5000, but not enough. Again, they had to match overwhelming numbers with innovation. They built successive lines of modern pā, like tiny Western Fronts, to block Cameron's advance; they launched a systematic raiding campaign against his lines of communication; and they managed to procure a battery of artillery to sink his steamships. At the first line, Meremere, they held him up for a remarkable three and a half months. Their cannon fired fast and accurately at his steamships, but they could get no proper ammunition, and makeshift projectiles such as grocer's weights hit but failed to sink the armoured vessels. On 31 October 1863, Cameron was able to outflank Meremere by water, though the Māori escaped without loss.

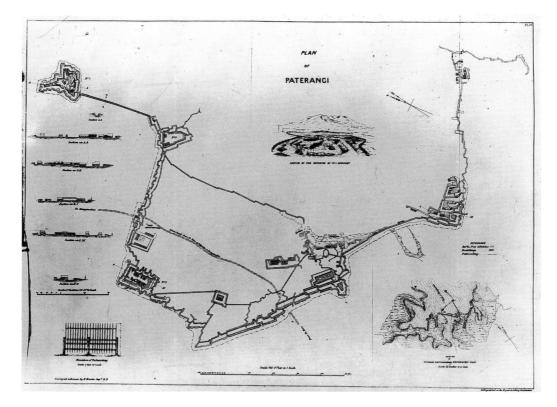

Vast and sophisticated Māori fieldworks at Paterangi, in 1864. *Alexander Turnbull Library*

Much of the Kingite army then had to disperse briefly for economic reasons, and in the interim it was unable to fully garrison the second Waikato line, at Rangiriri. On 20 November, Cameron stormed a weakly-held part of the line, and though no less than eight assaults on the remainder were repulsed, he was able to get possession by misusing a flag of truce. This was a heavy blow, and Cameron's brilliant outflanking of the third Waikato line, on 21 February 1864, was a still heavier one. Māori casualties were light, but they lost the rich agricultural district of Rangiaowhia, and this was followed by a strategically minor but tactically heavy defeat at Orakau at the beginning of April. The battered Kingite army sheltered behind its remaining lines, protecting Ngati Maniapoto and Ngati Haua territory, awaiting Cameron's final blow.

It never came. Cameron's objective, like Pratt's before him, was to win the war quickly and cheaply through a single decisive battle, annihilating a substantial Kingite force and breaking the Māori will to resist. Because the Māori would not engage in the open, and because modern pā could not normally be surrounded, this meant he had to storm a pā with the enemy still in it. Try as he might, Cameron was unable to do this. Though sometimes damaged, the Kingite army escaped from every action, and he despaired of decisive victory in Waikato. Then, in late April, a perfect opportunity

THE CHARGE OF THE NEW ZEALAND CAVALRY AT THE BATTLE OF ORAKAU.

'Charging' cavalry at Orakau. Their function was in fact to ride down fugitives. *Alexander Turnbull Library*

arose when the Tauranga Kingites built a pā — the 'Gate Pa' — on the coast, allowing Cameron to concentrate crack troops and a vast array of artillery against them. The general did everything right — in proportion to duration and the size of the target his bombardment may have been the heaviest in the world up until then — but his assault was repulsed with heavy loss. Cameron concluded that complete modern pā were an insoluble problem. His troops won a compensation victory in Tauranga against the incomplete pā of Te Ranga on 21 June, but this did not change his conviction that the desired 'decisive blow' was impossible. 'And if Her Majesty's troops are to be detained in the colony until one is struck', he wrote, 'I confess I see no prospect of their leaving New Zealand.' Despite pressure from Grey and the settlers, Cameron saw no point in continuing the invasion of Waikato.

The British were unable to destroy the King Movement, but they did defeat and gravely weaken it, and this was the great turning-point in relations between the two zones. The King Movement lost much of its capacity to protect Māori independence outside its own heartland, which still stretched from the Upper Waikato to the Upper Wanganui, and became known as the 'King Country'. This greatly reduced Māori unity and increased collaboration with the government. The Pākehā were therefore able to give the new evangelism more teeth, mixing it with military force, and to add two further measures: the Native Land Court and the Confiscation Scheme.

Established in 1865, the Native Land Court proved to be an effective mechanism of subtle conquest. Its purpose was to simplify the ownership of Māori land so that it could be sold more readily. If even a minority of owners took land before the Court, it would allocate title to ten of them, who could then sell to private Pākehā buyers. Manipulation, debt, and other pressures, which might not have worked when the Māori zone was stronger, ensured that many did.

Confiscation was conceived by Grey in July 1863 but administered by the settler ministry. It was designed partly to make the war pay for itself but largely to permanently cripple Māori independence by confiscating the best land of the key resisting tribes and allocating it to 'Military settlers', or soldier-farmers, some 5000 of whom were recruited. In practice, because British victory was so incomplete, the scheme was implemented partially and gradually — 'creeping confiscation'. As the wounds of war began to heal in a particular district, creeping confiscation would rip off the scab. This sparked off more fighting ironically helped by a new Māori religion, Pai Marire or Hauhauism. While fundamentally peace-oriented, Pai Marire sometimes had the effect of inspiring renewed resistance, or of creating bitter divisions within tribes. From 1864 the New Zealand Wars therefore entered a new phase of sporadic localized campaigns.

The Māori zone came to be divided between 'insiders' and 'outsiders', to use contemporary terms; those who engaged and negotiated with confiscation, the Native Land Court and the refurbished new evangelism, and those who did not. Insider territory tended to form a growing transition zone between the core Māori zone and the Pākehā zone. Insiders initially retained some autonomy, but state encroachment had full play on them. To avoid expensive campaigns, the government was often willing to 'return' some of the land it wished to confiscate, as 'Native Reserves' but only to those groups which 'came in' and negotiated with them, submitting to some degree of state control and laying themselves open to more. Many outsiders owned good land in the transition zone, but lost it to insider co-owners by boycotting the Native Land Court. The temptation to 'go in' and defend their claims before the Court was great. These levers prised many Māori from outsider to insider status.

The Māori did not supinely succumb to this range of pressures, but sought to match it with a range of response. Helped a little by the withdrawal of Imperial troops from operations in 1866, they employed three main strategies to protect their autonomy: military collaboration, and non-violent and violent resistance.

Kūpapa, Māori fighting on the British side, were not an important factor during the Taranaki and Waikato Wars. Thereafter, a few Māori joined colonial units, notably the 'Armed Constabulary' established in 1867, and served at one remove from the tribal structure, on the same basis as Pākehā. These 'pure' collaborators had their equivalents in Māori ranks — 'renegades' and army deserters, often Irish. Both groups were interesting but small. Normally, kūpapa fought on the basis of perceived

Mete Kingi Paetahi, of Whanganui, who manipulated his Pākehā allies at least as much as they manipulated him. *Alexander Turnbull Library*

hapū or tribal interest, not as turncoats or 'loyalists'. These interests rarely converged fully with those of the government. Kūpapa were allies, not subordinates, and they fought a different kind of war at different levels of intensity. The Wanganui chief 'General' Mete Kingi fought how he chose, when he chose, and as hard as he chose, drawing good wages for his warriors, equipping them with two government rifles each, and protecting his valued entrepôt of Wanganui — which he would have done anyway — at government expense. He drove his colonial paymasters to distraction — 'O that mine enemy commanded a Native contingent containing four Mete Kingis' — but they could not do without him. Moreover, no tribe was wholly or consistently kūpapa. The Arawa confederation came closest, but some even of them fought against the Pākehā. Ngati Porou were the staunchest of Kingites during the Waikato War, then the staunchest of kūpapa. Some chiefs, such as Tareha of Ngati Kahungunu and Topia Turoa of Wanganui, were both Kingite and kūpapa, depending on the context. Often, these changes reflected deep tribal divisions, the changing ascendancy of one faction over another, or the old necessity to protect 'their' particular Pākehā, but sometimes it was a bet each way. After the wars, kūpapa engagement with the state made them more vulnerable to the new evangelism and the Native Land Court, but their collaboration temporarily shored-up or even increased their independence.

The second Māori strategy, non-violent resistance, requires more research, but may have been more cohesive and pervasive than is generally assumed. Indeed, it may be legitimate to speak of a peace movement, or series of peace campaigns, dating from 1864. Te Ua Haumene, original prophet of Pai Marire, was the founding figure, and the movement was religious as well as political, involving a spiritual commitment to peace. Te Ua led passive resistance to the surveying Waitotara in 1864; tried to end a campaign in South Taranaki in 1865, and travelled around preaching peace in 1866. Te Whiti O Rongomai of Parihaka and until he turned to violent resistance, Titokowaru, can be seen as Te Ua's successors, and other prophet-peacemakers such as Te Maiharoa of Ngai Tahu may have been linked. The King Movement partly converted to Te Ua's creed. It still kept the boundaries of the King Country inviolate, and opposed gold-prospecting, the Native Land Court, and land surveying outside it. But 'goodwill was to effect all these', in Rewi Maniapoto's words, 'the sword was to be sheathed'. The peace movement had some success in slowing creeping confiscation, in protecting the Māori zone, and in building a cultural and spiritual bulwark against the new evangelism.

Non-violent resistance was the more effective because the Pākehā could never be quite sure of it. Some of its practitioners — including the Kingites, as we have seen — stopped short of Te Whiti's absolute commitment to peace. Repeated state encroachment could convert non-violent resistance into the third Māori strategy: continued violent resistance. Between 1864 and early 1868, this was at its low point of effectiveness, and the Pākehā could congratulate themselves on restoring nature's plan. Then, in mid-1868, two Māori religious and military leaders emerged who for a while threatened to reverse the result of the Waikato War: Te Kooti Arikirangi and Riwha Titokowaru.

Te Kooti campaigned across a large part of the eastern North Island between 1868 and 1872 after escaping from imprisonment in the Chatham Islands. A brilliant but sometimes unnecessarily ruthless guerilla leader, he could never master the modern pā, and was beaten when he tried to fight from one. In January 1869, he was permanently weakened by defeat at Ngatapa at the hands of Colonel George Whitmore, most able of the colonial commanders. Thereafter, Te Kooti miraculously evaded capture a number of times before taking refuge in the King Country, where he further developed his remarkable Ringatu religion. In military terms Titokowaru was more dangerous to the Pākehā, coupling most of Te Kooti's guerilla talent with mastery of the modern pā. Beginning in June 1868, with a tiny force, he swept south from the foot of Mount Taranaki to the outskirts of Wanganui, smashing two vastly larger colonial forces along the way, and creating a major crisis of confidence among the Pākehā. But at the vital moment, in February 1869, his force broke up over an internal dispute. Titokowaru escaped and remained independent in central Taranaki as an ally of Te Whiti, but the Pākehā reconquered south Taranaki by default.

All three of these strategies contributed to the survival of the independent Māori

A British military base in Taranaki, circa 1865. *Canterbury Museum*

zone up to and beyond 1872. The Pākehā attempt at military conquest had failed to that extent. But it had succeeded in removing most of the hard shell of Māori independence. The seeds for the destruction of the Māori zone; creeping confiscation, the Native Land Court, and a tougher new evangelism, had been planted and were sprouting fast. If Māori independence was a full bottle, then war took the top off it, allowing non-military subversion to slowly empty out the contents.

Māori independence should not be romanticized. Its features included tribal feuds, sometimes quite bloody, and killings for adultery and sorcery. But it was a dynamic expression of Māori vigour and identity, existing despite the Pākehā, not because of their disinterest or enlightenment. At its peak in the 1850s, interaction between the two zones was a tense but genuine partnership. The partners were autonomous in most respects, but economically interdependent, like Siamese twins with distinct identities who are firmly fused at the wallet. The partnership was not incompatible with Pākehā self-determination or reasonable material interests. It offered a chance of co-operative biculturalism, and one can understand why the Māori found it hard to forgive the Pākehā for not taking it. Of course, whether this was Timothy Sullivan's fault is another matter.

In the 1870s government-assisted immigrants with their families poured into New Zealand. Immigrants were a favourite theme of paintings, photographs and lithographs. Here they are shown arriving at Lyttleton in 1877. Their sailing ship had anchored out in the harbour and the immigrants completed their journey to land by steam tug. *Canterbury Museum*

5. *Railways and Relief Centres*
(1870–1890)

👥

RAEWYN DALZIEL

During the 1870s and 1880s the European colonizers of New Zealand came to feel they had at last made the country their own. Blood had been spilt in conquest; children born in the country had grown up and regarded it as their homeland; the settler Parliament ruled within its own territory. The Māori people, whether they had remained neutral, fought against the settlers or sided with them, faced the task of coming to terms with the permanency of European settlement while coping with a loss of fighting men, a loss of land, disruption to their economic life, poor health and high mortality. The two societies met in Parliament, in the land courts, in limited trading, occasionally in friendship and marriage, occasionally in hostility and conflict. However, separate development ruled as physical isolation, language barriers, the events of the past and attitudes of the present, made it impossible to conceive of a future in which Māori and European lives were entwined. The balance had fallen in favour of the Europeans who now were determined to shape the country as they wanted it.

In 1870 New Zealand was still in the age of sail, foot and horse traffic. The largest town, Dunedin, had a population of just over 14,000 people. Most Māori lived in rural kāinga; three-quarters of the Europeans lived in the countryside or in villages of less than a thousand people. Most of the new migrants who flooded into the country in the early 1870s travelled from their homes and villages in Britain and Europe to their port of departure by horse and cart. Rural migrants would have seen steam-operated farming machinery but they would have worked with hand implements; rural women churned butter by hand, gleaned corn in the fields, carried water from wells and washed clothes in streams. City migrants were more familiar with the steam engine and the railway but their environment too was still largely one of horse-drawn transport, candles and oil burning lamps, water drawn from hand-operated pumps and primitive sanitary arrangements. All the immigrants who travelled to New Zealand before 1874, and most of the cargo, came on sailing ships. In New Zealand there were scarcely any railways, a few coastal steamers and no telegraph connections with the outside world. Work was done by hand and with the simplest of tools — clippers in woolsheds, axes in the forest, picks and shovels on the roads, tubs and scrubbing boards in the laundry.

During the next twenty years technological change and innovation quickened the pace of life. There were more people, travel became faster, information could be spread more rapidly. The demands on individuals and on society collectively became greater. Māori cultivations and ancestral lands were taken over by European farmers; government and business faced new challenges — and on the whole did not handle these well; a revolution in communications started to link the settlers in a network of towns and villages. Most Māori people stood outside this network, in some cases deliberately, in others because they had no choice. They had networks of their own which did not follow the lines of the railway and the social pattern of the Europeans.

Making the decisions for this country of some 300,000 people in 1870 was an elected House of Representatives with seventy-six members. Since 1868 four of the members represented Māori electorates. In the nineteenth century politics and government sometimes seem to lack a direct connection with the life of the governed. However that impression is misleading for government and government policy helped determine the context of life even for those furthest from the seat of power. Relatively few participated in politics but the outcome of political decisions affected everyone.

Political life was at its busiest during the three or four months when Parliament sat in Wellington and the couple of months preceding a general election. Between 1870 and 1890 seven general elections took place, only the last two of which resulted in a clear indication that the government should change. Governments usually owed their position not to the consent of the governed but to factional shifts and bargains within Parliament. Despite the extensive coverage of parliamentary debates by the press and occasional rowdy meetings of voters, politics did not greatly excite the mass of the people in the 1870s. Only men could vote and before 1879 a requirement that voters must own some land imposed restrictions on European, although not on Māori, men. In many electorates the voters left politics to a coterie of influential men, established landowners and farmers, business and professional men. These men might split into two or even more groups, divided by personal and sectional interests, local or, more rarely, national issues. Organized political associations were electorate based and often the political activists were so united that only one candidate was nominated. Almost a quarter of the candidates were elected unopposed in the 1871 election. By 1890, however, more people viewed voting as a significant way of expressing an opinion and influencing the direction of events. Only half a dozen candidates were unopposed in the 1890 election. Whereas in 1879 only half the men enrolled bothered to cast a ballot, in 1890 nearly three-quarters of the eligible voters went to the polls.

The development needs of the electorates over-rode all other political issues, at least until 1887. Political associations were formed to advocate local causes — a railway here, a bridge there, protection for a local industry, free trade to help local farmers. Most politicians were quite unabashed about this. They were in politics to win a share of government expenditure in their region. William Rolleston, a Canterbury member of the House of Representatives, believed that Parliament was generally regarded as 'a place in which to scramble for loaves and fishes'. It has been said that politics 'ran on railway tracks'. Voters and politicians were occasionally roused by other issues. In 1875 politicians from Otago and Auckland joined forces to fight the proposed abolition of the provincial councils. Their leaders, Sir George Grey and James Macandrew, made fiery speeches against the centralization of power and the destruction of liberty and freedom, winning support from the champions of provincialism and those who hoped to squeeze as much from central government for their region as possible. Sometimes voters were swayed by religion. In 1879 William Fox reckoned that his views on government aid to denominational schools cost him the Roman Catholic vote and the seat of Wanganui. A business scandal could hurt a candidate, but personal morality rarely entered into politics.

Political leaders were, in most cases, amateurs. They knew that control of the Treasury benches meant control of development, but were neither sufficiently convinced of the importance of power, nor sufficiently enamoured of it, to organize their support consistently. Ministers and Opposition leaders would make a great show during the parliamentary session then retreat to their farms, sheep stations or businesses for months on end. Political programmes tended to be skeletal and developed haphazardly as issues arose. Nevertheless, some of the leaders were men of considerable stature. In 1877 Grey, the former governor, became Premier supported by a coalition of provincialists, radicals, businessmen and speculators. At sixty-five, the best of Grey's career was behind him. But he had lost none of his powerful flow of rhetoric and his obsessional hatreds. Despite the fact that his Auckland enemies habitually referred to him out of the House as 'the lunatic of Kawau', he was still impressive as a politician. As a leader he was hopeless and lucky to remain in office for two years. The South Islanders, John Hall, William Rolleston and Francis Dillon Bell were able and conscientious men, if lacking in flair. They regarded themselves as 'the true colonists', fair-minded men whose destiny was to put New Zealand on to a sound basis, protecting the interests of the 'natural' élite of landowners while making it possible for the rest to achieve a modest competency. Harry Atkinson, a Taranaki farmer, was highly respected except when he started on one of his fads. His main policy was prudent financial management. The two Hawke's Bay politicians, John Ormond and Donald McLean, worked together as a strong team. Ormond, a man of great prejudices who spread gloom all around him and McLean, once deeply religious and interested in Māori life, were by the early 1870s largely concerned with maintaining their control over Hawke's Bay and transferring large tracts of Māori land as peacefully and as rapidly as possible to European farmers and developers. In the later 1870s and 1880s another team of Robert Stout and John Ballance emerged. These two were interested in political ideas, in social justice, in urban poverty and land tenure; they also had shared business interests.

The Colonial Treasurer of the early 1870s, Julius Vogel, was closest to a professional political leader. He was an urban politician, a newspaper editor, with business interests on the side. With no learned profession to absorb his intellectual energy and no land to tax his physical energies, he viewed politics as a fascinating game through which he could influence events and further his own career. He was an extrovert, a convivial man but a landless, Jewish gold-rush migrant whose brash, pushy style alienated the political establishment. Rolleston thought him 'strongheaded, wrongheaded' and Edward Stevens regarded him as an 'impudent adventurer', but Vogel turned the tables on his opponents by ignoring them and seeking his support from the financial world. Through the exercise of patronage and a policy of development, he welded together the independents and newcomers who entered politics in the 1870s. A promise of a job, a trip overseas on some commission, a local bill given time in the House, a local project given funds: all of these were powerful means of winning and keeping support. Vogel towered over his colleagues in the early 1870s and established the political agenda for the next twenty years. Yet even Vogel, with his desire for office and his ambitious policies and programmes, saw no need to establish any kind of political organisation. He thought nothing of spending months overseas, neglecting his constituents and announcing policy without consulting his followers.

Pre-party politics had a certain in-built chaos. Politicians who professed to place their independence above all else, yet owed their election to their ability to gain government expenditure in their electorate, could be impervious to whips on issues unrelated to their major concerns. Men were in politics for specific and limited goals. Over a third of those elected to the House of Representatives between 1866 and 1890 served only one term. Resignations and by-elections occurred frequently in the 1870s. The lack of experience among members and the constant turnover in the House meant that a core of experienced politicians, influenced by one or two businessmen outside the House, most notably the Auckland financier Thomas Russell, could dominate policy making. In 1875 the Opposition coined the term 'the Continuous Ministry' to describe the Government that was formed by William Fox in 1869 and which, although undergoing several ministerial reshuffles, held office for most of the following eight years. The label was used thereafter by Opposition factions who wished to charge any government with inconsistency or with an over-long monopoly of power. It was a term applied to governments headed by Fox, George Waterhouse, Vogel, Atkinson, Frederick Whitaker and John Hall.

Political attention shifted decisively in the 1870s from the local to the national scene. The provincial councils, after contending for power with central government for twenty years, finally conceded defeat. Too parochial and under-resourced, they had failed in their task of regional development. All hopes now focussed on the local members of Parliament and Wellington. With the war no longer the central issue of concern, the role of government was to create the conditions for economic growth. Vogel was the man who had the clearest idea of how this was to be done. His Premier, William Fox, was an experienced politician but had little knowledge of finance or the economy. Fox believed that New Zealand needed to 'rekindle the flame of colonization' but he lacked the spark to undertake the task. He allowed the dominant

Cutting the line for the railway was one of the great engineering and labouring feats of the later nineteenth century. The men worked in the backblocks, living in camps, enduring harsh conditions while they pushed the line further into the country. *Alexander Turnbull Library*

young Treasurer to take the lead in policy. Vogel proposed a programme of government borrowing to finance development and immigration. The credit of the central state would be used to raise money on the London money market. The money would be spent on communications — roads, railways, telegraph lines — and on importing a labour force. More money would be spent on purchasing Māori land. This land would be resold to European developers and farmers providing the government with a profit, allowing European settlement to penetrate deeper into the country and the land to become part of the productive economy. Government expenditure would encourage private investment, jobs would be created, and New Zealand could look forward to an era of expansion and prosperity.

All of this occurred in the early 1870s. The Government had no difficulty in raising loans at reasonable interest rates and borrowed throughout the decade. The amounts were minuscule compared to later times but significant for those days, when governments did not lightly go into debt. Occasionally the financial press in Britain and the Opposition at home warned that the country was borrowing more than it could afford but such warnings did little more than create temporary hiccups in the borrowing programme. A financial structure was created in London with a representative, the Agent-General, usually a retired politician, responsible for raising the funds. The Bank of New Zealand, which operated the government account, found itself doing very well. Parliament decided that trunk railways should run the length of both Islands and a British firm, Brogden and Sons, was contracted to construct the tracks. Most politicians from small towns and farming districts tried to get a local railway added to the annual railway-building schedule. Often Parliament agreed, but few of these branch lines were actually built. Road construction went on all over the country. John Ormond, who tended to be careful about where the money was spent, ruefully commented that dray roads were being made where a dray was unlikely to travel for years. The telegraph system was extended to many remote areas. Even more marvellously, by 1876, New Zealand had a telegraph cable to Australia, cutting the time to receive news and information from Europe from days to hours. The Agent-General recruited immigrants in Great Britain and Europe. From November 1871 until 1880 they arrived in their thousands, in all some 100,000 people whose fares were partially or wholly paid by the government. Over half of the immigrants came from England, about a quarter from Ireland with fewer from Scotland and less than a tenth from the rest of Europe. Of the adults, men outnumbered women by some 8000. Most landed at Port Chalmers or Lyttelton, as the main centres vied for workers. The immigrants helped swell the European population from 256,393, in 1871 to 489,933 in 1881. Over 60% lived in the South Island. At the same time the Māori population declined from 47,330 in 1874 to 46,141 in 1881, most living in the North Island. Māori people suffered from high mortality rates, aggravated by a measles epidemic in 1875–1876 and a whooping cough epidemic during 1877–1880.

The new immigrants found jobs on the railways, road building, in domestic service, in the construction industry and in agriculture. The ideal was to get immigrant families settled on the land. 'Any fool', said one politician. 'can make a railway. But it requires a statesman, in the present condition of New Zealand to devise a satisfactory scheme of settlement of people.' Some settlers walked or were driven in carts to bush-covered backblocks where they lived in tents until the men had cut tracks through the bush and earned enough to put a deposit on a 40-acre farm purchased from the government. Others lived in immigration barracks until they could get jobs and meagre lodgings in the towns. But jobs, in the first instance, were plentiful and wages were relatively high. A domestic servant could get fifteen shillings a week plus board; a carpenter earned eight shillings to ten shillings a day and a labourer five shilling to eight shillings . These wages were all higher than in Britain and the cost of living was probably not very different. Meat and vegetables were cheap and abundant; housing and clothing were more expensive.

Roads, railways and bridges began to alter the appearance of the country and the lives of people. In 1871 the first Cobb and Co. coach arrived in New Plymouth, carrying the Premier and other dignitaries. All the shops were closed for the day, a triumphal arch was put up in the centre of the town and the buildings were decked

Cobb and Co. had a monopoly on coach traffic in the country. This photograph was taken after their first run to New Plymouth in 1871, outside the White Hart Hotel. Most of the town turned out to greet the coach but it is believed that the photo was taken on the following day. *Taranaki Museum*

with flags. An escort of fifty men rode out to meet the coach and its armed guard. Most of the townspeople assembled at its arrival point and in the evening the notable men gathered for dinner and toasts at the Masons' Hall. Similar scenes were re-enacted in towns all over the country. Turning the first sod for a railway development was another festive occasion. A young girl who watched such a ceremony in Wellington in August 1872 wrote in her diary that it was 'a grand affair' with the Volunteer Corps and the Constabulary turned out, the Governor and his family, the officers of the *Dido* and most of Wellington present; 'altogether it wasn't bad fun.'

Coaches ran to more places than trains but the trains made a greater difference to travel. The construction of the railway lines was a gigantic engineering feat and even the main trunk lines were not completed until the twentieth century. The nature of the landscape, the long thin islands, narrow coastal strips, jagged hills and mountain ranges and the wide changeable rivers, made the work slow. Often the men employed were new to navvying and they worked with picks and shovels. Most of the rolling stock was imported. So the tracks were opened in short sections, but again with the maximum of ceremony. The politician who attended a railway opening ceremony ensured his re-election.

860 PARLIAMENT HOUSES — WELLINGTON
BURTON BROS. DUNEDIN

Wellington was transformed in the 1870s, after it became the seat of government in 1865. Public buildings made an enormous impact around the Thorndon area. Parliament House had extensive renovations and additions, the first section designed by Edward Rumsey and then a new Legislative Council Chamber designed by W. H. Clayton. *National Museum*

Business boomed in the early 1870s, as the government hoped. The businessmen of Auckland embarked on land development in the Waikato, hatching heroic plans of draining swamps, sowing pasture and cutting up the land for small farms at vast profit. They formed timber and gold companies and companies to develop trade with the Pacific Islands. Wellington underwent a transformation as the government undertook harbour reclamation and building. The town was badly in need of the trappings of a capital. New Parliament Buildings, a new residence for the Governor, a new home for the Premier, government offices all went up. The building and construction industry was the major beneficiary. In Dunedin a similar activity had gone on during the gold rush days; Dunedin now settled into a more staid phase, consolidating its industrial and urban development. Some of the wealthier Dunedin businessmen, such as William Larnach, built themselves extraordinary mansions to display their wealth. In Canterbury pastoralists and business men banded together to

This photo of early Eketahuna was taken by James Bragge for an album capturing the development of the Wairarapa. His book was published in 1876. Scandinavian migrants settled the area and their work cutting and burning the bush is clearly shown. *National Museum*

form the New Zealand Shipping Company and the Kaiapoi Woollen Company, companies which reflected the symbiotic relationship between town and country in the pastoral areas.

As land became accessible and roads fanned out over the countryside, European settlers moved into areas which had previously been in Māori ownership or where there had been only one or two isolated European families or individual farmers. Villages started to multiply and in many places small towns began to appear. Places such as Palmerston North and Feilding in the Manawatu; Oamaru, Balclutha, and Kurow in Otago; Timaru and Ashburton in South Canterbury; Hamilton and Cambridge in the Waikato, all took off in the 1870s and 1880s. Some towns were carved out of great pastoral estates; some were established by the government as it purchased land and sponsored immigration. Other towns sprang up at crossroads, or river crossings, to service travellers or surrounding rural families. Pubs and post offices, sawmills, stock and station agents, breweries, tanning yards, sometimes a railway station, were established. Townspeople, anxious to be seen as progressive and community-minded and wanting to attract more residents and economic investment, joined to build churches, schools, town halls, athenaeums and even theatres. They formed brass bands, fire brigades, temperance associations, lending libraries, debating clubs and mothers' unions. Men in small towns lived a life structured around an eight- or ten-hour working day, six days a week. This still left them some leisure time in which they could cultivate the land around their cottages, growing vegetables, sometimes running a cow and hens. They spent time in the pub and they played sport. No small town was long without a cricket club and a football club and a few were ambitious enough to start racing clubs. Respectable women, and not all women were respectable, did not go to the pub, but they too developed leisure activities outside of the home. Many of these were associated with local churches — sewing bees, meetings and lectures, fairs and galas. A few women participated in sport. Tennis, which seems to have been introduced in 1876, was played by both men and women.

While these small towns struggled to establish themselves, the four main cities grew and changed almost beyond recognition. By 1891 Dunedin's population had reached over 23,000, with over 45,000 if its suburbs were included. And Dunedin was no longer the biggest city. Auckland in 1891 had nearly 29,000 people in the city and over 51,000 when its suburban fringe was included. Christchurch came next with a total of 44,688 and Wellington fourth with 33,224.

The original central city areas spilled out into new streets of cottages built to house the families of craftsmen, artisans and labourers, into semi-rural areas of the well-to-do, new boroughs and highway board districts. Horse-drawn buses and tram cars linked some of the inner city suburbs to the central business area. By the late 1870s the first steam-driven trams were puffing through the central city streets. Wellington had a public electricity supply by the late 1880s but most urban streets were lit, if at all, by gas lamps. The telephone arrived in the 1880s and all four cities had telephone exchanges, servicing a total of some 2500 subscribers. Impressive colonnaded, porticoed and turreted buildings such as the Australia and New Zealand Bank in Dunedin (1874) and the Public Library in Auckland (1887) altered the look of the towns. The huge four-storeyed government office building (1876) in Wellington was a massive statement of the increasing importance of central government. In the 1870s several new departments of state were created: Immigration, Public Works, and Education joined the Treasury, Internal Affairs, Native Affairs, Lands and Post Office. Harbour reclamations in Auckland and Wellington altered the shoreline forever and the extended docks were bustling jumbles of activity employing hundreds of men on a casual basis.

Rural areas prospered in the first half of the 1870s. Wool prices increased, and so did production. Pastoralists freeholded their leased land when they could, took their families on trips to England and built new station homesteads. The price of pastoral land increased and, as speculators entered the land market, continued to rise throughout the decade. Small farmers had more of a struggle. As yet they had no export market and most small farms were subsistence, family farms, or produced limited surpluses for the local market. To meet their commitments the men worked periodically on the roads, or for other farmers; the women helped on the land and by making cheese and butter, in addition to the work of housekeeping and child care. Small farmers, however, also saw their land increase in productivity and value as it was cleared of the bush and as roads and railways brought home markets closer.

Although export prices for farm products increased in the early 1870s, receipts from

This building, in the style of a French château, was opened as the Auckland Public Library in 1887. The money for the Library came from the City Council and a bequest from a relatively unknown Irish settler, Edward Costley. *National Museum*

exports were outweighed every year, except 1871, by the cost of imports. As yet few products were manufactured in New Zealand. The industrial sector was limited to a few clothing and textile factories, breweries, flour mills, sawmills, meat processing plants and agricultural machinery. In 1871 mining employed more people than industry.

High export prices justified the borrowing and the optimism of the early 1870s. By 1876 however there were signs that prosperity could not be sustained. Wool prices went into a long slow decline; and wool made up over half the total exports. There were tales of unemployment in Dunedin and Christchurch. Bank inspectors began to write gloomy reports about the prospects of their branches and their clients. Questions about the viability of the economy became more insistent. Perhaps more importantly, the politicians lost their nerve. Vogel was overseas on a government mission from mid–1874 to the beginning of 1876. In his absence more cautious politicians consolidated their support. Harry Atkinson rose to prominence, taking Vogel's place as Treasurer in 1874. Atkinson's view was that the pace of change had

The towns of the 1880s, although changing, still had a market town atmosphere. Victoria Street caters for the domestic needs of Christchurch residents. *Alexander Turnbull Library*

been too rapid and that borrowing should be restricted or a bust was inevitable. By mid–1876 Vogel could see that his policies had become unpopular. New Zealand had launched him on to a political career and he now decided to try his luck in a wider sphere. He resigned as Premier, was appointed Agent-General in London, leaving the field to Atkinson and his less daring colleagues.

Government activity slowed down. In 1877 Atkinson called for a 'political rest'. However in the private sector investors had too much at stake and were not ready for Atkinson's rest. They continued to pour money, usually borrowed money, into the economy, particularly into land purchase and development. In 1877 Atkinson was defeated in Parliament and replaced by Grey's government, with a new man, John Ballance, as Treasurer and the old Dunedin expansionist, James Macandrew, as Minister of Public Works. This government resumed borrowing, ordered more immigrants and drew up new proposals for spending on public works. In 1879 these plans came to an abrupt halt when the world economy went into a sharp recession. Land prices collapsed; landowners and mortgage holders faced certain loss even if they could find a willing purchaser for their property. New Zealand investors began to send their money out of the country, mainly to Melbourne where there was a building boom. Grey asked for and received a dissolution of Parliament, and went to the polls over a year early. The result was unclear, neither a victory for Grey, nor for the Opposition. A lot of political jockeying for position took place, with the ultimate victor John Hall, a Canterbury pastoralist. Atkinson was back as Treasurer. He immediately called for a reduction in government spending and introduced a tax on property. Assisted immigration was cut back savagely and public works proposals were abandoned. These measures did not make the government popular but it survived an election in 1881. The following year Hall gave up the Premiership and was succeeded by Whitaker and then by Atkinson who held the key portfolio of finance at the same time.

Atkinson's main aim was to balance the budget and in this he succeeded fairly well. However the government could do nothing to stop the slide of export prices which continued until the mid–1890s. Unemployment hit the country, most severely in the towns during the winter when casual work was scarce and itinerant rural workers drifted in from the countryside. Unskilled workers and men from the construction industry were those most likely to find themselves without a job. In 1880, 900 men were unemployed in Wellington. It was said that half the men in the building trades in Dunedin were out of work at any one time. Some of the unemployed men were able to get relief work from local bodies but this was spasmodic and poorly paid. Women and young people replaced men as lower paid workers in some factories. In the mid- and late-1880s, thousands of men and women shifted to Australia in search of work.

The depressed economy took a toll on family life. The problems of women without financial support and uncontrolled children seemed to escalate. The newspapers contained stories of young boys and girls roaming the streets, engaging in petty theft and generally disruptive behaviour. Homes for orphans and reformatories for undisciplined and delinquent children were overcrowded.

In 1884 the voters turned against Atkinson's policies and re-elected a Parliament with a majority in favour of a return to borrowing and development. A government was formed by Robert Stout and Vogel but they too found, within eighteen months, that the dangers of borrowing were more than they were prepared to risk. Their followers wanted to return to prosperity but expansion had lost its appeal as a policy. The era became known as the 'long depression' during which, despite a slight improvement in real incomes, contemporaries believed they were witnessing a prolonged economic downturn. Pastoral farmers who had freeholded their land wisely and who had diversified their economic activities came through relatively unscathed but others were not so lucky. The banks and mortgage companies which had lent money to pastoral farmers and land developers found they had to prop up these borrowers or take over assets they could not sell. This led to a squeeze on investment in other areas. The one bright spot on the horizon was the success of experiments in the new frozen meat trade. Urban businessmen saw their companies becoming unprofitable and their investments decline in value. Auckland remained ahead in the early 1880s, the timber trade holding its own. But in the later eighties Aucklanders too suffered and only a few businesses, such as breweries, continued to make a reasonable return.

While some tried to solve their problems by escaping across the Tasman Sea, others turned to new political solutions. In the early 1880s the Minister of Lands, William Rolleston, tried to promote various forms of land settlement — purchase of land on deferred payments, and perpetual leases of crown land — to enable families with limited savings to get on to the land. In 1882 Atkinson, concerned about the plight of the aged poor, proposed an insurance fund from government subsidies and from compulsory levies on all workers over the age of sixteen. This fund could be drawn on by contributors if they fell sick, or by their children if orphaned, and at the age of sixty-five all contributors would receive a weekly benefit of ten shillings. His proposal was well ahead of its time. The prevailing attitude was, if self-reliance and virtuous independence failed, that charity, not the state, was the only acceptable solution. The cautious Atkinson was branded as 'communistic' — a man who planned to sap the moral fibre of the nation. In 1888, a number of his political supporters left him when, back in the office of Premier, he imposed and increased tariffs on a wide range of imported goods, as well as imposing an excise duty on home-grown tobacco.

Changes to the franchise were advocated as another avenue of change. By the mid-1880s women, led by Kate Sheppard of the Women's Christian Temperance Union, were arguing that justice demanded they be given the vote. They also argued that if women had the vote they would be more effective in tackling social problems: they would use their vote to ensure that enlightened men were returned to Parliament and that social and economic reforms were enacted. In 1889 the plural vote, which had enabled landowners to vote wherever they owned land, was abolished. Māori people, dissatisfied with their token presence in the European Parliament, demanded a separate Parliament in which their concerns would be paramount and where their sovereignty, in their view an issue not clearly determined by the Treaty of Waitangi, might be expressed.

Men more radical than Rolleston and Atkinson proposed more far-reaching solutions to social and economic problems. Taxing the 'unearned' increment on land, the single tax as advocated by the American Henry George, was one of these solutions. Stout and Ballance were among those who supported the single tax. Some claimed that the Crown should stop selling land to private landowners and a few favoured land nationalization. The eight-hour day was supported in the towns and some workers, carpenters and engineers, railway workers, shearers and seamen, formed local unions. The Maritime Council, a federation of seamen and miners, became the most powerful of the working-class combinations and in August 1890 called its members out in an unsuccessful general strike. The Reverend Rutherford Waddell in Dunedin used the press and his pulpit to attack the conditions of women industrial workers and to demand legislation to protect working women and children.

For many people political solutions were impractical and too slow. They wanted to do something to relieve the distress immediately. Local committees of men and women, often affiliated to a church, set up soup kitchens and centres which distributed clothing. In Dunedin, the Methodists established a Central City Mission to help the poor. The Salvation Army provided a doss house for the homeless and a

Kate Sheppard, the women's suffrage organizer for the Women's Christian Temperance Union. Mrs Sheppard became a skilled organizer and politician and, after the winning of the women's vote, she achieved international stature as a speaker, writer and advocate of women's rights. *Canterbury Museum*

refuge for unmarried pregnant women. Members of the Women's Christian Temperance Union set up crèches in a number of towns, gave advice on how to stretch out meagre earnings, visited the sick and tried to help women in need.

In the main, the political and economic events discussed so far were in the hands of men, either as powerful or not-so-powerful participants. The ideology and the context of the time made it inevitable that this would be the case. European, and Māori society too, by this time, drew a fundamental distinction between men as the prime movers in the business of governing, trading and providing, and women as houseworkers, child minders and community workers. This division of responsibilities provided a way of organizing life and of ensuring that individuals knew what was expected of them. The rhetoric was that men and women each exercised power in their own sphere and that the spheres and the influence derived from them were complementary. For some, however, the domestic world of women was a poor second best to the public world of men and increasingly women sought, if not to change the way society was organized, at least to ensure that they were trained to understand the public world and be able, if necessary, to enter into it.

Besides ideology, other factors ensured that New Zealand was a society dominated by men. Among Europeans, men made up a large majority of the adults. In 1871 there were 89,032 men and 45,824 women over the age of twenty. In other words 66% of adults were men, and only 34% women. Men in mining camps, on sheep stations, backblocks farms and railway work sites rarely had normal social contact with women. Life was a cycle of hard physical work followed by bouts of gambling, boozing and fighting in the nearest town on pay days. In towns young single men in lodging houses usually repaired to the pub in their spare time. The disparity in the sex ratio worked against the family ideology that had always had a central place in colonizing plans. The 1874 census showed that 43,853 men over the age of twenty were single. At the same time just over 7000 adult women were unmarried. Even if one counted single women over fifteen, there was a shortfall of some 25,000. Thousands of men could never experience the reality of a marriage, home, and family. There is no doubt that the plight of the single male concerned respectable citizens, men and women alike.

Time would eventually alter the sex ratio but that was no answer to the immediate problem. Officially, and unofficially, the country wanted all the young women it could get. Free passages to New Zealand were available for single women earlier, and for longer, than any other migrant group. One bachelor wrote to another who had gone on a visit to Europe in 1874: '. . . I live in hopes of being introduced to Mrs H. next time we meet, it is no use your coming back here to the "old" Bachelor life . . . bring lots of young women with you. There are men enough for all.'

In the 1870s thousands of young women, orphaned, jobless or looking for adventure, decided to emigrate to New Zealand. Here they could get jobs as domestic servants at better wages than they could get at home, and it was said that there was more independence, better living conditions and the chance to get on. So they came, women from Irish farms, from London, from English villages and Scottish islands and found that domestic service was much the same everywhere. A dawn to dusk work day, repetitive cleaning, washing and food preparation, ever-present employers who expected docility and obedience, and little free time or independence. The one advantage was that the labour market for domestic servants seemed inexhaustible — even in the 1880s. If a woman didn't like the family she worked for, or the place, she could leave and soon find another.

The other escape route from paid domestic service was into marriage. An idea existed that domestic servants made good wives, skilled in household tasks, protected from the coarse environment of the streets or the factory, trained to obey. In fact, the months spent as a general servant in someone else's house were probably a reasonable apprenticeship in housekeeping but as a preparation for marriage they can have been of little use.

In 1874 over 14,000 women worked for wages. They could be found doing a variety of

Tennis made its first appearance in New Zealand in the mid 1870s. A game enjoyed by men and women it was both formal — see the clothing — and informal — the court and the play. *Alexander Turnbull Library*

jobs: making musical instruments, manufacturing furniture; working as carriers, as druggists and actors; even, the census noted, 107 women engaged in the 'criminal classes'. Over 3000 women worked in one or another branch of the clothing industry; 701 were reported as receiving wages for work in agriculture. However, in general, jobs were defined by sex and it was almost impossible for women to be employed in a male occupation. In the 1870s, 60% of women who worked for wages were domestic servants. About 20% of all homes employed a servant and almost all servants were women. Immigration agents reported a great need for servants, newspapers editorialized on the scarcity of housemaids, servant registries appeared in towns and middle-class women worried over how they were to find and keep good workers. Most young single women from working class families who needed to earn a living went out as general servants, helping their employer in the daily routine of housework and child care.

Few married women worked for a wage. However, they often supported the family economy by home production in country areas and in the towns by letting a bed or a room to a lodger, or by taking in washing or sewing. Middle class women had to protect their position and respectability and if they absolutely had to earn money they took in sewing, turned their homes into schools, became governesses or taught the piano. \

By the 1880s the young women born in the 1860s and those who came to New Zealand as children in the 1870s were looking for work. The hard times of the mid- and late–1880s sent more women into the wage-labour force. Hard times also meant fewer people risked marriage before they had some financial security, so there were more single women on the job market. Almost five times as many women were earning wages in 1891 as in 1871; in the 1880s the proportion of women who worked for money went up from about 20% to about a 25% of the women over fifteen. These new workers found it possible to get jobs outside of domestic service. The proportion of women employed in service had dropped to 46% by 1891. Women now worked in greater numbers as nurses, school mistresses, waitresses, laundresses, shopkeepers. The largest growth area, however, was in the clothing industry where three times as many women worked as cutters, machinists, dressmakers, seamstresses and milliners as in 1874. In the countryside too there was a considerable increase in the number of women employed. Most were relatives assisting on farms but there were also a few women shearers, rabbit catchers, kauri gum diggers, and women who ran farms and sheep stations on their own account. There were not as yet many new jobs for women — they had not made much headway in offices, or even in the new telegraph and telephone departments.

Although 45,000 women, some 2000 of them under 15, worked for wages by 1891, the propriety of women working for wages was still a subject of debate. Some people, from both the working and middle class, believed that progress and civilization could be measured by the number of women a nation could afford to keep at home. The majority of commentators, however, accepted that some women would, at certain stages of their lives, have to work for wages. They tried to improve the conditions of women in industry, giving little thought to the domestic, private environment in which most women operated.

The employment of women in factories was a matter of public concern from the early 1870s. In 1873 Parliament passed an act which prohibited women from working more than eight hours a day in factories and from doing night work. Five years later a Royal Commission investigating the working of the act, took evidence from employers, unionists and workers in Dunedin. It appeared that the legislation was generally observed in the clothing industry but not by the two laundries in town. The laundries operated eleven and twelve hour days, gave their employees only ten minutes for lunch and tea and paid no overtime. The real concern of the Commission, however, was not so much conditions of work, but whether or not married women worked and what happened to their children. This concern was shared by Henry Hogg, secretary of the Operative Tailors' Society. Hogg believed that many women workers were married and left their children either to take care of themselves or in the care of older sisters. He was clearly opposed to such behaviour. Not so John Richardson, a Dunedin politician, who in 1881 published a paper on the

Pubs were a focal point for men resident in the towns, but, as this photo of the Anchor Hotel in Wanganui shows, women were also involved in pub life, and children hung around the doors. *Alexander Turnbull Library*

'Employment of Females and Children in Factories and Workshops'. Richardson maintained that although past events had shown that women and children needed 'kindly sympathies and precious guardianship' women had 'a natural right to provide a living for themselves or their families, if married'.

During the 1880s, as more women entered the labour force, the debate over factory work intensified. In depressed conditions employers did all they could to cut their costs and women did what they could to keep their families afloat. Any job was better than no job. Conditions deteriorated, hours lengthened, the legislation was ignored. In 1888 and 1889 conditions in Dunedin factories were so bad that middle class reformers, led by Rutherford Waddell, Downie Stewart and Rachel Reynolds, banded together to investigate, organize the workers and force legislative improvement. Waddell became President of a Tailoresses' Union with Harriet Morrison first as Vice-President and then as Secretary. Their actions led to a Royal Commission being set up in 1890. This time the Royal Commission focussed on conditions and shocked the country by its evidence of long hours, poor pay and the exploitation of women and child workers. The Commissioners recommended that all places where people were employed on wages should be registered and subject to inspection; no boy or girl under the age of fourteen should be allowed to work in a factory, and no factory worker under eighteen should work for more than forty-eight hours a week or between six in the evening and six in the morning. They recommended that the government establish Boards of Arbitration and Conciliation with employer and worker representation and statistical bureaux that could collect and maintain information on industrial employment. The aim of their recommendations was to ensure the 'sanitary and other arrangements necessary for the health and morals of the workers'.

Although increasing numbers of women worked for wages, such work was transitional, occupying the years between the end of school and marriage, usually a period of, at the most, ten years. Marriage rates dropped in the 1880s and the average age of women marrying for the first time increased from 23 in 1871 to 25.6 years in 1891. However, the vast majority of women married eventually. By 1891 immigration of single women and the sexual balance among the native-born population meant a more even sex ratio — 56% of adults were male and 44% female; 58% of men over twenty and 77% of women were married.

For most women marriage meant a home of their own, usually rented, and children. The families of the 1870s and 1880s were large; seven to eight children was normal; families of ten or twelve not uncommon. Mary Rolleston, wife of the politician, William, married in 1865 and had nine children, the last one born in 1889 when Mary was forty-four. Both William and Mary worried about their large family, concerned about the toll it took on Mary's health and on the family income. William tried to cheer his wife up when she was pregnant with her seventh child by suggesting they 'make solemn vows for the future of celibacy and *keep them*.' Some couples must have taken more effective steps to limit conception: for instance the birth of Mary Vogel's fourth and last child in England when she was only twenty-seven suggests an active control over conception. Artificial means of contraception were not easily available but were known about; they must have been used by those who were growing up and marrying in the 1880s and 1890s. These young people began to limit their family size so that by the early twentieth century family size had fallen to an average of four children.

In the meantime, lack of contraceptive knowledge and technology and a relatively low child mortality rate, meant that women could expect to have a child every two years from marriage until their mid- and late-forties and to spend much of their life looking after children. Their first grandchildren were likely to be born while their own last children were still quite young.

The domestic work of women did not change much in the 1870s and 1880s although for well-off families there were some new appliances that made certain tasks more efficient and safer. Most houses, with the notable exceptions of those of the wealthy pastoral and urban business and professional families, were small three or four roomed cottages. They had wooden floors that caught the mud and dust in the cracks, rough plank walls, sometimes lined with hessian, newspaper or wallpaper, open fire-places and only occasionally running water. For some women cooking was made less

Rugby football was apparently first played in New Zealand in 1870, introduced by Charles Monro who had attended an English public school. The Wellington Club was formed in 1871 and its players adopted their own forms of nonchalance and bravura for the photographers. *Alexander Turnbull Library*

dangerous and cleaner by enclosed coal ranges, which by the 1870s were being manufactured in Dunedin by Henry Shacklock. Coppers for boiling clothes were making an appearance and wooden wringers were available to attach to the basic wooden laundry tub. Carpet sweepers had just been introduced. Perhaps the appliance that most changed women's lives was the sewing machine that was first imported to New Zealand in the 1860s. Sewing, making shirts, trousers, skirts and bodices, to say nothing of stitching household linen, had taken hours of women's time. It was a job that was never completed, and, often carried out by candle light or oil lamp at night, played havoc with women's eyesight. A sewing machine, if one could be afforded, meant that garments could be made more quickly and more neatly. Mass produced garments made in workshops became cheaper and a sewing machine in the home became a source of income for women who did not want to, or could not go out to work.

By the 1870s and 1880s some of the early women settlers were becoming matriarchs, and significant figures in their own communities. Their sons and daughters were now grown up and were producing grandchildren. Older women had an active part to play in the lives of these extended families. They often attended at the births of their grandchildren, and, even if they did not bring the children into the world, they stayed and cared for the family until the new baby was several weeks old. They were nurses to neighbours who took ill and took charge at times of crises, such as accidents or deaths. Some worried about the future of the children and grandchildren they saw around them. They were watching a new generation grow up as New Zealanders, barefoot, noisy and rumbustious colonial children. What would all these children do? Would there be enough land for them to farm? Would there be jobs for all? Would the young women find good husbands? These fears were related to the economy of the country and what were seen as changing attitudes. Older people were both proud of what had been achieved and fearful of the future.

Religion and the church was an area of life in which women, although unable to preach or take important positions in the church hierarchy, were becoming more prominent. In a sense this was a two-way movement, for one reason why women became more important in religious affairs was that men were forsaking the church. European settlers in New Zealand came from a culture where religion was in decline. Even the settlements where religion was to be the basis of the new society — Otago, Canterbury, Albertland — rapidly lost their religious character. Although most people, when asked by the census takers, could state a religious adherence, the percentage of regular church attenders was lower in New Zealand than in the Australian colonies. Not everyone had a church they could attend near them but the clergy became used to empty pews on Sundays. The sacrosanct nature of Sunday was being broken down. In 1874 the Dunedin Athenaeum club voted by a margin on 252 to 242 to open its library on Sundays. In the 1880s church committees found they had to compete with sightseeing, sports and visiting to get people to church. This is not to say that New Zealand was a hotbed of atheism. Diaries and letters, especially those of middle class women, show a deeply felt and spiritually moving religion. Among a number of Māori communities Christianity, often fused with Māori spiritual beliefs, was a central part of life. Revivalist preachers, for instance the Roman Catholic, Father Patrick Henneberry in the later 1870s and Brethren preachers in the early 1880s, had a great success. But church-going in the formal sense was increasingly becoming an occupation of women and children and clergymen of all denominations bewailed the loss of faith they perceived everywhere around them.

Many women, and some men as well, driven by religious conviction and a desire to make the world a better place, identified a number of moral changes that threatened New Zealand as much as economic problems. Indeed many of the country's economic problems were seen as having a moral cause. Prostitution, promiscuity, alcohol, violence, thriftlessness, high spirits and sheer non-conformity; all were marked out by the reformers as serpents in the new Eden. Men convened public meetings, sat on committees and discussed legislation; women tried to identify individuals in danger, to persuade the unruly to give up their old way of life and created homes and institutions for the vulnerable. Elimination, and if not elimination, control and regulation were their goals. The impulse had something to do with puritanism but it would be wrong to see these reformers as repressive killjoys or hypocrites. That they could not distinguish symptoms from causes was scarcely their fault. The women, in particular, lacked the intellectual training and the habit of challenging old modes of thought that might have led to a fuller understanding of the society they lived in.

While the church was losing its grip on the people, education was gaining.

When the central government took over the responsibility for primary education in 1877 school committees could compel all children between 7 and 13 to attend school. The response from these Palmerston North children to their educational experience seems rather mixed. *Alexander Turnbull Library*

Schooling was in the process of moving from local to central control and out of the hands of untrained but sometimes well educated men and women into the hands of trained and professional teachers. The process still had a very long way to go. In 1870 education was a regional matter with provincial councils picking up some of the responsibility and leaving the rest to private teachers. Inspection of council-funded schools usually showed that the buildings were inconvenient, classrooms lacked blackboards and books, the teaching was inefficient and the pupils inattentive. What to do about it was another matter. Schools were expensive and there was the vexed question of denominational schools and how they should be treated. How could the teaching be improved and how could you ensure that children attended and learned? The abolition of the provincial councils meant that the central government finally had to take the responsibility for these issues and this it did in the Education Act of 1877. The legislation set up a Department of Education and regional Boards of Education funded by the government. Education was to be secular and free and school committees were able, if they wished, to compel children between seven and thirteen, living within two miles of the school, to attend for at least half the time the school was open. If parents failed to send their children to school for the required number of days, they could be fined. Māori children could attend state schools if they wished but the system of 'native schools', established in the 1860s, co-existed with the new system.

By 1890 there were 1200 state primary schools in the country, sixty-eight Māori village schools, and 298 private primary schools. Over 130,000 children were receiving some form of education. The curriculum sounded interesting — all children were to be taught reading, writing, arithmetic, English grammar and composition, geography, history, and, if their parents did not object, science, drawing and singing. The girls got sewing, needlework and the principles of domestic science as extras and the boys had military drill. What actually went on in these classes however was usually far from interesting. The classes were large, controlled often by pupil teachers just out of their own school years. Books were uninspiring and the main teaching method was rote learning so that pupils could answer the questions of the departmental inspector on his visit. Children were cramped in long rows of desks, their slates in front of them, and their eyes on the teacher, endlessly repeating information or painstakingly making out words from readers and blackboards. Little wonder that truancy rates were high, especially at harvest time in the countryside, in bad weather and when anything more interesting was at hand. Alongside the state system there was still a less formal system in which children were taught in remote farmhouses by parents, older sisters, tutors and governesses. A network of religious schools, most of them Roman Catholic, also existed.

Beyond the age of thirteen relatively few children continued at school. By 1890 the main towns all had secondary schools for both boys and girls, but just over 2000 students were enrolled. To keep a child at school beyond the compulsory period was to forego their household help or their earnings, to say nothing of the expense of uniforms, books and school fees. The secondary schools were for those who wished to go to university, to enter business or a profession. They provided serious academic curricula, girls receiving much the same education as boys, although usually with inferior resources and with less attention paid to the classics and to science.

For the very few, there were three universities, or colleges by the 1880s. The Otago Provincial Council had decided in 1869 that it would establish a university and opened its doors, in a building originally designed as a post office but subsequently thought too grand for such a purpose, in 1871. Canterbury took its first students in 1874 and Auckland in 1883. The academic staff was imported from overseas and much of the teaching was in the evening and vocation oriented. The main degree was the B.A. and the main vocation of graduates, particularly of women graduates, was teaching. However before 1890, Otago and Auckland taught law, Otago developed a medical school and Canterbury had an associated college of agriculture.

Educational provision, although slow in coming, reflected the realization that if the country was to develop it needed an educated population. For a few people it betokened an appreciation of higher forms of art and culture and a widening of intellectual horizons. Among the early settlers there were men and women who were widely read and determined not to be diverted from the life of the mind by the pressures of colonial living. For most this meant a hungry devouring of an imported culture — the novels, the philosophical treatises, the poetry, the songs and music of Europe. It meant patronizing the visiting theatrical troupes, opera companies, and musicians who made regular visits to the main towns. For a surprisingly large number it meant performing themselves — in choral societies, amateur theatricals, elocution evenings, orchestral groups — and for a smaller number, creative work. William Fox, James Richmond, Emily Harris, Charles Goldie, John Hoyte were all talented painters working and exhibiting in the 1870s and 1880s. Dozens more belonged to the local art societies. The books of Lady Barker, Charlotte Evans and Vincent Pyke and the poetry of Thomas Bracken and William Pember Reeves were published in the same period. Countless others found the outlet for their pens in writing guide books on New Zealand.

In the 1870s and 1880s New Zealand became less totally absorbed in its own affairs and began to develop its links with the outside world, mainly but not entirely, within the framework of the Empire of which it was a part. The closest tie was still to Britain, the source of loans, immigrants, imports and, after all, the imperial power. But there were mutterings that New Zealand should be more equal in its relationship with the mother-country — that the Agent-General should by right be consulted on matters affecting New Zealand, that maybe New Zealand should have a representative in the House of Commons, or that there should be an imperial parliament determining matters of interest to Britain and all its colonies. The Australian colonies were friends and rivals. Migration across the Tasman was commonplace; inter-government negotiations frequent. The colonial governments conferred on constitutional issues, telegraph cables, steamer mail services, trade and the future of the Pacific. Some feelers were put out to closer ties with the United States. A shipping service to San Francisco was subsidized by the government in the early 1870s and an attempt was made to get the Americans to reduce duties on New Zealand wool. One or two New Zealand politicians visited the United States, rather to the chagrin of the British government whose diplomatic protocol forbade colonies engaging in such initiatives. New Zealand shippers, traders and financiers eyed the islands of the Pacific in the hope that they could develop business there and the government readily fell in behind these schemes. Any other nation venturing into the Pacific was looked on as an interloper, and Britain was regularly called on to defend the region against foreign interests. New Zealand itself placed a few guns around its coast after scares that war would break out between Russia and Britain in 1878 and again in 1885. The main line of defence however was the British navy, and the ships of the Australian Station, to which, after 1887, New Zealand made a financial contribution.

The most popular slogan in the political rhetoric of the 1870s and the goal of most settlers was 'happy homes and a prosperous country'. The era began with high hopes for economic growth, new settlement and peace. It ended in hardship, misery for some, and a feeling of being unable to get any further. New Zealand had provided the immigrants of the 1840s, as well as those of the 1870s, with the chance for a new life. The country was widely represented in migration and government propaganda as a

Utopia, a land of true social freedom, a land of equal opportunity and plenty. The experience of the 1880s cast serious doubts on this idealized view. Unemployment, poverty, the exploitation of women workers, ragged children in the streets, threadbare men on the tramp, damp dark cottages in mean alleys — these were old-world conditions. It was destructive to discover that idealism had not been sufficient to prevent these evils from contaminating the new world. Individual opportunities now seemed cut off; most of the good, fertile land was privately owned and there seemed little chance for new families to become independent and self-sufficient in the countryside. Urban growth made social differences more noticeable. The crowded cottages of Freeman's Bay in Auckland and South Dunedin were a stark reminder of the social distance between their inhabitants and the residents of the semi-rural villas and mansions of Remuera and Māori Hill. Somehow this southern Utopia had to be got back on to the right tracks.

6. *Centralization and Nationalism*
(1891–1912)

DAVID HAMER

The 'Liberal era' of 1891-1912 is often regarded as the beginning of 'modern' New Zealand. For instance, it saw the beginning of party government. In January 1891 a vote in the House of Representatives installed the Liberals as New Zealand's first party government, with John Ballance as Premier. The Liberals were to hold office for the next twenty-one years — which is still a record for continuous tenure of office by a New Zealand party. However, since New Zealand had not had party politics before, it took a considerable time for people to appreciate that a revolution in the relationship between the government and the people was in the making.

A dominant and accurate perception of this era has been that it saw the creation of the modern New Zealand State. A great deal of what was established then was to remain substantially intact for most of the next century — until the advent of the fourth Labour Government in 1984.

This period saw the beginnings of party politics. Initially there was not a party system because there was only one party — the Liberals. The Liberals convinced New Zealanders that the election of candidates pledged to support the leaders of a party in putting through a legislative programme, was preferable to a continuation of a régime of factions and independents who could not be relied on to support any government. It was the issue of effectiveness in government that brought the Liberals to power — their predecessors having discredited themselves by their inability (partly, it seemed, through lack of reliable parliamentary support) to respond effectively to the serious economic and social problems of the day — 'sweated labour', industrial unrest, the 'exodus' of population to Australia, land monopoly, lack of affordable credit for farmers, and so on.

The Liberals introduced the principle of party discipline, requiring a pledge from candidates before they were given the party nomination, and establishing a caucus as a mechanism for arriving behind closed doors at an agreed line to which all MPs were required to subscribe in public. There were frequent revolts against this discipline, but Seddon imposed it strictly and kept trying to purge the party's ranks of dissidents and independents.

The Liberals were much less successful in developing party organization outside Parliament and the party failed to nurture its grass roots. The Liberals' democratic philosophy made them unwilling to subject the movement to control by a party organization which would inevitably be dominated by a minority of enthusiasts. They preferred to govern in the name of an amorphous entity — 'the people' — which they never succeeded in mobilizing or institutionalizing in any form more substantial than ballot-box majorities.

A new democratic style of politics was forged by the Liberals, whose leader was 'King Dick' — Richard John Seddon, who replaced Ballance as Premier in 1893 on the latter's death, and who held the office until 1906. Seddon was born at St Helens, Lancashire in 1845. He migrated to Australia in 1863 and moved on to the West Coast of New Zealand's South Island at the height of its gold-rush boom in 1866. Unsuccessful as a prospector, he set up as a storekeeper and publican at Kumara and acquired his political skills in the rough, vigorous world of West Coast politics. His reputation was established by his work as a lay advocate in the Miners' Court. He never forgot his old mates on the coast. His later advocacy of old age pensions owed much to his personal knowledge of the destitution into which many of them had fallen.

Seddon combined a commanding platform presence, capacity for hard work, and relish for the often turbulent, scandal- and personality-ridden world of parliamentary politics. He did not wilt when under attack, and seemed to thrive under pressure, regarding his opponents' contemptuous dismissals of his fitness to head the government as a challenge to prove them wrong. His genius lay in making it appear that his critics were denying the fitness of the New Zealand people to govern themselves in the new democratic régime. In both his populist style and his rise to high office, Seddon epitomized the advent of a new democratic order. By his success he established the tradition of the populist Prime Minister in New Zealand. He had little interest in political ideas but much in making the people feel that the government was their servant. This meant that policies had to be acceptable to the broad mass of public opinion. Insistence on this democratic principle enabled Seddon to apply brakes to the aspirations of the more radical members of his party. The limits of reform in the Liberal era were defined as the limits which the people themselves wished to impose.

Seddon also stabilized politics by keeping on the backbenches anyone who would have tried to use office to force the pace of reform faster than Seddon believed the majority of the people were ready to accept. His Cabinet became filled with nonentities whose principal qualifications for being there appeared to be their subservience to Seddon.

In their use of the power of the state, the Liberals established a tradition of pragmatic interventionism. Although the word 'socialism' — usually qualified as 'state socialism' — was used to describe what was happening, the government did not

Seddon sought all the publicity he could extract from the initiation of public works and railway construction projects — a key to the government's hold on numerous rural electorates. *Otago Early Settlers Museum*

subscribe to, or see itself as implementing any doctrine. It intervened to deal with specific situations as these were drawn to its attention, usually through pressures generated by the newly established democratic system. As a result, the accretion of state functions developed on an ad hoc basis — a process which, as the Liberals were anxious to point out, had its origins in the pragmatism of the pioneers. The creation of a welfare state was not the goal of those who promoted old age pensions and other social reforms in this era. Nevertheless, Liberals were the pioneers of the New Zealand welfare state. It was not until the 1980s that a government decided to challenge this tradition of state intervention and radically revise the assumptions that had underlain the exercise of state power in New Zealand. For nearly a century the pragmatism established and practised so successfully by the Liberals reigned supreme.

That the Liberals favoured a major role for the central government in the development of the country certainly did not mean that they were antagonistic to capitalism. William Pember Reeves, the Minister of Labour in the early years of the government and one of the very few 'intellectuals' in its ranks, sometimes dreamed of a day when the competitiveness of the capitalist system would give way to the higher morality of 'socialism'. Most Liberals, and most New Zealanders, simply wanted the benefits of private ownership of property spread more widely than appeared to be the case in the 1880s. The Liberal view of the proper role of the state in the economy was grounded in a perception that private enterprise was weak. Much of the capital needed to develop the country, especially to buy land from the Māori and estate owners and to extend the communications and transport infrastructure begun by Vogel, would have to be procured and applied by the state. But that infrastructure was to serve the interests of private enterprise, not replace it.

The Liberals believed in a dominant role for central government. There was to be no going back to the provincial system — and few New Zealanders wanted that. There were too many districts dependent on the central government for development funds — there was a vast expansion of settlement made possible by the construction of roads, bridges, and railways. Paradoxically, this weakened provincialism, because thousands of settlers depended on the state for survival. Local government developed slowly and was not encouraged by the Liberal Government which preferred to maintain centralized control over the funding of public works. It was acutely aware of the valuable political leverage which this control afforded. It was a major device for ensuring the continued loyalty both of Members of Parliament and of districts that needed roads and bridges. Ministers loved to have their pictures taken opening a bridge or a railway extension — and Members of Parliament liked to be seen standing by their sides.

At first the Liberals hoped that New Zealand could get by without overseas borrowing. This policy, called 'self-reliance' by the first Liberal Premier, John Ballance, was tried for a few years, the government relying on budget surpluses generated largely out of customs duties, with some assistance from new land and income taxes to provide finance for development. From 1894 on there was a cautious

William Pember Reeves, Minister of Labour, 1891-6, and architect of numerous important labour reforms, including the Industrial Conciliation and Arbitration Act, 1894. Drawing by Vivian Hunt. *Alexander Turnbull Library*

revival of 'Vogelite' developmentalism, particularly by Joseph Ward who, as Colonial Treasurer, was notably successful in 1894 in arranging a loan in Britain to finance cheap state advances to settlers. Gradually there was a return to borrowing for public works. Many on the left of the party did not like this, but they had to accept it, as they appreciated that the survival of many settlers on the land depended on their receiving this kind of state assistance. If settlers failed on the land, they would have to move into the towns and cities, exacerbating problems such as unemployment and high rents for housing.

The Liberals inherited, and eventually added to, an enormous burden of debt. By 1896 the gross public debt was just over £43 million. Net indebtedness per head of the European population was just over £60. This was considerably higher than in New South Wales (£48) or Victoria (£39). By 1913 governmental indebtedness had risen to over £90 million. This was £84 per head of European population. Concern about the level of debt persisted, but there was a general feeling that unlike earlier loans, this borrowed money was used to a greater extent to increase productivity.

There was a great expansion of the apparatus of government. The Liberals created twelve new departments. This was an era of powerful civil servants, working closely with reform-minded politicians, for example Edward Tregear who was the Head of the Labour Department. There was more scope for them now than later because it took time for civil service rules to catch up with the impact of the revolution in the role of government in New Zealand life. There was considerable 'democratic' prejudice against an independent and powerful civil service, and widespread belief that in the fullest possible sense, the people should rule in a democracy. Because Seddon and other ministers did not like competitive examinations as a means of securing government jobs, they tried to circumvent them. Many 'temporary' civil servants were appointed, and there were allegations of excessive political interference with the process. But MPs regarded finding government positions for constituents and their sons and daughters as an important part of their democratic duty.

Unions were formed to protect government employees, for example the Public Service Association (1890), but the Liberal Government did little to reform the civil service. The issue was taken up by the opposition and as a result, gained the votes of many government employees in Wellington. They were further alienated by the Ward Government which dismissed 940 civil servants in the savage retrenchment of 1909. This, together with the sentiments against the civil service often expressed by Liberal politicians, made the government's employees yearn for more security in their employment. When the opposition took office as the Reform Party in 1912, it established the essential structure that the civil service was to retain until the State Sector Act of 1988.

One reason for the long duration of the Liberal Government was the weakness of its opposition which was discredited by its identification with the depression era. In the early years the Liberals concentrated on trying to frighten voters about the prospect of returning to the bad old days, seeking to establish belief in a connection between the depression and the state of politics in the days of what they referred to as the 'Continuous Ministry'. Few of the ministers had held office before and they disclaimed responsibility for what had gone wrong in the 1880s. It took time for a new generation of opposition leaders to emerge who were not tainted with the alleged sins of the 'Continuous Ministry'. Furthermore, what many opposition politicians were initially opposed to was the new system of party politics itself and this prevented them from adopting the same methods and discipline. There was no party with a name other than 'opposition' until 1909 when the Reform Party was formed.

The Liberals' philosophy and style made it very difficult for an effective and credible alternative government to emerge. The Liberals aspired to represent *all* the people. They were strongly opposed to class or sectional politics and argued that what had gone wrong with New Zealand politics in the past was excessive dominance by one minority interest — which they identified as the 'squattocracy'. This aspect of the Liberal creed enabled the party to appeal to a very wide range of New Zealanders. It also, however, put limits on the extent to which it was prepared to go to accommodate the demands of particular sections where these appeared to conflict with the general good. Dissatisfaction gradually increased amongst both organized labour and the Farmers' Union about the restraints imposed by what was in effect a liberal ideology (even if it masqueraded as anti-ideology). For their part, the Liberals found increasing difficulty in defining and retaining acceptance for a general community interest, to which sectional claims ought to be subordinated.

To begin with, public life was dominated by men from a generation which had experienced New Zealand before, as well as during, the depression of the 1880s. The indignation that they felt about the social hardships and economic problems of the 1880s flowed from their experiences as migrants whose reference point was the dreams and aspirations that they had brought with them. Their shock at what had gone wrong with their 'Promised Land' was traumatic and provided much of the emotional force behind the Liberal reforms.

Prices for wool, meat and dairy produce began a long upward trend after 1895. Prosperity slowly returned, and the standard of living rose to unprecedented heights. Indeed, it became one of the highest in the world. The key to this new prosperity was refrigeration and the ability of New Zealand producers, aided by the government, to respond to the challenge and opportunity offered by the new technology and the new consumer market waiting to be exploited at the other end of the world.

But occasional setbacks were given greater prominence and caused great alarm. Migrants such as Seddon were never able to take the improvements for granted. However, the gradual increase in the proportion and influence of native-born politicians was accompanied by a decline in the predominance of this depression-haunted frame of mind.

That New Zealand changed greatly in this period is undeniable. Although it is debatable to what extent these changes were attributable to the government's policies, the government naturally claimed much of the credit.

For example, in so far as New Zealand society became more 'democratic' this was to a large extent the result both of a reinforcing of characteristics which were already strongly established, and of a further weakening of resistance to these. The main difference was that New Zealand became one of the most self-consciously democratic societies in the world. Indeed, as far as politics was concerned, New Zealand *was* the most democratic country in the world, establishing universal adult suffrage many years before the United States or Great Britain. This was something of which New Zealanders were justifiably proud. It became an important ingredient in the developing sense of national identity. What democratic America was in the 1830s when Alexis de Tocqueville wrote *Democracy in America*, New Zealand seemed to become in the 1890s when another French student of politics, André Siegfried, wrote *Democracy in New Zealand*. There were even some Americans who visited New Zealand in the hope that it could provide lessons and new inspiration for what they saw as their own tired and corrupt democracy. Other visitors were equally impressed and spread abroad the reputation of New Zealand as a country where the most daring social experiments were being tried.

There continued to be a distinct wealthy class. But it became less conspicuous, withdrawing from public life, partly out of disdain for the new democratic ethos, partly as a consequence of a loss of esteem. Deference to wealth and position had never amounted to much in New Zealand, but the wealthy had had considerable influence at a time when few could afford the time or leisure to indulge in a public career. Now most Members of Parliament gained election as representatives of a party, not as local notables.

The Liberals had no wish to level all social distinctions. They admired the self-made man and reserved their condemnation for those who inherited and therefore had not earned their wealth. In their land policy they made much of the desirability of taxing the 'unearned increment'. The foundations of this policy were as much moral as economic.

'Democracy' had no enemies in New Zealand and met with minimal resistance or even criticism. Conservatism was weak, and therefore so was Old World radicalism. There were none of the enemies against which Old World radicals directed their anger — no established church, no titled aristocracy. There were attempts to invent substitute enemies of the people, such as the 'squattocracy' or the banks. The controlling feelings were those of migrants who had come to New Zealand in search of a better way of life. They were not going to be satisfied with a mere reproduction of Old World social structures. But they were happy with social hierarchy, as long as it was a dynamic structure with scope for unimpeded ascent by the hard-working and the morally worthy. The Liberals' policy aimed at removing barriers to social mobility.

Many wealthy squatters remained. But by adopting a more private life-style, they avoided the censure that they had incurred in the past, and the subdivision of estates took the edge off the anger of the land-hungry. The state assumed powers of compulsory expropriation of estates, but these were very seldom used. There were hardly any cases of stubborn resistance where land-hunger was strong, and so public opinion was seldom inflamed against landowners as it was in Ireland at this time. Indeed, numerous landowners found profit in subdividing, thus appearing to be accepting the trend towards small farming.

The force of indignation against 'land monopolists' gradually diminished. More and more people, especially labour leaders, who were concerned about the problems of urban society and the economy, became convinced that solutions to them had to be sought elsewhere — not in the promotion of land reform and closer settlement of the land. Slowly the appeal of the closer settlement of the land as a panacea for New Zealand's ills began to diminish — although it remained powerful for political reasons. Land reform was one of the few issues that continued to distinguish Liberalism as a political creed and so to unify the party.

Nevertheless, one of the distinguishing features of the Liberal era was the preoccupation of politicians with the land question. Legislation enabled the government to acquire and subdivide estates and by 1900 it had been offered nearly five million acres — 400,000 of which were selected for subdivision into small settlements. Increasingly the government had to borrow overseas to finance its

Lower High Street, Dunedin, 1907. Behind the Telegraph Building can be seen the tower of the Exchange Building. It was during the first decade of the twentieth century that Dunedin slipped from third to fourth place among New Zealand cities, being overtaken by Wellington. Its population in 1911 was 64,237. *Hardwick Knight Collection, Otago Early Settlers Museum*

purchases. This injection of funds into the land market raised land prices — as did increased expenditure on roads and bridges. As a result the government could afford to buy less and less land. By the time Ward became Premier in 1906, voices were being heard demanding a more stringent use of the land tax — originally fixed at a low level — as a device for enforcing the break up of estates. The government proceeded cautiously and pragmatically, subordinating its supporters' prejudice against large estates, to the economic necessity of maintaining large pastoral estates. In 1896 there were 732 estates between 5000 and 50,000 acres in size, comprising 31% of the occupied land, and 112 estates over 50,000 acres, comprising 30%. By 1911 the latter figure had fallen to 30 (20%), but the number of estates between 5000 and 50,000 had risen to 926 (28%).

The government made sure that it selected estates that it needed for closer settlement and that could be successfully subdivided. Even so it made a few, inevitably well publicized, mistakes, and there were even occasional suggestions of scandal, such as the alleged use of political influence by John McKenzie, Minister of Lands, to enable his sons to obtain the Bushey Park estate in North Otago, from the Bank of New Zealand Assets Realisation Board in 1897.

Ballots were held for the farms carved out of the estates and were great events in the districts in which they occurred. By 1914, 264 estates comprising about 1,500,000 acres had been purchased. On these 5,529 farmers had been settled. Stringent conditions relating to residence and improvement were laid down. In order to help poorer men to get onto the land, the government devised a new form of leasehold, called the lease-in-perpetuity, which had a fixed rental but no right of purchase. However, after more than a decade of intense controversy, this right was conceded by the Ward Government.

The policies of purchase and subdivision of estates must be placed in perspective. It has been calculated that government purchase was directly responsible for only 26% of the decline in acreage of estates of more than 10,000 acres between 1892 and 1910. Voluntary private subdivision was far more significant. Furthermore, most new farmers were not placed on land acquired under the Land for Settlements legislation, but were dairy farmers settled on Crown land in the North Island, much of which had been purchased from the Māori (3 million acres costing a mere £650,000, compared with the £5 million spent between 1893 and 1906 on purchasing land previously alienated to Europeans). Indeed, the South Island orientation of the policy of purchasing estates was frequently criticized in the north where there were demands for far greater expenditure on Māori land and on improving access to land already in the Crown's possession. Large numbers of South Islanders moved north to settle on the bush land there.

One group which regarded itself as having a special relationship with the Liberal Government was organized labour. The Liberals' success in the 1890 elections followed the failure of the maritime strike — a significant catalyst for change both in the political sphere and in the state's regulation of industrial relations. On the one hand, it made labour leaders aware of their weakness in direct dealings with employers and therefore ready to welcome and co-operate with state interference in industrial relations. On the other hand it had a traumatic effect on New Zealanders who thought they had left behind Old World evils, such as strikes and class warfare. They were ready for their part to accept an active role for the state in remedying this state of affairs.

The Maritime Council in 1890 was an attempt to form a national union organization. Its failure revealed the obstacles in the way of such a development.

The first refrigerated cargo to be conveyed from New Zealand to Britain was carried aboard the *Dunedin* which sailed from Port Chalmers on 15 February 1882. 4,460 mutton and 449 lamb carcasses arrived on 24 May. *De Maus Collection, Otago Early Settlers Museum*

There was no central trade union organization for most of this era, although local trades and labour councils held annual conferences and maintained close relations with the government whose policies favoured and encouraged the formation of unions and the giving of preference in employment to unionists.

For a brief time, New Zealand was the envy of the world for having apparently found the secret of industrial peace — a 'land without strikes', as the admiring American Progressive, Henry Demarest Lloyd, called it. Legislation passed in 1894 set up a system of industrial conciliation and arbitration. Disputes were to be dealt with by local Conciliation Boards — which often had clergymen as neutral chairmen. If their proposal to resolve the dispute was not to the satisfaction of either side, the aggrieved party would ask for it to be referred to the Arbitration Court where the determination was binding on all parties. Reeves, the architect of the measure, expected most disputes would be settled at the conciliation stage. This reflected the Liberal faith that conflict in society is capable of resolution if only the disputing parties can hear each other's point of view and take into account a wider community interest. However, of the 230 disputes dealt with between 1894 and 1908, 155 were taken on to the court. As a result, the court became overburdened and unions became dissatisfied with the consequent delays, arguing that employers referred disputes to the court to save money by delaying wage increases and improvements to conditions of work.

Unions had to register under the Act in order to benefit from awards of the court. Many unions came into existence for this purpose. In 1896 there were 65 unions totalling 9370 members; by 1908 the number had risen to 325 with a membership of 49,347. The court became a major New Zealand institution. Its awards were as significant as much of the legislation passed by Parliament and indeed had the effect of taking many contentious issues out of the political arena. For twenty years the expression of the divergence of class interests — which had erupted into open strife in 1890 and was to do so again in 1913 — was predominantly through law.

The overall Liberal approach to industrial matters emphasized a balance between labour and capital. Since labour was generally regarded as significantly weaker than capital at the beginning of the 1890s, there was considerable support for policies that appeared to be pro-labour, although this largely reflected a view that labour had a good deal of 'catching up' to do. The early awards of the Arbitration Court seemed to implement this philosophy.

However in the early twentieth century the cost of living began to rise, and workers found the court unwilling to deal with the problem. Liberals defended the apparent change of stance, saying it reflected the advent of balance in labour-capital relations. Some unions then began to consider the possible advantages of withdrawing their registration and negotiating directly with employers concerning wages and conditions of work.

In their relationship with the state unions were satisfied to act as pressure groups. The Liberals made gestures about a special relationship with labour, for example by calling their party organization the Liberal and Labour Federation in 1899. The Liberals received strong electoral backing from workers. A few union leaders were elected to Parliament and were known as Lib-Labs, but they did not form a separate party. With direct access to Reeves and then Seddon as Minister of Labour the unions backed the Liberals rather than risk disrupting the Lib-Lab majority and bringing to power a much less sympathetic régime (as indeed did happen in 1912). On most of the issues of the day labour leaders saw eye to eye with the government, or at least with the left wing of the governing party.

However there were tentative efforts to remind the government that it should not take its labour support for granted. In 1904 the conference of the Trades and Labour Councils passed a resolution calling for the formation of an independent labour party. But the new Political Labour League was not a success and it was not until 1908 that David McLaren in Wellington was elected the first independent Labour M.P. But even McLaren won only with the support of Liberal voters who supported him on the second ballot when their candidate was eliminated on the first (the second ballot system was introduced in 1908 — and repealed in 1913). In 1910 the Trades and Labour Councils conference set up a New Zealand Labour Party, and five Labour members were elected in 1911. They too owed their election to the second ballot system. Several benefitted from tactical voting by Reform supporters following their leaders' strategy to ensure the defeat of Liberal candidates. Through this period the growth of political labour was successfully contained by the Liberals. As in Britain, the shattering of the Lib-Lab alliance was not to come until the First World War.

There was a parallel growth of employers' organizations. There was only one such organization in 1896; by 1908 there were 122 with 3918 members. Like the growth of trade unions, this was principally a response to the new role of government creating a need for lobbies and pressure groups, and groups that were not so organized were at a disadvantage. Sectionalism — often described by Liberals as a menace to the general welfare — began to become tamed and incorporated into the fabric of New Zealand government. The arbitration system was a prime example of this.

Most New Zealand workers were not employed in large factories, for New Zealand was not an industrial country yet — and there were many who hoped it never would be, not wishing to see reproduced in New Zealand the evils associated with Old World industrialization. Most industries were associated with the preparation of raw materials for the export market. Numerous local industries produced consumer items such as boots and shoes, clothing, beer, and biscuits. Many workers were employed in extractive industries such as flaxmilling, kauri gum digging and processing, timber-milling, and gold and coal mining.

Output of coal rose from just over 700,000 tons in 1895 to a pre-war peak of over two million tons in 1910. The work-force in the coal-mining industry rose from 1799 in 1895 to 4599 in 1910. Coal was not a significant export commodity and in the period 1896-1913, it never accounted for more than 1% of the total value of New Zealand's exports. As annual consumption usually exceeded production, some coal was imported. In 1901 the government passed the State Coal Mines Act and took over two mines on the West Coast. The aim was not the eventual nationalization of this industry but rather the introduction of competition in the hope of lowering the price.

Kauri gum was in demand for use in the manufacture of oil varnishes. At its peak in the mid-1890s it was responsible for 5% of the country's exports. The kauri-milling industry was at its peak also. There was great demand for the timber throughout Australasia, used, for example, in the woodwork of fine homes built for wealthy businessmen on both sides of the Tasman.

The flax industry flourished, being a major activity in the Shannon district of the Manawatu, for example. But it was typical of the fundamentally predatory nature of these industries; no thought was given to conservation. Swamps rapidly disappeared, although drainage for cultivation also had a good deal to do with this. It was an industry characterized by many small firms, often poorly managed and undercapitalized.

The extractive industries changed with the arrival of investment in new technology. The day of the gold prospector working a solitary claim gave way to an era of sluicing and dredging, providing access to gold deposits that individual gold seekers could never hope to exploit. Syndicates of capitalists were formed, and gold towns such as Waihi became company towns where most people worked for wages paid by large

Flax mill at Waitahuna, Otago, 1904. The flax industry had played a major role in the settlement of districts in Otago in the 1880s when there was a strong demand for binder twine. *Hocken Library*

companies. Tensions developed, and unions were formed whose militancy was often accentuated by the isolation and grimness of the locations.

With the extractive industries spread permanent settlement as many workers stayed on to farm the land. In Northland gum-digging provided a supplement to income that was vital to the survival of many settlers. Village settlements were deliberately located on the fringes of gumfields so that the farmers could earn extra income in their spare time. Timber milling helped to clear land. The construction of public works, notably the North Island main trunk railway (completed 1908), created the nuclei of settlements especially through the centre of the island. Towns such as Taihape and Hunterville began as camps for construction workers and evolved into service centres for new farming districts.

Technological changes also transformed the farming industry. All sorts of new-fangled, labour-saving devices were enticingly displayed at fairs and shows and drawn to farmers' attention in literature mailed to them by distributors.

Despite extensive help from the government, farmers' spokesmen decried 'socialism' and extolled individual self-reliance. When the government sought to enforce standards of quality and hygiene, farmers complained, disliking the 'snooping' around farms by inspectors that this entailed. But New Zealand was becoming too dependent on meat and dairy exports to be able to afford any doubts concerning the quality. Farming leaders asserted distinctive positions on many of the major issues and policies. They were powerful enough to prevent the application of labour laws to farm workers, arguing that costs of farm production had to be kept as low as possible.

Many farmers wanted 'free trade' — the removal of duties on imported machinery, farm equipment, barbed wire, etc. There was much concern about the activities of American trusts which threatened to take over the markets for harvesters, using techniques similar to those employed brutally and successfully in the United States itself. The government followed a compromise policy. Moderate tariffs were imposed to assist New Zealand manufacturers of these products and provide employment for New Zealand workers. Farmers resented the tariffs as they meant high prices for imported products and a cheaper but often inferior domestic equivalent. Protection of domestic industry was an issue that united manufacturers and unions against the farmers. The opposition decided not to adopt a full free trade policy as it needed the votes of the urban middle class.

The rise of the Farmers' Union, founded in 1899, shows the farmers' increasing capacity to promote their sector. Pioneer farming was often a very isolated life that provided scant opportunity for farmers to get together to develop a sense of common interest. The dairy industry did much to alter this state of affairs. It necessitated frequent meetings of farmers. For example, dairy farmers had to go almost every day to creameries and skimming stations which were very numerous because of the shocking condition of many country roads. Much farmer organization also arose out of the mobilization of support for the formation of dairy factories and co-operative dairy companies.

There was a good deal of animosity in this period between 'town' and 'country'. Aggressive spokesmen for the 'country' interest attacked the 'parasitic' cities. There was strong pressure from many towns for the subdivision of large estates in their vicinity and for the promotion of more intensive settlement. In the struggle to grow and achieve dominance in their district, the towns needed as many settlers as possible to provide customers for their businesses. Their MPs could sound quite radical in their attacks on 'land monopolists'. Within the Liberal coalition their MPs were allies of the city radicals, but often uneasy ones. Fundamentally their outlook was pro-'country': their aim was to ensure the successful and prosperous settlement of farmers on the land. Often therefore they joined with the farmer members in Parliament to oppose and condemn the anti-'country' attitudes of city representatives.

The movement of population — and of young adults in particular — from the country to towns and cities aroused increasing concern. It was a world-wide phenomenon, but there seemed something wrong, even 'unhealthy', about its occurring in a 'new country', one of whose chief characteristics was supposed to be its abundance of land. By 1911 the urban population had exceeded the rural. The

This Burton Brothers photograph of Symonds Street, Auckland, shows the close juxtaposition of the homes of the rich and poor that was a feature of the 'walking city'. *National Museum*

population of Auckland nearly doubled between 1896 and 1911: from 51,000 to nearly 103,000. By 1911 30% of New Zealand's Pākehā population lived in the four main centres. Nearly 38% lived in towns and cities with populations over 8000. The trend caused much anxiety. Politicians endlessly discussed its causes and proposed remedies such as the more vigorous prosecution of land settlement and the breaking up of estates. Many believed that it was fundamentally a negative phenomenon, that people would prefer to live in the country but were compelled to go to live in the cities because of the unavailability or inaccessibility of land. There was a great reluctance to accept that there was anything about city life that might actually attract young people. The government tried to think of ways to make country life easier and more attractive. One answer was to make telephone services available in rural districts.

Yet, New Zealand did not appear to be a 'citified' country. The four largest towns in the 1896 census had non-Māori populations ranging from 51,000 (Auckland and Christchurch) to 42,000 (Wellington). These four contained over 25% of the population. Outside these centres there were only seven boroughs with populations in excess of 4000. There was much comment on the difference between the

The east side of Princes Street, Auckland, in the mid 1880s. This is typical of the tendency for the homes of the well-to-do to be arranged along Auckland's ridges. *Auckland Public Library*

Australian and New Zealand situations. Some saw the state of affairs in New Zealand as healthy in contrast to the way the population of Victoria had crowded into Melbourne or of New South Wales into Sydney. Others asked whether New Zealand might not have too many towns and suffer from its lack of one large city. There were those who saw the development of New Zealand as handicapped by the absence of one big centre where resources and energy could concentrate.

The North Island population continued to grow and it overtook the South Island around the turn of the century. By 1911 the non-Māori population of the North Island was 563,991 and of the South only 444,477. Between 1869 and 1911 the North's share of the non-Māori population rose from 48% to 56%.

Another characteristic of modern New Zealand gathered momentum in this period: the rise of Auckland province. There had been a long period of South Island ascendancy, resulting largely from the gold rushes and the prolonged struggle to break the hold of Māori tribes on North Island land. One healthy aspect of the growth of Auckland province was that only 37% of its population was urban (compared with Wellington's 57% and Otago's 51%). This reflected the great growth of the farming sector in Auckland province: Auckland's urban growth was 'healthy' in that it was based on a rapidly developing hinterland.

The cities themselves were being transformed by the growth of suburbs. They were no longer 'walking cities' in which most people could walk from home to work each day. In the central and originally settled parts of the cities, people of widely varying social and economic situations had lived in close proximity to one another, their locations differentiated mainly by variations in the terrain, with the rich occupying the heights (The Terrace in Wellington; Parnell and Princes Street in Auckland), and the poor the gullies and lower-lying, less salubrious areas (such as Thorndon in Wellington, Freemans Bay in Auckland). In the suburbs, class distinctions were far more visible and were indeed often a selling point. Suburbs were promoted by real estate agents in terms of a way of life with particular appeal to middle class people anxious to flee the increasingly congested inner-city. There was intensive and speculative subdivision of farmland surrounding and often very close to the original central cores of the cities.

Because of better roads and transport, the cities were becoming less dependent on farms in their immediate vicinities for their supplies of fruit and vegetables, milk and meat. For example, the Wellington suburbs of Kelburn and Brooklyn were originally farms, but much of the food supply for Wellington was produced in the Horowhenua-Otaki districts after the completion of the Wellington and Manawatu Railway. New forms of transport evolved to enable people to live in the suburbs and work in the city during the day, for example the Wellington cable car (1905) linking the new suburb of Kelburn with Lambton Quay. The government itself endeavoured to promote suburban development through the Workers' Dwellings Act of 1905. It acquired land at Petone and elsewhere, built houses, and rented these to workers. Financial considerations limited the application of this particular scheme, but it was a precursor of the state housing policy that was introduced by the first Labour Government.

A major concern of the government was unemployment. Levels fluctuated. The number assisted stayed reasonably steady between 1700 and 3100 between 1897 and 1905, then rose very sharply to a peak of 10,391 in 1910. This reflected the impact of the ending of work on the North Island main trunk railway. It then declined to a pre-war level of about 5700. With no welfare state and no dole unemployment was a very worrying prospect. Irregular employment was very common, and saving money difficult. That was one reason why contributory pension schemes had to be rejected. Many workers just did not enjoy regular enough employment to be able to save for their retirement.

As early as 1894 a select committee of the House of Representatives recommended that all persons who had resided in New Zealand for the last twenty-five years be granted a pension on reaching the age of sixty-five. Overhanging the evolution of this policy was the shadow of the British workhouse. The pension was presented as the alternative to a workhouse system and as being, not charity, but the citizen's right, earned by years of payment of taxes (most of the tax revenue was derived from

A typical scene at the post office when old age pensions were being paid out. Henry Demarest Lloyd observed the first payment of pensions in Christchurch in 1900: 'Punctually upon the opening of the door at nine o'clock the little corner of the office in the Post-Office Savings Bank Department set aside for this payment was filled with old men and women. Entering with anticipation and not infrequently anxiety on their faces they came out in happier mood.' *Canterbury Museum*

indirect taxes levied on basic items of consumption). Finally in 1898 a pension was introduced. It was payable by the state and was non-contributory, but it was restricted to the completely destitute or those who were on the brink of destitution. Furthermore, there was a moral test: a recipient was required not to have reached this condition through any defect in his or her own character or behaviour. Pensioners were supposed to be the *deserving* poor.

The government tried hard to appear not to be financing public works as a way of finding work for the unemployed. It feared that such a policy would become impossibly expensive and attract unemployed workers from Australia. It offered closer settlement of the land as its main solution to the unemployment problem. This was of little help to city workers whose main problem was irregular employment. The government addressed this problem to a small extent through the provision, on the outskirts of cities such as Christchurch, of suburban allotments on which workers could subsist when not employed.

Immigration slowed down considerably. It was at a low ebb in the 1890s, but picked up again after 1900, reaching a peak in 1908 of 14,261 immigrants. After assisted immigration was reinstated (it was suspended in 1892) 1751 assisted migrants arrived in 1905. The figure rose slowly to 4953 in 1909, fell off and then rose again to 5064 in 1914.

The Liberal era was a time of consolidation and resistance to large-scale immigration. New Zealand's problems were blamed on the excessive migration in the 1870s. There was less attempt to promote New Zealand as a migrant destination, more emphasis on encouraging the investment of capital. The vision of New Zealand's future that predominated in the Liberal era was not one that desired rapid growth — although there was an increasingly confident challenge to this state of mind from Joseph Ward who tried to assume the mantle of Vogel. Ward's own business vicissitudes (which included being declared bankrupt in the mid-1890s) continued to be a reminder of the risks of the sort of 'plunging' economic policy with which he was identified.

There was a gradual increase in the proportion of the native-born in the European population. By 1901 it was nearly 60%. But one has to bear in mind that a far higher proportion of those born outside New Zealand than of the 'natives' was adult. In 1896, of the 441,660 Europeans who had been born in New Zealand, 330,032 were under the age of twenty-one. That this was a generation of overlap and transition is reflected in the parallel tendency to form two types of organization — on the one hand, New Zealand Natives Associations which were supposed to be confined to people born in New Zealand, and, on the other, Early Settlers Associations which were designed for the 'pioneers', few of whom had been born in New Zealand.

There was a growing interest in defining and using symbols of New Zealand's distinctiveness and New Zealand was one of numerous places which laid claim to being 'God's own country'. There was an emerging awareness of New Zealand's (European) history, with the publication of such works as William Pember Reeves's *Long White Cloud* (1898), and the development of state-supported collection and publication of documents related to early discovery, exploration, and settlement, such as Robert McNab's *Historical Records of New Zealand* (1908; 1914). The pioneers were admired and their contribution to the founding of a nation marked by, for example, the rhetoric that accompanied the enactment of old age pensions in 1898. As more and more districts reached such milestones as the fiftieth anniversary of the arrival of the first settlers, there were many pioneer celebrations. Most early settlers had been young people, yet the modern image of them tends to be one of venerable greybeards. This image was formed during the many celebrations of the pioneer achievements, and lamentations over the poverty and distress into which some of the surviving pioneers had fallen. With the passing of the pioneer generation and the slowing down of immigration, the population 'aged'. Nostalgia for the pioneer era reflected an awareness of how much New Zealand had changed.

This nostalgia and concern for the welfare of the aged survivors of the pioneer generation went hand in hand with attention to child health and maternity questions. Although there was a world-wide decline in fertility, in New Zealand it assumed special significance through being linked to the passing of the pioneer phase of the country's development. This trend, coupled with a high infant mortality rate (in 1903,

Some of New Zealand's first Plunket babies. The Plunket Society was formed in 1907. In the same year the first Karitane Hospital was opened in Dunedin. *Plunket Society Archives, Hocken Library*

81 deaths per 1000 births), had worrying implications for the nation's future. The early twentieth century saw a growing emphasis on the need for support for motherhood, virtually its endowment, by the state. The government took steps to improve maternity care. This reached a peak with the creation of the Plunket Society in 1907.

An indication of New Zealand's maturing national self-consciousness was the appearance of a literature of its own. Much earlier writing about New Zealand had been designed to attract migrants and investors and was largely uncritical in character. Although books such as those written by William Pember Reeves, New Zealand's official representative in London from 1896, were still primarily addressed to an external audience, they did aspire to greater objectivity in their appraisal of features of New Zealand's development such as the wars of the 1860s and the borrowing of the Vogel era. In writing about New Zealand by New Zealanders, there was a strong note of pride in what had been accomplished. The Liberals associated their reforms with the concept of New Zealand showing the way to the rest of the world. This notion proved very appealing to New Zealanders and it has remained an abiding feature of their understanding of their country's purpose. (For example, it reappeared in the 1980s in justifications of the creation of a nuclear-free New Zealand.) There were connections between Liberal politicians and writers on New Zealand themes, especially the new generation of historians. Robert McNab, W. P. Reeves and T. L. Buick were all Liberal parliamentarians. Thomas Bracken, author of popular verse celebrating New Zealand — including 'God defend New Zealand' — was approached at one point to be the principal Liberal organizer.

New Zealand's popular literary, musical, and theatrical culture was still largely derivative. Many New Zealanders with artistic or literary talents left to seek opportunities to develop them that were not available in New Zealand. The best known are Katherine Mansfield and the painter Frances Hodgkins. However, there was a beginning of 'literary nationalism' with a few writers and journals, the composer, Alfred Hill, and painters such as Gottfried Lindauer and C. F. Goldie, endeavouring to construct a distinctive New Zealand style and subject matter. Writers such as Reeves, the poet Jessie Mackay, and the novelist William Satchell chose New Zealand themes and celebrated its distinctive landscape and bush, sometimes with a nostalgic reflection on what was already 'passing'. For most, New Zealand was an empty land in human terms with a 'dying race', rich in legend and poetry, giving way to a new race whose potential was as yet unknown. Lindauer and Goldie specialized in portraits of idealized and 'noble' Māori. In this period the face of the Queen was replaced on postage stamps with pictures of New Zealand scenery. In association with the emerging tourist industry, there was much experimenting with motifs of national distinctiveness such as the fern and the kiwi.

In the days before the world was shrunk by jet aircraft and television, New Zealand was still an exotic and little known tourist destination. The development of the tourist industry was heavily dependent on state promotion. A Tourist Department of Railways was established in 1900 and in 1906 a Department of Tourist and Health Resorts was set up. Rotorua had been created by the government as a tourist resort in the mid-1880s, although traffic to the hot lakes was deterred for some years by the Tarawera eruption of 1886. From 1894 there was a train service direct from Auckland to Rotorua. Whakarewarewa became a very popular tourist attraction. This was the great age of the spa where people went to 'take the waters' and New Zealand catered to this trade at the thermal springs of Waiwera, Rotorua, and Hanmer Springs, while Wairakei was just beginning its career as a tourist resort.

In the Liberal era, New Zealand's place in the world began to change significantly. What had been a colony at the start of this period was a Dominion by the end and in 1901 even acquired a colony of its own — the Cook Islands. Having failed to avail itself of the opportunity to join the new Australian Commonwealth, New Zealand was setting forth towards a 'national destiny' of its own.

New Zealand gained a reputation as one of the most loyal of the British colonies.

Troops of the Third Contingent marching through Christchurch prior to departing for the South African War, 17 February 1900. *Otago Early Settlers Museum*

But its politicians were calculatingly 'imperial', using the opportunities which the imperial connection afforded in increasing abundance at this period to establish a place for their fledgling nation on the world stage. But if New Zealand's needs did not coincide with those of the Mother Country, as when Joseph Chamberlain, British Colonial Secretary from 1895 to 1903, sought New Zealand's co-operation in the promotion of free trade within the Empire, New Zealand was not prepared to give way.

An event which may appear to be a prime example of New Zealand's unhesitating devotion to the cause of Empire — the South African War (1899-1903) — was in fact a major stimulus to New Zealand national pride. New Zealand sent 6495 men in ten contingents to the war with public subscription actually financing two of them. In proportion to its population, New Zealand sent more men to the war than any other British colony. Praise for the courage and quality of the New Zealand troops was reported back home. The war was followed closely and there were innumerable patriotic fêtes and parades. The mood of intermingled imperialistic and nationalistic sentiment was exploited to the full by Premier Seddon. Historians who have studied the development in New Zealand of a male culture based on war and rugby, have traced many parallels between support for the soldiers who went to South Africa and the fervour with which New Zealanders followed the All Blacks who toured Britain in 1905 — and lost to Wales by one famous and henceforward hotly debated try.

There was also continuing fear of the intrusion of international rivalries into the South Pacific. The division of Samoa between the United States and Germany in 1899 aroused great anxieties. New Zealanders, such as Seddon, felt that they were more devoted to the cause of Empire than many in England where there was always a strong current of anti-imperialist sentiment, especially in the British Liberal Party. Every effort was made to reinforce Britain's commitment to the defence of the region. New Zealand's imperial 'loyalty' appeared again in 1909 when Ward attended an Imperial Conference in London and offered to pay the £2 million cost of a 'Dreadnought' battleship for the British navy. As he had made the promise without consulting Parliament, there was a storm of protest back home.

Communications developments such as postal services unified the country as never before. This was the golden age of the local post office. The number of post offices rose from 856 in 1880 to 1700 in 1900. Post offices were important local institutions because they linked remote rural communities with the outside world. It was at post offices that old age pensions and other state benefits were paid out. The late 1980s was to see the brutal termination of that aspect of life in many communities in New Zealand.

In the country the backblocks settlers were — justifiably — obsessed with the construction of roads and bridges. This was the principal criterion that most of them used to judge whether or not their local MP deserved a further term in Parliament. For dairy farmers in particular economic survival depended on getting produce to the skimming station or dairy factory before it deteriorated. Road-making techniques were primitive by our standards but gradually improved. Shingle was spread on roads and left to be worked in by the traffic. In the early part of the new century there was a gradual adoption of the practice of rolling metal into the surface with a traction engine. For many years asphalt was rare in the cities: Queen Street, asphalted in 1902, long remained Auckland's only street in that condition.

Despite the many hazards of country roads, it was during this era that the motor-car began to make its impact, for example in election campaigns. In the cities the speed limit was by the standards of today absurdly low. In Christchurch it was four miles per hour, although in 1914 a magistrate decided that twenty miles per hour was safe. Hitherto any speed of that kind had been hazardous on account of the looseness of the metal on the roads. The motor-cycle was another invention that began to catch on. The bicycle became popular for recreation and was extensively used for travel around Christchurch by early in the new century. The towns saw a transition from horse and buggy to motorized delivery of goods. The horse that had dominated the

The first motor cars to arrive in Dunedin, c. 1900. The first car to be imported into New Zealand arrived in 1896. A car was defined for the first time in legislation in the 1902 Motor Car Regulation Act. Car registration was made compulsory in 1905. *Otago Early Settlers Museum*

urban scene since New Zealand was first colonized was on its way out but still ubiquitous, and a major reason for limiting the speed of cars was to avoid frightening horses. Electricity replaced horses as the source of motive power for urban trams and between 1902 and 1905 all four of the main cities introduced electric trams. Telephones began to revolutionize the handling of business while reducing the isolation of rural life. The number of telephones rose from 5000 in 1896 to 12,000 in 1904.

Society changed in other ways. New Zealand was celebrated as the first country in the world to give the vote to women (in 1893). Yet within New Zealand the direct consequences of this are not easy to trace or define. Women may have been granted the vote, but they could not yet be members of Parliament, let alone Cabinet Ministers. Behind the scenes wives of leading politicians such as Ballance, Seddon, Stout, and Reeves were able to exercise considerable influence, and there were some very influential and effective women government officials such as Grace Neill, Assistant Inspector of Hospitals. But for the most part, issues that were of concern to women had to be filtered through a system in which every position of power was held by a man. What emerged bore a close resemblance to what men thought was good for women rather than what women themselves may have thought. There was no attempt by the political parties to mobilize or appeal to women as a distinct political force, and no women's parties emerged to exploit on women's behalf the fact that they had received the vote. One reason why male politicians had been so ready to make the concession of the vote was that they were confident that women would not behave politically in this way. Much of the debate on giving the vote to women focused on the likely consequences for the temperance cause, it being assumed that they would vote overwhelmingly for a cause so strongly identified with the protection of family life. But the predictions were not borne out by any massive increase in the vote for prohibition. The emphasis in policy directed towards women was on the strengthening of the family unit rather than on the vote serving as some sort of lever to promote female emancipation, and women's organizations were on the whole prepared to support this.

This bias towards emphasizing the domestic role of women was powerfully reinforced by Dr. Truby King, founder of the Plunket Society, who propagated what was virtually a cult of motherhood. The doctrine that motherhood was women's destiny received little challenge even from the feminist movement of the day, and advocates of women's interests tended to concentrate on ensuring that women were given more assistance by the state in fulfilling this role.

Women's place in the population was changing dramatically. The demographic profile characteristic of a pioneer generation was disappearing. In 1861 the ratio of females to males was 62 to 100; by 1901 it was 90 to 100. Indeed, by this time there was an excess of women over men in the cities, especially in the fifteen to thirty-five age bracket. In part this reflected a migration of young women from rural areas into the cities where employment prospects were considerably greater. While Truby King and the state sought to encourage women to stay in the home and concentrate on bringing up healthy future citizens, significant new employment opportunities were opening up for women in fields such as nursing, teaching, typing and secretarial work. One consequence of this was to diminish still further the attractions of domestic service. The number of women employed in nursing increased from 1018 in 1891 to 3403 in 1911; and as teachers from 2617 to 5053. The point of reconciliation between these trends and the requirements of the Truby King ideology is the fact that most women viewed work as a transitory phase prior to marriage.

Seddon, who had recently won his fifth successive election victory as Liberal leader and Premier, died in 1906 on his way back from a visit to Australia. He was succeeded by Joseph Ward who proved much less skilful at holding together the vast range of interests that had accumulated under the capacious umbrella constituted by the Liberals' anti-sectional creed and style. A growing loss of confidence by labour in the arbitration system and the reappearance of strikes were a blow to the Liberals'

A scene outside a polling station in 1893, the first election after women received the vote. The new mayor of Onehunga was Mrs Elizabeth Yates. *Canterbury Museum*

prestige. In 1907 there were twelve strikes, while in 1908 there was a widely publicized strike of miners at Blackball on the West Coast of the South Island. What was noted here was the involvement of 'outside agitators', militants such as Robert Semple from Australia. The government's response to this, such as increasing the severity of penalties for striking while an award was in force, only further alienated sections of the labour movement from both the government and the arbitration system. However, the Liberals tried desperately to make conciliation work and to maintain the credibility of the Liberal creed of the ultimate reconcilability of sectional interests.

The Liberals lost power in July 1912 after a stalemate result in the general election of 1911. Ward resigned in February 1912 and was succeeded as Premier by Thomas Mackenzie, a former critic of the government who had joined it only four years earlier. This desperate last-ditch effort to give the government a new image was unconvincing and unavailing. Several Liberal members crossed the floor of the house to help put out the government. The opposition, led by W. F. Massey, a farmer from Mangere, had reorganized itself as the Reform Party in 1909 and concentrated on convincing voters that it could be trusted not to undo the major features of the Liberals' reform accomplishments. It gained the support of people who had hitherto supported the Liberals but became disenchanted with the government, either because of bungles and scandals in its administration or because they regarded it as having become too susceptible to left wing and socialist influence. Electorally the Reform Party put together a coalition which foreshadowed the electoral base of the National Party — farmers plus the urban middle class whose desertion of the Liberals was far advanced by 1911. The Liberals retained significant strength well beyond this era in provincial and country towns where their emphasis on state funding of development had great appeal.

7. Ancestral Voices
Māori Prophet Leaders

JUDITH BINNEY

In the oral traditions from the East Coast of New Zealand, Te Toiroa is still remembered as the seer who it is said, three years before the advent of James Cook, predicted the coming of white men to the land. A direct descendant of Ngatoro-i-rangi, the tohunga who guided the Arawa canoe and called up the fires of Tongariro, Toiroa stands in a continuous line of the prophetic leaders of the pre-European Māori world. As a very old man in 1865, it is known that he witnessed the onset of the wars in Poverty Bay which he had foreseen.

From the start of European settlement, other prophetic leaders would emerge in different parts of New Zealand. They were both men and women, and they sought to direct the history of their particular followers in rapidly changing circumstances. This form of leadership, which derives from the belief that the matakite (seer) is able to communicate with the ancestral spirits, is common in many oral societies. The wisdom of the ancestors is received either in dreams and visions, or in cryptic oral pronouncements spoken in a trance-like state. These are thought of either as experiences undergone by the soul in communication with the dead spirits, or as spirit possession. The strange spoken voices, often whistlings, are those of the ancestors. Such visions have stood, as the Bible once did in Western societies: they contain the unchallengeable (although often equivocal) truth, and the knowledge they convey is believed to stem from divine authority.

The role of the prophet in colonial Māori society would be reinforced rather than undermined by the introduction of Christianity. The Old Testament prophetic tradition was an integral part of the early Protestant teaching, while the situational parallels between the Māori and the Israelite tribes became imaginatively potent as conflicts over land and sovereignty developed in the mid-nineteenth century. Māori leaders often took for their baptismal names those of the Old Testament visionaries — Moses, Zerubbabel, Daniel. Living in a pre-Darwinian world and needing to explain their different appearance and culture from that of the settlers, they chose to

Papahurihia (Te Atua Wera), naked except for a small white loin cloth, his buttocks and thighs tattooed, at the centre of a hari (war dance) performed for the arrival of visitors at Waima, Hokianga, 1847. *Auckland Public Library*

associate themselves with the early Israelites, probably because they shared a tribal history of migration. This identification appeared in the first of the visionary movements that grew in the new world of cross-cultural fertilization, the Papahurihia faith (which originated in the Bay Islands in the early 1830s), and it would continue in all the subsequent movements. The Israelite tradition became embedded in Māori history, and shaped the actions and the understandings of many of its participants. In situations of tension or conflict, it led to a defiance of the Christians and their crucified saviour.

Papahurihia was the name of both the visionary leader and the god whom he worshipped. The name has been variously translated. It possibly derives from papa (a medium) and the Reverend Henry Williams in 1834 commented upon the name Papahurihia as meaning one 'who relates wonders'. It could also mean to turn the earth (Papa) right over. Papahurihia, the man, taught his followers that they were Hurai (Jews) and thus they worshipped on Saturday, assembling at night. From the beginning Papahurihia claimed the power to be able to converse with the dead. He held seances where he spoke with them in the whistling voice. He was undoubtedly a ventriloquist, like his father, the matakite Te Whareti, from whom it is said he derived many of his skills including the power to transport himself over vast distances in an instant. But equally important was his line of direct descent from his ancestress Taimania, remembered as a famous 'sorceress'.

Papahurihia was a traditional Māori matakite, but his specific teachings were a response to the changing circumstances of the lives of the northerners. He was particularly hostile to the Protestant missionaries, whose earliest mission station had been founded among his people, Te Hikutu of Rangihoua and Te Puna in the northern Bay of Islands. He called them 'He kai Kohuru' (deceitful murderers) of New Zealanders, and attributed the high number of Māori deaths to their practising mākutu (witchcraft). He warned against the Prostestants' heaven: it being, he said, little better than their hell as it contained 'nothing but books to eat'. His teachings consciously rejected the written Scriptures, but he had also absorbed some of their precepts. The ariā (manifestation) of his god was the biblical serpent, nākahi. Nākahi was not simply the serpent of Genesis; it was also the fiery serpent on the rod of Moses, which gave the promise of life to the Israelites in the wilderness. Nākahi became the active intervening agent summoned up by Papahurihia in the manner of previous Māori tohunga, and in shape he was not dissimilar to the ngārara (lizards) called upon by such men. His was the voice that spoke through Papahurihia in seances.

The Papahurihia movement spread rapidly upon its emergence in 1833 and attracted many of the chiefs from the northern and central Bay of Islands, and subsequently the Hokianga. It provided a focus for opposition to the newly developing Wesleyan and Anglican communities there. Later the Roman Catholic missionaries encountered its teachings and found that their doctrines seemed to be more acceptable to Papahurihia — or Te Atua Wera (the Fiery God) as he was known to them. Catholicism, because of its later arrival in New Zealand, often opposed the dominance of the Protestant community leaders in the politics of inter-hapū feuding. Papahurihia may have seen it in a more sympathetic light for this reason. But he had absorbed some of its basic metaphors as early as 1834, four years before the arrival of its missionaries. He taught that the judgement tree, which his followers climbed to the sky, was the true trunk — a recurrent image used by the Catholics, for whom the Protestants were the twisted branches. The Protestants, Papahurihia said, fell from the thin branches of a curved tree into the burning abyss below. Nākahi ignited the fires into which they tumbled.

Papahurihia was originally a young chief in the hapū which had protected the Anglican missionaries from 1814. As he turned against the Anglicans, so he also instigated the killing of two Wesleyan converts preaching in the Mangamuka district in January 1837. He gave a cask of powder and a musket (which he had inscribed in hieroglyphs made of red sealing wax, thus rendering it tapu) to a Hikutu chief, Kaitoke, to be 'medicine' for the missionaries and their followers. It was said that the gun would assure victory to the attackers while making them invulnerable to their enemies' fire. The war he had incited would quickly escalate to involve all the segments of Ngapuhi, and peace was only re-established after the deaths of several major chiefs.

Papahurihia was still only about thirty years old when he became Hone Heke's chief tohunga in the Northern War of 1845. But by then he was the major prophet leader of Ngapuhi, dominating all others in influence. He had acquired considerable wealth — in guns, cattle, horses. He had emerged from the shadows cast by the high-born chiefs of Ngapuhi, and in so doing revealed a pattern of alternative leadership to the senior chiefs, a role which some of the later prophets also established for themselves.

Heke consulted him on the eve of battle at Puketutu, and the most famous account of Papahurihia's advice derives from this occasion:

> the *Ngakahi* spoke in the night to Heke and his people, by the mouth of the Atua Wera. 'Be brave and strong, and patient. Fear not the soldiers; they will not be able to take this fort — neither be you afraid of all those different kinds of big guns you have heard so much talk of. I will turn aside the shot, and they shall do you no harm; but this *pa* and its defenders must be made sacred (*tapu*). You must particularly observe all the sacred rites and customs of your ancestors; if you neglect this in the smallest particular, evil will befall you, and I also shall desert you. You who pray to the god of the missionaries, continue to do so, and in your praying see you make no mistakes. Fight and pray. Touch not the spoils of the slain, abstain from human flesh, lest the European god should be angry, and be careful not to offend the Maori gods. It is good to have more than one god to trust to.

Heke's defeat came when he forgot the warning words. At Te Ahuahu in June, he seized a cartridge box from a fallen man. As he ran he saw the prophet, his mere raised, trying to rally the fleeing defenders of the pā. When Papahurihia noticed the blood on the box, he knew that the Māori atua, the spirits of the dead ancestors, were now aligned against them. All he could do, when Heke fell wounded, was to make the chief's bearers invisible so that they might carry him safely from the field of war. This was an ancient skill of tohunga known as tūmatapōngia. Later, at Ohaeawai, he was able to predict victory, and the hari he then composed terrified the retreating enemy with its open hatred of Christ:

Ka whawhai, ka whawhai, e	Fight, fight!
Ka whawhai, ki roto ki te awa, e	Fight in the valley,
Puare katoa ake nei, e	They are all exposed there,
Ka whawhai.	Fight.
Kihai koe i mau atu, ki to kainga.	You will not return to your village,
Ki Oropi, e.	To Europe.
I te ainga mai a wharewhare.	Because of the driving force of the fighters.
Ki a Ihu Karaiti,	To Jesus Christ,
Me te pukapuka,	And the Book,
Ki taka ki tua,	I will turn my back,
Ki taekaukau o taku kumu kei raro. — i, i.	And empty my bowels upon them!

Papahurihia's religion has been described as millennial, and he was the first in the line of such leaders in New Zealand. There is, in fact, no evidence that he offered a millennial vision of salvation. However, his 'heaven' was filled with the material goods that the Europeans had brought and whose supply they largely monopolized: guns, ships, flour, sugar. The Papahurihia movement was a cargo cult, promising the tangible wealth of the Europeans to its followers in the afterlife, but it saw no need for an imminent new world. Millenarianism was to grow from the seed-bed of war and land confiscations in the 1860s.

In the late 1840s and early 1850s a primary concern of Māori visionary leaders was the high mortality of their people. Many local healers emerged, claiming the traditional ability to heal the sick, but now their powers derived from two cosmologies. Some adopted the Christian notion of sin, and, following the Protestant missionary teachings, used it as the explanation for the recurring epidemics. An old woman, Te Hura, from Hawke's Bay became an influential medium in 1850, with the voice of her dead child speaking through her. The dead child (a common spirit medium) was accompanied by the Jewish prophet and lawgiver Moses when it visited her on a high hill. The spirit came in the form of a thin sharp hau (wind). It told her that 'the Natives, who had hitherto died in such numbers since the introduction of the Faith, were now about to be pitied, and that she was henceforth appointed to heal the sick & diseased'. She was instructed to seek out the local Māori Anglican teacher and be washed in hot water to remove the tapu of the old gods from her. This done, she took up her mission to cleanse others. She used a bed of heated stones and steaming herbs, while reciting over the sick person the words, 'O Lord O Lord steal away out of this person his stink & rottenness for Jesus Christ's sake Amen', uttered in a 'very peculiar and rapid manner'. The steaming remedy was traditional, as was the appeal to divine forces, for sickness in the Māori world was believed to be supernatural in origin. Missionary teaching reinforced such views, although now God was the source of all ills. Te Hura was acting as a spiritual healer, but she had violated her Māori tapu (the state in which the gods are present) in order to make her eligible, as she understood it, to seek out the mana (power) of Christ.

The flying dragon (tarakona), 29 November 1855. The dotted areas named (presumably the path of the dragon) are in the Hokianga and Whangarei districts. On the right there is a structure described as the 'house of evil on the water coming hither', with which the dragon contends. *K.A. Webster Collection, Alexander Turnbull Library*

A similar movement, which may have been derived from Papahurihia but which did not reject Christ as saviour, appeared in the Bay of Islands and Hokianga in 1855. The prophet is unknown by name, but he resided at Waimate. The winged dragon, which seems reminiscent of the nākahi, was his guardian ariā. It was to be the protector of the people from a new 'deadly malady', which would descend on them shortly. Talismanic drawings of the dragon were found in homes among most of the local tribes. The tohunga, who had distributed these 'books', communicated with the spirits from the top of a high hill near Waimate. He taught that he was the Māori brother of Christ. He explained the deaths and depopulation of the north as due to the neglect of the old gods and sacred places. He urged as the solution the destruction of tapu in all those perilous places. The power of the old had to be negated so that the new god could reign.

The problems with which these early visionary leaders wrestled were similar: the conflict of two universes and the apparent triumph of the Christian god over the Māori deities. The solutions they offered to temporal problems were inevitably conceived in spiritual terms: mana, life, and death had always been dealt out by the gods. In the new world of two peoples, it was no longer possible for Māori to believe solely in the old gods. Whether to appease them, or to negate them (if possible) was to remain a continuing dilemma. How to make the new god smile on the tribes was a further problem. When war was forced upon many tribes in the 1860s, it became a matter of acute urgency to discover how this god belonged to them.

The earliest of these movements was the Pai Marire or Hauhau faith, whose roots lay in the land conflict in Taranaki. The prophet Te Ua Haumene Tuwhakararo (originally baptized as Zerubbabel, the Seed of Babylon) was from the Taranaki tribe. In 1861 he became a leader there in the Kingitanga movement for Māori autonomy. In 1862 he experienced a series of visions. The Archangel Gabriel was his messenger, and the annunciation he brought was the special relationship between God and the Māori people, for this land 'is Israel'. Atua Marire (the God of Peace) promised to 'tana iwi wareware, tū-kiri-kau, motu tū-hāwhe' ('his forgetful, naked-standing people in the half-standing land') that they would be restored in their land. Te Ua equated the Māori people with the Israelites in their Babylonian exile. He reminded them of the promises given to Abraham that Canaan would be returned. In September 1862 he drew on the vision of St John in Revelation when he wrote:

> i kitea hoki e ahau i kohiwi ko Tamarura ko nga ingoa kei a ia hoki te Hiiri o te Atua ora. Ka karanga ia ka mea, kaua e whakakinoa te motu kaua te iwi ka hiiri hoki ahau i nga pononga a te Atua ki o ratou rae.

> I saw a figure whose name was Son-Ruler, having with him the Seal of the living God. He called out saying, do not hurt the land or the people till I seal the servants of God on their foreheads.

While the basis of the new faith was scriptural, many of its practices were bizarre to European recorders. The faithful frequently worshipped on the Jewish sabbath, called themselves Tiu (Jews), and like Papahurihia's followers erected tall flag-poles for their rituals. The poles they called 'niu' and they resembled ships' masts. Indeed, the earliest was said to have come from the vessel, the *Lord Worsley*, whose wreck instigated Te Ua's first vision. On the ropes of the niu, the faithful hung many flags as statements of religious identity and, in some cases, of their allegiance to the Kingitanga. The term 'niu' has been variously explained. It may simply be the 'news' pole, for the hau (breath of wind) moving on the ropes was believed to bring messages from God. It was also probably a deliberate adoption of the name of divinatory sticks traditionally used by tohunga. Gabriel had first instructed Te Ua to build a niu. From it the 'Spirit of God passing with the winds' would teach the people the 'gift of languages', together with all the different forms of religion. The services around the poles were therefore conducted in glossalalia, a mixture of tongues, filled with

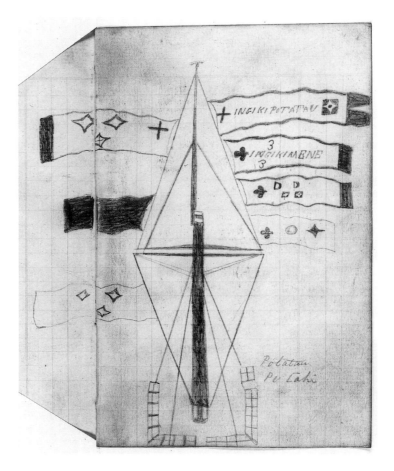

A drawing of a niu pole at Te Putahi, from the pages of a notebook which recorded the teachings of Te Ua. The flags indicate the community's loyalty to King Potatau, 'Ingiki Potatau', the second Māori King. 'Ingiki Mene' is less certain but probably it is 'King of Men'. The fallen club (taken from playing cards) refers to scriptural texts concerning the promised restoration of the kingdom of David on earth. The three diamonds represent the three islands of Aotearoa, the name recently given to the entire land by the Kingitanga. *Auckland Public Library*

purposeful references. Recurrent ritual phrases were derived from English military jargon (seen as phrases of power) and Protestant and Catholic religious services. This was a form of Pentecostalism, which consciously rejected the 'religion of England' and its missionaries.

The two names by which the faith became known were derived from phrases reiterated by the worshippers in their prayers. 'Pai Marire' means 'Goodness and Peace', and describes the attributes of God. 'Hauhau' refers to the winds, and also to the breath of life, the spark of spirituality given by God to humans. Central to the teachings of Te Ua were the mediating archangels, Gabriel and Michael. Te Ua called

A depiction of the Archangel Gabriel was found in 1867. It is one of a series depicting Gabriel-Ruler (as Te Ua called him). Here the winged angel wears a Pai Mārire flag around his body. The horse presumably represents one of the four horses of the Apocalypse. *Alexander Turnbull Library*

Gabriel Kaparierarura (Gabriel-Ruler) and he appeared to Te Ua as he did before the prophet Daniel with his vision of the end of time. Anahera Ariki Mikaera (Angel Lord Michael), who also appeared to Te Ua in his first vision, similarly served as he had for Daniel. He is the angel of war, predicted to defend 'the children of thy people'. The fighting flags of the Pai Marire, which were named Riki, probably represented Ariki Mikaera. Te Ua created a religion which was intended to serve in both peace and war.

By 1864 he had, in fact, set up not only a theology of defence and deliverance but also an evangelizing mission which was to reach out to the four corners of Canaan. The first attempts to spread the word, however, caused his message to be interpreted as instigating war. In April a party of soldiers in Taranaki, on a crop-destroying expedition, was ambushed by a group of Pai Marire, among whom was Te Ua. According to their views, they acted in the legitimate defence of their tribal lands. In the ambush the captain, Thomas Lloyd, was decapitated and then, on instructions from Kaparierarura, the head was preserved. The head uttered the tenets of the new faith, and was taken first to upper Whanganui by Matene Rangitauira, whose kinsmen had helped the Taranaki people at the renewal of the war there in 1863. Its arrival served to provoke old inter-tribal rivalries, leading to war in Whanganui. Te Ua later wrote that Matene had misused the head. It was meant to be circulated 'properly' through the four quarters of the land — Whanganui, Taupo, Urewera and ultimately reach the East Coast and the ariki there, Hirini Te Kani a Takirau, whose lines of descent were said to bring together all the tribes. The purpose was to make a ritual circle to 'kia kati katoatia nga tatau o te motu kenana' (bind up all the doors of the land of Canaan) and unite the tribes.

The emissaries sent out by Te Ua to the other corners of the land also became the harbingers of war. It was not that Te Ua preached a war of liberation against the Pākehā, nor that his message of peace was distorted by local politics, as has been argued. Te Ua was a religious leader in the Judaeo-Christian tradition, who preached deliverance from oppression in apocalyptic terms. God's messengers were the sword-bearing angels. Te Ua turned these scriptural stories to Māori ends at a time of land confiscation. His emissaries brought the message of deliverance to the regions, where almost inevitably it took on different forms.

At Tauranga, the millennial aspects manifested themselves immediately. The emissary Te Tiu (Jew) Tamihana arrived in December 1864, telling of immediate temporal salvation. The year, which had begun with a military invasion and had brought massive land seizures, would, he prophesied, bring the end of Pākehā control. Ngai Te Rangi flocked from their homes to hear the message of hope. They stressed to the local Pākehā authorities that there was 'no design on their part to provoke hostilities', but those authorities invariably saw the Pai Marire faith as a seditious doctrine. The Ngai Te Rangi chief Hori Tupaea, who had quickly adopted Te Ua's idea of setting up aukati (territorial lines of separation) between Māori and Pākehā so as to retain some Māori autonomy, was seized and held prisoner. An uneasy local peace held until the land surveys began in earnest in 1866.

At Opotiki, conversely, the two Pai Marire emissaries sent by Te Ua in February 1865 were direct catalysts of war. Patara Te Raukatauri and Kereopa Te Rau fired the anger of the Whakatohea people against their Anglican missionary, Carl Volkner, whom they knew had acted as a government spy. Volkner paid with his life, and the eastern Bay of Plenty tribes paid with much of their land.

Similarly, on the East Coast Patara and Kereopa were to become the catalyst for a civil war among Ngati Porou, which paved the way for armed European intervention and subsequently, as the war spread, further land confiscation in Poverty Bay and Hawke's Bay.

The Pai Marire doctrines were invariably divisive, as are all apocalyptic visions. At its height in 1865, about one-fifth of the total Māori population accepted Te Ua's gospel. From the north, however, Papahurihia (now a Wesleyan convert and government assessor) wrote condemning its fanatical teachings. At Turanganui (Gisborne), Hirini Te Kani a Takirau refused to assume the leadership. Nevertheless, he allowed Te Ua's missionaries to preach, seeing no sedition in their words. The converts there stressed that their religion did not mean a commitment to war. Anaru Matete, a leading chief of Ngati Maru who adopted the faith in 1865, told the oldest established European settler at Turanganui:

> Stay. Why leave your places? We have joined the Hauhau because we think by so doing we shall save our land (te Ao) and the remnant of our people. We have no quarrel with the settlers. . . . All our chiefs . . . say the settlers shall and will be protected.

But civil war came to Turanganui with an invasion of Ngati Porou fighters, together with European reinforcements, seeking out Pai Marire refugees from the north. The protracted siege of the Pai Marire at Waerenga a Hika pā in November 1865 marked the onset of a war which would last for seven years. The Pai Marire prisoners captured there and elsewhere would be shipped off to Wharekauri, one of the Chatham Islands. They would become the followers of the new prophetic faith born on the island, the Ringatu.

Te Ua himself surrendered to the government in February 1866, having become convinced that the expanding wars were disastrous for the Māori. He had developed a religious doctrine of deliverance from suffering, which had become a part of the active politics of war. He taught that Atua Hau (God-Wind) and his angels would restore the 'undivided holy soil of the Canaan' to the Māori. Until that day of deliverance he urged that the tribes separate themselves behind their own aukati. As a Kingitanga leader and warrior, he certainly accepted the legitimacy of their defensive wars. But he did not seek to instigate 'a final war at the end of the world'. He handed himself over in a vain attempt to stop the fighting. In July just before his death, he wrote to those whom he had earlier seen as his spiritual successors, Te Whiti o Rongomai and Tohu Kakahi, renouncing the faith itself.

The Pai Marire doctrines were the fount of many of the new religions which followed. Some of the most direct connections were derived from the early spread of the faith within the Kingitanga. In August 1864 the second Māori king had come to southern Taranaki where he was re-baptized by Te Ua with the name, Tawhiao (Hold the World). Te Ua composed the 'Lament for King Tawhiao', which sealed their compact under God, called Rura (Ruler). He taught Tawhiao and the Waikato chiefs who accompanied him that 'New Zealand is Canaan. The Maoris are Jews. The books of Moses are their law.' These teachings were taken back to Waikato. The very concept of the Rohe Potae itself (the encircling boundaries of the King Country) stemmed directly from Te Ua's notion of placing aukati, seen as lines of peace, between Māori and Pākehā. As Tawhiao said in 1865, the 'bloodshed arose from Pakeha's hands. It will not be right to bring that blood hither, leave it where it is.' As a consequence, until 1883 no Pākehā could enter the Rohe Potae without Kingitanga permission.

After his re-baptism, Tawhiao himself became known as a prophet, the mana being considered as bestowed from Te Ua. Later, he developed his particular form of the Pai Marire teachings, which in 1875 he called Tariao, a name he used for Venus as the morning star (or Tāwera). The Resident Magistrate in the Waikato commented that Tariao was a revival of the Pai Marire form of prayers, first introduced by Te Ua but subsequently abandoned. In so doing, he added, Tawhiao was stressing the 'promotion of peace'. The adoption of the name Tariao was a conscious statement of a new dawn, a new and peaceful era. It was also a deliberate reference to the Book of Revelation, asserting Tawhiao's lineage as the son of God in the line of the Jewish kings: 'I am the root and the offspring of David, and the bright and morning star.' The faith centred on a message of deliverance foreseen by Tawhiao's prophecies. It remained an integral part of the Kingitanga rituals, and would be actively revived again by Princess Te Puea in the early twentieth century.

In Taranaki itself, the faith was transmitted directly to several prophetic leaders. The visionary Titokowaru of Ngati Ruanui had accepted Te Ua's message that the wars must end. He declared that 1867 was 'te tau tamahine, tenei te rau o te Rameti' (the year of the daughters, the year of the Lamb). But the reality was a confiscation of land that rendered Ngati Ruanui virtually homeless. Titokowaru's war of 1868-1869 in southern Taranaki was fought to create adequate boundaries for their survival. But his support collapsed when he violated the strict codes of the Pai Marire and Kingitanga fighters against pūremu (adultery). As a religious leader his crime was doubly great and it stripped him of his tapu. His successful fighting forces simply melted away, bringing the war to an unexpected end.

In 1866, Te Ua had seen his nephew Te Whiti as standing in the light of God. He regarded Tohu, Te Whiti's brother-in-law, in the same manner. They in turn named 1867 the 'year of the Lamb' in the Pai Marire tradition, and with this message founded a new community at Parihaka, at the foot of Mount Taranaki. From its beginning it was committed to the path of peace. As Te Whiti specifically said, 'The wars of the past even unto the present shall not be renewed', and the people wore white feathers in their hair as a statement of their peaceful ways. For this reason the Parihaka community did not give its support to Titokowaru (any more than did Tawhiao). But the once disgraced Titokowaru would take his shelter at Parihaka and there erect his meeting-house.

Te Whiti making his monthly address on 17 January 1880. Carte de visite. *Canterbury Museum*

The Parihaka community was founded in the midst of confiscated land. Te Whiti never recognized the legitimacy of those confiscations. There were many specific aspects to his objections, not the least being that the confiscations were justified on the grounds that the Māori tribes had rebelled. This he rightly denied. From 1869 he began preaching the ultimate return of all confiscated Māori land, and repudiated the authority of the laws over the Māori. That year he named 'te tau o te takahanga' (the year of the trampling underfoot), the year in which he initiated the tactics of peaceful non-co-operation. His objective was not simply the restoration of the seized lands. As the Reverend T.G. Hammond observed in 1880, 'Land he wants, but a recognition of his independence he wants more.'

In 1878 the surveying of the disputed land in Taranaki began. Te Whiti and Tohu opposed the action, calling it the theft of land that had been promised to them. And indeed in the official confiscation map of 1873 the Crown's claims there had been marked 'Abandoned'. Under the direction of Tohu, the Parihaka challenge began in May 1879. The men went out in small groups to plough the land to assert their ownership. Day after day they were arrested, and day after day they were replaced by others. The population of Parihaka grew rapidly as tribes from other parts sent their representatives: from Patea, Whanganui, and Waikato in particular.

The Parihaka community, 5 November 1881. The people are crowded together on the marae (centre right), where they had been waiting since midnight for the assult. Te Whiti and Tohu were sitting together in front of one of the small raupō whares which looked directly into the marae. The wooden gabled building at the top left is Te Whiti's new meeting-house, Miti Mai Te Arero, begun in 1881. Photograph probably by W.A. Collis. *Alexander Turnbull Library*

Te Whiti made the issues plain in his monthly speeches to the Parihaka community: 'The Government is attempting to keep the chieftainship (rangatiratanga) from Israel and I am striving to prevent the Government from becoming our masters for ever and ever. . . . No law of the Europeans shall govern the Maories. . . . Do not let us think the Europeans can make laws to rule us, they cannot; nothing can stand that they make.' He also made clear his plan for the lands: 'The settlement to be by Europeans and Maories, the Maories on their reserves and the Europeans on the remainder but the Maories being owners of the soil to receive "takoha" (tribute) from the Europeans'. He sought to make Parihaka, Israel, the new kingdom of the Māori. He hoped to make a binding covenant with the government, replacing the Treaty of Waitangi (which Taranaki and Ngati Raunui had never signed), recognizing the Māori as the owners of the soil and their right to take tribute. As Hammond, who left an account of the monthly meetings, observed, 'Should we consent to all this, truly the chieftainship will have returned unto Israel.'

It was the extensive links which Parihaka had established with other tribes which led the government to seek its destruction in 1881. On 5 November Parihaka was occupied by force. All the 'outsiders' were subsequently expelled (about 1600 people) and their homes destroyed. Te Whiti, Tohu, and Titokowaru were arrested, and all three spent six months in jail in New Plymouth awaiting Supreme Court trials. But Titokowaru's case — the charge, unlawful obstruction by sitting still on the Parihaka marae on 5 November — was considered by the judge to be absurd. As a consequence, the government abandoned the prosecution, and rushed through special legislation to allow them to keep Te Whiti and Tohu imprisoned indefinitely without trial. This legal chicanery did not destroy Parihaka. Released after two years, Tohu and Te Whiti returned to Parihaka in 1883 and began its reconstruction. The community was born again as the new Jerusalem in Canaan. The conflicts over the land and the laws did not cease, and nor did Te Whiti's terms change. Both he and Tohu would be arrested again. Parihaka remained a centre of conscious non-violent resistance to the yoke of the settler's manipulative legislation until the deaths of the two leaders in 1907.

Te Whiti had called himself variously the 'mouthpiece' of Jehovah and 'a small Christ', the messiah for the days when it was prophesied that 'the small people should rule the island'. This emphasis on the ordinary people (or the 'shoemaker', the 'carpenter' and the 'blacksmith' as Tawhiao put it) would be sustained by Te Whiti's successors. But Te Whiti also claimed to be the sole ruler: 'It is all to be left to me, the judgeship and ordering of the earth so that all people may see that I am the son of God.' He had turned the Pai Marire teachings of deliverance into a statement of Māori Christianity under his authority.

A separate faith, but one which had also been influenced by the Pai Marire teachings, was that led by the South Island prophet, Hipa Te Maiharoa. In 1877 he lead a heke (migration) of over a hundred followers back to their ancestral lands at Te Ao Marama (Omarama), in north Otago. The people called themselves Israelites. They denied the validity of the vast South Island land purchase of 1848, and claimed the interior as their own. It was their promised land. But the wealthy runholders protested and in 1879 the Ngai Tahu exiles were expelled by an armed police expedition.

Te Maiharoa's ideas were shaped by the spread of Te Ua and Te Whiti's teachings. Among Te Maiharoa's followers in 1879 was a Taranaki man, Tuaha Matenga, while at least one Ngai Tahu kinsman was among those arrested at Parihaka. The religious practices were resonant of the Pai Marire beliefs. In particular, the Ngai Tahu Israelites adopted the ritual of circling the places of worship as the Pai Marire had circled the niu poles. Tapu-lifting rites were an important aspect of Te Maiharoa's teachings and they derived, in part, from the Israelites' codes of ritual cleansing, directed against the presence of dangerous Māori ancestral spirits. Te Maiharoa also insisted on the circumcision of male infants, contrary to Māori practice. He claimed to be a prophet but not a messiah; he predicted that his work would be completed by another, 'a little child', who would 'come forth from under Mount Taranaki'. After his death in 1885, his school of learning at Korotuaheka was razed by his followers so that it should never be desecrated.

The only faith which was born out of the wars but which rejected its association with

Pai Marire was Ringatu. Its founder was Te Kooti Arikirangi Te Turuki, who was first arrested by the government 'on suspicion of being a spy' at the siege of Waerenga a Hika in 1865. Te Kooti was born within the chiefly ranks of Ngati Maru of Poverty Bay, but had been known mostly for his youthful trouble-making. Caught up in the civil wars at Poverty Bay, he had fought for the government with reluctance, like most of the Turanganui 'loyalists', who believed that the war had been forced upon them unnecessarily. Released for want of evidence, he was rearrested in March 1866. He had been picked out as a potential source of disturbance when the land was confiscated. Despite his request for a trial, he was sent with the Pai Marire prisoners to the island of Wharekauri. There, in the 'Wharepononga' ('House of Bondage'), the message of deliverance was brought to him.

Te Kooti recorded the visitations of 'te Wairua o te Atua' (the Spirit of God) in a diary which he kept on the island. The first entry was on 21 February 1867: 'Ko te marama tenei i nui ai toku mate 21 o nga ra ka hemo au' (This was the month in which my sickness increased, on the 21st day I became unconscious). But the spirit, he said, raised him up in order to make his name known 'ki tona iwi e noho whakarau nei i tenei whenua' (to his people who are in captivity in this land). The spirit, a voice, visited again when he became unconscious with fever on 21 March. Then on 21 April he appeared in the likeness of a man. He was clothed in white, and wore a crown and girdle like the rising and the setting sun. His fan was like a rainbow and his tokotoko (staff) was of colours never before seen. This spirit of God, probably derived from Revelation, told him that he would teach him, warning him not accept any books, as they were written only by mortals. He also gave him two signs, which he was to reveal. One was a ngārara in a form he had never before seen. In the traditional Māori cosmogony, the ngārara is a lizard that travels between the worlds of the gods and humanity, bringing either life or death. The other was a flame which did not burn, and this he showed to the prisoners in a service he held on 18 June 1867. By July accounts of the new religion had reached Māori in Turanganui, while it was this incendary act which finally caught the attention of the Resident Magistrate on Wharekauri. He reported that Te Kooti was deceiving the prisoners with phosphorus from matches. Te Kooti was therefore prohibited from holding services and placed in solitary confinement in June 1868. The oral traditions of the Ringatu narrate how he escaped every night to hold prayers secretly amongst the whakarau (the prisoners). He also planned (and predicted) their escape from the island in July.

On Wharekauri, two religious traditions had been transformed into one as the culmination of many years of predictive history. As the old Ringatu tohunga Eria Raukura put it:

> In the year 1766, three years before the arrival of the pakeha
> in this land, Ariki-rangi was disclosed by Toiroa, and all the
> conditions of life in this world. He it was (Toiroa) who
> renewed the Covenant and conducted it according to the

guidance of the Spirit. It had been maintained quite differently by the ancestors during the lengthy years which had gone by in between. More than 1000 years had passed since that migration out of Canaan. . . . At Wharekauri the Angel of the Lord appeared to him. There the Ringatu Covenant, and all the prophetic sayings were revealed; the first prophetic sayings, and the pattern also of the prophetic sayings of the creation of the World, and also the sayings from Abraham right until Christ. . . . At the very time of Te Kooti, only then was it made very clear, the joining of the first things of the past, that is the Maori's hold on Io, and the pakeha's hold on the gospel of Jesus Christ.

In this manner the most distant ancestral past was specifically yoked to the earliest Christian teachings. Toiroa had predicted the coming of Arikirangi, and the times of trouble that this child portended, with the ominous song, 'Tiwha tiwha te pō (Dark, dark is the night). He had performed the tohi (naming ceremony) over him, recognizing him as Arikirangi, the one foreseen, and dedicating him to Tu-matauenga, god of war and of man. From his prophetic ancestors, Te Kooti inherited his visionary powers. But it is also believed that when the Māori left Canaan at the last dispersal of the children of Israel they brought with them the knowledge of Io (Jehovah). It was in Aotearoa that the 'first things of the past', the Māori relationship with Io, were married with the Christian faith. The full significance of this covenant for the Māori was revealed to Te Kooti.

In the oral traditions, it was the warrior angel Michael who appeared before him to tell him of the covenant. Through this association, Te Kooti becomes the leader of a war for liberty. On 4 July 1868 the whakarau — 163 men, 64 women, and 71 children — escaped their bondage by capturing a supply ship. They landed on the 10th at Whareongonga, a stony beach south of Turanganui. Here they gave thanks for their deliverance by God, raising their right hands in an act of homage instead of kneeling in submission. From this deliberate gesture the name of the new faith was born: the Ringa-tū, the Upraised Hand.

Their purpose was to go inland. Te Kooti said that he sought no fight with the government, although they had all been kept imprisoned without trial and for longer than had been originally determined. He intended to go into the Rohe Potae and there challenge Tawhiao for the spiritual leadership of the Māori. But because the whakarau were armed, they were to be inexorably pursued by the colonial forces, who thus created a formidable guerrilla leader, and a war which lasted until 1872.

It was because Tawhiao rejected Te Kooti, warning him formally on 29 October that he would be repelled if he attempted to enter the Rohe Potae, that Te Kooti turned back to attack the settlements in Poverty Bay. This decision, which gained him his particular notoriety, derived from the fact that he had nowhere else to go. He was being pursued by the militia. Ahead lay the Urewera, but the Tuhoe, whose

Tokanganui a Noho, about 1887. This photograph shows the original paintings on the doorway, a style which Te Kooti initiated. The house was begun in 1873 for King Tawhiao, and was completed and opened on 2 January 1883, when Te Kooti gave it to the Maniapoto chiefs, whose relationship with Tawhiao had become strained. Photograph by F. Stewart. *National Musuem*

permission to enter their lands he had similarly sought, would wait until March 1869 before they fully committed themselves. He disguised his need for a sanctuary with the prophecy that 'God would give the Turanganui country, and all the best places of the Europeans, back to him and his people.' Once there, the killing of ordinary Māori and Pākehā, and the taking of large numbers of Māori as prisoners, meant that from this point on he would be hunted as a wild beast, and that his pursuers would now include many Māori.

The Tuhoe finally supported Te Kooti because they saw him as the leader of those (like themselves) who had been dealt with unjustly. In turn, their remaining lands were subjected to a ruthless scorched earth policy. To curtail these attacks on homes and crops, in July 1869 Te Kooti crossed into the Rohe Potae, seeking out King Tawhiao. His aim now was to be conciliatory. Again he was rejected. As Tawhiao's chief advisor, Tamati Ngapora, said plainly, Te Kooti's 'purpose in coming amongst them was to lower their chieftainship, and to destroy their Atua; and that they would not bow down to his Atua'. Nevertheless, when he left he would be accompanied by some of the major Kingitanga fighting chiefs, including Rewi Maniapoto. But his losses in the Taupo district in September (observed by Rewi) ended any possibility of an alliance.

Eventually he would take his sanctuary in the Rohe Potae, living under the protection of Ngati Maniapoto from May 1872. But it was not until September 1873, when he accepted Tawhiao's doctrine of pacifism, that he was reconciled with the King. From that date, he said, 'I ceased strife. . . . I came into the presence of Tawhiao, and will not withdraw myself from it.' In that month, Te Kooti supervised the carvings and decorations in the great meeting-house Tokanganui a Noho which was being erected for Tawhiao in Te Kuiti. This house became his gift to him.

Tawhiao formally established the Tariao faith in 1875 and it is probably not coincidental that in the same year, while he was living at Te Kuiti, Te Kooti began to lay down the rituals and the structure of the Ringatu. He initiated the First of January as a major celebration then, and from 1876 celebrated the First of July as the second 'pillar' of the faith. January marked the beginning of the year; July the beginning of the seventh month, the sabbath of the sabbath. In 1879 he introduced the huamata (planting rites) and the pure (harvest rites) as annual rituals, thus completing the four 'pillars' of the year. Then, in 1888, after he had left Te Kuiti, he set up, in addition to the Saturday sabbath, the Twelfth of the month as a holy day. It celebrates, among other aspects, the passover, or the safe return of the Exiles from Wharekauri. From these beginnings the church would grow.

The Ringatu, unlike any of the earlier movements, was able to transform itself into an institutionalized faith, partly because it was structured for survival by its founder. It was Te Kooti himself who composed its songs, its prayers and hymns, and its scriptural texts. These were taught orally; but on his instructions, they were also written down. So were his prophecies. As a consequence, the Ringatu possess a large body of doctrine. Further, just before his death, in 1892 he devised the organization of church officers. Although there have been (and still are) regional differences, together with rivalries over leadership, the local church structure has remained intact in the areas where the faith is still practised.

The covenants of the faith today recount the histories of the Jews and state that the faithful believe in the promises made to Abraham, to Moses and to David, which shall be fulfilled at the time when Christ shall appear for a second time on earth. Te Kooti's task had been to link all the prophesies. The Ringatu also believe that the fallen tabernacle of David shall be re-erected, and that his house shall be confirmed for ever.

After his reconciliation with Tawhiao, Te Kooti committed himself to the paths of peace. His teachings emphasized his acceptance of the law. Only the law, he said, can be set against the law. After his governmental pardon, on 12 February 1883, he was able to leave the Rohe Potae, and he sought meetings of reconciliation with his former enemies. But increasingly he spoke out against his rival prophets, particularly Tawhiao and Te Whiti, or the 'whare whakakeke' (houses of resistance) as he called them. Shortly after his pardon, he directly intervened to assist in the arrest of Te Mahuki Manukura, the Ngati Kinohaku prophet who had founded a community at Te

Te Mahuki and (right) Paru Kau, a follower of Te Whiti, at Te Kumi, 4 June 1885. The community, imitating Parihaka, had raupō houses facing directly into the marae. Photograph by Alfred Burton. *National Musuem*

Kumi within the Rohe Potae. Te Mahuki was a staunch follower of Te Whiti, and had been driven by the troops from Parihaka in 1881. He had returned home to recreate there its replica. He and his followers called themselves the Tekaumarua (the Twelve) after the twelve apostles and the twelve evangelists whom Tawhiao had created in 1866 to proselytize the Pai Marire faith and had sent to give support to Parihaka. In March 1883, Te Mahuki seized the surveyor Charles Hursthouse, who was then working within the Rohe Potae by permission of the senior Maniapoto chiefs. Hursthouse had earlier been directly involved in the charges brought against Te Whiti and was distrusted. Te Kooti, accompanied by some of the Maniapoto, broke into the whare where Hursthouse was being held prisoner, Te Kooti announcing himself first, 'It is I! it is I! my children'. This was his confirmation of the agreement he had reached with the government. He named it the 'maungārongo' ('the long abiding peace').

Commitment to peace was an essential component of almost all the later religious movements because fighting had led to bitter defeats. Stemming from Tawhiao, it became intrinsic to the Ringatu from 1873. It was at the heart of Pai Marire teachings under Te Whiti. It was fundamental to all those who would claim the succession to Te Kooti. One of the least known movements in this tradition was the Pao Miere faith. It developed as a rejection of the opening of the Rohe Potae to surveying in 1883, 'Pao Miere' meaning 'Refuse Honey', or the sweet taste of land money. In 1887 two

Te Miringa Te Kakara, about 1905. In the foreground is a truncated niu pole, one of three rows which stood facing the entrances. Photograph by Leslie Hinge. *Auckland Institute and Museum*

tohunga, Te Ra Karepe and Rangawhenua, directed the construction at Tiroa of a cruciform-shaped house, which became their centre of teaching. It was called Te Miringa Te Kakara, the name being taken from an older house of learning, dedicated to the worship of Io, which had been built on the same site in the 1860s. The movement combined elements of the worship of Io, the Māori supreme deity accepted by the Kingitanga, with some Pai Marire beliefs. It is said that the four doors were to admit the four winds of the world to unity. Niu poles were erected outside the four doorways. The area is regarded as a place associated with peace and according to the oral traditions of Ngati Rereahu (who have always been closely associated with the schools of learning of Te Miringa Te Kakara) it was there in 1869 that Te Ra Karepe rejected Te Kooti's original message of war. After his death in 1894, Te Ra's book of teachings were placed under one of the pillars of the meeting-house Tokanganui a Noho when it was shifted to its present site in Te Kuiti. In this manner the prophetic traditions of Tawhiao, Te Kooti, and Te Ra concerning peace were ritually joined.

In the Hokianga in the 1880s, three women prophets emerged. Women taking this role were relatively unusual, but there was scriptural (as well as Māori) precedent. Miriam (also known as Maria), the sister of Moses, was a prophetess. In 1885 Maria Pangari, granddaughter of Pangari, a leading chief from the Waihou river, founded a settlement near Kaikohe into which Ngati Hao of the upper Waihou poured in the expectation of the destruction of the world at the end of March. After the failure of her prediction most returned home, but the movement continued in the Waihou.

Upon Maria's death, the leadership passed, in 1887, to her father, Aporo (Apostle) Pangari, and her sister, Remana, but their authority was challenged by a rival, the prophetess Ani Kaaro. Ani, as the granddaughter of the Ngati Hao senior chief Patuone, was the tribe's political leader. Ani had visited Te Whiti, and claimed to possess his spiritual mana, but Remana contested it with her. At Remana's camp

The interior of Te Miringa Te Kakara, 1983. The house had been renovated in 1931 but still contained many of the original tōtara beams, adzed by hand, and inscriptions, including the words on the southern poutahū (ridge post) 'NGARE O KAHA 1887' ('FAMILY OF DIVINE LINEAGE'). The house was deliberately burnt down by its keeper in 1983. Photograph by Gillian Chaplin.

near Okaihau, the people only wore white. Inside the fenced enclosure, which they named Mount Zion (the predicted place of deliverance), stood two flagpoles from which fluttered small white flags. All who entered within this tapu place, be they man or beast, had to be clothed in white as a statement of peace. The colours red or black, said Remana, were signs of danger, and they seized and bound the local Araturi storekeeper when he blundered in in the fog, burning his clothes and boots. As a consequence of his complaints, combined with the feuding with Ani Kaaro, the community was invaded by an armed police force on 22 July 1887. Remana and her father were among those arrested and subsequently imprisoned for assault and resisting the police.

The issue at stake between the women was the leadership of Ngati Hao at a time when the upper Hokianga was being reopened for extensive timber milling and settlement. It was a particularly unsettled period in the political history of the north, as the Treaty of Waitangi Kotahitanga (Unity) movement took its origins from there. Ani Kaaro had persuaded Ngati Hao into a compact with the Kingitanga in 1885, whereas other local tribal leaders wished to keep the initiative in the north. Ani and

The arrest of the Waima leaders, 6 May 1898. Hone Toia stands with his arms folded. The others in the foreground are Romana Te Paehangi; Hone Mete; Wiremu Te Makara, who had been arrested with the prophetess Remana in 1887; Rakene Pahe. *Alexander Turnbull Library*

Remana disputed for both the mantle of Te Whiti and the most effective way to hold the land closed.

However the government-assisted settlement of Hokianga continued, and by 1896 the Māori there had become outnumbered by Pākehā. The centre of protest shifted to Waima, where the prophetic leader Hone Toia claimed to be communicating with the nākahi. Papahurihia had died in 1875, but his ariā returned in the form of the serpent's whistling voice, summoned by the new seer. He created a separate community of followers drawn mostly from the Omanaia and Waima river valleys, where Papahurihia had lived. Hone Toia led a movement directed against the new rating laws on Māori property near public roads, and the tax on dogs. The dog tax was imposed locally in 1896, and fell heavily on rural communities like Waima, impoverished by the decline of the gum-digging industry. Māori also argued that they had owned dogs long before the Pākehā had arrived. A number of men chose imprisonment (rather than payment) in 1896 and in 1897. Under their new leader, they sought the advice of Te Whiti and Tohu, who in 1897 were themselves sending the Parihaka ploughmen out, also protesting against the dog tax and a law of 1892, which had asserted Crown control and leasing rights over all the Māori reserve lands in Taranaki. In 1898 about fifty Waima and Omanaia families again refused to pay their taxes, and prepared themselves for a siege.

Te Kooti Arikirangi, 1887. Pencil sketch by Reverend Richard Laishley. *Alexander Turnbull Library*

Hone Toia said directly, 'We will never pay taxes. We will not obey your laws.' The government responded with artillery and a gunboat. In the end, Waima surrendered unconditionally, the men being persuaded by the northern Member of the House of Representatives, Hone Heke, to give up their few guns. Although it is not certain whether they had ever intended to fight, Hone Toia had told the local settlers that he had no quarrel with them. He had also sent a message to those stalking the approaching soldiers not to fire. Te Whiti's message of peaceful resistance was adhered to at Waima, but sixteen men, including Hone Toia, were charged and subsequently imprisoned for levying war against Queen Victoria.

The politics of the prophetic leaders were oppositional because they interpreted their people's colonial history as the recurrence of the cycle of oppression of the Israelites. They understood that the words of Moses were for them and their children: 'The Lord made not this covenant with our fathers, but with us, even us, who are all of us here alive this day.' Some of the Māori prophets adopted the millenarian tradition of salvation, which had developed later in Israel's history. Te Ua had taught the belief of the coming of the new Jerusalem on earth, which some of his emissaries expounded in its fullest form, preaching the resurrection of the Māori ancestors and with it, their command of all forms of knowledge, including the English language.

It was Te Kooti who, in a series of predictions, specifically developed the expectation for a successor, one greater than himself, who would complete his work. These predictions contained warnings of rivalry, but also the promise of the Māori Messiah. In one recurring vision he saw a star, which would appear in the east, telling the advent of the new leader. By 1880 he spoke of two stars striving against each other; in 1885 he reiterated that the star in the east was the star to consent to. In 1892 he saw a great cloud, whose 'glory is constant', and out of which he heard a voice saying, 'This is my beloved son, hear him.' Thus he predicted Christ's coming in the words of the evangelist Luke. Finally, in April 1893, as he lay dying, he said that the leader would arise within the next generation: in twenty-six years, or perhaps less, depending on the faith of the people.

There would be several claimants to be the promised leader. The first was Te Matenga Tamati, who was a faith-healer from Ngati Kahungunu. He came from Putahi in the upper Wairoa, a region that had given support to Te Kooti in the wars, and took the Ringatu teachings to Te Kooti's former opponents on the lower reaches of the river. In 1894 he revealed that for the children of Israel to receive their blessings and renew the covenant with God, they must first build the tabernacle of David in their land. This became his mission, and the faith Te Kohititanga o Te Marama (The Rising of the New Moon) was born. Twelve great tōtara logs were cut from the forests of upper Wairoa and named after the twelve children of Jacob, the ancestors of Israel. But Matenga had also said that the final journey of the logs from the milling site to the chosen land on the coast, Korito, must not done by human hands. Faith alone must move the logs, and in 1904 a great flood brought them down river to their destination — all save 'Joseph', who wandered into a 'distant land' some miles along the coast, and had to be hauled back to join his 'brothers'. Matenga then told the people that the completion of the tabernacle belonged to the next generation and to a new leader. Matenga finally claimed no more power than that of a prophet and the twelve logs still await their destiny at Korito.

The man who claimed the title of Messiah, and who did erect the tabernacle in his own community, was the Tuhoe prophet Rua Kenana Hepetipa. His claim was based in the 1885 prediction of Te Kooti that the leader would come from the land lying between Nga Kuri a Wharei and Tikirau, that is, the boundaries of the Mataatua canoe tribes of the eastern Bay of Plenty. He emerged in 1905 after experiencing a vision on Maungapohatu, the sacred mountain of the Tuhoe. The archangel Gabriel appeared before him, and told him he must ascend the mountain. There he encountered the Tuhoe ancestress Whaitiri and, in some versions of the myth, Christ. It was Whaitiri who revealed to him the sacred diamond, the mauri (talismanic stone and life principle) of the people. Its bright light was concealed and protected by Te Kooti's

The prophet Rua standing at the entrance gateway to his new Jerusalem at Maungapohatu, 1908. The lettering reads 'MIHAIA' ('MESSIAH'). The two moving stars are depictions of (left) Kōpū, or Venus, as the morning star, and (right) Halley's comet, which represent the two sons of God, Christ and Rua. The standing clubs are emblems for Rua as the predicted King in the line of David. The four-pointed star above the gateway refers to the prophecy of Te Kooti, telling of the advent of his greater successor from the east. Photograph by George Bourne. *Auckland Institute and Museum*

shawl. Rua is the last to have seen the diamond; its power still remains to be revealed in the latter days. From this beginning, whereby his annunciation was made by both Gabriel and Whaitiri, he set out to establish himself as the one foreseen by Te Kooti. Consequently, in 1906, he went with all the leaders of Tuhoe to Turanganui to meet King Edward VII. This act was in fulfilment of Te Kooti's prediction of 1884 that the man who would appear would come to Turanganui in the faith — thus achieving what Te Kooti himself could not, having been permanently exiled from his home by the government. In Gisborne, when King Edward failed to appear, the inner meaning of Rua's pilgrimage was explained:

> 'When will the King come, Rua?' the people said after three days. He answered, 'I am really that King. Here I am, with all my people.'

At Turanganui in the waters of the Waipawa, Rua was baptized by Eria Raukura, with a name that had been predicted by Te Kooti for the leader to come: Hepetipa (Hephzibah), the one who would make the land fruitful again. Rua then moved into the interior, re-enacting the journey into the wilderness before the re-entry into the promised land, Maungapohatu. There, in 1907, the construction of Jerusalem began. The two major buildings were called Hiona (Zion) and Hiruharama Hou (New Jerusalem). Hiona was a conscious re-creation of the temple of David's son, King Solomon. It was the community's meeting-house and the 'throne of mercy'. Hiruharama Hou was Rua's house, as the King in the line of David, or 'the bloodline of the Lord'. But as the covenant with God has to be collectively renewed by each generation, so the history of the Israelites (as the people of Maungapohatu now called themselves) would be marked by difficulties and failures, forcing at various times the abandonment and rebuilding of their Jerusalem at Maungapohatu (like Parihaka before them). Maungapohatu was a community consciously committed to the 'long abiding peace', the compact of Te Kooti with the government. As a consequence, its major conflict with the law would occur in the First World War, when its men refused to volunteer.

Rua had actively discouraged volunteering because Te Kooti had said that 'War won't reach New Zealand. It is a holy land.' Rather, he had reminded that 'My Son who is coming is the man of peace, who will finish what I have started.' This commitment to peace was construed as seditious, but because refusing to volunteer was not illegal Rua was pursued with other charges. Maungapohatu was assaulted by an armed police expedition on 2 April 1916 ostensibly to arrest him for illicit grog dealing. This was an issue about which Rua had protested, because the law in this respect treated Māori unequally. As a consequence of the police assault, two men were shot dead, one of whom was Rua's son. Rua was tried for sedition but was imprisoned only for earlier 'morally resisting arrest'!

After the assault the belief that Rua was Christ was confirmed amongst his followers. The stigmata of his wounds could be seen; that he had been shot but did not die became a firmly entrenched conviction.

> That's the place where the spear went in Christ. But no bones broken, nothing. Just like Christ. Rua told the policemen, 'Well if you are going to put me to death, I want you people to shoot me, once. One shot. If you don't kill me with one shot, that to let you people know that I am the Son of the living God.' So they shoot him all right.

Maungapohatu was reconstructed after Rua's return from prison in 1918. First, Hiona was demolished, and Rua himself lived apart from the main settlement, to test the people's strength. Then, in 1927, he directed the rebuilding of all the houses in anticipation of the end of the world in a fall of burning stars. When God did not appear, Rua explained to his followers that the failure was of their own making. The millennium was postponed. He died in 1937 predicting his resurrection from the tomb; a few believers still live in that hope.

Millennial politics inevitably have a limited life because they focus on the one unobtainable event. The politics of Exodus, or the journey of suffering and liberation through the labours of the people, can be more readily renewed with each generation. Tahupotiki Wiremu Ratana was the prophet who understood this best and gained the greatest Māori following. He was of the Taranaki and Ngati Raukawa tribes, and was brought up closely associated with Parihaka. His aunt Mere Rikiriki had lived there, and was considered a faith-healer and 'Prophetess of Peace', in the line of descent from Te Whiti. She founded the Haahi o Te Wairua Tapu (Church of the Holy Ghost) at Parewanui, which Ratana attended, and in 1912 predicted the coming of a child, or chosen man, who will be 'kahore ona whanaungatanga ki te tangata' (more than a man). Later she identified her nephew as the one whom the wairua (spirit of prophecy) would enter.

In 1918 the voices began to speak to him. In an early vision, on 8 November 1918, a voice out of a cloud identified itself as the Holy Ghost, and told him that he had appointed him as 'hei Mangai moku' (my Mouthpiece) in order to unite the people. Later that evening, in a blaze of light, the angel Gabriel appeared before him to confirm this task.

Ratana based his teachings on two texts: the Bible and the Treaty of Waitangi. Behind him lay the vision of the Te Popoto prophet Aperahama Taonui who, in 1863, told the chiefs of the north:

> . . . He ra ano kei te haere mai ka kite koutou i tetahi tangata
> e mau mai ana e rua ana pukapuka: ko te Paipera me te Tiriti
> o Waitangi. Whakarongo koutou ki a ia.

> . . . There is a man coming, however, who will carry with
> him two books: the Bible and the Treaty of Waitangi. Listen
> to him.

Aperahama had become a major leader of the Treaty of Waitangi Kotahitanga in the 1880s, and was considered by many of the Hokianga chiefs to be the inheritor of the prophetic mantle of Papahurihia. Ratana claimed to be the man Aperahama had foreseen and, with his acknowledgement of the Treaty, broke with Te Whiti's ideas. Ratana's work had two specific aspects: temporal and spiritual, which he called the ture tangata and the ture wairua, and by delineating these tasks he made clear the political as well as religious goals of his movement.

He emphasized the spiritual side first. He quickly gathered a mass support as a result of his response to the heavy mortality of the Māori in the 1918 influenza pandemic (seven times greater than that of Pākehā). He acted as a spiritual healer — as had most of the Māori visionaries, including Te Kooti and Rua. Lieutenant-Colonel Carmichael of the Salvation Army, who visited the mushrooming settlement at Ratana pā in 1921, claimed that 3147 people had already professed to be cured of their illnesses through Ratana's help. Among those who came in November 1920 were 1000 people from Te Kumi, who returned home to build a Ratana centre. By 1925 Ratana had developed his own form of worship. His creed states that the members of the church accept Ratana as the Mouthpiece of Jehovah (the role Te Whiti had earlier claimed). It asserts that the prophets speak by the inspiration of the Holy Ghost, and that the Faithful Angels are the workers and messengers of God. The emblem of the faith is a five-pointed star and crescent moon, Te Whetu Marama. The points on the star represent respectively the Father, the Holy Ghost, Te Mangai (the Mouthpiece), the Faithful Angels, and the Son of God. The star also represents the western star seen by Te Kooti, which in the Ratana tradition is accepted as the prediction of their leader. The moon is the māramatanga, or the spiritual knowledge revealed to Ratana. Alpha and Omega, the beginning and the end, are also marked at its points. The Ratana faith, therefore, wove together many strands of the Māori prophetic tradition and became immediately the largest indigenous church. By the 1926 census nearly 19% of the Māori population said they were believers.

This rapid success indicates that Ratana had tapped real needs. He created a common identity, using a name that had already been adopted for the Māori by Te Ua, and thereafter by Te Whiti and Te Kooti, that is, Nga Morehu, or the remnant of the people, on 'whom the Lord shall call'. But with Ratana it took on a particular emphasis: that of the ordinary people and the detribalized, the 'carpenters' and the 'blacksmiths', whom he predicted (following Tawhiao) would come to power. The name rejected the primacy of tribal affiliations. It carried a renunciation of the leadership of the tribal chiefs and the educated Māori parliamentary representatives, who seemed to have betrayed the people. Ratana also worked actively to extirpate the old Māori powers of mākutu and tapu, still seen as the two main sources of illness.

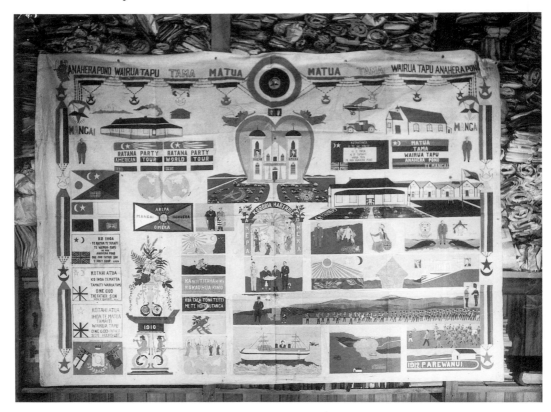

An example of the large painted cloth charts which are used by the Ratana church to narrate its history. At the top it reads symmetrically: Faithful Angels, Holy Ghost, Son, Father. In the centre at the top is the pattern of concentric circles that depicts the eye of God, and within it is the five-pointed star and crescent moon, Te Whetu Marama. On the sides of the cloth Te Māngai (Ratana) is depicted. Directly below the eye of God is the tabernacle of the Ratana pā, opened in 1928. At the bottom right, there is a reference to the prediction of Mere Rikiriki made at Parewanui in 1912. The small aeroplane, with a ladder descending into a waiting car, depicts the descent of Ratana, in 1928, from his spiritual mission to his political mission. Hall Raine Studios. *National Museum*

This was the old dilemma. Rua had set out to destroy all the ancient tapu places in the Urewera, and rejected the practice of ancestral carving. Ratana similarly created new visual symbols for his faith, which were painted and not carved. He placed particular reliance on the guardian angels in the struggle of māramatanga (knowledge) against mākutu (darkness). They acted as ancestral ariā, but were God's messengers. The religion appealed to those who felt they had been left outside the concerns of the powerful. The traditional community leaders were discredited, the Kotahitanga had failed to make any impact on New Zealand society, and the main churches were firmly in the hands of Pākehā ministers. Ratana's commitment to the two spheres of activity expressed the widespread Māori view that the two were interdependent, and that their particular needs, as Māori, were still to be met.

Ratana actively took up the temporal sphere in 1928. As he said then,

> I have admonished you to unite as one before God, and then having done so support the Treaty of Waitangi. You will now be aware that I have descended from the law of the Scripture to the law of the country created by man. . . . The Temple is now complete, the church is established, the organisation surrounding it is secure, [therefore] I wish to state here again that I desire a confrontation with the laws of the country. I repeat again that I wish to divide my body into four quarters.

The four quarters were to be the four seats in Parliament, which Ratana set out to capture. This parliamentary strategy finally brought the Ratana political thrust into an alliance with the Labour party in 1935. The Piriwiritua (Campaigner), as he called himself in this capacity, met the new Prime Minister Michael Savage and presented him with four objects: a potato (the ordinary person); a greenstone tiki (the mana of the Māori); a huia feather (the leadership); and a broken gold watch. The watch represented the laws relating to the Māori, and as Te Whiti had first said, only the law can repair the law.

Ratana was the first of the visionary leaders to bring the autonomist demands of the Māori into the mainstream of parliamentary politics. He sought recognition of the Treaty as a statement of Māori independent rights. He sought ultimately the establishment of Māori self-government. This desire, the recovery of the autonomy of the people or the power to shape the laws that bound them captive, had been the consistent goal of all the prophets. If Ratana was successful in achieving some social gains (better Māori housing and pensions) through his political alliance with the Labour party, he failed in his larger objective.

The Māori visionary leaders all claimed spiritual descent from those who had gone before them. There is a lineage of mana — a family tree — which the oral histories recount. They narrate how, and to whom, the spiritual power was transferred. The mana is seen as a gift of God, held in trust by the leaders of each generation. Through God's direction, it may be transferred to the next. But the oral histories which tell the stories of succession also reveal the problems of rivalry. The prophets challenged each other. As Te Kooti rejected both Tawhiao and Te Whiti as 'the houses of obstruction', so Te Whiti claimed that he alone was God's mouthpiece: 'it is left to my hand alone to heal the sick to weld the broken iron to build the houses and to raise the tree. . . . I will build and complete the house of the world in this generation.' For the Ringatu, the star in the west foreseen by Te Kooti is the star of ill-omen and dispute, but for the followers of Ratana the same prediction serves to confirm that the source of his authority is divine. The prophets often rejected the Māori temporal leaders and most refused to participate in attempts at political unity, such as the Kotahitanga of the Treaty of Waitangi, and thereby helped to undermine their effectiveness.

Of all the prophets, Te Ua and Ratana gained the greatest following, each rapidly breaking through tribal differences to gather in about a fifth of the Māori population. In the 1981 census Ratana remained the largest indigenous faith and the third largest religion among the Māori people, after the Anglicans and the Roman Catholics.

All the prophets tried to establish a common identity for the Māori as Israelites, cutting across the tribal divisions while still accepting them historically. They drew on traditional Māori concepts of the cosmology, and particularly on the intervening role of the ariā, the spirits of the ancestors, who may appear to the living in many forms. The ancestors were and are believed to speak with the mouth of the gods, and to be able to remember what has not yet happened. These Māori concepts of cyclic history were brought into the framework of the Judaeo-Christian faiths, and created the new religions. The prophets believed, like the Israelites, that God moved with people through time. Only some were messianic in their vision; in other movements, the leaders taught directly that the freedom of God's people lay in their own hands.

The politics of Exodus remain an active guiding principle in the world of the Māori today.

8. *The Farmers Take Over*
(1912–1930)

MILES FAIRBURN

Most historians have seen New Zealand's past as a story of progress. Its history does not consist of decline and fall, of cycles, of movement back to a golden age, or even a meaningless sequence of events, but of cumulative improvement. Progress is seen as change for the better in six key areas. They include achievements in the arts and literature, the growth of national independence, the development of better race relations, strong and stable economic growth, the extension of civil rights, and the expansion of governmental responsibility for the prevention and resolution of such 'problems' as social injustice and inequality.

The history of New Zealand's progress, however, is not viewed as a rising straight line but as an extremely erratic movement within a long-term upward trend. In some periods the line is disappointingly flat or barely climbs at all. In others it ascends at a more satisfactory pace. In the 1890s and late 1930s it positively soars. But over the years from 1912 and 1930, the subject of this essay, it plunges more precipitously than at any other time, with the possible exception of the Great Depression. The only 'progressive' trend that historians discern in the age was the rise of the Labour Party.

New Zealand's degeneration between 1912 and 1930 is not attributed to the usual things associated with a society's decline — such as the excessive power of the trade unions (which is often taken as the 'British disease' since World War II) or moral decadence (New Zealand was hardly an effete and overcivilized country), but to something quite different — rural idiocy. The claim is that farmers wielded more control over the economy, politics, and social attitudes at this time than at any other. Farmers, historians imply, were the 'ruling class' (they provided four of the five Prime Ministers from 1912 to 1935 and the Farmers' Union was the most powerful pressure group); and farmers' ideas were the ruling ideas (the popular saying of the time was that farmers were the 'backbone' of the country).

Yet, the literature suggests that farmers were incapable of exercising their domination with wisdom — with prudence, objectivity, detachment, knowledge and reason. The outlook of most farmers — especially the smaller, the newer and those living in remote areas — was twisted and cramped by the combined effect of the economic instability of their livelihoods, their deficient leisure and education, cultural poverty, social isolation and material squalor. Less than 30% of dairy farmers, for instance, had been educated beyond standard six, only 16% had septic tanks attached to their homes, 23% had no running hot water, 26% of their wives worked on the farm at least forty hours a week and half belonged to no leisure organization at all (except perhaps a church), and over a quarter of the children of sharemilkers were assessed as educationally backward. By force of circumstances, in other words, farmers were unfit to rule. Unlike the Liberals of the 1890s and the Labour men of the late 1930s who were townsmen, the farmers had a perspective on New Zealand society that was crude and unbalanced. Inevitably, therefore, New Zealand went downhill from 1912 to 1930 because its interests were in the hands of rural barbarians, of backwoodsmen, 'know nothings' who had little comprehension of how to run a society which was becoming more modern, more urban, more complex.

The unprogressive character in these years of farmer rule is frequently linked to the disasters of the succeeding period. Farmer rule helped create a moral, social, and political climate which was hostile to innovation. The climate of conservatism in turn prevented New Zealand from adapting to a changing world and left it ill-prepared for the Great Depression. Originality, talent, and the expression of differences were all stifled by oppressive mechanisms of conformity. The sanctions of the law and of public opinion had never operated so vigorously to enforce a rigid moral code based on the work ethic and 'wowserism'. Displays of skill, talent, and individual self-expression received the strongest acclaim when they focussed on the coercion of deviance. It was accordingly in this field of endeavour that the country's most enterprising and dynamic institutions operated. One outstanding example was the prohibition movement, which almost succeeded twice (in 1911 and 1919) in winning referenda on the outlawing of alcohol. Other than this, the society only permitted creativity and recognized achievement in sport, war, growing grass, do-it-yourself hobbies and pastimes, petty acquisitiveness, the art of frugality through improvisation, and (for women) in cooking and care of the home.

Does the period deserve its black reputation? The remainder of this essay will suggest that it does not. It will argue that the orthodox views exaggerate the significance of what they regard as the key indicators of national decline characterizing the period.

The notion that the society slid back over these years is based, first of all, on the observation that they witnessed an unprecedented assault on civil rights. In 1913 the authorities seriously curtailed the legal capacity of trade unions to strike. During World War I other freedoms were attacked. Censorship regulations were imposed in 1914; conscription was introduced (New Zealand was the first Dominion to do this); and in December 1916 the War Regulations on 'sedition' were stiffened to include such things as the incitement of class ill-will, interference with war production, and the encouragement of opposition to the war, all of which led to the arrest of several labour leaders who spoke out against conscription. The Expeditionary Forces Amendment Act of December 1918 deprived conscientious objectors of their civil rights for ten years. From 1919 to 1922 other freedoms were restricted.

Also taken as a key sign of the withering of the country's spirit was its export of its artistic geniuses, most notably Katherine Mansfield, who left New Zealand for good in 1908, followed by the painter Frances Hodgkins in 1913. In the 1890s the first hesitant steps had been taken in literature to define a New Zealand identity, but apart from the contributions of Jane Mander and the young poet R. A. K. Mason, the 1913–1930 period did nothing to take the development further. The critics and reading public greeted Mander's novels with outright hostility, and ignored Mason's verse. Sales of one of Mason's collections of poetry, *The Beggar* (1924), were so miserable, that in despair he threw unsold copies into Auckland harbour.

The third indicator of progress which historians see as going in the wrong direction is the performance of the economy. From 1895 to 1907 New Zealand had experienced twelve years of strong and uninterrupted economic growth accompanied by full employment, rising real wages and diminishing inequality, without the costs of inflation or excessive borrowing. Thereafter the rate of growth was slow, highly unstable, and attended by all the problems missing in the earlier period. A recession brought rising unemployment in 1908–1910. World War I then created a boom and rising employment; but at the cost of falling real wages, a sharp increase in the national debt, high inflation, and growing inequality. The boom peaked in 1920 with a frenzied burst of land speculation. This was fuelled by the massive injection of money into the uncontrolled land market by ex-servicemen, spending their cheap government 'rehab' loans on the purchase of farms. With the ending in mid–1920 of the 'War Commandeer' (the acquisition during the war of all New Zealand's export production by the British Government at fixed prices) and the crash of international commodity markets, the economy slumped in 1921–2. Unemployment soared: a third of the soldier settlers, unable to service their debts, and all too frequently settled on poor country or lacking farming experience, walked off the land. Although the economy grew again during the early 1920s, this was partly stimulated by heavy government borrowing for rural development. This phase was succeeded by another slump in 1925–26, again producing high unemployment. True, the late 1920s witnessed a recovery; but this time unemployment did not fall; it rose until the onslaught of the Great Depression in 1930 cruelly revealed the fundamental nature of the problems underlying the previous twenty years of relative economic difficulty.

It is the failure of political vision and will, however, which historians see as being at the core of the country's malaise during the period. Dominating the political scene was the Reform Party which first came to office in 1912 and stayed there for another sixteen years (though in coalition with the Liberals as a wartime contingency between 1915 and 1919). Reform's inability to arrest and reverse the waning vitality of the society is epitomized by the stunted outlook and limited background of W. F. Massey,

The failure of New Zealanders in the 1920s to recognize the talents of the poet R.A.K. Mason (photographed here as a young man) is one of the signs historians have taken that this was a period of sterility. *Hocken Library*

Prime Minister from 1912 until his death in 1925. A Mangere small farmer by occupation, a British Israelite by conviction (British Israelites believed that the British were one of the lost tribes of Israel), and an Ulsterman by birth, Massey never had an original idea in his life. Nor over his very long political career, did he ever question his belief that New Zealand should always remain a loyal, Protestant, family-centred, rural society where every man was his own landlord. His successor, Gordon Coates (a Kaipara farmer), won a large majority for Reform in 1925 with an unparalleled display of electoral hype. But he lacked experience, and became bogged down in a squabble within his party over an ill-fated scheme by the Dairy Board in 1926/27 to sell cheese and butter in Britain at fixed prices.

Reforms resisted experimental legislation. Its power base consisted of the two most conservative elements in the electorate, the urban professional and business élites and, most of all, farmers, supposedly the largest component in the voting population. To these groups the only legitimate function of government was to stay out of business, protect the status quo (especially from trade unions) but treat the farmer as the 'backbone' of the country.

In addition, the government's inertia is taken as a legacy of the extraordinarily long time Massey and his lieutenants had spent on the opposition benches before coming to power in 1912. Massey himself had languished there ever since entering Parliament in 1894. Once they had at last won the prize of office, their natural desire to keep it made them very cautious about acting in advance of public opinion. The front bench contained more than its share of time-servers, but Massey refused to demote them because of the debt he owed them for sticking by him ever since he became opposition leader in 1903.

Some commentators suggest that the government's poor legislative record was not entirely its own fault. The problems of administering the war effort distracted Reform for five of its sixteen years of rule. So did the fact that for a cumulative total of another eight years or so it had a narrow and tenuous parliamentary majority. Some historians also concede that the Reform era was not totally devoid of achievement. It restructed the civil service in 1912 and eliminated the 'evils' of ministerial control over promotions and appointments. It established primary producer boards in the 1920s which introduced greater efficiency in the sale of exports. A few of its cabinet ministers are also recognized as having ability. For instance, Sir James Allen, the Minister of Defence, managed the war effort almost single-handedly during the lengthy intervals Massey was out of the country; Gordon Coates, Minister of Native Affairs, took initiatives to rectify Māori grievances; and Massey distinguished himself in his conduct of foreign relations.

But these accomplishments, according to most writers, were heavily outweighed by the damaging repercussions of an otherwise sterile rule. For a start, Reform's resistance to state intervention is frequently condemned for retarding the development of the welfare state. The progressive steps the Liberals had taken between 1891 and 1912 towards creating a humane, egalitarian society were not continued by Reform. Apart from a tiny provision for child allowances in 1926, it did nothing to build a stronger framework of state protection and care. Because of its negligence, the poor and the needy suffered all the more deeply when the depression came in 1930.

It is also implied that by neglecting social legislation, Reform was unable to conciliate unionists after their defeat in a bitter round of industrial conflict in 1912 and 1913. Had it reversed the economic inequalities brought by the war, Reform would have prevented hatreds from persisting and saved the country from a resurgence of working class protest between 1917 and 1920. Instead, Reform attempted to suppress the unrest by curtailing civil liberties, and this was a measure of its political bankruptcy.

Its one field of vigorous endeavour lay in pandering to the farming electorate. Borrowing heavily abroad, Reform intensified and extended the policies of its predecessors of fostering rural development. Thousands of returned servicemen were put on the land, investment was poured into bringing electricity to the countryside, ever greater sums of cheap mortgage money were made available to farmers through State Advances, and great strides were taken in building roads and bridges in the backblocks. As the blatant purpose behind all this was to buy votes,

Reform debased the currency of politics. Public concern for principle and the long term interest of the country diminished, cynicism and greed increased. To raise their chances of winning elections, the other two parties had to outbid Reform in making promises to borrow and spend.

The degeneration of public life allegedly reached a squalid and bizarre climax at the 1928 general election when in his opening campaign address Sir Joseph Ward, leader of the United Party (the Liberal remnant), misread his speech notes and pledged that he would borrow and spend £70 million within a year of coming to office (he meant to say it would be over ten years). This was a huge sum, about ten times the amount normally borrowed in an average year over the 1920s. After observing that the public responded to the speech with wild enthusiasm, Ward did little to correct the error and won the election, ending Reform's long spell in power. The onset of the Great Depression, however, compelled United to stop borrowing and cut government spending, and in 1931 it coalesced with Reform to complete this arid exercise, killing the political reputation of them both, a fitting act of historical retribution.

But Reform's most infamous contribution to New Zealand's decline is seen as its economic mismanagement. Its policies not only aggravated the structural problems which caused the low and unstable economic growth of the period, but they also worsened the subsequent effects of the depression. One such problem was the overdependence on the British market (which took 80% of New Zealand's exports) where New Zealand's products faced increasing competition, at a time of sluggish consumer demand, from margarine, Danish butter, and Australian and Argentinian meat. A further and related problem is said to have been the overdependence on agriculture itself. Reform allegedly reinforced both problems with its programmes of rural development.

Yet another structural imbalance, according to some, was the excessive amount of government borrowing. This arose from Reform's reluctance to offend its electoral base by paying for rural development and the costs of the war out of taxation. The difficulties of servicing government debt after 1930 led to savage spending cuts which added greatly to the misery of the common people.

Finally, Reform has been indicted for lending too much money to farmers and failing, at the time of the 1920 land boom, to control the land market. These things encouraged farmers to speculate in land. The evil of land speculation was that it saddled farmers with large debts which became unmanageable when export prices fell. This happened to the soldier settlers after the war; and it happened to the whole farm sector during the depression.

What has been put forward so far is the conventional view of the period. But is it plausible? Did farmer rule stifle innovation and lead to national decline? Can national decline be measured by a poor record of civil rights, literary and artistic endeavour, economic growth, and state activity?

To answer these questions it is intended to examine the period from another

Hand-milking was still a common practice in the 1920s especially on the smaller and poorer dairy farms. Although women had always played a vital role in the running of the family farm in New Zealand, a dimmer view of the long hours spent by women and children in milking cows emerged in the 1920s. *Hocken Library*

perspective. The first claim is that the defining characteristic of the age was civil strife, and that the strife stemmed largely from circumstances that long pre-dated 1912 and were outside New Zealand's control; moreover, farmers had little to do with it. The second claim is that after 1921 the strife was controlled then completely eradicated, and that this was a major achievement. From 1912 to 1921, Pākehā New Zealand was wracked by the worst years of collective conflict in its history, but by the end of the period unity and peace prevailed within the framework of a new consensus. The third claim is that astute political management played a vital role in moving New Zealand from conflict to consensus. The final claim is that the things that brought stability were linked to the defects that commentators identify with the period; indeed the defects were the price the society had to pay for the harmony and consensus it so desperately needed.

Although in the early part of the period New Zealand was filled with fanatical protest movements, two stand out as the most powerful and menacing. One was a right wing Christian fundamentalist organization called the Protestant Political Association (PPA), and the other consisted of various extreme left wing groupings in the labour movement. A precondition for the rise of both was the rapid integration of individuals into a growing variety and number of communities and organizations in New Zealand from the 1880s. Most of these had mixed memberships; but some did not. They were enclaves — isolated cells — where people of a particular class, ethnic group, or religion, stuck to each other, thus retaining or acquiring separate beliefs and values. Under ordinary circumstances, the enclaves lacked the will to assert themselves politically. But unfortunately for the unity of early twentieth century New Zealand, the countries with which it had the greatest contact were swept by ideologies embracing paranoid delusions and idealistic dreams, which expressed the frustrations and fears of isolated social groupings which had counterparts in New Zealand. Inevitably, these ideologies were imported into the country. It then took only a few precipitating factors, most notably the chance emergence of charismatic leaders, to induce the members of these enclaves to translate the imported ideologies into mass action.

The enclave from which the PPA derived most support was the Orange Lodge. Brought to New Zealand in the early colonial period, the order devoted itself to preserving the culture of the Irish Protestant minority by keeping alive fears and hatreds towards 'popery' and Irish nationalism. Before 1914, it had very occasionally interfered in politics but never with success, since its members were widely scattered across the country in a multitude of small branches. But by 1917 the situation had changed dramatically. The beast of Protestant bigotry stalked the land.

One reason for the change was that since the turn of the century there had been an upsurge in America, England, and Australia of organizations composed of fundamentalist Christians hostile to the Roman Catholic Church. Their views, conveyed to New Zealand by travelling preachers and a torrent of literary propaganda (much of it grotesquely offensive and abusive), gave the Orangemen additional rationalizations for their anti-Catholicism, and the feeling that their convictions were shared and approved by large sections of international opinion. Another reason for the change was the increasing assertiveness of the Catholic Church, which like the Orange Order, was an enclave in New Zealand society. A Papal decree of 1908, *Ne Temere*, invalidated mixed marriages unless performed before a priest. Spearheaded by the Catholic newspaper, the *Tablet*, and the Catholic Federation (a political lobby group formed in 1913), the church made strident claims for state aid to its schools and against the demand by a coalition of Protestant churches for compulsory Bible reading in state schools. All this appeared to confirm the worst fears of Lodge members that Protestant New Zealand was being attacked by Rome.

Then a series of events during the patriotically charged years of the war whipped the paranoia of the Orangemen into a frenzy. Abroad, the Papacy declared its neutrality in early 1916 and the Easter Rebellion broke out in Ireland in April 1916. At home, Sir Joseph Ward (a Catholic) was made deputy Prime Minister in the coalition government at its formation in 1915; members of the Marist Order obtained exemption from conscription in late 1917 following intense pressure from the church; and elements in the Irish Catholic community became openly supportive of Sinn Fein, the revolutionary Irish nationalist movement.

It took, however, the emergence of a charismatic leader, Howard Elliott, to transform fear into a mass political organization. Elliott was a Baptist minister in Auckland. He had developed rabidly anti-Catholic attitudes in Australia before he immigrated to New Zealand in 1909. An electrifying orator, he first came to the attention of the Mount Eden branch of the Lodge in mid–1915 with sermons alleging that the war was an international conspiracy by the Papacy to extend its temporal power. He became the unofficial chaplain of the branch and soon dominated it, persuading the branch early in 1916 to form a Committee of Vigilance. Using the committee as his power base, Elliott then disseminated his message in a furious propaganda and speaking campaign mainly around the Auckland area, experimenting with techniques of crowd manipulation and winning national press coverage in the process. Next, he induced the Grand Orange Lodge (the national body of the Orange Order) to establish a political movement (the PPA), with a central office in Wellington and Elliott as the National Lecturer. Exercising his enormous powers of energy, organization and persuasion, and backed by the resources of the Grand Lodge, the Baptist minister travelled all over the country forming branches of the PPA, recruiting from the vast majority of the Lodges' widely scattered membership. By 1919 he claimed the movement had 225 branches and 200,000 members. Many recruits came from outside the Lodge, especially from the Baptist, Church of Christ and other fringe Protestant sects. A twisted sense of patriotism and varying degrees of anti-Catholicism drove them to join the PPA, as did, most of all, Elliott's sensational methods of stirring up hatred.

The most notorious example of this skill was displayed at a huge demonstration in Auckland held by the PPA in July 1917. After fulminating in his standard manner against Rome's plot to use the war to take over the world, Elliott accused the New Zealand Post Office of illegally censoring the PPA's inward mail, and read out some of the letters supposedly delayed by the Censor. One 'correspondent' asked if it were true that the results of an inquest into the drowning of a Taumarunui nun had been suppressed, and if a dead body of a child had been found buried in the grounds of an Auckland convent. The allegations of censorship were intended to embarrass Ward, the Postmaster-General. They led to stormy debates in Parliament, and a Commission of Inquiry where Elliott read out more such letters which he said had been the object of illegal Post Office censorship as well. Although the enquiry rejected Elliott's claims and condemned the PPA for inciting sectarian strife, he managed to come out of the affair looking as if he had been attacked for standing up for the rights of free speech.

By the end of 1917, the PPA had enraged the Catholic community so much that social tension reached breaking point and spontaneous acts of violence broke out between the two groups. Elliott was knocked down by several men and horsewhipped; two Protestant clergymen were beaten up after a PPA meeting; a mob stoned a house where Elliott was staying; and a group of PPA supporters violently seized a town hall

Howard Elliott. *Private collection*

after being told they could not use it. On other occasions Elliott was under police protection, and had to leave meetings by the side entrance to avoid riotous crowds of Catholics. A PPA deputation had great difficulty restraining its rank and file members from taking reprisals.

For tactical reasons, Elliott started to shift the PPA towards the far right of the political spectrum. He increasingly added to his scurrilous revelations about Rome, extreme attacks on the 'disloyal' Left, on the 'Bolshevistic' Labour Party, on radical unionists and socialism of any kind, exposing their role in the Papal plot. The object was to tap the welling up of conservative anxiety over the renewal of working class radicalism and of dissatisfaction with the coalition government: the PPA was to replace Reform as the official party of the New Zealand Right.

The by-election of October 1918 for Wellington Central gave the PPA its first major opportunity to prove to conservative opinion that it could save New Zealand from its enemies. The association threw its monumental resources behind an independent candidate in a strenuous effort to defeat both the Labour candidate, Peter Fraser, and the coalition contestant. Fraser won, and Elliott took the fateful step of directing the PPA to back Reform candidates at the forthcoming 1919 general election (he was to do the same in 1922). He calculated that if the PPA mobilized popular support at the local level for every such candidate, it could reasonably expect to increase its already high level of influence over Reform's customary voters and inside Reform's hierarchy. His objective, in other words, was to turn Reform into a PPA front.

Massey's conservative rule from 1912 to 1925 is often unfavourably compared with the two periods of reform under the Liberals (1890-1912) and under Labour (1935-1949). His main achievement, however, was to help bring to a peaceful end the acute class and sectarian divisions in New Zealand society. As the photograph suggests, Massey liked to present himself as a man of the land; indeed he was commonly known as 'Farmer Bill'. He was the first leader of a conservative political party to become a 'stump politician'. *Hocken Library*

As it happened, the PPA's support did help Massey. He won by a landslide in 1919 and held on by the skin of his teeth in his 1922. It also played a major part in the rapid demise of the Liberals up to 1928. Ward was the most effective politician the Liberals had, and the PPA did so much to destroy his public reputation, that he lost his seat in 1919 and was unable to return to Parliament until 1925. But the policy of backing Reform failed totally to attain its objective: the PPA went into a steep decline from about 1921 and vanished in 1934.

Certain sections in the labour movement posed the second major threat to New Zealand's political stability. As with the Christian fundamentalists on their extreme right, these sections were drawn from small enclaves in the society. However, most of the enclaves were not formally constituted as the Orange Lodge was, but consisted of weak informal groupings. Belonging to these groupings were a large minority of the country's unskilled workers, bunched together in a multitude of settings like the coal mines of the West Coast and Huntly, the boarding-houses of the main urban centres, in the Manawatu flax mills, public works camps, timber mills, and the larger shearing

This picture of Harry Holland, the Australian-born leader of the New Zealand Labour Party, was taken in 1912 or 1913. *Private Collection.*

gangs. During the decade or so before the World War I, these populations were heavily represented by new immigrants who poured into New Zealand from Britain and Australia carrying with them traditions of working class culture and protest that were far stronger than those in New Zealand. In any other set of circumstances, the presence of these more class-conscious immigrants would not have fostered an upsurge in worker radicalism; the unskilled tended to be extremely footloose, and, as 'here today and gone tomorrow' sort of people, were difficult to unionize, indoctrinate and control.

Conditions between about 1905 and 1913, however, were exceptional. For one thing, new ideas celebrating strike action as a means of short term improvement and ultimately of revolution (anarcho-syndicalism) were inspiring the working classes in other parts of the world. Inevitably, these were imported into New Zealand through the printed word (particularly the material put out by the Chicago left wing publishing house of C. H. Kerr and Co.) and the effort of visiting lecturers, journalists and international working class leaders like Tom Mann, Ben Tillett, Harry Scott Bennett, Charles Edward Russell, R. S. Ross, and H. E. Holland. The message appealed particularly to the recent immigrants since it accorded with their experience of class and their status as outsiders in New Zealand society.

For another, the population of unskilled immigrants happened to contain a disproportionately large number of potentially charismatic leaders such as M. J. Savage, Bob Semple and Paddy Webb. They had sufficient energy, rhetorical skill, and organizational ability to overcome the difficulty of recruiting footloose workers into a movement.

Finally, the agitators were able to exploit a variety of dissatisfactions that had accumulated and intensified since about 1905. The Arbitration Court (a wage setting mechanism established by the Liberals in 1894) had not permitted wage rates to keep pace with prices, employers were attempting to change long-standing work practices, and the Liberal Government was no longer pro-labour.

All these circumstances generated a burst of unionization of the unskilled. A successful but illegal strike by the Blackball coalminers early in 1908 led by the revolutionaries, allowed them to take over the miners' unions and form a militant Federation of Miners later in the same year. From this base they were able to erect another umbrella organization in 1909, the Federation of Labour (FOL). It was charged with the responsibility of intervening in the industrial disputes of its affiliated unions. In 1911 the federation formally adopted the revolutionary principles of the American based anarcho-syndicalist movement, the Industrial Workers of the World (IWW), of using a general strike to destroy capitalism and replace it with a shop floor Utopia. At its peak in the middle of 1912, the federation, or 'Red Feds', represented one-fifth of total trade union membership, though only a fraction of them shared the revolutionary goals of the agitators.

In 1912 and 1913 New Zealand came closer to class war than at any other time in its history. Just before the Reform Party came to office in July 1912, the Waihi gold miners who were affiliated to the 'Red Feds' had gone on strike in protest at the formation of a breakaway union, and the company had closed the mine. After the molestation of the dissenting unionists by picketing federationists, Police Commissioner Cullen sent a strong police contingent into Waihi to restore order, and the strike leaders were prosecuted and imprisoned. The company then went on the offensive and reopened the mine in October, recruiting scab labour for the purpose. Tension mounted. Under full police protection the scabs gained in confidence. On 12 November, after a week of street battles with the federationists, the scabs sacked the Miners' Hall, where George Evans, a 'Red Fed' miner, was clubbed to death by a policeman he had shot in the stomach. Next, they conducted a terror campaign against the federationists, running them out of town, which brought the strike to an end.

Alarmed by the failure of its affiliates to aid the strikers effectively, and fearful of further state intervention in disputes on the side of employers, the FOL retreated ideologically and reorganized. It took initiatives to strengthen the solidarity of the whole labour movement. A Unity Congress in mid–1913, with the approval of all but the most conservative trade unions, founded two organizations: a new political party, the Social Democratic Party (SDP), having parliamentary socialism as its goal, and a new union umbrella (the United Federation of Labour), which accepted strike action but not as a revolutionary instrument.

The employers, however, who wanted to smash the union base of the new

The Waihi strike of 1912 was perhaps the most bitter and turbulent strike involving a single employer in New Zealand history. With the protection of the police, and the connivance of the mining company, a break-away union resorted to violence to remove the miner's union affiliated to the radical Federation of Labour. *NZ Herald*

movement before it had time to consolidate, precipitated a lock-out of the Wellington waterside in October 1913. After the locked out men occupied the wharves, the Massey Government enrolled special constables, recruited chiefly from farming areas ('Massey's Cossacks'), to evict them, producing riots and the occasional use of firearms by the strikers. The UFL then declared a general strike, but capitulated after six weeks. What defeated the strike was that only a tiny proportion of unionists supported it (primarily the miners and the unskilled Auckland unions). Also the government legislated to make unions which were not registered under the Arbitration Act liable for civil damages caused by striking; and a decision by the Supreme Court ruled that it was illegal for an Arbitration union to use its funds in support of a strike.

After the disaster, the two new labour organizations crumbled. The working class was not to achieve unity again until the late 1930s. Even so, defeat left the unskilled workers sullen and embittered, and this predisposed them to lead the radical revival between 1917 and 1921. Triggering the revival was a surge in the cost of living, the result of inflationary government war expenditure and the international commodity

The smashing of the 1913 waterfront strike called by the United Federation of Labour was actively supported by Massey's Reform Government. The Government recruited special constables (principally from farming areas) to break up picket lines and street demonstrations by striking workers. *NZ Herald*

boom. An unmarried general labourer paying 18 shillings for a weekly stay in a boarding house in 1913, was charged 22 shillings six pence by 1918. Although pensions and wage rates went up too, they lagged behind inflation. The government lacked the resources for welfare spending, and the practice of wage setting under the Arbitration system meant that wages were only adjusted at two yearly intervals.

Other grievances fed the revival. One was the low level of allowances for the families of servicemen. Another was the growth of inequality as profits and farm incomes, benefitting from the inflationary conditions, soared ahead of wages. Inflammatory, too, was the failure of the government, mainly because it lacked adequate administrative machinery, to control profiteering or to use the taxation system to redistribute incomes. Although it was initially popular, conscription nonetheless engendered resentment because of the apparent inequality of sacrifice it entailed: workers were conscripted, while profiteers went unchecked. After the bloodletting of Gallipoli, war weariness set in. It was harder for people 'to do their bit', and to tolerate the selfishness of the wealthy. There were successful campaigns against conscription in Australia (two referenda were rejected in late 1916 and 1917), and along with the international rise of socialist movements from 1917, these

The boarding house areas of central Wellington and Auckland provided the recruiting ground for radical trade unions from 1908 to 1913. A disproportionately large number of the unionists were transient labourers who had recently immigrated from Australia and Britain. *Alexander Turnbull Library*

encouraged protest.

The new outbreak of working class radicalism took diverse forms. One was protest against conscription, which, before the government repressed it using the 1916 War Regulations, principally expressed itself in two Anti-Conscription Conferences held early in 1916 and 1917. Another was the return of industrial unrest. After falling to an historically low point in 1915, the number of strikes rose rapidly until 1921, despite the fact that striking violated the War Regulations. Most troublesome were the miners who engaged in a series of strikes and 'go-slows' from 1916 to 1918, winning (to the fury of conservative opinion) major concessions. The unskilled unions reorganized in national federations, and in 1919 the Alliance of Labour was formed. It had the same anarcho-syndicalist ideology of the former FOL. The strongest sign of the revival was the explosive growth in electoral popularity of a new socialist organization established in 1916, the Labour Party. It won three by-elections in 1918, and at the 1919 general election received more than doubled the proportion of votes the various labour and socialist candidates had won in the previous general election of 1914.

In contrast to the 'Red Fed' years, the new phase of working class protest was devoid of social violence, and had none of the viciousness and unruliness associated with the

PPA's antics. But it destabilized society by causing a marked shift to the right in middle class political opinion thus allowing the fanatical PPA to expand its influence. The Labour Party was particularly responsible for the shift. Although Labour rejected revolution as its instrument, its avowed ends were revolutionary, for they amounted to nothing less than the abolition of capitalism. In 1919 it translated this principle into a concrete programme of gradual but total land nationalization. In the context of the party's accelerating growth, such radical intentions naturally produced a reaction of right wing extremism, a situation somewhat akin to that occurring later in many parts of Europe with the rise of fascism (although the PPA had a sectarian not a racialist ideology). The 'Red Fed' background of most of Labour's leaders and the sympathetic utterances by some about the Russian Revolution also did little to alleviate middle class apprehension.

By the mid–1920s, however, the politics of left wing radicalism were clearly on the wane. The number of strikes and of unionists per worker dropped substantially, to levels far lower than those in Britain and Australia. The branch membership of the Labour Party, which had risen sharply from 1917 to 1921, stagnated thereafter. Although the share of the vote for the left in general elections rose from 10% in 1914 to Labour's 24% in 1919, the party made no further electoral progress for the next twelve years. Even in the depression year of 1931, it could only muster 35% of the vote. In response to its chronic electoral failure Labour effectively abandoned its commitment to socialism by throwing out its programme of land nationalization. It moved towards the political centre, declaring that now its aim was to improve capitalism, not to abolish it. Focussing on rural development and overseas borrowing, it adopted the policies of its rivals. The second threat to political instability in the period was dead.

Why did the PPA and the radical tendencies in the labour movement subside? Many factors were involved but the principal one was the political skill with which W. F. Massey, the Reform Party's leader, managed social conflict.

To some extent the PPA's demise can be attributed to good fortune, to events outside New Zealand's control. The victory of the Allies in late 1918 meant that Elliott could no longer portray the war as a Papal plot for world dominion. Similarly, the settlement of the Irish question in 1921 when Britain granted Ireland its independence while retaining Ulster, deprived Elliott of the capacity of playing patriotic fears of Irish-Catholic disloyalty.

To a degree, too, the decay of the Christian fundamentalist organization was self-induced. Elliott made a fatal error in deciding to throw the PPA behind the Reform Party in the 1919 general election. By working so hard for Massey's landslide in 1919 (the largest majority Massey ever won), Elliott found it more difficult to whip up fears that the country was imperilled by a Catholic-Bolshevik set of bogeymen. He could no longer claim that Joseph Ward was aiding and abetting the Roman Catholic Church from inside the the citadels of power, for Elliott had succeeded all too well in politically destroying this folk devil of the Orangemen. By helping to set up a strong conservative government he pushed the PPA to the periphery as the scourge of the Left.

Massey had to tread very carefully in dealing with the PPA. He could not afford to antagonize it, let alone repress it. The movement was too powerful, and too many of Reform's high ranking personnel belonged to it, including the Chief Whip, the General Secretary, and half the Auckland Executive. Also 'Farmer Bill', like many of his followers, broadly sympathized with the sentiments of the movement. At the same time, Massey had to recognize that under the leadership of the rabid but gifted Elliott, the PPA had become a danger to the internal safety of New Zealand. As a prolific generator of hatreds and turmoil, it could in the end make New Zealand ungovernable. For this reason the Prime Minister appears to have adopted a two part strategy for bringing it under control.

The first part consisted of using the PPA to bolster the power of the Reform Party. Once Elliott had decided to back Reform, Massey cultivated him and gained his trust in a series of secret meetings. Through these contacts, as well as through exchanges between the two groups at other levels, Reform and the PPA seem to have co-ordinated their campaigns for the 1919 election. Having used the PPA to win his landslide victory, Massey then put the second part of his strategy into operation. Between 1919 and 1922, the Reform Government appeared to take a strong line against the power and privileges of the Roman Catholic Church in lay society. An education act withdrew the right of pupils at denominational schools (most of which were Catholic) to win state scholarships and to receive free rail passes. The Marriage Act of 1920 countered the effect of the 1908 Papal decree *Ne Temere* by outlawing statements or suggestions that any persons lawfully married were not truly and sufficiently married.

Over the same period, the government implemented a series of apparently tough measures to crack down on 'disloyalty'. Wartime censorship laws were revived to stem the inflow of Sinn Fein and socialist literature. Teachers were obliged to state an oath of allegiance to the Crown. Flag raising ceremonies were made compulsory at schools. A Roman Catholic Bishop, Liston, was prosecuted (unsuccessfully) for sedition in 1922 for reportedly saying that the suppressors of the 1916 Irish uprising were 'murderers'. The government refused permission to the Post and Telegraph Employees' Association to join the Alliance of Labour.

These activities have been criticized for eroding civil rights. But they were largely symbolic, more a matter of style than substance. The effect they were designed to achieve, moreover, outweighed their costs. As intended, they undercut the appeal of Elliott as a rabble-rouser and eased sectarian tensions. By appearing to act resolutely against the PPA's enemies, the Prime Minister pacified and soothed right wing Protestants, weakening Elliott's influence over them. Their incentive to join the PPA or to stay in it diminished, for the state looked as if it was acknowledging their concerns and had become their protector to an extent it had never been before. Massey gave right wing Protestants a sense of security they had not enjoyed for over a decade. Their paranoia thus receded. The subtlety of the Reform leader's symbolic authoritarianism lay in the fact that at the same time, it deceived Elliott into believing that the government was his ally; eroded the popular base of his movement; and did not sufficiently harm the independence of the church or the Left to provoke them into taking desperate countermeasures.

The final reason for the shrinking appeal of the ultra-right was that from the early 1920s, working class protest itself declined, and the Labour Party, unable to make ground at successive elections, moderated its policies. Massey's skill as a political manager of social conflict was involved in this process also.

As with the PPA, the dissipation of labour radicalism owed much to circumstances outside the control of any individual. The first was the disunity of the labour movement. The most powerful union organization of the 1920s, the Alliance of Labour, scorned parliamentary action, and hence denied the Labour Party its support. The second was that the many sharp recessions of the period produced a relatively large surplus of labour which helped to discourage strike action. The next was the small scale nature of New Zealand society. This severely limited the growth of working class consciousness on a scale which few historians have recognized.

During these years only about a third of the population lived in the four main centres. The rest dwelt in a host of tiny hamlets, townships, small towns and on isolated farms. Even the suburbs surrounding the main centres tended to be like villages in contrast to the sprawling, amorphous character they have taken on today. Workplaces were correspondingly small. For example, just a third of total factory employees were engaged in units with over one hundred hands, and the ratio of employers to employees was appreciably greater than in Australia and Britain. The consequence was that most New Zealanders were forced to associate across class boundaries. In Wellington, for instance, almost half the brides whose fathers were manual workers selected grooms whose fathers had middle class occupations. Almost everywhere in New Zealand, the two most popular sports, cricket and rugby, very rarely had teams that were purely derived from one particular socio-economic group. Detailed research has found the same pattern with the class composition of neighbourhoods of towns and suburbs; in the ten largest provincial towns and in a cross-section of Labour-held electorates, a minuscule fraction of wage-earning households resided in streets consisting wholly or predominantly of fellow wage earners.

Under these conditions most workers and their families were heavily exposed to the social pressures of their middle class friends, employers, leisure companions, relatives and neighbours. As the political opinions and attitudes of the middle classes were overwhelmingly conservative — hostile to trade unions, strikes, socialism, and the whole labour movement — the effect of cross-class mixing was to make 'working class Tories' of a large number of wage-earning people. It was partly because of this that the Labour Party's electoral growth stagnated after 1919. At every general election

The period saw a rapid growth in secondary schooling, especially for girls. The technical high school played a vital role in this trend. King Edward Technical College, Dunedin. *Hocken Library*

in the 1920s the party received only about 25% of the total poll at a time when manual workers and their adult dependents comprised about 60% of the voting population. Even in the so-called Labour strongholds, the inner city electorates, which were 66% to 80% manual workers in composition, the party obtained an average of only 54% of the vote. A study of a typical year, 1925, has shown that in the ten largest provincial town seats the discrepancy was even greater. Here the proportion of manual workers in the voting population ranged between 56% and 64% (with an average that was exactly the national average), and yet the poll for Labour varied tremendously between 8% and 47% with an average of about 20%. (The outcome was little affected by three-cornered contests.) A simple process of deductive reasoning suggests that, with the exception of the mining and timber milling seats, the gap in the rural constituencies was worse still.

Labour's leaders had little idea that the key reason for the party's electoral failures was that half or more of its 'natural' supporters rejected it. Nor did they understand the social mechanism that partly lay at the root of the problem. Instead they mistakenly believed that the party had won over nearly all wage earners, but as these were only a minority of the electorate, it had to broaden its class appeal, to drop its socialist image which antagonized the majority — the clerks, small business people, and most of all the farmers (who, along with their adult dependents, actually comprised a mere 14% of the voting population). To this end the party made the historic decision in 1927

A key thrust behind the repatriation of returned servicemen after World War One was their settlement on 'rehab.' farms. Land was either bought by the Government or purchased by the men directly with cheap loans borrowed from the Government. The scheme was one of the greatest disasters in social planning New Zealand has ever known, and has contributed to the view that this was a period of failure. The land was often of poor quality and the men frequently lacked the appropriate skills. The scheme triggered a massive land speculation boom and the 'rehab.' farmers were left with huge debts which could not be serviced when primary prices collapsed in 1921-2. *Alexander Turnbull Library*

to abolish the land nationalization policy, effectively renouncing its doctrinaire socialist principles, and moving towards the political centre.

But if Labour in its ignorance of social facts did a lot to bring political polarization to an end, Massey with a more intuitive grasp of social realities, did even more. Belying its reputation for selective inertia, the Massey Government had an activist social policy which centered on the promotion of home ownership and secondary education opportunities.

Although its administration of education was based on the reforms of the previous Liberal era and was generally not innovative, the government was highly sensitive to the growing demands by parents that their children be equipped with the qualifications enabling them to enter skilled trades and white collar jobs. It invested strongly in the provision of places at secondary schools with the consequence that enrolments leaped. Before 1914 about one-third of primary leavers went on to secondary school; by 1930 slightly more than half did so. Enrolments grew most rapidly at technical high schools, and most of their pupils came from the lower socio-economic strata.

With home ownership, thousands of ex-servicemen who had been without property before the war, obtained cheap urban housing finance through the government's open handed administration of the 1915 Discharged Soldier Settlement

The suburban sprawl of Dunedin was characteristic of all the main centres by the 1920s and grew rapidly at this time. Multitudes of better-off wage-earners borrowed cheap loans from the Government to buy a 'home of their own' on suburban sections. *Hocken Library*

Act. (The success of this has been obscured by the failure of farm settlement scheme under the same act.) An even greater number of workers were tempted to buy their own homes through Reform's vigorous implementation of the 1906 Advances to Workers Act, which allowed wage and salary earners below a certain income to borrow money from the state on favourable terms. Although the supply of funding was cut to a trickle during the war, it poured out after 1919, especially after amending legislation in 1923 raised the maximum possible advance to 95% of the value of the property.

So active was the state in the promotion of home ownership that it became the largest mortgagee in the country. In an average year it lent a sum equivalent to about two-thirds of the total value of new urban housing. With all this stimulation the proportion of wage and salary earners householders who owned their houses climbed from 36% in 1916 to about 50% in 1926. By that year New Zealand had probably the highest rate of ownership in the world.

Unlike its repressive handling of the strikes of 1912–1913, Reform's intervention in education and housing went some way in providing a permanent solution to working class discontent. As education standards improved, the proportion of white collar employees increased and the proportion of unskilled workers fell significantly. Over the long term these changes weakened the labour movement. They whittled away the

The cult of domesticity had a central place in New Zealand ideology during the 1920s. It helped to keep down the proportion of women engaged in paid employment. *Hocken Library*

population base from which the movement had drawn its most radical supporters and leaders.

On top of this, the intervention weakened radical tendencies because it gave working people greater access to long term satisfactions. In this context, better education probably did less to fulfill desires than did the possession of a home of one's own. Whereas education beyond the rudiments had never been an aspiration of colonial workers, acquiring land had always been a central desire. Their proprietorial appetites had been whetted by the land surplus of the frontier (one-third of workers with households owned houses in 1892) and by a state tradition of making land available. A core theme in immigration propaganda presented New Zealand as a labourer's paradise where the industrious were invariably rewarded with the joys of property. Land had also played a critical role in the wage earner's material culture; small scale production of food for subsistence purposes and sale had acted as the equivalent of a welfare state, giving workers and their families something to fall back on during the frequent bouts of unemployment and in the years of retirement. These economic functions of land owning became less important as people moved to the towns. The home came to be valued more as the place of family affection and warmth, of 'Merry and Laughing Children gathered round Loving Parents' as Walter Nash, the General Secretary of the Labour Party, put it in 1922.

For the wives of working class men who bought 'cosy homes' in this period, intense pleasure came from the pride of ownership. A women writer for the 'Home Circle' page in the *Maoriland Worker*, a labour weekly, described the feeling this way:

> Every woman at the back of her mind, cherishes one dear dream — that some day she will have 'a home of her own.' It doesn't matter a scrap whether we work in a shop, an office, a factory, or in some one else's house, we're all 'sisters under one skin' in this matter of The Big Dream. A 'Home' of some kind is an absolute necessity to the woman who IS a woman.
>
> So the 'Roomer' piles her cushions and books, hangs her curtains and pictures, and pictures, and plays 'Let's Pretend.' By and bye, if Fate is kind, she will attain the Reality!
>
> I wonder if we ever remember that we are putting little bits of our own identity into these Homes of ours — whether they are permanent, or just temporary make-shifts?
>
> For it is absolutely true, that houses and rooms Do acquire some Aura or atmosphere from those who inhabit them . . . .
>
> What a fascination there is in a New House — a house that is Ours, even if it is only a two roomed whare, just made for us, and for nobody else, with its walls all fresh, and uncontaminated by the worries, perplexities and unhappiness of other people. Just a sensitive film on which we print all our own records.

The narrow focus of these (obviously real) satisfactions was the inevitable product of a society that continued to believe that a woman's place was in the home. Mothers were taught to be professional child carers, and girls learnt home craft in schools. Women, especially working class women, were given limited scope for fulfillment outside family life. Women's occupations had diversified considerably since the turn of the century. Domestic service, the traditional mainstay, diminished in relative importance and office jobs, nursing, teaching, and working in shops had increased. But the proportion of female school leavers designating the 'home' as their destination remained very high, at around 33%. Very few women still worked after marriage. The fraction of all women actively engaged in the work-force remained at around 17% to 18% from the turn of the century until the 1930s, with a brief rise to 20% after the end of the World War I.

The rise of working class home ownership destroyed radicalism not only by giving contentment but also by imposing restraints. In Massey's words, it allowed New Zealand to 'have VERY MUCH LESS OF THIS BOLSHEVISTIC NONSENSE'. The families who purchased houses with the Reform Government's assistance or believed and hoped that they would be able to do so, had something to conserve. Labour's objective of abolishing capitalism had little appeal to these small capitalists or would-be capitalists and worse still, Labour's detailed programme of land nationalization was a direct threat to their petit-bourgeois interests and sentiments. Similarly, workers became more averse to taking strike action, for strikes made mortgages difficult to service, and placed at risk the collateral — the savings represented by the home.

To sum up, the period saw outstanding success in one fundamental area of civilized life. It began with social conflict and ended with a new found consensus. Although this achievement was obscured by the country's lurch into economic depression, it was not forgotten by Massey's spiritual descendants, the National Party, from the 1950s to the 1970s. The National Party used the promotion of education and home ownership opportunities, with the additional refinement of full employment, to keep themselves in office and to give New Zealand another long period of political stability.

It is true that Massey financed the rise of New Zealand as a property owners' (or mortgagors') democracy by borrowing overseas, and that the demands of the accumulated debt load forced the government to slash spending with such painful results in the depression. But to condemn him (and the subsequent United Government which did the same) for worsening the depression is to blame them for not having historical hindsight.

The historical convention that Reform was simply a farmer's party without a social policy is not true. Certainly Reform failed to deal in a positive fashion with working class discontent before 1919, which gave it no option but to repress the discontent by restricting civil rights. But its hands were tied by the demands of running a war administration in harness with the Liberals (Ward had the finance portfolio), by the draining of the government's financial resources into defence expenditure, by Massey's long absences abroad from 1915 to 1919, and by the likelihood that any concessions to radical opinion would intensify the middle class flight towards the PPA. Furthermore, the 'Red Feds' were so intractable that it is doubtful if any gesture would have worked. Another historical convention which is wrong is that through the period New Zealand was rigid with conformity. The reverse was obviously the case, at least up to the early 1920s. The social strife brought by the PPA and the militant Left is proof positive that there was too little conformity, not too much.

Finally there is the charge that the period when the farmers took over is largely a sterile one in literature and the arts. Although this cannot be denied, it overlooks the work of a consummate and neglected political artist though not a very attractive person, W. F. Massey, a farmer whose talent contributed so much to the healing of a society's wounds.

A demonstration of the unemployed in Christchurch. What was unique was the extent to which the unemployed blamed their plight on an unjust social system, and demanded the right to work. *Hocken Library*

9. *Depression and War*
(1931–1949)

ERIK OLSSEN

This period began with depression and ended with the fear of depression exorcized. It began when the fastest mails still travelled on land or by sea, and ended in aircraft. It began with the most limited forms of assistance available to the unemployed, the destitute, the sick and the homeless; it ended with the welfare state securely in place and accepted by both political parties. It began in a mood of insular complacency which had stultified writers and artists for almost twenty years; it ended with a renaissance. During this period New Zealanders endured a massive depression and yet another world war; in the process they elected a Labour Government which transformed the fabric of New Zealand society and helped produce a new sense of pride in New Zealand as a nation. By 1949 New Zealanders were again convinced that theirs was the most just and prosperous society in the world. By 1949, however, the world was frozen into the Cold War, India had won independence, and the Communists had triumphed in China. Still more momentous, perhaps, the nuclear age had begun in 1945.

By 1932 everybody realized that the depression was more severe than anybody had expected. Export prices had collapsed and unemployment had soared. By October 1933 around 80,000 people were unemployed. The Unemployment Act (1930) had required all unemployed Pākehā men over twenty years old to register and pay an unemployment levy. The Government's attempt to balance its budget forced the Unemployment Board to keep cutting relief rates and making relief work scarcer. Women and youths were not entitled to benefits. Voluntary societies and hospital boards, which in the past had attempted to provide assistance to the unemployed and the destitute, could not cope with the tidal wave of human suffering.

In March 1932 several concerned citizens formed a Vocational Guidance Committee to assist young men not eligible for relief. They could do little. By 1934 some 600 boys had been placed on farms. Their wages were extremely low and many boys refused to go. Little more was done for women. Well-meaning citizens tried to

Pickets outside a looted tobbacconist's premises at the entrance to His Majesty's Arcade, Auckland. Shopkeepers later advertised in ways that made clear their sympathy with the rioters. *NZ Herald*

equip unemployed women with domestic skills such as dressmaking, cooking, and embroidery. The National Council of Women opened a register but there was little point in registering. The Māori fared little better. Most Pākehā believed that 'the communal method of living in pahs' allowed the Māori to survive unemployment without much hardship. Although Māori men were not required to register and pay the unemployment levy, about 8000 did so. They described relief work as mirimiri rori — stroking the road. Unlike unemployed women and youths, however, most of the Māori unemployed lived in rural areas, and a large number — about 5000 by 1938 — were employed under Sir Apirana Ngata's Development Schemes.

By the end of 1931 the Unemployment Board ran six relief schemes. Regardless of which relief scheme offered assistance, no relief was provided without work, the rates of pay were less than those in the private sector, and every fourth week saw all relief workers stood down. During that fourth week the unemployed depended on private charity and the Hospital Boards. Everybody had their own ideas. The *New Zealand Observer* suggested that Auckland's unemployed should be sent north to Ninety Mile Beach to clear away the shells of dead toheroas so that Wizard Smith could have a better chance to break the world land speed record!

Although only a small proportion of unemployed men were sent to relief camps, the camps themselves became symbols of the Coalition Government's heartless indifference to human misery. *NZ Herald*

Government retrenchment had already contributed largely to the ranks of the unemployed but after the election of 1931 and the formation of a Coalition Government retrenchment gathered momentum. Relief rates were again cut, the Government proposed camps for the unemployed, and civil servants suffered a second 10% wage cut. Pensions were also cut for the old and for returned servicemen, including the disabled. The Government also proposed to abolish compulsory arbitration in order to allow private-sector wage levels to be forced down. In this ugly context a number of Hospital Boards, notably Otago's, refused to provide any form of relief over the Christmas holiday period. These boards, like government and local councils, had to juggle increasing demands and falling revenues. The unemployed reacted violently.

By 1932 some 13,000 unemployed had joined the Unemployed Workers' Movement. The UWM also formed women's branches. The Communist Party, many of whose members were active in the UWM, also established a women's division which published its own paper. Many women became very active. The riots of 1932 exploded quite unexpectedly in Dunedin, Wellington and Auckland. Queen Street shops had their windows broken and many were looted. Mounted police attempted to chase the

"J. Edwards addressing the demonstrators." A vast crowd had followed a procession of civil servants, protesting at their second wage cut, with mounting excitement. Rumours of police attacks were rife. Shortly after this a constable clubbed Edwards as he rose to urge the crowd to disperse, and the Queen Street Riot began. *NZ Herald*

rioters from the streets. In Wellington mounted police attacked unemployed demonstrators. Although no rioting occurred in Christchurch, the bitter tramway strike of 1932 led to violence. In all the cities special police were recruited to strengthen the hand of law and order. Some proposed establishing a New Guard modelled on a paramilitary organization in Sydney. And for weeks the country asked:

'Where is Jim Edwards hiding?' Edwards, a member of the Communist Party, had helped to organize and lead the great demonstration by Auckland's unemployed which resulted in mayhem when he, climbing onto a soapbox to ask his followers to go home peacefully, was struck down by an excited constable. Inside the Town Hall, where civil servants were denouncing their latest wage cut, somebody cried 'There is blood in the streets!' A group of women invaded the stage and began singing 'The Red Flag'.

By 1949 the riots came to be seen less as a threat to civil society than as an understandable human reaction to misery. Even during the depression, radicals reproachfully observed 'that the dreadful fact about Mr. Depression's [victims] is not their revolt but their apathy'. Most New Zealanders, however, did not take this view in 1932. The Government reacted by postponing the next election from 1934 until 1935 and passing the Public Safety Conservation Act. Special police were mobilized. Some small effort was made to assist unemployed women. It also promoted with more vigour the idea of despatching unemployed men, including married men, to rural camps. The churches spearheaded resistance to this last proposal. The values of domesticity helped to define the limits to government action. Several local bodies made small plots of suburban land available in the hope that the jobless would become independent; often, however, the garden plots were miles from home.

The militant unemployed — encouraged by Labour — had tried to frighten the government into moderation. Perhaps they succeeded. New relief schemes, such as the goldmining one, worked quite well. Many young men had a marvellous time. Most did not. The unions, scared, offered little help. The seamen, the miners and the freezing workers resisted wage cuts by striking; they failed. Other unions lost most of their members. The Auckland carpenters, for instance, had 1000 members on its books in 1933 but could not find half of them and only sixty were 'engaged fully at the trade'. Young men no longer signed on for apprenticeships. The unemployed bore the brunt of the suffering. Breadwinners could not earn bread. Their wives had to make do as best they could, improvising clothing out of sugar sacks, trying to feed their families, scrounging and begging. They also had to keep their homes clean and tidy to impress the voluntary inspectors who checked to make sure that families really needed assistance. One man, Bill Richards, recently a father (and deaf from a baton blow in Cuba Street), received a lecture on the need for self-control. For good measure he and his wife were told to get rid of their canary. He was to devote the next thirty years of his life to the destruction of the hated system.

The UWM, and the less-militant alternatives that emerged after the riots, tried at times to organize resistance. When bailiffs moved in to move families out for falling behind on their rent, the UWM often shifted the furniture back in. They tried to organize strikes by relief workers. It was impossible to win. Yet, for the first time ever, large numbers of the unemployed denounced the capitalist system for their fate, demanded award wages for relief workers, and upheld the banners of human dignity. The militant among them — women and men — were to become the fulcrum for a revolution, although not of the sort that many of them expected and wanted.

Unemployment did not preoccupy everybody. Large numbers of people were scarcely aware that unemployment was a major problem. For people who had jobs or lived on fixed incomes, life was certainly no worse than it had been in the 1920s and for many it was better. The cost of living fell. There was also plenty of other news. The death of Phar Lap (the great racehorse) in April 1932 attracted almost as much attention as the riots from the daily newspapers, all of which fully supported the Government. The body-line cricket series in Australia, where England's fastest bowler aimed at the batsman's head rather than the wicket, attracted enormous publicity. Many blamed the unemployed for their own plight. It came to be believed that the leading figures in the Coalition Government shared such a view. Coates, whose imaginative attempts to grapple with the depression have only recently been recognized, was widely reputed to have told a delegation of unemployed that they could eat grass.

The Government's strategy for dealing with the depression was simple; it tried to reduce the internal cost structure and to balance its own books. Coates devalued the pound and established the Reserve Bank. Mortgages were investigated and reduced in many cases. In 1934 the Unemployment Board began paying a dole for those physically unfit, and to all men older than fifty years who had been on the largest relief scheme, No. 5, for over twenty-six weeks. Coates established a scheme to encourage the revival of the construction industry. Under this scheme subsidies were given and in 1934-1935 these were extended successfully. Otherwise, the captains of industry were left to their own devices. In 1935, however, the government made a modest attempt to expand its public works programme.

But between 1933 and 1935 many New Zealanders blamed either politics or the government's interventionism for the depression. The rapid rise of the New Zealand Legion in 1933 fed on a widespread feeling, especially among the educated middle classes, that the politicians, in their miserly search for political advantage, had failed to grapple with the crisis. The formation of a Coalition Government — based on the wartime precedent — did not appease these people, in part because Labour had stood aside. Dr. Campbell Begg, the founder of the Legion, was politically naïve and had no solution to the depression. The Legion grew spectacularly (and terrified many in the Labour Party who believed that it was a fascist movement), and disappeared as quickly as it rose. The yearning for national unity and leadership did not die so quickly. Community events — fairs, parades, festivals and sing-songs — remained the major vehicles for expressing this mood. Coates was the most likely leader, but his economic nationalism was unpalatable, partly because it had no impact on unemployment and because it hurt the pockets of many. Devaluation, in particular, outraged many people. Importers and merchants were most upset. In 1935 they formed a new right wing party, the Democrats, to punish Coates and the Coalition. In the absence of political leadership, people flocked to see the new aviators, especially Kingsford Smith and Jean Batten. Here, at least, was a promise that the old values of individualism could master the new machine — industrial society.

By 1935, however, the Government could do little right. A majority of New

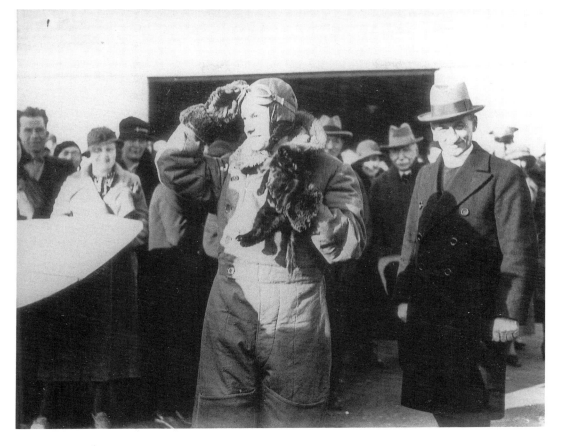

Jean Batten was the first woman to fly solo from England to Australia, in May 1934. Over the next three years she made a number of record flights, including one from England to New Zealand in 1936, and became a national hero. *E.A. Phillips Collection, Hocken Library*

Zealanders now agreed with the UWM that the unemployed could not be blamed for unemployment; instead they laid the responsibility with Government. Indeed the rise of the Douglas Social Credit movement reflected a growing conviction, particularly strong in the middle-class suburbs and in dairying regions, that the depression itself was unnecessary. In 1932 W. N. Field wrote *The Story of the Slump: who caused it and why*. The Labour Opposition also put forward the same message. Labour leaders insisted that New Zealand had the resources to provide everybody with work, food and housing; only the political will was lacking. Equally important in creating a new mood was the growing knowledge concerning the impact of unemployment on individuals and their families. Reports about sub-standard housing, malnutrition, and crime appeared in the newspapers and the weeklies.

The growing belief that the depression should never have happened and that the problem of unemployment ought to be the government's first priority reflected in part the changing composition of the unemployed. In 1929/30 some 8% of the unemployed lived in the four main cities and 65% of them were unskilled workers. By 1935, by contrast, only 40% of the unemployed were unskilled and over 60% lived in the main cities. Although the proportion of unemployed clerical and shop workers increased from less than 5% to only 7%, their children could not get jobs.

Even some professional men were unemployed. By 1935 1200 teachers were receiving rationed work and being paid at relief rates. Many others received no help at all. Equally important, the age structure of the unemployed changed. In 1929 almost one quarter of all unemployed men were younger than twenty-five years old; by 1937 (the next year for which figures are available) this proportion had fallen to just over 5%. In 1929 around 29% of the unemployed were older than forty-five years old; by 1937 this proportion was almost 52%. Worse still, of course, whereas in 1929 relatively few of the unemployed had been in that state for more than a year (and most for less than three months) by 1937 not only had the great majority of unemployed been without work for more than a year, but the older one was, on average, the longer one had been without work.

Relief depots, schools, churches and hospitals also provided the contexts in which the more fortunate came in contact with the unemployed and could see for themselves the material and moral consequences of unemployment. Photographs of relief camps where the jobless lived in tents, helped spread the UWM view that these were fit only for slaves. The medical profession, politically right wing, agreed that some form of national insurance was essential to help the poor afford their services. By 1935 most of the churches in New Zealand had concluded that full employment ought to be the main task of Government. Even the Anglicans, never known for radicalism, decided that full employment must be basic to a just and Christian society. The rapid growth of the free milk schemes for schoolchildren in 1935 reflected the new mood. Henry Kelliher's *Mirror*, an influential weekly, played a lively role in promoting the free milk scheme. Some went further. The Auckland Clergy Group, which consisted of six clergy from different denominations, announced in September 1935 that 'our faith in God renders it impossible to believe that the present economic situation is in accordance with his will . . . ' .

The belief that New Zealand had been the world's social laboratory undoubtedly contributed to the mental revolt against the government. Although in comparative terms unemployment was much less in New Zealand than in Australia or Britain (not to mention the United States or Germany), by 1935 it had created a much greater sense of outrage. In *Man Alone* (1939) John Mulgan's tramp cried: 'I knew Absalom, oh Absalom, and Seddon, I knew Seddon. They are no more now, no more.' A new mood of social realism emerged. Organizations were founded to provide the public with facts. Individuals, such as Dr. E. B. Gunson of the Auckland Hospital Board, conducted their own investigations and publicized the results. In 1934 the UWM-sponsored march of the unemployed from Gisborne to Wellington attracted sympathetic national publicity. Ironically, with the exception of a handful who graduated from Otago's Faculty of Home Science, New Zealand's universities produced no sociologists or social statisticians. The only sociological work of note, H. C. D. Somerset's *Littledene* (1937), evoked nostalgia for the close-knit rural society that some still believed was central to the New Zealand way of life. That view, however, became less tenable during the depression when urban realities slowly forced themselves onto the nation's attention.

Social realism also dominated the arts. The documentary became a major vehicle for artistic expression in the American film industry. The work of British and American documentary photographers was also well known. The *New Zealand Observer* published some excellent investigative journalism and used photography to capture the reality of such events as the riots. In fiction the same mood was apparent. In *Children of the Poor* (1934) John A. Lee, the Labour MP, savagely depicted the consequences of poverty for a young child. In *The Hunted* (1936) he pursued his analysis. In Lee's hand, social realism was a catalyst for change; he wished to shock people into a recognition that the present economic system had failed to deliver human welfare and decency. In *Man Alone* (1939) John Mulgan also depicted the consequences of the depression for his solitary hero and used his imaginative sympathy to reassess the significance of the riots, unemployment, and the depression. The other important novelist of this period, Robin Hyde, also used social realism. She, unlike the other two, had worked as a journalist and wrote many investigative pieces for the *New Zealand Observer*. In two powerful novels she explored, through the life of James Douglas Stark, the impact of the first World War and the depression.

Although social realism provided the techniques and methods for these novelists, in all cases it was designed to provide a dramatic contrast between promise and reality. Seddon, long dead, became a shorthand symbol of what had been promised and in an earlier period achieved. The young historian, J. C. Beaglehole, was not alone in feeling dismay and shock at the distance which had opened up between the promise of 'God's own' and the reality. The writers of the thirties were also nationalists, determined to explore and celebrate New Zealand. The young Frank Sargeson, whose *Conversations With My Uncle* (1936) used the techniques of social realism to explore New Zealand life detached from the events of the 1930s, was to become the best known.

The belief that New Zealand was destined to become a copy of Britain became less relevant during the depression. Many intelligent young people rejected the idea altogether. Ian Milner spoke for many when he wrote in *Tomorrow*, a radical periodical, 'Two years ago I left New Zealand to "go Home" but two years in England as a New Zealander has failed to convince me that this is other than a foreign land.' The apparent irrelevance of the old dream helped to release new energies. Although the quest for cultural identity had been pursued for a long time, young artists and poets began afresh (almost as though nobody else had ever lived here). Young poets — Denis Glover, R. A. K. Mason, Allen Curnow and A. R. D. Fairburn — rejected the view that they should celebrate natural beauty, a sort of literary arm to the landscape painting tradition, and instead chose to explore the human predicament in these islands and the islands themselves. The dominant tone was caustic and critical.

Allen Curnow was one of the brilliant young poets of the 1930s. He became not only the most influential literary critic, but also the architect of a New Zealand poetic tradition, and even of a sensibility. Photograph by Clifton Firth. *Clifton Firth Collection, Auckland Public Library*

The depression also brought a change in the way that realist painters viewed their world. Until the 1930s this world had seemed quite simple; increasingly artists sought for a solution within a framework that bordered on socialism. Christopher Perkins — *Silverstream Brickworks* and *Taranaki* (1931) — and Rita Angus painted industrial landscapes. Russell Clark — *Saturday Night* (1934) and *Late Night* (1942) — painted manual workers in the towns. William J. Reed and A. Lois White used their painting as a vehicle for protest against social conditions. More important in the long run, however, was the way in which young artists — Rita Angus, Toss Woollaston, Colin McCahon — dismissed romanticism from landscape painting. Clarity and harshness now dominated the genre.

In November 1935 the country went to the polls. In some societies people waged war to effect the sort of change that occurred; New Zealand has elections. M. J. (Micky) Savage led Labour to its historic victory. In Auckland large crowds shouted with glee 'off with his head', as each Tory was defeated. In the various Trades Halls around the country the partying went on for days. The new government had won overwhelming support within the urban working class and had also swept the suburbs and the secondary towns. In the more recently-settled dairying regions of the North Island Labour also did much better than it ever had before. Shortly after the election

Michael Joseph Savage on election night, 1935. He may look tired and thoughtful, but Labour's followers were ecstatic, and in many towns the revelling lasted for days. *NZ Herald*

Labour also came to an arrangement with the Ratana Church. As a result the three Ratana members joined the Labour caucus. Vast crowds flocked to the country's railway stations to cheer the newly-elected Labour members as they headed for Wellington.

The new government moved with speed. The unemployed were given a Christmas bonus. In 1936 the Reserve Bank was nationalized; a guaranteed price was introduced for dairy farmers; the old age pension was restored and then increased; a state-owned broadcasting system was established (and one channel undertook the responsibility for broadcasting the proceedings of Parliament); compulsory arbitration was restored and compulsory unionism introduced; the Arbitration Court was instructed to introduce the forty-hour week when possible and to provide a minimum wage for all workers sufficient to support a man, his wife, and three children. The Teachers' Colleges were re-opened and the five year-olds went back to school. Relief workers were given award wages. A housing scheme was established in order to provide every New Zealander with 'a house fit for a Cabinet Minister', as Walter Nash, the Minister of Finance, put it. More startling still, the Reserve Bank was instructed to provide interest-free credit to finance the housing scheme. Bob Semple, ex-Red Fed and now the Minister of Public Works, symbolized the new mood of optimism and confidence when he climbed into a bulldozer and demolished a great stack of wheelbarrows. Instead of using the most labour-intensive methods in order to make the work go further the new government had resolved that if a job was worth doing, it was worth doing at award rates of pay and as efficiently as possible. Conservatives still feared that the country would be bankrupt; they were frightened.

Savage's Government had won office at the right time. Although 47% of the voters chose Labour candidates, divisions within the Coalition gravely weakened the old government. Besides, export prices were recovering and the old Coalition Government, successful in balancing its budget since 1932, had also hoarded a tidy nest-egg of sterling which Labour cheerfully spent on public works. The extent of the change which occurred in 1935 is difficult now to recapture. Savage and his Cabinet appear to have put New Zealand back on its true course as the most advanced and humane society in the world, to have fulfilled the original dream. This was not accepted by everybody in 1935. Five of Savage's Cabinet, including Savage himself, were Australians. Six of them had belonged to the old 'Red' Federation of Labour. Four (John A. Lee, who became under-Secretary to the Prime Minister is included) had graduated from industrial school (the Borstal's predecessor), the school with the largest representation in the Labour Cabinet. Four of the new government had also served at least one prison sentence for subversion or advocating violence. There had not been such a turning of the tables, such a dismissal of the old order, since 1890. Despite the dominance of Australians in the new government, or perhaps because of it, it was vigorously nationalistic. In *Labour Has A Plan* (1935), written by Lee, this note was stridently trumpeted:

> New Zealand, with its temperate and sub-tropical zones, with its potential water power, its timber, coal and iron resources, its fisheries, its holiday resorts, can be made the centre of a new civilization. Under Forbes Coates we 'follow Britain' to intensify misery. Under the Labour Government we shall use our own physical resources and apply the progressive genius that has been dormant in these past decades and erect the new social state that will once again cause New Zealand to inspire the world . . . This Policy was made in New Zealand by New Zealand citizens who know New Zealand conditions. It is not exotic, but native to our problems.

Unemployment began to fall; prosperity to return. The housing scheme symbolized the fulfilment of that promise. By March 1937 Fletcher Construction Company had two state-built joinery factories working twenty-four hours a day producing timber for the new houses. Land had been bought in all the main cities and a host of small towns. The first nails had been driven in Labour's new houses. Wherever possible all the materials to be used were to be New Zealand-made. Conservatives still muttered in public that such a scheme could never work. In private many agreed with George Forbes that houses built 'with the highest paid workers in the world, at the lowest cost heard of, makes our policy of orthodox finance seem almost prehistoric'. Hope returned. Even defeat at the hands of the Springboks in 1937 did nothing to slow the emotional recovery of New Zealanders. In 1938, when Savage announced to the tumultuous cheers of the Labour Party Conference that his government would provide social security from 'the cradle to the grave', the promise of Labour had been delivered. 'Applied lunacy,' snorted the Opposition. 'Applied Christianity,' replied the Prime Minister.

In foreign policy too Labour asserted a new pride in the independence of New Zealand. Savage appointed William Jordan, an ex-Cockney policeman, as High Commissioner to London and the League of Nations. Jordan's strictures upon the devious diplomats of the old world won him an international reputation in the 1930s. One historian of the League compared him to one of Oliver Cromwell's Roundheads because of his genius for blunt speech and simple moral judgement. Ironically, New Zealand's independence attracted enormous attention. Labour stood against appeasement. The government rejected the Anglo-French attempt to recognize the Italian conquest of Abyssinia. The government insisted that aggressors be dealt with firmly by the League, even when they were powerful states such as Japan. Labour believed that there was nothing wrong with the League except that its members had betrayed the ideal of collective security.

In defence policy too the new government struggled to define the interests of New Zealand and the military capacity required to protect them. Here it was less successful. The rise of totalitarianism in Europe and Asia deeply outraged not only the Labour Government but the Labour movement. For this reason alone, Labour was willing to reconsider its long hostility towards the Empire and the navy. In 1939, when Savage sadly announced that New Zealand was again at war, his motives were more complex. New Zealand's government entered World War II without question, because it had long been convinced that the peace-loving nations of the world should band together to defeat aggressors. In a quavering voice the dying Prime Minister invoked the heritage of loyalty to Britain: 'Where Britain goes we go, where Britain stands we stand . . . ' . According to his private secretary, the Irish-Australian Savage, on the verge of his conversion to Catholicism, was reluctant to use the famous sentence.

The outbreak of war helped bring a long-simmering dispute within Caucus to a head. The flamboyant and truculent John A. Lee, also an important novelist, had long resented his exclusion from Cabinet. Savage neither liked nor trusted him. The Prime Minster considered *Children Of The Poor* in parts disgusting. Lee had spearheaded a rebellion against Cabinet in a number of areas, notably economic policy. As one of the architects of 'insulationism', Lee had long favoured the introduction of exchange and import controls as part of a strategy to insulate New Zealand from the booms and busts of international capitalism. Only behind the ramparts of 'insulationism', he believed, could New Zealand develop a more diverse economy and ensure that gains in welfare could be kept. Nash, a kindly man of infinite industry, never accepted this policy although events compelled him further and further along Lee's road. On 7 December 1938, in response to the rapid exhaustion of the country's sterling reserves, Nash had reluctantly instituted exchange controls and import controls. Only with the war, however, were these controls effectively implemented.

At the end of 1938 Lee claimed that the controls represented a major step towards a planned economy; Nash said they were a temporary expedient to deal with the short-term crisis. Lee's discontent had surfaced during the 1938 election. He attempted to make socialism the issue (an attempt which the Opposition happily assisted until Labour won). *Socialism in New Zealand* (1938) was Lee's most ambitious attempt to prove that socialism was indigenous to New Zealand and that the government had no alternative but to keep moving forwards towards a planned and insulated economy. Lee had become extremely critical of Nash and wrote a letter to all members of caucus summarizing the conflicts of the past and damning Nash as incompetent. This issue became public early in 1939 and at the Labour Party Conference in April, Lee was censured. The same conference elected him to the National Executive.

With the outbreak of war Lee urged that a returned soldier, such as himself, should be elected to Cabinet. Savage refused. He himself was dying of cancer, and should have undergone surgery before the 1938 election but had refused. He wanted to ensure his government's triumph and believed, probably rightly, that only he could provide the necessary leadership. In December 1939 Lee published an article in which, without naming Savage, he attacked the Prime Minister as mentally incompetent. Lee was sacked as Under-Secretary and the factions began manoeuvring for the Conference of 1940. Savage was a man of indomitable will. Just as he had postponed his operation and fought the 1938 election in great pain, so now he refused to die until the 1940 Conference. The startled and affronted delegates heard Savage's report read. The dying Prime Minister complained that Lee had made his life 'a living hell'. Others rose to say that Lee's article had killed Savage. The mood was heightened by regular bulletins concerning Savage's triumphant death. The conference voted to expel Lee. A handful of other delegates, including Norman Douglas, a one-armed trade union official, left with him. They promptly formed a Democratic Labour Party.

Peter Fraser succeeded Savage. The decision to send an expeditionary force abroad had already been taken and in June 1940, with remarkably little fuss, conscription for the forces and civilian needs was introduced. Fraser also moved to reduce dissent. The most remarkable consequence of the war, however, was to rescue Labour from the deteriorating economy of the late 1930s. The war created a political climate in which the government could impose a range of controls that would never have been tolerated in peacetime. The war also helped to consolidate the great reforms of the Savage Government, notably social security. The doctors had fought this measure until the end and then had refused to implement key sections of the act. Savage forced

Devonport children doing air-raid drill. After Japan's assaults on Pearl Harbour and Singapore, New Zealand prepared for attack. Blackouts, building air-raid shelters, and air-raid drill made everyone aware of the danger. *NZ Herald*

some concessions by threatening to allow Jewish doctors to migrate to New Zealand, but his death removed their most vigorous opponent. Fraser had never favoured key elements of the Social Security Act and negotiated an agreement with the doctors which allowed them to severely modify parts of the scheme. That compromise also contributed to wide acceptance of social security. The housing scheme, which had to be suspended when war began, had also won wide acceptance. In 1940 the National Party instructed all members to cease publicly attacking a scheme which enjoyed such extraordinary popularity. It was not only popularity at home but attention from abroad that helped to win public acceptance for these reforms.

The government's principal task between 1940 and 1945 was the war. Fraser and his Cabinet were determined, however, to avoid the mistakes that the Massey Government had made during World War I. In 1940 they instituted stabilization of prices. When this proved inadequate they convened an important conference and introduced a comprehensive price stabilization scheme, including subsidies where necessary on such staples as bread and butter. With price stability guaranteed the government and the Federation of Labour worked to maintain wage stability. Various products, such as petrol and later butter and other staples, were rationed. Import controls and shortages of shipping saw a remarkable growth in manufacturing. Rubber products, tanks, an extraordinary range of war materials were made in New Zealand. This growth came unplanned and unco-ordinated. From the sidelines Lee stridently urged a number of policies to introduce the planned development of industrial growth, but without success. Although some unions were disgruntled most accepted Labour's policy. Indeed the Federation of Labour, which Fraser had helped establish in 1937, played an important role in contributing to industrial harmony.

The war reinforced traditional gender roles even as it briefly opened new opportunities. Unlike in 1914-1918, however, nobody questioned the need for women in the armed forces (although not in combat roles). Nor did couples postpone marriage until the future looked more certain. Instead the marriage rate rose rapidly. As more and more men were conscripted, the government began urging women to undertake work traditionally done by men. Women ran farms, drove trucks and buses, worked as tram conductors and took over many of the lower-paid jobs. A system of Land Girls was set up to recruit young women for farm work. Women did many jobs once defined as un-feminine. The 17,000 American marines, not to mention visiting American sailors, helped to reassure women that they had not been unsexed. 'Over-paid, over-sexed, and over-here' was the male complaint. New standards of courtship became fashionable. The Americans provided the cutting thrust to an international process which re-defined femininity as sexual allure. The advertisers exploited the new possibilities. Although sex education was not available, Vital Books, run by John A. Lee and Norman Douglas, published *Bio-Sex F* and *Bio-Sex M* on the grounds that sexual happiness was necessary to mental health and happy marriages. The new definition of femininity survived the war but with peace the women were driven out of their wartime jobs. Queen Elizabeth was soon to remind women that their main duty now was to rebuild family life.

The war was also a contradictory experience for Māori. By and large Labour had dismantled the laws that discriminated against the Māori. *The Māori Today* (1940), edited by I. L. G. Sutherland, documented the dramatic gains and spelt out the continuing Māori demand for greater participation in decision making and the administration of policy. In October 1939 the Government agreed to establish an infantry battalion for Māori. Within three weeks 900 Māori had volunteered. The Government decided not to apply conscription to the Māori for fear of inflaming old wounds. It became necessary, however, to increase the Māori war effort — if only to disarm Pākehā critics.

In May 1941 Cabinet gave Paraire Paikea, a member of Cabinet since 1940, responsibility for recruiting. Paikea next offered to create a list of all adult Māori — the Native Department did not have one — and set up the Maori War Effort Organization. This nation-wide organization, operated and controlled by Māori, dealt with all war issues. Even the Tuhoe and Waikato took part, despite their bitterness over confiscations in the 1860s and conscription during the Great War. The tribe and the hapū became the administrative units. Paikea, and the national and tribal leaders, worked to build a united Māori front. Taha Māori was the way. Cabinet

Land Girls on Ruakura State Farm, Waikato. Women entered many occupations previously closed to them but this scheme was in part designed to train wives for farmers. *NZ Herald*

agreed to recognize tribal leadership in the armed forces. Recruitment proceeded and the MWEO's tribal committees expanded their functions. They ran the Māori manpower scheme and in 1942 appointed welfare workers to help young women sent to Wellington and Auckland. The government, despite Fraser's sympathy, only tolerated this remarkable experiment in self-government because of the war crisis. In 1945 the Maori Social and Economic Advancement Act ended the experiment. The government insisted — and many Pākehā agreed — that it had given the Māori mana motuhake. Many Māori disagreed.

The most exciting developments were abroad. The fall of France wiped out the earlier mood of euphoria, a mood that fed on the victory of HMS *Achilles* over the *Graf Spee* (a German battleship). The New Zealand Division had gone to Egypt in 1940 and had fought rearguard actions against the Germans in Greece and Crete in 1941. Indeed Fraser, after Greece and Crete, went to Europe to inform the British in no uncertain terms that the New Zealand Division was a national army; its total annihilation or capture was unacceptable. As in World War I, New Zealanders at home took an enormous pride in the exploits of their Division. John Mulgan, shortly

Reg Stillwell's Welcome Club, 1943. The arrival of American troops and the large military camps generated anxiety and anger among New Zealand men, but it was a momentous 'invasion'. *Canterbury Museum*

before his suicide and after the battle at El Alamein, wrote: 'Perhaps to have produced these men, for this one time, would be New Zealand's destiny.' The attack on Pearl Harbour in December 1941 and the fall of Singapore early in 1942 created a sense of crisis in New Zealand. The Home Guard was mobilized. Black-outs and air-raid drills became mandatory. The attack on Pearl Harbour persuaded the Australian government to withdraw its divisions to the Pacific. Fraser favoured the same step but was dissuaded by Churchill. In return a division of American marines arrived to defend New Zealand while the New Zealand Division remained in the Middle East and Italy throughout the war. In order to meet its responsibilities in the Pacific — and to Australia — the government agreed to mobilize another division.

The inability of Britain to defend New Zealand against Japan's southward thrust, uncertainty about Japan's intentions, and the arrival of a division of American soldiers all sharpened the deeper sense that New Zealand was embarking into a new and unknown world. The poets captured this mood superbly. John Lehmann claimed that only in New Zealand during the 1930s had there been a group of writers 'of more than local significance.' He featured a number of them in his Penguin anthologies. As Allen Curnow noted in his influential anthology *A Book of New Zealand Verse*

Home Guard, Mercury Bay. The mobilization of the Home Guard was New Zealand's desperate response to the risk of invasion, but the arrival of the Americans did more to quieten public fears. *NZ Herald*

1923-45, the depression had called in question so many inherited certainties that it sharpened the critical imagination. Loyalty to Empire and the desire to re-create British forms in the south seas no longer seemed satisfactory or sensible. The war raised the same questions with greater urgency. These poets spoke to the human condition by addressing such local questions. The landscape and the seascape became metaphors for exploring ideas and values.

New Zealand's centennial of 1940 had been overshadowed by the outbreak of war. For all that it provided an opportunity for celebrating 100 years of progress and interrupted prosperity. Thousands visited the centennial exhibition in Wellington and schoolchildren were brought in from all over the country. A number of important works were commissioned for the centennial. Eric McCormick's *Art and Letters in New Zealand* (1940) and Monte Holcroft's *The Deepening Stream* not only celebrated but provided a sensitive critical perspective of what had been achieved and in the process illuminated what might yet be achieved. The fortnightly national surveys, entitled *Making New Zealand*, proved enormously popular. Many authors contributed but they shared the belief that New Zealand could best be explained by looking at what had happened in New Zealand. It fell to a public servant, one of Coates's bright young men, W. B. Sutch, to write a brief interpretative history. This assault upon the nation's past earned Fraser's displeasure and he tried to prevent the book from being published. In 1941 the Wellington Co-operative Book Society published it as *Poverty and Progress in New Zealand.* J. C. Beaglehole's *Discovery of New Zealand* and F. L. W. Wood's *New Zealand in the World* proved less contentious. A number of young photographers, notably David Hall and John Pascoe, also began working in the realistic mode in order to capture on film not merely the reality of New Zealand's scenery but what it was to be New Zealanders. The poets, artists, critics, historians, and photographers were usually third or fourth generation New Zealanders. Their roots were here and they had a strong sense of place. They wished to grasp and communicate that sense. In the 1940s there was a large audience for their works.

The establishment of the Progressive Publishing Society in 1941 heralded the birth of cultural nationalism with a pink tinge. Sutch played a large role, and was conscripted into the army for his pains. He saw the Society as 'a synthesis of left-wing and "New Zealand" impulses', but in reality they represented competing interests. This radical intelligentsia published poetry, discussions of post-war reconstruction, various cultural analyses, and contemporary left wing political comment. The New Zealand New Writing series attracted the most controversy in part because the selection of stories and poems raised political issues; what was the correct stance? Some wanted proletarian art, others (less zealous) social commitment, yet others talked of vitalizing popular culture. In the end no political litmus test was used. The dream of creating a socialist-popular culture persisted, however, and the PPS published a remarkable range of work by New Zealanders. In 1945 Harry Tombs published the first *Arts in New Zealand Yearbook* 'with quiet assurance and national pride'. For all that, however, A. H. Reed picked the popular mood best as he expanded his publishing firm by including in his list a sizeable number of books about New Zealand. His own *Story of New Zealand* (1947), a celebration of the past as a moral fable, proved enormously popular. The radical intelligentsia, many of them employed in the University, was becoming isolated.

The government also moved vigorously in the 1940s to subsidize culture and to make it widely available to everybody. Labour's leaders had long wanted to improve the lot of working men and women. It is often forgotten that this meant to them making available the finest cultural products of western civilization. Resources were poured into the education system. The opening of the National Art Gallery symbolized the new resolve. In the 1940s the government created the National Film Unit (Fraser did it in 1941 under his wartime emergency powers by Cabinet minute after being greatly moved and impressed by the film *Country Lads*). The *Weekly Review*, a war-information newsreel, was produced by the Unit. The government also established the National Symphony Orchestra and the State Literary Fund. Some poets, notably Fairburn, bitterly attacked the growing role of the State in the creative arts. For Fairburn, the artist had to be alone and isolated; suffering, poverty, and rejection marked the path to achievement. The Labour Government had a more comfortable and pragmatic view. State patronage made up for the absence of private patronage. But the state was active in cultivating areas where there had already been remarkable private initiatives. The poets and artists of this period played a large part in defining both identity and purpose.

With the surrender of Germany, the New Zealand Division, mired in Italy since 1943, raced to Trieste to confront the Yugoslav Communists. Fraser would willingly have gone to war; Cabinet refused. Reconstruction now dominated Labour's agenda. New Zealand's excessive manpower commitments had bled the economy. Thousands of women had entered the workforce to do jobs that men previously had done. The government now wanted them to go home. Over 100,000 servicemen had to be integrated back into New Zealand society. Labour debated the wisdom of embarking upon an ambitious scheme for settling servicemen on farms. Some thought that New Zealand did not need more farmers. Others thought that more farmers would weaken Labour's political base. Despite such arguments the government launched an ambitious land settlement scheme. It also opened up educational opportunities to returned servicemen. Rationing and controls remained, however, as a gesture of solidarity with Britain.

Fraser and many in the Party, not to mention the increasingly vigorous National Party Opposition, now hoped that the Commonwealth would provide New Zealand with the security which Britain had failed to deliver. Fraser and Nash also played a vigorous role in international affairs. Fraser, quick and forceful, enjoyed considerable influence during the debates over establishing a new international organization, the United Nations. Nash was involved in planning a post-war economic order that would guarantee price stability and prevent the wide and erratic swings of the past. Although he played his part in establishing the International Monetary Fund, the Labour Caucus refused to endorse New Zealand's entry.

The desire to create a better world, more just and decent, permeated New Zealand society. The young especially were filled with brave new ideas about a brave new world. Although the welfare state was fully accepted, many people wanted to move forward. In state housing areas citizens banded together to form co-operative shops and community organizations. In Lower Hutt a group of young men and women planned an exciting venture in town planning and modern architecture. E. A. Plishke, an Austrian architect and a refugee from the Nazis, was the prophet of 'design and living for a modern age'. His impact on the Town Planning Division of the Housing Department had been considerable. His book, *Design and Living* (1947), was the manifesto for the new movement. His more exciting proposals now seem rather quaint and the politicians emasculated them. Some of his houses for private buyers, however, helped introduce modern design into New Zealand architectural practice and proved much more influential in the long run. The Fabian Society was revived by younger members of the Labour Party such as Dr. Martyn Findlay and Ormond Wilson. The Party itself lurched left briefly in the excitement. Despite Nash, the Bank of New Zealand was nationalized. In 1945 a motherhood endowment was introduced and a minimum wage provided for all workers not registered under the Arbitration Court. This last measure also provided a fortnight's annual holiday for all non-arbitration workers. Resources were also poured into schools and housing. New Zealand suffered a shortage in many areas because of the war.

The key to post-war New Zealand was the dramatic growth of the North Island and especially Auckland. By 1926 one-third of all New Zealand farmers were in Auckland province. The forced growth of manufacturing to meet the needs of war had not only led to the articulation of the doctrine of 'import substitution', but had seen urban Auckland grow dramatically. Rural electrification and the introduction of the motor truck had allowed the integration of an increasingly large and prosperous rural area into Auckland's economy. By 1949 Auckland had become the nation's manufacturing heartland for clothing, textiles, footwear, foodstuffs, domestic appliances, building materials and engineering. The port, the largest in the country, handled 26% of all trade although the chief exports were still butter, frozen meat, milk products, tallow, hides and skins. The city was also a major military base. In the 1940s the growth of the central plateau region — electric power, agriculture, and forestry — strengthened Auckland's position. The new towns — Tokoroa, Murupara, Tauranga — and Auckland's burgeoning suburbs were to provide the revitalized National Party with a new base.

Labour's leaders believed they had created a socialist society in which all people were guaranteed freedom from want, fear of illness and sickness. During the war, full employment had become a major objective of Government policy and in the late 1940s, despite fear of another depression, full employment remained. The main problems that the Government faced were generated by the persistence of wage controls and rationing in a period of rapidly rising expectations. The most highly-organized unions, notably the Auckland Watersiders and Carpenters, chafed at the restraints. For too long, these men believed, they had foregone their just deserts in the national interest. The Government responded with a heavy and at times draconian hand. Such measures merely deepened the rift. Outside the union movement, many other New Zealanders now chafed with the persistence of wartime rationing and regulations. In his memoir, *Hot Water Sailor*, Denis Glover caricatured the degree of bureaucratic interference in the life of ordinary citizens. The novelist Bill Pearson, in '*Fretful Sleepers*', a celebrated essay on New Zealand culture, described it as a 'busy-body state' which institutionalized the nosey-parker traditions of a small Protestant community. Government regulations determined almost everything. A man who wanted to build a house for his family found that the number of rooms he could build, the types of materials he could use, the height of the stud and various other matters were controlled by bureaucrats. National capitalized upon the growing frustration and Labour's inability to deal with the industrial unions effectively. Led by Sid Holland, a progressive businessman from the Christchurch suburbs who rejected the tradition of Forbes-Coates, National came close to defeating Labour in 1946 and finally accomplished the miracle in 1949.

The conflicts within New Zealand had their own long and complex histories. The waterfront industry, the powder room for the great upheaval of 1951, would require a book to have its history told. Although these conflicts had indigenous roots, they also seemed to mirror the increasing polarization of the world between communism, symbolized by the Soviet Union, and freedom symbolized by the United States. Although the Labour Government tried to deal firmly with union unrest, it could

Massey House, Wellington. Plishke was not the first architect in New Zealand to design buildings which expressed the spirit of modernism, but he became the best known prophet and practitioner of architectural modernism. *Alexander Turnbull Library*

never entirely forget that its own strength as a party depended upon union support. Although Fraser and his cabinet also strongly supported the developing Cold War strategies of the United States and Britain, National skilfully linked Communism abroad to industrial unrest at home. Many within the Labour Party were sceptical of Cold War rhetoric. These issues fused in 1949 when Fraser, persuaded that the Third World War might well begin within eighteen months, persuaded first his Cabinet and then a reluctant caucus to accept peacetime conscription. He toured the country and addressed the trades councils in the main cities; in each a motion of no confidence was passed in his face. The Labour Party Conference of 1949 reluctantly agreed to conscription if a majority of the voters indicated their acceptance of it in a referendum. Fraser had never been tolerant of dissent and the government's heavy-handed management of the referendum campaign did little to cheer its supporters and nothing to allay the fears of its enemies. The complex inter-relationship of issues, skilfully exploited by National, brought Labour down. The reforming government had become managers of the status quo; had cut itself off from the new currents of radical thought. National's promise of freedom and a forward march towards prosperity and a united New Zealand community won the support of most voters.

The voting nation in 1949 had experienced at least one world war and a depression. A sizeable minority had lived through two world wars and a depression. Nor, looking backwards, could the 1920s have been said to have compensated for a lifetime of deprivation. Not only had expectations risen but people were impatient to return to the domestic certainties which life had so far denied them. For many women and men, marriage, a family, and a house and garden in the suburbs was the consummation of their dreams. Their children might later describe the suburban utopia that flourished in the 1950s as boring, but to large numbers of New Zealanders such boredom was what they wanted. Life had given them more than their share of excitement.

Between the riots of 1932 and 1949 New Zealand society was transformed dramatically. By 1949 the depression itself was universally denounced by New Zealanders of all political persuasions. Even Holland promised that a National Government would never allow such a depression to happen again. The myth of a man-made depression where all had suffered equally now provided the coping-stone for the welfare state. Labour's partisan arguments of the 1930s had become part of a national consensus. National made it absolutely clear that if elected it would not attempt to undo any of the great welfare reforms. What they did promise, however, was to release New Zealand from its bureaucratic and regulatory shackles and to distribute the new consumer wealth more widely. Full employment remained an implicit goal of government policy. These remarkable changes and their rapid acceptance also helped re-establish the belief of most New Zealanders that theirs was the most just society in the world; once more the social laboratory. Scholars came from abroad as they had in the 1900s to study the miracle.

These extraordinary challenges to views that had been unquestioned in 1929, also released a powerful current of creative energy. The remaking of New Zealand society and politics was only the most dramatic expression of this. In all the arts young men and women struck out to find new ways of seeing the world they had inherited, new ways of defining what that world meant to them. For over 100,000 men and women who served in the armed forces, the voyage home was undertaken gladly. They had seen no other country that met their expectations. The establishment of *Landfall* in 1947 heralded the growing maturity of New Zealand cultural life. Yet for the majority of New Zealanders plays, operas, poems and novels were not what they most wanted from peace. They returned to the traditional pastimes of New Zealanders such as horse-racing, gardening, picnics, cricket, and rugby. Although a very successful New Zealand cricket team toured England in 1949, the trek of the All Blacks on the South African veldt that same year perhaps struck the strongest warning note about the voyage yet to be made. In order to accommodate the racist attitudes of white South Africans, Māori players were excluded from the team. A few protested. And then the all-white All Blacks lost every test.

Ironically, while the Second World War and the United Nations thrust isolated New Zealanders on to the world's stage, the effect of this broadening of the national experience only confirmed our insularity and complacency. The success of the welfare state in rekindling the image of New Zealand as uniquely just and fair, no less than prosperity, turned New Zealanders back towards self-satisfaction. Nowhere was this more clear than in immigration policy. James Thorn, an ex-unionist and now a Labour member of Parliament, chaired a Parliamentary Committee on Dominion Population in 1946. The Committee recommended against any policy of wholesale immigration 'at the present time or in the immediate future'; immigrants should be selected 'for their occupational aptitudes; and assisted immigrants should, as in the past, be recruited only in Britain.' Both parties agreed that immigration policy should be controlled to enhance and consolidate New Zealand as a British society. The unions had long favoured such a policy, the radical intelligentsia agreed, and so did National. Only a small number of refugees were admitted. 'We were on to a good thing' and determined to keep it. 'We're alright mate' might have been the nation's anthem. Instead, in a popular decision made in 1940, 'God Save the King' remained New Zealand's national anthem.

Recruiting office, Auckland. Enlistment was voluntary until 1916 when conscription was introduced.
Auckland Museum

10. *New Zealand in the World*
(1914-1951)

MALCOLM McKINNON

In 1914 the connection with Britain was the dominating reality of New Zealand's external relations. New Zealand was a British colony with Dominion status — recognition that it was self-governing. Most of its population of less than a million people were of British descent with relatives in England, Scotland, Ireland and Wales. New Zealanders were a different people — colonials — but they were Britons too. The British were not foreigners, a point that was clearest when they were set alongside the French, the Germans, the Russians or even the Americans. 'Native races' — Asians, Africans, Polynesians — did not even enter into this way of thinking.

Conservative opinion saw the Empire and the Empire connection in a benign light. Britain's preparedness to use its power against unruly natives, dissident socialists and foreign rivals reassured them. Both the Liberal and Reform parties supported spending on defence preparedness including the introduction of compulsory military training and subsidies for the British Navy. The Massey Government could stress its loyalty to the Crown and Empire because it agreed with British policies. Even within the labour movement there was support for the British connection, particularly the British tolerance of New Zealand's restrictive immigration policy and its exclusion of low wage Indian and Chinese labour. Their exclusion it was believed, ensured the country would remain the 'paradise of the working man'. However some socialists were unconvinced by this argument and were critical of the British connection, arguing that it helped the capitalists in New Zealand more than the workers.

Pro-British sentiment, for the majority who did feel it, was underpinned by self-government and by the facts of New Zealand's livelihood and security. Although New Zealand was politically within the Empire, it administered its own tariff and immigration policies as well as all aspects of its domestic policy. The colony had been self-governing for decades and the politically aware had always been alert to any evidence that its interests were being overridden. The first colonists inveighed vigorously against the Colonial Office for what they saw as its dilatory approach to settler self-government and control over land purchase. However, once self-government had been granted and Māori resistance overcome, there had been little friction over the demarcation of responsibility between the British government and the colony.

Economically, Britain provided the most significant overseas market for New Zealand's production. British investors provided most of the overseas capital borrowed by government or private concerns, British business sold to New Zealand a majority of the country's imports, as well as important services like insurance and shipping. As New Zealand had one of the highest per capita figures for overseas trade in the world, the significance of overseas investment far overshadowed domestic investment. In the late 1880s and early 1890s New Zealand's indebtedness created friction between the money-hungry colonists and cautious British investors, but the return of prosperity later in the decade solved the problem.

The British navy dominated the waters around New Zealand and saved New Zealand from having to provide for its own defence. The Anglo-Japanese alliance shored up Britain's position in the Pacific, keeping its northern flank in friendly hands.

'In such a compact,' wrote André Siegfried in 1904, taking all aspects of the Anglo-New Zealand relationship into account, 'has [New Zealand] not everything to gain and is it not an invaluable asset to have at her back a proud and mighty people to support her?'

The history of New Zealand's foreign relations in the four decades after 1914 is the history of how the all-embracing association with a dominant and capitalist Britain was challenged, changed, but also maintained through first a world war, then an era of disarmament, a severe economic depression, another world war, and a brief interlude of peace before the advent of yet another global conflict, the cold war. The challenges and changes came from events and developments both outside and within the country and by 1951 New Zealand's relations with the rest of the world were greatly altered. But there were also some important continuities.

Britain's declaration of war on behalf of the whole Empire on 4 August 1914, was accepted by most New Zealanders. The loyalty of New Zealanders, comments Paul Baker,

> went without saying . . . quite transcending the morality of Britain's position. It was nevertheless strengthened by the belief that Britain's declaration of war on 4 August was both 'righteous' and 'unavoidable'. That Britain had "stood consistently for peace", but had been forced by Germany into war, became an instant orthodoxy.

There was scope for debate about just what values and institutions New Zealand should be loyal to: the Empire or British justice? the Royal Navy or no standing army? But even amongst labour groups there was widespread support for Britain, whilst for his part Massey released the 1913 strike prisoners, and other labour leaders assured the government of their loyalty. If Britain were defeated New Zealand would fall under German rule: 'German officers would swagger in the streets of Auckland and New Zealand women would be treated as the women of Belgium have been treated,' as the *Auckland Weekly News* expressed it.

Unity was maintained in the initial months of the war. The war was good for the farmers, who enjoyed high prices. Rising farm incomes benefitted other businesses. Nor was New Zealand itself in danger. The German navy remained locked up in European waters, endangering British shipping but not posing any direct risk to New Zealand. The New Zealanders and the Australians fanned out quickly into the Pacific to pick up the German booty: Samoa, Nauru, the northeastern part of New Guinea. The helpful Japanese ally convoyed New Zealand and Australian troops to Egypt where they were to train.

In April 1915 New Zealand forces went into a major action, against Germany's ally Turkey. The British wanted to open the southern maritime route to their ally Russia, to cut off Germany from the Middle East. New Zealand along with British, French, and Australian forces were sent to 'the Straits'. The Turks ably defended their own territory, Britain got a bloody nose, New Zealand and Australia got something more — some 2700 New Zealanders died on Gallipoli and some 4700 were injured. The enterprise was abandoned, a failure, at the end of the year. Although there was criticism of the British command, of British decisions, of British soldiers, the commitment to the war, to the wider cause, did not falter. Instead the loss became a rite of passage — New Zealand had been blooded. The young lion cub, New Zealand, did not rebel against the lion, Britain, but took his place at his father's side. Recruiting in New Zealand picked up in the face of the twin shocks of both Gallipoli and the sinking of the *Lusitania* off the Irish coast, with the loss of over 1000 people, mostly civilians.

From the Mediterranean most of New Zealand's forces were moved to Germany's western front, one of the two principal war theatres. It had become a war of attrition, of two gigantic military forces locked in mortal embrace along a thousand miles of trenches, wire and fortifications, neither able to make significant headway against the other. Battles were not really battles as that word had been understood in the past, but rather bloody lashings out by combatants neither of whom could administer a fatal blow to the other, both of which turned out to have blood and yet more blood to expend. For New Zealanders the banal places and place-names of northern France and Western Belgium — Armentières, the Somme, Messines, Passchendaele, the Ypres salient, Le Quesnoy — were invested with heroism and bravery but also with injury, illness, death and the waste of young lives. In 23 days during the July 1916 Somme offensive 1560 were killed. To gain ground measured in metres not

A New Zealand dressing station at Gallipoli. *Auckland Museum*

kilometres, 640 were killed at Passchendaele on 12 October 1917.

The rhetoric of Empire, of unity, of New Zealand doing its bit, grew more fervent as the toll of war mounted. New Zealand's leaders, Massey and Ward, travelled to London, and sat in an imperial war cabinet. They spent from late 1916 to the middle of 1917 in England, and returned again in June 1918. The stress of war had enhanced the status of the Dominions — New Zealand, Australia and Canada. They earned a voice with the sacrifice of their young men.

As in all wars a siege mentality came to dominate, the British drew the bonds of Empire tighter. Economically there was investigation, planning, direction — these resources here, those resources there, all for the greater good of the imperial war effort. New Zealand was caught up in it, its leadership particularly.

Back home a few rejected the notion of being involved in the war at all, but they were small in number, the most notable were the Waikato people for whom England was still the conqueror, not the liberator. Amongst other Māori people, such as the Arawa, there was eagerness to participate. Some Irish New Zealanders, particularly after the suppression of the Easter 1916 uprising in Dublin, felt similarly to the Waikato people — it was England's war.

Potentially more significant was the widespread concern about the cost of living, about profiteering, about the introduction of conscription late in 1916. They all bore on the country's commitment to the war effort too, called into question the logic of the

Although Sir Joseph Ward (leader of the opposition Liberal party) and W. F. Massey (leader of the Reform Party and Prime Minister) loathed eath other, they were compelled to share power in a war-time coalition government. Both men (especially Massey) spent long periods overseas during the war. *Auckland Institute and Museum*

entire endeavour and the assumptions which underpinned it. The prospect of conscription helped unify the labour movement and led to the formation of the New Zealand Labour Party in the middle of 1916. Opposition continued after conscription was introduced, but without success: many accepted conscription believing it was fairer than volunteering. The local body elections in May 1917 delivered only limited support for Labour's stand. Conscientious objectors generally were badly treated and a group of Waikato Māori were imprisoned in Auckland for resisting conscription.

When the United States entered the war and provided an enormous and much closer source of fresh manpower many in New Zealand were ready to reduce its military commitment, which was proportionately higher than that of any other Dominion. Fewer troops meant lower taxes and more labour at home — strong economic advantages in favour of abating the commitment. There was also anger and disillusionment after the heavy losses in October 1917, a suspicion of incompetence on the part of the command. A dramatic reduction in the reinforcement rate was approved not long after.

A month later the revolutionary socialist Bolshevik party seized power in Russia, took that country out of the war and became *de facto* allies of the Germans. In New Zealand, the government increased its attacks on the Labour party which had praised the Bolshevik approach to Russia's problems. The Labour leader, Harry Holland, in response accused the government of 'Prussianism', of undemocratic practices. Labour's gains in 1918 by-elections showed that voters were at the very least sceptical of the extent to which the war had been fought with a true equality of sacrifice.

When the war ended it was the defeated countries — Germany, Austria, Hungary, Russia, which experienced radical political dislocation and change. The victor countries (with Italy a partial exception) did not. In New Zealand Massey and the Reform party interpreted the victory as an affirmation of continuity, in external relations as in other respects.

Yet alongside the British Empire there was now not just Lenin's expectation of an international Communist revolution, but also President Woodrow Wilson's dream. He envisaged an international order grounded in law and principle rather than in what he saw as the bankrupt and self-interested power politics and secret diplomacy of the European powers. An end to war, an end to the rule of one people by another, an end to governments' taxing and impoverishing and policing their people to maintain standing armies, and corrupt courts and aristocracies. The vision of a League of Nations was in its own way as powerful a vision as Lenin's — Wilson was mobbed by Europeans when he visited the continent for the peace treaty negotiations and the establishment of the League in 1919.

The Dominions signed the Versailles Peace Treaty with Germany separately and as member states of the British Empire. They acquired individual membership of the League. These were striking demonstrations of the increased status their participation in the war had conferred on them. However, New Zealand opinion was cautious — apprehensive of loosening the benign protection which the British connection was seen to provide.

Challenging to the League's vision, new Empire positions were being staked out in the Pacific. New Zealand acquired, with Australia and Britain, a direct stake in phosphate-rich Nauru. New Zealand reluctantly acquired Western Samoa. These territories were taken from the Germans and in terms of the constitution of the new League, this was betrayal of the rights of the local people. The mandates system was established but in the case of Nauru and Samoa a 'C' class mandate which reduced the supervision of the League to the bare minimum. By its actions, New Zealand showed its loyalty — the League might be all right but the Empire was more valuable. While these matters were being sorted out, New Zealand sent an armed contingent to Fiji when a strike by Indian labourers led to rioting and some bloodshed. The colonial governor requested the troops 'to assist in protecting European residents if so required', but the strike ended without any intervention by the New Zealanders.

Meanwhile in Britain's new Middle Eastern territories, New Zealand troops also helped keep 'the natives' under control. New Zealand forces had been active in the Palestine campaign in the latter part of the war. In 1919, before returning home, New Zealand forces helped the British suppress riots in Egypt. The workings out of the new ascendancy produced trouble with Turkey in September 1922: the Chanak crisis. Like Gallipoli, Chanak (Canakkale) was on the Straits. It almost looked as if the Empire

New Zealand troops going ashore at Apia to take possession of Western Samoa in 1914. *Alexander Turnbull Library*

would be going to war again. In New Zealand there was agitation, enthusiasm, and also criticism from the League of Nations Union and the Labour party, but the crisis faded almost before it had begun.

As before the war, most workers believed they had a stake in the status quo. The Immigration Restriction Act of 1920 had refined the country's rigid immigration law by introducing a system of individual permits for all immigrants not of British or Irish descent, even for British Indians. This reinforcement of existing immigration restriction measures was popular. The same watersiders who refused to coal the vessel taking troops to Fiji until they received assurances they would not be used as strikebreakers, resolved not to work boats carrying Indian immigrants from Fiji. 'The immigration bill,' said Massey

> is the result of a deepseated sentiment on the part of the huge majority of people in this country that this Dominion shall be what is often called a 'white' New Zealand, and that the people who came here should as far as is possible for us to provide for it, be of the same way of thinking from the British Empire point of view . . . and that they shall be people who will be loyal to the Empire, loyal to the Crown, and loyal to this country when they become its citizens.

At the Imperial conference in 1921 the Indian government accepted that dominions had the right to restrict immigration but not to discriminate against legally resident Indians, and so its wrath was directed only at South Africa. The Chinese consul for his part unsuccessfully lobbied against the discriminatory terms still imposed on Chinese immigrants, in addition to the new legislation.

The government took steps to limit the influence and impact of the dissatisfied, the dissentient. The Undesirable Immigrants Exclusion Act 1919 was directed primarily against ex-enemy aliens but also against the disaffected or 'disloyal' of whatever nationality.

Labour took a quite different approach to foreign relations matters from the other two parties. It condemned the Versailles peace treaty with Germany and the League as a victor's peace and a victor's organization, a violation not an endorsement of Wilson's programme. In answer to a question in Parliament about the Labour party cabling congratulations to the British Labour party on British worker support for Russia, Massey claimed that

> 95 per cent of the population . . . were thoroughly loyal and were opposed to Bolshevism, Sinn Feinism, IWWism [a reference to the Industrial Workers of the World, a revolutionary socialist organization] and all the other 'isms' with which the civilised world had been afflicted in the last few years. He knew perfectly well that the people of this country were prepared to stand by the Imperial Government in every possible way to prevent the disintegration of the Empire. . .

In a St Patrick's Day address in 1922, the Catholic Coadjutor, Bishop Liston of Auckland, reportedly described Irishmen as having been murdered by foreign troops. The government prosecuted him for sedition. Liston claimed he had not been talking about the 1916 rebellion but about more recent actions by British forces. He was not convicted but there was popular approval of the prosecution.

The government might have faith in a New Zealand continuing to circle peaceably in the orbit of the power and prosperity of British capitalism, but faith was not enough to maintain either. Both the security of New Zealand and the security of its livelihood were in question in the immediate post-war period too. Yes, Britain was a victor power, a great power, a great naval power. But the Pacific Ocean was further away from Britain than any other waters, and there Britain was weak, and not just in comparison with British strength elsewhere. The real naval powers in the Pacific were Japan and the United States — neither exhausted by war as was Britain. The Americans did not like the Anglo-Japanese alliance as it meant their main rival in the Pacific, the Japanese, had the protection of the British. But when Admiral Jellicoe wrote a report on New Zealand's naval defences in 1919, he identified Japan as the only possible nation in the Far East, except the United States, which would be in a position to inflict any permanent injury on the British Empire. The United States, he considered, could be omitted from the calculation.

Because New Zealand feared the Japanese, Massey wanted to see the Anglo-Japanese treaty survive. But at the Imperial conference in 1921 and the Washington Naval conference in late 1921/early 1922, New Zealand had to accept the end of the Anglo-Japanese treaty even though it was seen as a protection for Australia and New Zealand. A common fear of Communism, and radical nationalism in China, helped Japan, Britain, and the United States reach agreement. Harry Holland had spoken out against Britain's implicit support for Japanese designs on China, but it was not clear that the new arrangement would be better for China than the old. Others, worried about Japan for other reasons, took comfort from the evidence of Anglo-American friendship. As one Reform minister put it:

> perhaps more valuable than the treaties is the fact that America and Great Britain have come together in a way that we have often desired, and as they have never come together before . . . Britain and America today have ten units of naval power to six or seven for the rest of the world.

Once the wartime emergency had passed dreams of closer imperial economic relations turned out to be just that. Imperial preference was a popular cause only with the Conservative party in Britain and its tariff proposals effectively put it out of office at the 1923 election. Massey was upset at this blow to imperial economic unity but New Zealand as a whole seems to have been less exercised, perhaps because it was realized that it wanted to and did import from other countries, and because there was no consensus for abandoning New Zealand's own protective tariff. Moreover, the Anglo-American debt settlement in 1923 seemed to indicate that the welcome pre-war patterns of international commerce and finance were being restored.

The 1923 election in Britain put a minority Labour government into office — Britain's first ever Labour government — with Ramsay Macdonald as Prime Minister. The ideological character of the pro-British sentiments so vigorously and repeatedly voiced by Massey and the Reform party were exposed to view. Now it was the government rather than the Labour party which found itself critical of British foreign policy — of the Macdonald Government's interest in closer relations with the Soviet Union, of its enthusiasm for the League of Nations, and in particular of its support for the Geneva Protocol (an attempt to stiffen the disputes settlement provisions of the League's Covenant). Massey thought the Protocol went too far in involving foreign countries in matters of domestic concern such as immigration policies. In addition, Massey objected to the British government cancelling a proposed base in Singapore.

The Conservatives had planned this as a strong point for British naval power in Asia, one which would compensate for limitations Britain had accepted at the Washington Naval Conference. In the naval estimates for 1923 Massey had provided for a substantial contribution to the project.

The British Labour government lost office to the Conservatives again in the 1924 election but change still occurred. Canada, South Africa and Ireland wanted Britain to recognize the independent status that they felt had been achieved by the Dominions as a result of war. At the 1926 Imperial conference they got their way. The Balfour Declaration said what they wanted to hear and Great Britain committed itself at the 1930 Imperial Conference to giving it statutory form, a commitment discharged in the Statute of Westminster 1931. New Zealand, like Australia, held back.

The New Zealand government was cautious about Britain's commitments to the Locarno pacts concluded between Germany and its western neighbours — as cautious as it had been of the abortive Geneva Protocol, and like the other Dominions left it to Great Britain to assume the formal obligation. There was more enthusiasm for the revival of the Singapore base project and in 1927 New Zealand budgeted £1 million for it. Labour was critical again.

The government's deployment of marines in Samoa in 1928 showed that it took its determination to maintain control there seriously. The fracas in December 1929 when eight Samoans including one of the royal heads of the country, Tamasese, were shot dead by New Zealand armed police led to another marine intervention early in 1930.

The return of economic bad times from the second half of 1926 had widespread effects. Under pressure from labour opinion, assisted immigration from Britain ended in 1927. Attempts were made to find new export markets. Confronted with rock bottom prices, and having failed in a controversial attempt to manage the British market single-handedly, the dairy industry looked anywhere else, everywhere else, for sales. A trade treaty was signed with Japan. Although expectations were not realized, it was an interesting demonstration of the changed political and economic attitudes towards that country. New Zealand got into the Canadian market as a by-product of the 1925 Australian-Canadian trade agreement. But in 1930 the New Zealanders were shut out. Neither the Australian nor United States markets were any more open, despite the quite substantial buying New Zealand did from both countries. Interest groups and politicians continued to be divided over the respective merits of protectionism and free trade — the supporters of free trade often somewhat contradictorily hoping for helpful protective action from Britain. Labour was moving away from socialist economics but only beginning to advocate other alternatives to economic orthodoxy.

New Zealand's United Government was upset when the British Labour Party took office in June 1929 and slowed down work on the Singapore base. But the mood in New Zealand was changing as anti-war and pacifist sentiment increased in significance. The Great War had been labelled 'the war to end wars'. From 1924 on, the settled international climate suggested that the goal had been achieved.

Disarmament was a prominent part of the diplomatic agenda, the wastefulness and futility of war a common theme in both literature and public discussion. Even farming and business interests, resistant to higher taxes, were antipathetic to defence spending. It was against this backdrop that compulsory military training was ended in 1930. The Minister of Defence, John Cobbe, explained that while the reasons were partly economic it was also because of the strong feeling against militarism.

Of the major political parties, the Labour party was most sympathetic to such thinking. It had changed its mind about the League of Nations, seeing it now as a progressive force in international relations. Labour also argued that New Zealand, like the other Dominions, needed to assert its independent status within the Empire. Apart from the belief that it was appropriate to the country's independent status that it act in its own interest, Labour had its own understanding of those interests, both political and economic. Harry Holland continued to champion the Samoans despite the complex nature of the anti-New Zealand movement there — part indigenous rights, part local commercial interests, but not much socialism.

It was possible in the later 1920s to envisage a slow but profound change in the character of the Empire: disarmament, the increased importance attached to the League, the recognition of the independence of the Dominions. Maybe a new international order was being born, even if much opinion in New Zealand was still attached to the patterns of the old.

More than any other event, the great depression of the early 1930s called into question the predominant patterns of New Zealand life. Inevitably the country's external relations were affected too. This was most evident in the economic sphere, but the election of a Labour Government at the end of 1935 ushered in changes in political relations too, changes that built on Labour's thinking in the 1920s but were given a new dimension by the world-wide deterioration in international relations.

Initially the commonest response to the deepening economic crisis was to see New Zealand's salvation in a closer relationship with Britain. What had passed for the open world of international economic relations in the 1920s seemed to be breaking up. The Americans were taking refuge in protectionism, the French were reducing their trade and accumulating gold. The British financial crisis in August 1931, although providing unprecedented evidence of that country's economic weakness, was seen as ushering in a new era of imperial economic unity and the hopes of New Zealand's primary producers were pinned on the Ottawa Economic Conference scheduled for the middle of 1932. At Ottawa New Zealand did conclude a trade agreement with Great Britain which provided some preferential access, over and above that of foreign suppliers to the British market. In exchange British commercial opportunities in New Zealand were enhanced.

But the agreement was a fragile reed. The British government had obligations to its own producers which took precedence over those to the Dominions. And it could not realistically put important trading partners like Argentina and Denmark completely out in the cold either. In early 1933 the British proposed quotas for butter imports. The New Zealand dairy industry was shocked and angry. But as Coates, Minister of

Joseph Gordon Coates. He became Prime Minister at the high point of the 1920's prosperity (1925) and lost office against a backdrop of rural depression and growing unemployment. *Auckland Public Library*

Finance in the Coalition Government pointed out, 'In 1882 we discovered in Great Britain a bottomless market: in 1932 we discovered that the market is not a bottomless one.' In 1934 the British made similar proposals in respect of meat. Despite Coates's domestic diplomacy the New Zealand government supported its farmers and stonewalled on both butter and meat quotas — as did the Australians. Eventually the British relented and dealt with their own farmers' problem by way of income support.

Nonetheless, such episodes helped shatter assumptions about New Zealand's place in the international economy. While secure access to the British market remained a central goal of New Zealand policy-making, there was much more discussion of diversification, and industrialization, both strategies for reducing New Zealand's vulnerability.

Such ideas overlapped with more radical thinking about New Zealand's external economic relations. In the Labour movement, critical thinking about international monetary relations and the burden of debt, had a powerful hold. Sometimes the focus was on the City of London, sometimes on the bankers in New York and Paris who were credited with bringing down sterling in 1931, sometimes on what was seen as an international Jewish financial community, sometimes on all of the above. Adjusting debtor-creditor relations was a powerful domestic issue in New Zealand and it influenced attitudes towards external relations. For some socialists the way forward

The British threatened butter quotas. Coates told the farmers the British market wasn't bottomless but told the British the quotas were unacceptable. *NZ Herald*

was to overturn capitalism completely. Others, including the Labour party, took more limited approaches, seeking reform rather than revolution.

The severity of the depression revivified radical politics. The Communist party, which had only taken on a stable organized form in late 1920s, became active in trade unions and amongst the unemployed, both in the cities and in the labour camps. The Labour party, now with power within its grasp, was a vigorous adversary. Labour appealed to the nation as a whole, save only holders of what it regarded as undue economic power, such as bankers. Nonetheless, the language and thinking of politics generally had shifted to the left, as individuals like Coates recognized. If capitalism and parliamentary democracy did survive — and it seemed questionable at times in 1932 and 1933, not just because of what was happening in New Zealand but also because of events in Germany, France, the United States, even England — then it was widely accepted it would be a very different kind of capitalism. It would be more like the organized version with which New Zealand had become acquainted in the First World War than it would be like the nineteenth century ideal of *laissez-faire*, the unrestricted market economy with a minimal state.

Nazism, German fascism, with its employment and rearmament policies vigorously implemented against a backdrop of repression of trade unions and other opponents of the new régime, offered one controversial solution to the crisis of contemporary capitalism. Another solution was present in the Soviet Union whose economy was isolated from the international depression and was embarking with great fanfare on its first Five Year Plan. Enthusiasm for Russia became widespread even outside the radical left and the perils of Stalinism were overlooked by many old and new enthusiasts. The Soviet Union joined the League of Nations not long after Germany left. The cause of peace and disarmament flourished, in New Zealand as in other British countries, and overlapped with sympathy for the Soviet Union. The potential contradictions between a peace policy and an anti-fascist policy which might mean war, were not fully appreciated.

When New Zealand elected the Labour Government at the end of 1935, it was inevitable that there would be change in external and external economic relations — inevitable because of not just Labour's own beliefs but because of the country's experiences before and during the depression.

In its attitude to international relations the Labour Government placed strong reliance on the League of Nations and this appealed to those who believed that the League had the capacity to emancipate international relations from the conflicts of power politics. When Labour took office the League, under the initiative of Britain and France, had imposed sanctions on Italy because of its invasion of Ethiopia. British government support for a League policy met with the agreement of both the Coalition Government and the soon to be elected Labour party. Only the left was sceptical, its scepticism seemingly vindicated when the British and French Foreign Secretaries, in complete contradistinction to League policy, proposed concessions to Italy. The newly-elected Labour Government dissented, in a private communication to the British government. Although the outcry in their own countries led the British and French governments to revert to sanctions, the League itself lifted them in June 1936 in the face of Italy's completed conquest. It was a decision which New Zealand was reluctant to accept.

New Zealand's stand on Ethiopia was the precursor to a number of differences between the New Zealand and British governments. New Zealand took the League more seriously than did Britain which was unsure of the extent to which it wished to pursue hard line policies against those powers — Italy, Germany and Japan — challenging the League.

Nonetheless the Labour government wanted it to act, but failing that, was prepared to accept that in the final analysis it was British power that was necessary to preserve international order. On issues where the League was not directly involved, the New Zealand government was also cautious. Over the Spanish Civil War, the New Zealand government was anxious to see the League play an active role in resolving the dispute, but it was reluctant to become identified with left wing activity in New Zealand on behalf of the Spanish Republican Government.

It is revealing that at the 1937 Imperial Conference, whilst Savage implicitly criticized the British government's appeasement policy, he also criticized Canadian isolationism. For the New Zealand government the conference marked something of a watershed, after which it came to accept that Empire defence would be as important (if not more important) than the League in fighting fascist aggression. On his return to New Zealand, Nash argued that rearmament could not ensure permanent peace and that the only permanent way of achieving that was through the League. But if other countries

> determine to use their coercive powers to dominate the members of the British Commonwealth then at that point there is justification for defending the principles of the Commonwealth . . . .

During the Munich crisis of September and October 1938 New Zealand tolerated the British and French negotiation with Hitler, including their acquiescence in the annexation of large parts of Czechoslovakia by Germany.

On the economic front, the later 1930s saw a slow and cautious rapprochement between France, Great Britain and the United States, expressed in the 1936 currency stabilization agreement and the November 1938 Anglo-American trade agreement. Both were welcomed by the New Zealand government in an era when co-operation between the democracies in all spheres of relations seemed desirable. New Zealand itself however found little opportunity to diversify its trade either amongst the capitalist democracies or with other countries such as Germany or the Soviet Union. Its energies remained focused on the one hand on negotiating a special economic relationship with Great Britain, and on the other seeking to build up a more protected economy in New Zealand. These two policies were potentially in conflict with each other and this became evident in 1939 when New Zealand's external payments situation required the government to seek financial assistance from Britain. The New Zealand government defended its policies as necessary to the building of a better New Zealand, the British wanted to teach the Antipodean 'socialists' a lesson. The onset of war helped solve the disagreement. It increased New Zealand's importance to Britain and it legitimated New Zealand industrialization, because it made the country more useful to the war effort.

The shift of focus from League to Commonwealth had not meant unqualified support from the New Zealand government for British foreign and defence policy. In the months before the war there was some feeling in New Zealand that the country would not be able to participate directly in the fighting in Europe because of the need to assure its own defence in the event of a possible threat from Japan. There would not necessarily be an expeditionary force as there had been in the First World War. This attitude overlapped with strong opposition in the Labour party to any thought of reintroducing conscription. A strong segment of the labour movement, having opposed conscription in the First World War, was determined that a Labour Government should never introduce it.

As in 1914, conservative opinion supported entry into the war in 1939. It also made sense to most Labour supporters. Savage's address did not speak solely in the language of pro-British patriotism, and he abjured hysterical anti-German sentiment. His famous line 'Where Britain goes we go' was often instanced subsequently as evidence either of the lack of any independent New Zealand thinking, or to give bipartisan credibility to the actions of National party governments. Read in context it was a sober and not at all jingoistic statement, identifying Britain as a defender of universal as well as national values in a way that was obviously calculated to appeal to the government's supporters as much as its domestic opponents.

Throughout the war New Zealand stayed within the framework of the British war effort. But there were two important changes that made the Second World War a very different war from the First. Soviet and American participation in the war and commitment to post-war collaboration promised a more successful transformation of international relations than had been managed after World War I by either the League or international socialism. And war against Japan forced New Zealand to conduct its own diplomacy, to establish a high commission in Canberra and an embassy in Washington. New Zealand was forced to think in terms of international rather than purely Commonwealth relations.

But in the first year of the war these considerations were remote. This was a war against Germany fought by France and England — even in Europe most countries were neutral. The hesitation about Japan's intentions apparently vanished with war's outbreak. Having received assurances from the British Admiralty about Japan, New Zealand agreed to organize an expeditionary force which would train in Egypt, then be ready to fight in France.

Two dimensions of New Zealand's participation in the conflict — the pro-British and the anti-fascist — did not always coexist easily despite the unity with which the country had entered the war. The differences had been manifest even in the different ways the Labour and National parties responded to the outbreak of the war. The National party caucus resolved to remember the slogan of the last war: 'to the last man and the last shilling' while Labour predicted the inevitable triumph of 'justice, democracy and socialism'.

Within the labour movement concern grew that the war would turn against the Soviet Union. Certainly there were no holds barred in the rhetorical fury which descended on the Communist party, which after some initial hesitation condemned the war as a struggle between capitalists of which socialists should not have a bar. The Soviet Union's collaboration with Germany in partitioning Poland, and then its move against Finland in November 1939 increased the hostility. To conservative opinion in New Zealand opposition to the war was a phenomenon of the left, of intellectuals, pacifists, trade unionists and the like.

The government vented its hostility on the Communists but it was also conscious of unease amongst its own supporters about the war. Through the summer of 1939-1940

Savage speaking at Otahuhu in 1939. At the outset of the war Savage stressed there would be no conscription. He died in March 1940, and the decision to introduce conscription was made at the end of May. *NZ Herald*

while the Soviet Union was being castigated the armed peace continued on the European western front. In February the joint council of the Federation of Labour and the Labour party released a statement of war aims calculated to reassure their supporters. It stressed that

> the British government was at last standing for collective security as New Zealand had repeatedly advised; it would now be 'politically irresponsible or worse' if New Zealand Labour did not give Britain fullest support. The six peace aims of British Labour were endorsed: no revengeful peace, but restitution to victims; rights of all nations to self-determination; the outlawing of war; rights of minorities; an effective international authority; an end to colonial exploitation and trade monopoly.

The events of May and June 1940 changed the character of the war. But with the blitzkrieg, the fall of France, Italy's entry into the contest and Britain itself under attack, ambivalence about the war diminished. New Zealanders in the RAF were involved in the Battle of Britain and in the subsequent bombing of German cities. In response, New Zealand introduced conscription and suppressed two newspapers — the Communist *People's Voice* and the radical *Tomorrow*. There were war-related economic difficulties in the 1940-1941 export season, but many commentators noted what little effect the war had on domestic life in New Zealand.

It was in April 1941 that New Zealand forces in large numbers went into combat, in the abortive Greece and Crete campaigns that provided a strategic echo of Gallipoli. Crete in particular saw the New Zealand forces overwhelmed by Germans who gained command of the air, the airfields, and inevitably of the island itself. Over 1600 prisoners were taken on the mainland and nearly 300 died. On Crete the New Zealand force of 7700 saw 671 killed and 1943 captured. The government was well-informed — Fraser was actually in Egypt during the Crete campaign. The New Zealand public knew less until the casualty lists started to be released. As during Gallipoli, the campaigns seem to have reinforced the commitment to the war effort.

In November 1941 that New Zealand forces went into battle again, against the German and Italian armies threatening Egypt, a campaign which lasted on and off until the Axis armies were driven from Africa. In the first round there were over 900 killed and over 1900 taken prisoner. New Zealand forces became involved in this campaign again in June 1942. The loss of life and numbers taken prisoner were not dissimilar to the earlier episode but in this case there was success. With victory at Alamein at the beginning of November 1942, the way lay open to Tunis which was reached in May 1943. The Māori Battalion, recruited on a volunteer basis, played a prominent part in the desert war. Although dominated by recruits from some iwi rather than others, there was support for the Battalion throughout the Māori community, even amongst the Waikato and others who had resisted becoming involved in the First World War.

Eighteen months before the victory in Africa, Japan's victory at Pearl Harbour transformed New Zealand's situation and its part in the war. The outbreak of conflict in Asia did not come as a surprise to New Zealanders but the rapid collapse of British and American positions in Asia and the Pacific did. This underlined what was already likely, that the war would become primarily one between the United States and Japan with Australia, New Zealand and other allies in subordinate roles.

Although the war in the Pacific was closer, most New Zealanders remained more involved with the conflict in the Middle East and subsequently Europe. In early 1942 when New Zealand was directly threatened by Japan, the British and Americans resisted allocating shipping to allow New Zealand forces to return from the Mediterranean. The Government agreed that an American division provide New Zealand's defence instead. Thereafter New Zealand's own security was not under threat. Although the war was seen initially as America's war the Australian and New Zealand governments met in Canberra in January 1944 and the resultant pact asserted their rights to a say in the peacemaking with Japan. The pact also warned the

New Zealand soldiers at Suda Bay, Crete. The campaigns in Greece and Crete in the Second World War were both initiation and débâcle for the New Zealand forces. *NZ Herald*

United States off treating wartime occupation of islands as a basis for post-war claims. The Americans were annoyed, the British pleased.

New Zealand land forces did fight in three Pacific campaigns in the Solomons, on Vella Levalla, Green, and Nissan Islands during 1943 and early 1944. The numbers involved were much smaller than in the Middle East, and the loss of life much less, but the tropical conditions were not benign. Manpower shortages hastened the decision to withdraw the men and concentrate manpower either with the Second Division, now in Italy, or on the home front. There was no longer a direct threat in the Pacific, the soldiers were as useful, maybe more useful in Italy than they would have been in the unhealthy islands. The RNZAF and the RNZN did continue to play a role, though, in the Pacific war. That war drew New Zealand attention to the Pacific, to the many islands and their strategic significance for New Zealand. But attention faded away again once the war was over, only to revive in the 1970s.

The commitment to the British war effort remained and intensified later in the war. The decision to keep the New Zealand forces in the Mediterranean theatre was also indicative of a responsiveness to British priorities. As part of the British Eighth Army, the New Zealanders fought their way up the Italian peninsular across a landscape often reminiscent of home. In lives lost and prisoners taken, the campaigns were much less costly than the early battles in the desert. The New Zealanders were now part of an alliance on the offensive, in Italy as elsewhere. The ancient Benedictine abbey of Montecassino was the most distinguished victim of the New Zealand advance, bombarded by the Allies because the Germans may have fortified its strategic site. At Trieste in the far north-eastern corner of Italy the New Zealanders found themselves almost by accident involved in keeping the city out of the hands of the Yugoslav Communist army at the end of the war. Fraser endorsed the decision to get involved. He was already sensitive to and apprehensive about Soviet ambitions and interests in the post-war world.

New Zealand also supported the British war effort from late 1943 by introducing more extensive rationing of butter, meat and other commodities in short supply in Britain. Yet at the same time from at least 1943, victory felt assured, the sense of urgency weakened. This undercurrent was given most dramatic expression in the furlough episode in 1943–1944. Enlisted men, who had returned to New Zealand after three years active service in the Middle East and Italy, refused to return to the front. They had come back to a country in which the war seemed remote, in which there seemed to be many able-bodied men who hadn't seen active service. The men were technically deserters, but the government backed down and the men were dealt with fairly leniently. The episode was a sharp reminder of the divisions that appear in a community under stress of war, of the difficulty of achieving that equality of sacrifice so often invoked.

Germany invaded its erstwhile friend the Soviet Union in June 1941. Soviet entry into the war had significant reverberations in New Zealand's foreign relations. The progressive character of post-war goals had already been set out in the Atlantic Charter in August 1941, agreed to by Roosevelt and Churchill. The participation of the Soviet Union, the revolutionary power of the 1920s, the 'rogue' country of 1939–1941, in a post-war international order was confirmed in the Moscow Declaration in October 1943 and in the meeting of Churchill, Roosevelt and Stalin at the end of November 1943 at Tehran.

Soviet participation in the war however had surprisingly little impact on the domestic political climate, and this was to be significant after the war. Although the Communist party in New Zealand threw itself energetically into the war effort, the Labour party remained suspicious of its activities, and conservative city authorities and politicians even more so. For mainstream opinion the fact that the Soviet Union was an ally suggested more that the Soviet Union had changed not that the political objectives of the war had, nor that radical social change should be contemplated in New Zealand: 'they'd joined us, we hadn't joined them'.

Attention turned to the shape of the post-war order. The great powers unveiled a

The bombing of Montecassino. *NZ Herald*

scheme for a united nations organization. The Prime Minister, Peter Fraser, vigorously opposed the possession of a veto power by the great powers. But it is not clear that this was a major cause of concern to the population at large. Public opinion did certainly welcome the prospect of an end to war and conflict. It placed great emphasis therefore on the maintenance of friendship between the Soviet Union on the one hand and the United States and the British Commonwealth on the other. Even Sid Holland, the National party leader, could find nice things to say about Russia, although his domestic anti-Communism was as strong as ever.

The nations of the world reached agreement on the charter of the United Nations Organization, at the San Francisco conference in April and May 1945. The government believed the values which it embodied, even with the veto, were touchstones for the new age and the new world. This commitment was reflected in the stances it took on a number of issues in the first eighteen months after the war. In respect of Japan, of atomic energy, of peacemaking in Europe — the government approved of efforts to reach arrangements that would be based on the collaborative model embodied in the United Nations itself. It took trusteeship in general, and the commitment to advance Samoa to self-government in particular, seriously. It wanted, like Australia, to see a new commitment to political, social and economic development in the South Pacific generally. At the Commonwealth Prime Ministers' meetings in April and May 1946, Nash, like the Australians Chifley and Evatt, frequently found himself taking exception to the strongly anti-Soviet line of the British government. It seemed to augur badly for the maintenance of 'one world', the dream of San Francisco and was a surprising indication to Nash, who represented New Zealand, of the preoccupations of the British Labour government. Some of the British ideas, Nash wrote to Fraser, indicate 'the difficulty of reconciling [Commonwealth relations] with our loyalty to the United Nations Organisation'.

However the New Zealand government took more traditional stances itself, for instance in working with Australia and the United Kingdom to involve the United States in the security of the South Pacific. This was an interesting shift of emphasis from wartime when the New Zealand and Australian governments had been concerned about overweening American power. But American attention had shifted away from the South Pacific; it had control now both of Japan and the former Japanese-occupied islands north of the equator. So the plan for a pact fell by the wayside.

New Zealand attitudes to the new world order were strongly moulded by the fact that the United Kingdom was one of the architects of the system and that therefore the new world order did not entail the sort of radical changes it might have otherwise. Indeed it was quite characteristic for New Zealanders to see the new United Nations as the Commonwealth writ large, or at least to believe that intra-Commonwealth relations provided a model for the new world body. Despite the official importance attached to good relations between the great powers and in particular to good relations between the Soviet Union and the Western powers, the Labour Party continued to keep the Communists at home at arms length.

On the economic front the new world order was largely designed by the United States and the United Kingdom with the former having the clout to call the shots. The Soviet Union, not a participant in the international capitalist economy between the wars, played a more peripheral role. New Zealand opinion generally approved of the principle of Anglo-American economic collaboration but was apprehensive about some of its applications. Labour opinion was worried that the United States would attack New Zealand's system of controlling external trade which assured full employment. National opinion was more anxious that the United States would demand an end to Empire preference and the Ottawa arrangements. The Cabinet decided New Zealand should join the International Monetary Fund and the World Bank, but neither the Labour nor the National caucuses were in favour, despite the fact that Britain itself had agreed to join. Many felt that Britain had only agreed under duress, in exchange for the $3.75 billion dollar loan that the American Congress finally approved in July 1946.

V.J. Day celebrations in Auckland, 1945. There was little enthusiasm in New Zealand for further military participation in the war against Japan and corresponding relief when the war ended. *NZ Herald*

New Zealand's failure to join the two institutions did not have any immediate effects on its foreign relations. Neither became as powerful as some had hoped and others feared. Controls of all sorts remained characteristic of the post-war era despite American pressure to remove them. Trade talks dragged on without resolution. Meanwhile New Zealand prospered. Bulk contracts provided for the sale of all the meat and dairy produce it could produce to Britain, a marked contrast to the uncertainties of the 1930s. Wool prices were high. New Zealand, which had been nearly insolvent in 1939 donated £10 million to Britain in 1947.

In the 1946 election the National party did not even have a foreign policy plank in its platform, whilst its defence policy rested on the principles of Commonwealth and United Nations collaboration. The Labour party shared the same outlook. In 1945 and 1946 there were officially no enemies — there were the victorious united nations which had set up a global organization to which all countries were invited to attend, and to which it was envisaged that the defeated countries would eventually be admitted. But over the following two years New Zealand foreign relations were to be reshaped, to retreat to a narrower channel than that carved by the establishment of the United Nations.

In 1947 it became clear that not only could the great powers not agree on the shape of the post-war order but that they could not even agree to disagree, to say 'that's yours and this is mine'. On the one hand, the United Kingdom and the United States, and the Soviet Union on the other chose to see their former partner(s) as having designs on their own sphere of influence and on the political, social and economic order in those spheres. The near economic collapse of Europe in the northern winter of 1946–1947 gave credence to these fears as well as emphasizing the differences between the reconstruction policies of the different powers. When President Truman declared in an address to Congress in March 1947, that the United States faced a totalitarian enemy, when in June the Soviet Union rejected participation in an American recovery plan for Europe, it was clear that co-operation had died and enmity had replaced it.

For the most part, New Zealanders supported the changed orientation of American and British policy, which had been foreshadowed since the war's end. For conservative opinion there was no problem. It had always felt awkward about collaboration with the Soviet Union, a professedly revolutionary power and had no deep-seated wish to accommodate its diplomatic, let alone its ideological demands. Moreover, the *entente* with the Soviet Union reduced the value of foreign policy as a weapon in domestic politics.

The government was in a slightly more invidious situation, one not dissimilar to that it had faced in 1939–1940. Should it accept the official Anglo-American line of hostility to the Soviet Union? or should it take a distinct stand? Pursuing a pro-British rather than a pro-American policy was impossible because of the close collaboration on foreign policy, especially in Europe, that had been established between the Attlee Government and the Truman administration by the end of 1947. In fact there was little doubt about which side the New Zealand government would come down on. The government's attitude to domestic communism had hardened, not least because of differences of opinion about the government's stabilization policies. And the fact that a British Labour government was taking the lead in confronting the Soviet Union helped. So too of course did the evidence of undemocratic practices reported from Eastern Europe, most especially the coup in Czechoslovakia in February 1948 and the blockade of the Western sectors of Berlin imposed by the Soviet Union in June of that year. 'In the past two years,' noted a CIA report on New Zealand in the middle of 1949, 'after much equivocation on the Communist issue, Labour politicians, particularly Fraser and Semple, have become vigorous campaigners against Communism.'

In respect of Europe and the Middle East, the government's role in 1947 was primarily to welcome and supplement the support the United States proffered Britain in the form of Marshall Plan aid. With the collapse of sterling convertibility in August 1947, the government launched New Zealand's own Aid to Britain campaign, which remained active through 1948 and was headed by F. P. Walsh, the dominant and vigorously anti-Communist union leader. The United States accepted that international trade would be subject to controls for the foreseeable future, at least until Europe's balance of payments problems were overcome. The post-war schemes for economic reform and stabilization — the IMF and the American loan to Britain in particular — had failed to solve this problem. Ambitious plans for an international trade organization had been abandoned, ironically because of opposition within the United States to the concessions it made during the negotiations. Even a relatively limited trade agreement was greeted with suspicion in New Zealand. But the country's trade was already protected through import controls and export contracts and in 1948 the government ratified the General Agreement on Tariffs and Trade, GATT as it was called.

It was in that same year that New Zealand became more directly involved with Britain's rearmament and its defence against what it saw as a Soviet and Communist threat. New Zealand provided three Dakota air crews to help maintain the airlift to Berlin. Australia, New Zealand and Britain discussed the security of the South-east Asia region and in particular the British position there. New Zealand's wartime defence commitment to Fiji was revived in 1948. And New Zealand accepted a British request to reach a state of readiness that would allow it to despatch an expeditionary force to the Middle East in the event of war. The Middle East had been a contentious area in 1947–1948 as Britain attempted to slough off its responsibilities in Palestine whilst also maintaining its influence in the region generally. Fraser had been a supporter of the Jews but in the event did not recognize Israel until the British themselves took that step in January 1949.

The most debated consequence of the decision to prepare for war was the introduction of conscription. Even more than in 1939–1940, it was a divisive issue in the labour movement. The American Legation, which monitored Communist activity over the issue, recognized that 'the opposition to compulsory military service in peacetime has far deeper roots' — in other words it was not just the Communists who were involved. The referendum victory which Fraser won in August 1949 was achieved at the cost of a rift in his own party. While Fraser strongly defended the cold war foreign policy and was supported in this by the National party opposition, there was bitter division within the labour movement, which reinforced tensions over domestic issues. Steps too were taken to remove people suspected of pro-Communist sympathies from sensitive employment in the public service, another expression that the country had returned to a wartime mentality. Cabinet, encouraged by Ernest Marsden, the Director of the Department of Scientific and Industrial Research, sought British Prime Minister Attlee's opinion on whether New Zealand should develop its own atomic energy pile, although it was not intended that it should be capable of producing a bomb. Nonetheless in the eyes of Fraser and others it had a defence significance, especially in allowing for the dispersal of the resources of the Commonwealth in this sensitive area.

The formation of NATO raised questions similar to those that had surfaced in the Second World War. Would Australia and New Zealand be left out of policy-making — forgotten even? Maybe there should be a Pacific pact to match the Atlantic one? The Americans were not interested, however. Their policy towards Japan continued to arouse anxiety in New Zealand although at least some officials and politicians accepted that Japan had to remain allied to the West and could not therefore be treated too harshly. At the very end of the period, the Communist victory in China pointed the way to a new cold war in Asia. New Zealand attitudes to the defeated Chiang suggested that this development was less likely to engage New Zealand opinion than the tension in Europe and the Middle East, and Chiang elicited none of the sympathy in New Zealand that he had found in the United States. But the other big event in Asia — Indian independence — seemed a triumph for British policy, especially when India decided to stay in the Commonwealth as a republic. This latter decision disappointed Fraser and others, but the disappointment should not be exaggerated. It was believed that in staying in the Commonwealth India was in some fashion committing itself to foreign policy co-operation with the other member states, and that was the substantive goal.

The government finally ratified the Statute of Westminster in 1947 — it had been committed in principle to ratification since taking office but had delayed. The parliamentary debate on ratification found government members defending themselves against opposition charges that they were 'disloyal', that is disloyal to Great Britain. But the substance of the statute had been accepted since 1935 and no one believed National would reverse ratification.

National took over the reins of government at the end of 1949. It saw the world very similarly to Fraser: the Communists, the Soviet Union were the enemy; the British and the Americans were friends, the world would only be safe if they stayed united and prevailed. There was some residual anti-Americanism over economic matters but with prosperity and buoyant export prices, it had little significance. Prosperity also made it easier for National to remove import controls.

Encouraged by Fraser, the new government refused to recognize the Peking government, in this respect parting company with the British. F. N. Doidge, the Minister of External Affairs, became absorbed with the new dangers to South-east Asia — the armies of a Communist state were on the borders of French Indochina and that much closer to British Malaya.

But that concern was overshadowed in June 1950 by the outbreak of war in Korea. New Zealand and other Commonwealth countries provided political and military support to the Americans in Korea. At the time of the North Korean invasion the Soviets were boycotting the Security Council and as a result, resistance to the invasion came under UN auspices. This fact gave additional rationale for New Zealand's participation.

In November however the war turned sour. The Chinese intervened when UN forces came too close to the Chinese border and something close to a rout of the United States and its allies followed. American opinion was both angry and confused. There was talk of using the atomic bomb, of war with China. For New Zealand there was a twofold consequence. On the one hand, the United States became receptive to the notion of a South Pacific security arrangement, something Australia and New Zealand had hoped for since the end of the Second World War. 'It was of supreme importance to New Zealand,' Doidge told the rest of the Cabinet at the end of March 1951, 'that we obtain a guarantee of our security from the United States of America.

The United Kingdom no longer had the strength to protect us: "Britannia no longer ruled the waves." ' In London, the Prime Minister Sidney Holland, anxious about the prospect of the United States reverting to isolationism, proclaimed his determination to stick with the United States, through thick or thin, right or wrong. But on the other hand, opinion in New Zealand became rather apprehensive about just where American foreign policy was headed. Even at a time of conflict, most New Zealanders could envisage future relations with Communist China, provided it stayed out of other people's — particularly Britain's — backyard.

However, in April 1951, when President Truman officially announced the plan for a treaty between his country, Australia and New Zealand, he had only weeks before sacked General MacArthur. American foreign policy seemed set in a saner mode. New Zealand apprehensions about America's determination to sign a peace treaty with Japan were allayed. It was fairly evident that the Americans would not be pulling out in a hurry and New Zealand did not mind Japan being a gigantic aircraft carrier, as long as it was an American one, not a Japanese one. The government and much press opinion was more concerned with New Zealand's own military commitments. The text of the security treaty, released in July, was reassuring in its recognition that Australia and New Zealand had Commonwealth obligations outside the treaty area. As Britain seemed almost on the brink of war with Iran over oil investments, that was a timely reassurance. New Zealand, for the first time in its history, entered an alliance without Britain.

There was talk of economic organization for war too: the possible world war as well as the local one in Korea. A battery of committees was established in Washington, mostly to assure Americans access to commodities at reasonable prices. They pushed the New Zealanders and Australians for a year to abandon free enterprise, in particular the wool auction system. The New Zealanders — producers and government alike — as stoutly rejected that proposal as they chastised Britain for tying them to the price clauses of their meat, butter and cheese contracts, the security of which they had so welcomed when they were extended for seven years in 1948. So if international economic collaboration was a little fractured it had its good side for New Zealand as commodity prices went up and up and up. The pain would come later.

The Labour party agreed with the government's new departures in foreign policy. When in government, Labour had wanted a treaty with the United States and it believed the Soviet Union was an adversary. Fraser had gone, but his policy survived him. There was criticism of course, from intellectuals, from some unions. The historian Willis Airey argued in May, an echo of Harry Holland in 1921, that the proposed peace treaty with Japan was 'based on promotion of the cold war and is a negation of the United Nations . . . . We are being committed to American policy; and American policy gives Japan enormous bargaining power.' But it was a minority view even within the Labour party. As for the unions, between February and June 1951 the radical segment of the labour movement was beaten to the ground over the waterfront dispute. Both government and watersiders claimed that the other was the agent of a foreign power. In fact both anti-Communist conservatism and union activism were home grown. The victory of the former did however entrench what was already the dominant orientation of the country's foreign relations.

At the beginning of September the government won an election called ahead of time to exploit the economic good times and its victory over the watersiders. An American diplomatic officer wrote that:

> while the Government was unable to reveal any direct link between the Kremlin and the militant unions, it did manage to convince many people that the left-wing labour elements in the country were, consciously or unconsciously, serving the interests of Moscow. It was easily demonstrable that the tying up of the country by crippling strikes had crippled New Zealand's capacity to ship food to Britain and train troops for Korea and Commonwealth defence.

The same week in San Fransisco, New Zealand put its name to both the peace treaty with Japan and the security treaty with Australia and the United States, ANZUS as it came to be called. The cold war consensus was underlined both at home and overseas.

In 1914 New Zealand was a satisfied part of a liberal and capitalist British world. Nearly half a century later that was only partially true. New Zealand possessed an international personality of its own, its own foreign service, its own membership of a host of international institutions. As much as this development reflected changes in the international environment where British power had declined, it also expressed strong impulses within New Zealand. World War One enhanced the status of all the Dominions and the pressure from the most assertive produced a codification of this change by the end of the 1920s, a change welcomed by the Labour government elected in New Zealand at the end of 1935. In the meantime the depression had administered a shock to New Zealand's assumption that Britain provided a 'bottomless market' for New Zealand exports — although it remained by far the most significant market for another generation. For New Zealand itself the Second World War was even more significant than the First, as events in the Pacific in particular required the country to conduct its own diplomacy with countries outside the Commonwealth, in particular the United States. Unlike its reluctant participation in the League of Nations, New Zealand's involvement in the United Nations was vigorous. The patterns of wartime diplomacy reappeared with the advent of the cold war — New Zealand had two important allies, Britain and the United States, not just one.

So there was change. But there was also continuity — New Zealand a member of the

The Second World War showed Britain could not protect New Zealand. The 1951 security treaty filled the gap with an assurance of American protection against Japan or any other threat. *NZ Herald*

Empire, of the Commonwealth, of the United Nations, of the free world under American leadership; the names changed, but much else did not. There was an enemy of global significance, there was a need to marshal resources, both economic and military, there was a need to defend the forward area, and secure the rear ones, to maintain imperial, British, capitalist, non-Communist, allied, call it what you will, influence — in Europe, in the Middle East, in Asia and Africa, and even at home, wherever the enemy might strike. It seemed to be the condition of existence, and even if the enemy changed its name and beliefs, the pattern remained the same. In the First World War the Bolsheviks were believed to be in league with the Kaiser, in 1939 Stalin did make a pact with Hitler and totalitarianism, but the common character of Nazism and Communism was exposed for all to see. There were disgruntled nationalists within the Empire after the first war, within the Commonwealth during and after the second. The French were difficult in the First World War, difficult after it, unreliable in the second, unpredictable after it. It might be that New Zealand's interests were not always looked after by the British — let alone the Americans — but most New Zealanders went along with them all the same. So for anyone born before the First World War and growing up in New Zealand in the first half of the century, there were plenty of reminders of the world of their childhood in an era when conscription was introduced for the third time and plans were made for participation in the event of another war. The Middle East was the likely theatre of action, a reminder of 1915 and 1941.

There was also institutional continuity. Amongst the practitioners of foreign relations — the government's senior advisors and in the politicians of both parties — there was a large measure of consensus. The same names recur over lengthy periods with the 1935 election providing a break for politicians, but not for civil servants. In the economic interest groups and in the dissenting groups, the same names reappear again and again. New Zealand may have been a society organized for war three times in this half century, but it remained itself a society at peace, not invaded, not attacked. The story of most people's lives was of continuity or at least of expected change, not of the disruption and dislocation usually associated with war.

At times it did seem as if there would be more transformations. World War One produced dissent, but as it was tied closely to the politics of the war itself, that dissent proved less able to force changes in foreign relations once the war was over. It was in the 1920s that more wide-ranging change seemed to be occurring. Anti-war sentiment became more pervasive, a feeling that new patterns in international relations were necessary. The depression brought still more changes and new thinking about international economic relations in particular. When Labour took office it did seek reform in both the economic and political spheres. But it had travelled a long way from its socialist rhetoric at the end of the First World War and the changes were not as great therefore as might have been expected. The most evident sources of friction, both with conservative opinion in New Zealand and with the British, were over policy in the League of Nations in 1936–7 and over economic matters in 1939.

Although the Second World War returned the country to a more traditional mode, the fertile thinking of the 1930s exercised an influence during the war, especially with the establishment of a close Anglo-American political collaboration from 1941. This culminated in the plans for the United Nations and other institutions of global order. The initiative came from outside New Zealand but was widely welcomed in New Zealand. Although the cold war did not end the dream of the United Nations, it did administer a blow to the hopes invested in it, and much of the pattern of the earlier conflicts returned.

11. *The National Governments and Social Change*
(1949-1972)

BARRY GUSTAFSON

The political scene in New Zealand between 1949 and 1972 was dominated almost totally by the National Party governments of Sidney Holland (1949–1957) and Keith Holyoake (1957 and 1960–1972). Those governments and Prime Ministers embodied and articulated the concern for normalcy, security, prosperity and comfort which pervaded New Zealand society throughout the 1950s and, to a somewhat lesser extent, the 1960s. After twenty years of depression and war there was a widespread desire among tired but hopeful New Zealanders that the next twenty years would be far less stressful.

Soldiers returning from overseas and wives who had been in effect solo mothers during the war years longed to be reunited with loved ones and rebuild their family lives. Some men, of course, found it difficult to fit back into civilian life and some women found it just as difficult to leave the workplace and become housewives again, but in the late 1940s and early 1950s they were the exceptions.

For most New Zealanders in the fifties and early sixties it was simply enough to be with one's family and friends; to own a home or rent a state house; to build a farm or business; to have a secure job; to take advantage or see one's children take advantage of the unprecedented opportunities for education and upward social mobility; to buy from the growing array of material goods available; to repair and clean one's second-hand car, cut the lawns, put down a vegetable garden, lay concrete drives and paths, paint the house, and paper the lounge; to go to the local picture theatre, the beach, the races, the pub (before 6 pm); to have a family Sunday lunch followed by an afternoon nap; to take part in community activities, establishing kindergartens, playcentres, schools, churches and sports clubs in the new suburban housing estates which began to sprawl across the urban hinterlands.

The post-war era saw a suburban sprawl. The Parade, St Heliers, 1964. *Auckland Public Library*

The desire for normalcy did not mean that New Zealanders were depressed or apathetic in the post-war era. There was an enormous intellectual energy and excitement and an outburst of creative activity throughout the country. There was an optimistic consensus that New Zealand should be a prosperous and fair society, free from fascism, depression, war and want. Everyone would have a job, a home, security in illness or old age. It was recognized that education, and not just through schools and universities but throughout society as a whole, held the key to the future. The post-war baby boom made New Zealand a society oriented very much towards the needs of children. Writers and artists, who believed that society was at its most perceptive and articulate in literature, painting and music, started to depict and interpret the New Zealand landscape and society and to question that society's apparent uniformity, conformity and cultural colonialism.

Both New Zealand's somewhat mediocre dominant mass culture and its more élitist minority literature, art and music have always been derived from the cultures of the overseas societies which provided New Zealand's narrowly selected immigrants, its higher education, books, magazines and comics, music, plays, motion pictures and radio programmes. Those influences were reinforced in the sixties by the advent of television and the dependence of that medium on entertainment and information

Most of New Zealand's leading performing artists travelled overseas to further their careers; for example, Kiri Te Kanawa and Inia Te Wiata. *NZ Herald*

programmes produced in the United States, Britain and Australia, and reflecting the values, biases, preoccupations, outlooks, judgements, heritages and environments of those English-speaking but increasingly foreign societies. New Zealanders tended to read love stories, murder mysteries, westerns and historical romances set in Britain and the United States. They watched films from Hollywood and Ealing Studios. They rocked and rolled or twisted to the records of Bill Haley and his Comets, Elvis Presley, Cliff Richard and the Shadows, the Beatles and the Rolling Stones. They responded to the protest ballads of Joan Baez, Bob Dylan and Peter, Paul and Mary.

The best of New Zealand's performing artists during the 1950s and 1960s still had to go overseas for training, work and recognition. They performed international music for international audiences. The New Zealand singer Oscar Natzke, who died in 1951, provided a role model for Inia Te Wiata, Donald McIntyre, Kiri Te Kanawa, and a large number of other fine singers. Ballet dancers such as Rowena Jackson, Alexander Grant and Bryan Ashbridge also sought fame in London rather than Auckland. Talent such as theirs could not be adequately supported by New Zealand's small population, despite brave attempts to do so by the National Symphony Orchestra founded in 1946, the New Zealand Ballet formed in 1953 by Poul Gnatt, and the New Zealand Opera Company launched in 1954 by Donald Munro. In 1971 the latter two combined to form the New Zealand Ballet and Opera Trust. New Zealand's few gifted composers, such as Douglas Lilburn, Edwin Carr and Jenny McLeod, stayed in New Zealand but struggled to interest a largely apathetic New Zealand population in their music.

Attempts to establish a professional national theatre group also proved very difficult. The New Zealand Players, created in 1953 by Edith and Richard Campion after their return from the Old Vic Theatre in England, fought high costs throughout the rest of the decade before being finally destroyed in 1960 by a controversial and financially disastrous tour of Samuel Beckett's *Waiting for Godot*. More successful were attempts to establish metropolitan theatre groups such as Auckland's Community Arts Service and Ngaio Marsh's Canterbury Players from the late 1940s, Wellington's Downstage Theatre in 1964, and Auckland's Mercury Theatre in 1968. Very few of the plays were written by New Zealanders or reflected a New Zealand way or view of life. The notable exceptions were Bruce Mason's *The Pohutukawa Tree* (1957) and *The End of the Golden Weather* (1959). The first explored the clash between the European and traditional Māori lifestyles and the latter, a solo work, was performed by Mason almost a thousand times before his death in 1982.

In literature, the 1950s and 1960s saw the further development of a countervailing cultural nationalism tentatively and sometimes self-consciously exploring New Zealand and the people who inhabited it. Small, co-operative coteries of intellectuals located in the university cities shared somewhat élitist, often dogmatic and sometimes arrogant certainty of what was 'good' in literature and art. Openly contemptuous of traditional forms of painting, writing and music, they praised the experimental, even if it was also imitative and rather tame by international standards. Some regarded themselves as the consciousness and the conscience of society, commenting with assumed authority not only on the arts but on New Zealand history, politics, economics, foreign policy and society.

The economics of publishing became a little easier during the fifties and sixties. Although novelists such as Frank Sargeson and Janet Frame continued to publish largely in London or New York, they and others were assisted by the establishment of the State Literary Fund in 1946 and of the Arts Advisory Council in 1961. The Council was renamed the Queen Elizabeth Arts Council in 1963. New periodicals appeared to publish and comment on the growing volume of poetry being written: *Landfall*, founded in 1947 and edited for the next twenty years by Charles Brasch; *Here and Now*, established in 1948 to foster the free discussion of politics, literature, art and public affairs; and *The New Zealand Poetry Yearbook*, edited from 1951 to 1964 by Louis Johnson. Various private sponsors also provided encouragement with the Watties Book of the Year Awards and the Benson and Hedges and the Kelliher Art Prizes.

The major poets of the 1950s and 1960s had established themselves in the 1930s and 1940s: A. R. D. Fairburn, Allen Curnow, R. A. K. Mason, Denis Glover. Those older, more traditional poets were associated with the Caxton Press, set up in Christchurch in 1936. They were joined by groups of younger poets: in Wellington W. H. Oliver, Louis Johnson, and Alistair Campbell; in Auckland, Keith Sinclair, Kendrick Smithyman, M. K. Joseph and C. K. Stead. In time, Sinclair and Oliver were to become New Zealand's leading historians. Hone Tuwhare made a considerable impact with his collection *No Ordinary Sun* (1964) and a number of women poets were prominent, notably Gloria Rawlinson, Fleur Adcock, Ruth Gilbert and Janet Frame.

James K. Baxter, who published his first volume of poetry, *Beyond the Palisade*, in 1944 and who died aged 46 in 1972, was between those years *the* figure of New Zealand poetry, more so than Fairburn who died in 1957 or Curnow or Smithyman. In a diverse range of early poems, Baxter revealed a fresh insight into and a robust vision of New Zealand. His growing spirituality and his deep commitment to help those damaged by alcohol and drug addiction were reflected in his later poetry as well as in his personality and practical social work.

Perhaps even more impressive than the poetry of the fifties and sixties were the novels and short stories written by New Zealanders. Some reflected wartime experiences and emotions and reinforced the themes of collective identity and collective responsibility which pervaded not only much of New Zealand's literature but also debates on its society, economy and politics. Dan Davin's *For the Rest of Our Lives* (1947) and *The Sullen Bell* (1956); Guthrie Wilson's *Brave Company* (1951); M. K. Joseph's *I'll Soldier No More* (1958); Errol Brathwaite's *Fear in the Night* (1959) and *An Affair of Men* (1961), were such novels. Brathwaite also explored the Māori-European land wars of the nineteenth century with a trilogy of novels published between 1964 and 1967, and Noel Hilliard's *Māori Girl* (1960) revived the theme of race relations in New Zealand.

New Zealand had a number of excellent short story writers, some of whom also became successful writers of novels. They included Maurice Duggan, O. E. Middleton, Maurice Shadbolt and Frank Sargeson. Sargeson, notable for using New Zealand colloquial language in his earlier writing, became one of the most influential prose writers of his generation. He often dealt with solitary, socially marginalized misfits, as his titles suggest: *I Saw in My Dream* (1949), *I, For One* (1956), *Memoirs of a Peon* (1965), *The Hangover* (1967), *Joy of the Worm* (1967). He and some of his contemporaries criticized the puritanism which they believed inhibited the development of both healthy individuals and a healthy collective New Zealand society. Davin and James Courage were others who wrote about deviants and explored the stress and conflict which grew out of narrow and arbitrary constraints, which they argued were imposed particularly on the creative young and the divergent individual by an authoritarian, conformist and stultifying New Zealand society with its restrictive religious and sexual codes of conduct.

The theme of alienation is found also in the search for identity and the unhappy fate of those lonely individuals on the dividing line between sanity and insanity who people the novels and short stories of Janet Frame. Frame, whose first book of short stories, *The Lagoon*, appeared in 1951, published her first novel, *Owls Do Cry*, in 1957.

Frank Sargeson's use of ordinary New Zealand language and his protrayal of social misfits influenced a generation of New Zealand writers. *NZ Herald*

She went on to become arguably the most important New Zealand prose writer of her day, gaining a substantial international reputation with seven further books during the 1960s: *Faces In the Water* (1961), *The Edge of the Alphabet* (1962), *Scented Gardens of the Blind* (1963), *The Adaptable Man* (1965), *A State of Siege* (1967), *The Rainbirds* (1967), and *Intensive Care* (1970).

Many other New Zealand writers contributed to the impressive quantity of quality prose written during the fifties and sixties. Shadbolt, whose *Among the Cinders* (1965) was to sell over 150,000 copies, continued to produce accomplished novels and short stories spread over the following quarter of a century, as did Maurice Gee, who explored the more violent side of New Zealand society. Ian Cross's *The God Boy* (1958), R. H. Morrieson's *The Scarecrow* (1963), Joseph's *A Pound of Saffron* (1962) and *The Hole in the Zero* (1967), Bill Pearson's excellent regional novel *Coal Flat* (1963), and Stead's *Smith's Dream* (1971) were all, in terms of plot and character development, universal in appeal but parochial in setting. Barry Crump's popular books, starting with *A Good Keen Man* (1960), were written in an anecdotal style and New Zealand idiom. In 1972 Witi Ihimaera emerged on the literary scene with *Pounamu Pounamu*, the first collection of short stories published by a self-consciously Māori writer. Although not as significant or successful as Frame, other women writers made substantial contributions during the period: Sylvia Ashton-Warner's *Spinster* (1958), *Incense to Idols* (1960), *Bell Call* (1964), and *Greenstone* (1967); Ruth France's *The Race* (1958) and *Ice Cold River* (1961); Marilyn Duckworth's *A Gap In the Spectrum* (1959); and Joy Cowley's *Nest in a Falling Tree* (1967).

The 1950s and 1960s saw an initially small group of potters such as Len Castle, Peter Stitchbury, and Barry Brickell pioneer the development of pottery as New Zealand's premier craft.

As for painting, the revitalizing of the public galleries (especially the Auckland City Art Gallery under the directorships of Eric Westbrook from 1952 and Peter Tomory after 1956) in respect of purchasing policies and lively presentations of exhibitions, was enormously important. So was the arrival of active dealer galleries which challenged the overall conservatism of the arts societies, gave public exposure to younger painters, and encouraged the work of abstractionist painters such as Rita Angus, Toss Woollaston and John Weeks. Some long overdue energizing of the art schools took place and a useful 'modishness' about buying works of art spread through a section of the community with the power and desire to purchase paintings. Experiment could at last be considered more than eccentricity and provided a challenge to the much greater mass of representational painting by such technically gifted artists as Evelyn Page and Peter McIntyre.

One factor in the transformation of the art scene was the arrival of 'modern art' in the primary school syllabus during the late 1940s. Future artists and appreciative audiences were thenceforth prepared to experiment with and appreciate diverse forms of art. This artistic revolution owed much to officers of the Department of Education such as Dr C. E. Beeby and Gordon Tovey, to the art lecturers in Teachers Colleges, and to itinerant art specialists who went out evangelically into the primary schools and the district high schools. Secondary schools were much more resistant to change, in spite of spreading ethusiasm for child art and the patronage in the late forties of the Prime Minister Fraser and the Governor-General Sir Bernard Freyberg.

The most controversial painter of the period was undoubtedly Colin McCahon, who in 1948 created some striking religious paintings such as *The Virgin and Child Compared* (1948) and landscapes such as *Takaka: Night and Day* (1948). McCahon's interest in religion and landscapes continued, though his style changed from a cubist technique in the 1950s to a more hard-edged look in the 1960s. His use of scriptural texts and word paintings provoked strong derision and hostility as well as fervent admiration and praise, as did the work of other prominent abstractionists such as Milan Mrkusich, Gordon Walters, Donald Peebles and Ralph Hotere. One modernist painter who returned from overseas, Patrick Hanly, had a profound local influence. Although an expressionist he used abstraction in a number of powerful moral works on the theme of the nuclear holocaust.

Don Binney, Robin White, Brent Wong and Michael Smither pursued a new brand of realism. Binney's birds, landscapes and seascapes were among the most widely appreciated and acclaimed paintings of the 1960s. Gretchen Albrecht impressed with her joyful use of colour, as did Robert Ellis with his semi-abstract patterns of colour and light. Para Matchitt's *Te Kooti* (1967) advanced the use of Māori motifs, but Matchitt and other Māori painters were to face a struggle and considerable Māori opposition in reconciling European skills and styles with traditional Māori art forms.

Physical prowess, however, has always been admired and often rewarded more than intellectual achievements in New Zealand and most New Zealanders during the 1950s and 1960s were more interested in rugby, racing and beer than the works of Baxter, Frame and McCahon.

Sport was probably the major catalyst and the most visible expression of New Zealand's emerging sense of national identity during the fifties and sixties. For a small country, New Zealand produced a surprisingly large number of world-class athletes over a wide range of sports. Yvette Williams, who won a gold medal in the long jump at the 1950 Empire Games in Auckland and was to win three, for the long jump, discus and shot, at the Vancouver Empire Games in 1954, became the first New Zealand woman to win an Olympic gold medal when she competed in the long jump at Helsinki in 1952. In 1956 some 60,000 people at Eden Park in Auckland saw the All Blacks beat the Springboks in the fourth rugby test by 11–5, thus winning the rubber for the first time in sixty years. In the same year New Zealand's cricket team, playing the West Indies, won its first ever test match. At the 1960 Rome Olympics, Peter Snell won the 800 metres and Murray Halberg the 5000 metres and at the 1964 Tokyo Olympics Snell won both the 800 metres and the 1500 metre golds. In less publicized sports, Ivan Mauger became the world's motorcycle racing champion, the golfer Bob Charles won the British Open, and Denis Hulme, Bruce McLaren and Chris Amon were among the world's top motor-racing drivers.

Although it is unlikely most men and women found New Zealand in the 1950s as dull and conformist as some historians and most writers have suggested, certainly during the 1960s many younger New Zealanders did feel cramped on an isolated island nation with its small, relatively homogeneous population and narrow and authoritarian collective outlook. Never having known war, depression or real economic deprivation, a few younger New Zealanders questioned the traditional consensus and started to identify and challenge some of the problems which were to become even more evident in the 1970s and 1980s. The relative calm of the 1950s and early 1960s was replaced by the gathering storm clouds of a much less certain and much more turbulent era.

New Zealand in 1949 was governed by a Labour Government that had been in power for fourteen eventful and stressful years. Peter Fraser, the Prime Minister, was within a year of his death and the other Labour leaders were ageing and understandably weary. They had brought New Zealand out of the depression of the 1930s, created a comprehensive social security system, competently led New Zealand during six years of war, and successfully rehabilitated tens of thousands of returning servicemen back into the economy and society.

People's memories are short, however, and their expectations of what are their

Peter Snell's athletic achievements and the success of many other New Zealand sportsmen and women were a major factor in New Zealand's emerging nationalism. *NZ Herald*

reasonable needs are constantly being revised upward in comparison to what they see the more fortunate in society enjoying. The electorate's gratitude to Labour for its past actions was by 1949 more than balanced by resentment at the continuation of inflation, shortages and rationing of consumer goods, scarcity of housing, and restrictions, regulations and bureaucratic controls of every conceivable kind. Many voters disliked the government's unwillingness or inability to oppose industrial militancy, especially on the waterfront. When the government did move in 1949 to deregister the Auckland Carpenters Union, that divided the Labour Party's active membership. So did the much more controversial Government decision to hold and support a referendum that led to the introduction of compulsory military training in peacetime. Women, concerned at the rising cost of living and housing shortages were a particular target of the National Party Opposition which won the 1949 election gaining 46 seats to Labour's 34.

The new Prime Minister, Sidney Holland, who for the next five years was also to hold the post of Minister of Finance, had been more than any other person responsible for creating, unifying and bringing the National Party to power. A vigorous man, Holland was no theorist but he knew clearly, simply, firmly and instinctively rather than intellectually what type of society he believed was best for New Zealand. Whereas Labour had emphasized egalitarianism and collective responsibility, Holland and the National Party stressed equality of opportunity for the individual and a more meritocratic system of rewards. Private and individual freedom, initiative, enterprise, responsibility, and reward were paramount, though during the 1940s, partly in recognition of electoral realities, Holland and his party had tempered their political conservatism and economic pragmatism with a strand of social humanitarianism. He promised that the social security system and full employment would be maintained and that, in addition to prosperity and security, New Zealanders could have personal freedom as well. Holland's leadership peaked with the 1949 and 1951 elections when he led his party to its first victory, survived a traumatic industrial challenge that tore apart New Zealand society, and consolidated National's hold on office by calling and winning decisively an early election.

Unlike the Labour Government it replaced, which had been dominated by men born and raised in Britain and Australia, or even the 1957–60 Labour cabinet, almost half of whose members had been born overseas, all but one of Holland's sixteen member cabinet had been born in New Zealand. The exception, the Australian Fred Doidge, had lived in New Zealand since 1902. Over half National's Members of Parliament were returned servicemen. Most were farmers, businessmen, lawyers or accountants. Clearly the new National Government was representative of a different generation, a different socio-economic stratum, and a different set of values and vested interests to those from which the first Labour Government had been formed. Labour had dominated the late 1930s and the 1940s and imposed its doctrines, ideas, methods and style on that era. With two brief, three-year intervals of Labour administration, National was to do the same during its long tenure of office over the following thirty-five years.

Holland's Government moved swiftly in 1950 to abolish the Labour-dominated Legislative Council, the appointed and largely ineffective upper house of the New Zealand Parliament, thus making the legislature a unicameral one and paving the way for a further increase in executive power. But the new government did not act as decisively in regard to its 1949 election promise to abolish compulsory membership of a trade union. One reason for Holland's hesitation was that, after April 1950, the New Zealand trade union movement was bitterly divided between the more conservative Federation of Labour and the Communist-influenced Trade Union Congress, the major component of which was the Waterside Worker's Union who favoured direct action rather than the arbitration system in settling wage disputes. This challenged the economic stabilization and firm wage control policies of both the post-war Labour and National Governments. In 1950, a record 271,475 workdays were lost through strikes. The *de facto* leader of the Federation of Labour in 1951 was its vice-president, the able but vicious Fintan Patrick Walsh, who was to assume the Federation's presidency from 1952 until his death in 1963. Walsh developed a close and effective working relationship with the National Government's Minister of Labour Bill

Sidney Holland, who more than any other man was responsible for bringing the National Party to office in 1949. *NZ Herald*

Sullivan, and later with Sullivan's successor Tom Shand.

In February 1951 the shipowners refused to give a 15% wage demand to the watersiders who proceeded to ban overtime. The owners retaliated by putting men off work for two days for every day they refused overtime. The watersiders rejected arbitration. The government proclaimed draconian emergency regulations. The armed forces moved in to work the wharves. Other unions, such as the miners, drivers and freezing workers, stopped work in protest. New Zealand's economy and society were disrupted by the longest and most costly industrial dispute in the country's history. After 151 bitter days, at the height of which some 20,000 men were involved, the strike was broken. The Labour Opposition, which had adopted a somewhat ambivalent position regarding the dispute itself, was incensed at the government's use of regulations to prevent donations to strikers and their families, to censor publications putting the worker's viewpoint, and to ban meetings including some to

The 1951 waterfront dispute divided the country and gave the National Government the opportunity to call and win a snap election. *NZ Herald*

be addressed by Walter Nash, the Leader of the Opposition. Labour claimed in Parliament that Holland and the National Government did not have the support of the majority of New Zealanders in the way it had handled the dispute. In reply, Holland called a snap election on 11 July 1951, winning 54 per cent of the vote and 50 of the 80 seats in Parliament.

Between 1949 and 1954 the National Government gradually started to de-regulate the economy. Rationing was ended. Import controls were considerably relaxed. A free market was established in land and buildings. Home ownership was encouraged. Inflation, however, continued to be a problem and there was every prospect that National's large majority in Parliament would be reduced or even destroyed at the 1954 election. In the event, National dropped from 54% to 44% of the vote, a little less than Labour polled, but the major beneficiary of National's eroded support was the new Social Credit Political League, which gained a surprising 11%. That was insufficient to win Social Credit a seat and because of the three-way split, National clung on to office with a reduced but still comfortable majority of ten seats over Labour.

Walter Nash, Prime Minister 1957-60, a politician from an earlier generation, with Keith Jacka Holyoake, the outstanding politician of the sixties. *NZ Herald*

Over the next three years the National Government's new Minister of Finance, Jack Watts, attacked inflation by cutting government expenditure, reducing the availability of credit, raising interest rates, and encouraging capital investment rather than consumption. A decision was also made to change the collection of income tax from a single, yearly, terminal payment to a Pay As You Earn (PAYE) system.

The National Party was pessimistic about its chances of winning the 1957 election. The inevitable erosion of support after eight years in office; the changing demographic reality that New Zealand was becoming more urban and industrialized, thus reducing the number of safe rural National seats and steadily increasing the number of urban Labour strongholds and marginals; the threat of further inroads by Social Credit into some of National's rural strongholds, all made the task of holding office difficult. More serious, however, were two other problems: Holland's health and, as export prices for butter, wool and cheese started to collapse, the prospect of a serious balance of payments crisis. The impending economic crisis was deliberately and successfully kept from the public until after the election, but Holland's illness could not be concealed and weeks before the election he was replaced by his deputy, Keith Holyoake.

Labour, under the leadership of Walter Nash, by then 75 years old, polled 4% more of the vote than National at the 1957 election and sneaked back into office with 41 seats to National's 39. With the appointment of a Speaker, Labour effectively had a one-seat majority. Labour's victory was not just the inevitable rejection of an incumbent government, nor can it be explained simply by Nash's election promise to refund up to one hundred pounds of tax following the introduction of PAYE. Labour's election policy included a number of other very attractive proposals, notably the increase of family benefit payments, which could be capitalized for home purchase, and a system of state loans at 3% or 5% interest to families wishing to build a house. Some of Labour's more perceptive leaders such as Arnold Nordmeyer, a politician of great ability and integrity who became Minister of Finance, and Phillip Holloway, a young and charismatic MP who became Minister of Industries and Commerce, also recognized the need to start restructuring New Zealand's economy.

Although New Zealand had been ready for economic change after World War II, the development and growth that took place was very much along traditional lines: export-oriented farming for wool, meat, butter and cheese; a heavily protected manufacturing sector; and a service sector largely funded from taxation. The Bulk Purchasing Agreement with Britain ended in 1954, but in 1952 the British agreed to duty-free access for New Zealand meat to the British market until 1967 and a similar arrangement for dairy products was concluded in 1957, again until 1967. Those guaranteed markets, combined with the incredibly high prices paid for New Zealand wool in the early fifties during the Korean War, confirmed New Zealand's continued optimism about its traditional products and markets and delayed radical economic reform. Initially, the emphasis was on increasing agricultural production by developing marginal lands, placing some 10,000 rehabilitated ex-servicemen on their own farms, and increasing productivity through aerial top-dressing and spraying, mechanization, stock improvement, and better farm management.

The boom prices paid for agricultural exports, especially wool, did enable New Zealand during the 1950s to liberalize import licensing and effectively to subsidize some development of secondary industry aimed primarily at maintaining full employment but also hopefully in the future providing additional export earnings or at least saving foreign exchange through import substitution. A number of existing New Zealand industrial firms grew considerably, such as Fletchers, Watties, Fisher and Paykel, Alex Harvey and Todd Motors. Carpet manufacturers such as Feltex and Kensington started processing New Zealand wool.

Tasman Empire Airways Ltd (TEAL) changed from using Solent flying boats to land-based DC6 aircraft in 1954 and became wholly New Zealand owned in 1961 when the New Zealand Government bought out its Australian Government partner. In 1965 TEAL changed its name to Air New Zealand after extending its service to the West Coast of the United States the previous year. Air travel during the 1960s was to supplant almost completely travel overseas by sea. By 1973 there were no passenger liners coming regularly to New Zealand. Increasing numbers of young New Zealanders flew off overseas for working holidays, returning to New Zealand and questioning why some of the more attractive amenities and services they had found in Britain and Europe did not exist in their homeland.

Two large companies made timber a major New Zealand industry. In the centre of the North Island, New Zealand Forest Products built the town of Tokoroa and a mill nearby at Kinleith, and in 1953 commenced producing pulp from forests planted during the 1930s. In the eastern Bay of Plenty, the Tasman Pulp and Paper Company, set up in 1952 to mill the government-owned Kaingaroa Forest, started producing newsprint in 1955 at its Kawerau mill. In 1959 exports of pine logs to Japan through the port of Tauranga commenced and by 1972 some seventy-five million board feet of timber were being cut annually at Kawerau and Murupara.

The fifties and sixties were also the decades during which most of New Zealand's hydroelectric power projects were completed: Maraetai (1952–1954 and 1970–1971), Whakamaru (1956), Atiamuri (1958–1964), Waipapa (1961), Manapouri (1963–1971) and Turangi-Tokaanu (1965–1974). A geothermal field for electricity generation was built at Wairakei (1956–1959) and the Kapuni No. 1 Well in Taranaki was developed between 1959 and 1962 with gas pipelines to Auckland and Wellington being constructed between 1966 and 1971. Further gas and oil were found at Maui I in 1969.

The Nash Labour Government of 1957–1960 was faced from the start with a wide diversity of insatiable expectations, the difficulties of governing with a majority of one, and the limitations imposed by the now evident balance of payments situation. New Zealand, without borrowing, held only sufficient overseas reserves to pay for six weeks worth of imports. The implementation of Labour's election promises, especially in social welfare and housing, would also undoubtedly increase both government expenditure and inflation. The import controls which National had been systematically and perhaps over-optimistically dismantling were reimposed. Nordmeyer introduced a controversial 1958 budget. It increased social security benefits, provided for state loans for private housing at 3% and 5%, and hurt least those taxpayers on lower incomes and with dependent children. But the budget also increased both direct and indirect taxation, including dividends and company profits, and raised the price of cigarettes, beer and petrol, thus hitting the modest pleasures of many wage-earners.

For the following two years, Holyoake mounted a sustained and incredibly effective attack on what he labelled 'the Black Budget'. He claimed that it had been caused not by economic factors outside the Government's control, but by the need to fund what he alleged were Labour's reckless and unprincipled election bribes, such as Nash's one hundred pound tax rebate. Labour's increase in the rates of taxation was compared to National's reduction of the rates in seven of the eight years it had been in office. The criticisms were accepted not only by National supporters and the press but also, partly because of the hostility of the Hotel Worker's Union to Nordmeyer, by many Labour party voters and members. In two years the membership of the Labour Party was halved. It was to erode further during the following decade to a mere 13,476 financial members in 307 branches in 1970. National, on the other hand, entered the 1960 election with a record membership of 230,000 in 1300 branches making it, compared to the size of the electorate, the largest mass-based party in the Western world.

The 'Black Budget' dominated the 1960 election campaign but there was also considerable disappointment among traditional Labour voters at the Labour Government's refusal to introduce price controls; at its apparent inability to improve significantly the social security system; at its cautious and orthodox foreign policy, especially in relation to the testing of nuclear weapons and the recognition of Communist China; and at the Prime Minister's refusal to become involved in the controversy caused by the exclusion of Māori on racial grounds from a New Zealand rugby tour of South Africa. At the 1960 election Labour activists were fewer on the ground than at any time since 1943. The non-vote was especially marked among Māori manual workers. National swept back into office with a majority of 4% in the popular vote and 46 seats to Labour's 34.

Holyoake, who won four successive elections in 1960, 1963, 1966 and 1969, was a pragmatic conservative who was always conscious of the effect of government policies on people. He strove not only to achieve and maintain prosperity but also to foster co-operation and consensus rather than division and conflict. Undoubtedly one of the ablest politicians in New Zealand's history, his gifts were those of a chairman, manager, negotiator and tactician. Around him he built a formidable team of lieutenants: John Marshall, Harry Lake, Ralph Hanan, Tom Shand, Norman Shelton, Brian Talboys and, after 1967, Robert Muldoon. A patient listener and superb communicator at an individual level, Holyoake was not a particularly charismatic public speaker. It can also be argued that his reactive, consensual style delayed New Zealand seeing and preparing for some of the economic problems that were to become much more evident and critical in the 1970s. However, it was no accident that Holyoake, with his 'steady does it' approach, presided over a period of considerable economic growth, material prosperity, cultural liberalism and upward social mobility. He articulated the mood of his times, although as one protest song of the sixties noted, 'the times, they are a-changing'. In no area of policy was that truer in the 1960s than in foreign affairs and defence.

New Zealand traditionally had enjoyed a bipartisan foreign policy based on a recognition of New Zealand's tiny population and isolated geographic position. The economy was almost totally dependent on access for its primary exports to overseas markets and the German and Japanese navies had shown how fragile those trade links were. The devastating potential of nuclear weapons and the spread of Communism into Asia reinforced New Zealand's sense of strategic vulnerability and made reliance on a major military ally and an emphasis on collective security and forward defence even more self-evident. By the end of World War II the United States was more able to fill the role of protector than was Britain.

The signing of the ANZUS Treaty at San Fransisco on 1 September 1951, set in the context of the Cold War between the United States and the Soviet Union, the reconstruction of Japan, the emergence of Communist China, the Korean War, the explosion of the first Soviet atom bomb, and the decolonizing of South-East Asia by the British and the Dutch, was welcomed in New Zealand by all but the inconsequential extreme Left. Although the treaty involved consultation rather than automatic involvement by the signatories in the event of hostilities against one of them, there was a clearly implied and understood commitment by the United States to defend Australia and New Zealand against any future aggressor. In return New Zealand, by and large, went along with America's foreign policy lead even when New Zealand had reservations, as for example over the non-recognition of Communist China and its exclusion from membership of the United Nations. The Manila Pact which set up SEATO in 1954 was also accepted uncritically by both Government and Opposition and most New Zealanders.

There was little opposition to New Zealand's military involvement in the United Nation's forces in Korea (1951-1954) and in the Malayan Emergency (1955–1960). Only volunteer soldiers were used and there were relatively few casualties. In Korea, 3794 soldiers were involved over a four-year period. Casualties were 33 dead and 79 wounded. In Malaya the forces were even smaller, with only 7 dead and 7 wounded.

The Anglo-French invasion of Egypt in 1956 raised the first real concern about New Zealand support for its major allies. Although New Zealand voted with Britain in the United Nations, it clearly found itself embarrassed by the British action and by American condemnation of it. There was never any serious consideration that New Zealand troops should become involved. The ambivalence shown by New Zealand reflected a growing sophistication in foreign policy and a clash between the still deep-seated instinct for collective security and an increasing desire for independence. While New Zealand diplomatically and militarily saw itself still as part of the Western, English-speaking world, it was slowly coming to recognize that geographically it was a South-West Pacific nation.

The collapse of European empires in Asia and the Pacific during and after World II created considerable instability and tension in the region. After the expulsion of the Japanese and the French, Vietnam was divided into two parts; the North under Communist control and the South under an anti-Communist regime. Increasingly, during the 1960s the United States found itself being dragged into a civil war between its ally, the South Vietnamese Government, and South Vietnamese Communist guerillas backed by the North Vietnamese regular army, which was supplied throughout the struggle by the Soviet Union.

In May 1965, the New Zealand Government announced that it was sending combat troops to South Vietnam at the request of the South Vietnamese Government. In fact the Holyoake Government was responding to United States pressure on its allies to intervene. New Zealand had already sent a non-combatant engineering unit and a medical team in 1964, but in May 1965 a New Zealand artillery battery attached to Australian infantry was despatched. In 1968, soldiers of the Special Air Service were also deployed. Holyoake himself had serious misgivings about New Zealand involvement in Vietnam, though he never expressed them publicly. He accepted,

New Zealand's involvement in the Vietnam War resulted in massive protests which started a realignment in New Zealand politics. *NZ Herald*

however, the arguments of a majority of his cabinet led by more hawkish ministers such as his deputy, John Marshall, that ANZUS was an insurance policy and that New Zealand's involvement in Vietnam was a premium paid on that policy. New Zealand's action would confirm its place as one of America's most dependable allies, whose strategic security and economic well-being should be resolutely protected. Holyoake was never fully convinced and, in marked contrast to the United States and Australia, New Zealand's contribution in Vietnam was kept to a minimum of volunteers. In total only 3500 New Zealanders served in Vietnam between 1965 and 1972 and never more than 550 at any one time. The casualties comprised 35 dead and 187 wounded.

Even the limited New Zealand involvement in Vietnam, however, provoked a strong reaction. Many younger and some older New Zealanders saw the American and New Zealand involvement as indefensible in what was essentially a civil war. The United States itself was bitterly divided over the war. Into New Zealand living rooms came American television news exposing both the war in all its depraved viciousness, and the large and sometimes violent anti-war protests. New Zealanders became emotionally divided on the issue and the traditional bipartisan approach to foreign affairs and defence disintegrated. The United States itself, and not just the war in Vietnam, started to be criticized by some protesters.

The Labour Opposition came out immediately and apparently unequivocally against New Zealand's involvement in the war. Nordmeyer, who in 1963 had succeeded Nash as Labour's leader, for the first and only time in New Zealand's history recorded in Parliament an Opposition's condemnation of a Government committing New Zealand to military action. He argued that Parliament, not the Cabinet, should have made the decision and he promised that a Labour Government would immediately withdraw the New Zealand contingent from Vietnam. Nordmeyer, however, was replaced shortly afterwards by the Labour Party President, Norman Kirk, who initially was less committed than Nordmeyer to an anti-war position. Kirk believed that the stand could cost Labour the 1966 election if Vietnam became the major issue. He instructed Labour's candidates to avoid debating Vietnam during the election campaign and tried to keep the government's alleged economic mismanagement as the paramount issue.

National's victory at the 'no-change' election of 1966 appeared to confirm both Kirk's fear and the National Government's cautious and limited involvement in Vietnam. But it also marked the beginning of an electoral realignment on generational and educational lines that was eventually to reshape party politics in New Zealand. The campaign against the Vietnam War continued. Teach-ins such as the 1968 'Peace, Power and Politics Conference' started to mobilize the predominantly young, affluent, well-educated opponents of the war. Protest marches became more common, such as that on 30 April 1971 when over 35,000 New Zealanders took to the streets. Even before the election of the third Labour Government in 1972 brought home the last New Zealand soldiers from Vietnam, the National Government itself had from 1970 started reducing its minimal commitment.

During the first half of the 1960s New Zealand's farm exports enjoyed high prices overseas and manufacturing expanded at a record rate. Real Gross Domestic Product rose by almost a quarter between 1960 and 1966 and the terms of trade improved also. The raucous debate over Vietnam from 1965 tended to distract attention from a deterioration in New Zealand's economy and the emergence from about 1967 of unemployment following a disastrous collapse in the wool price a year earlier. In 1967 New Zealand devalued its currency by just under 20% and a new Minister of Finance, Robert Muldoon, started to introduce mini-budgets, with the budget of May 1967 resembling Nordmeyer's famous 'Black Budget' in its increased indirect tax on petrol, motor vehicles, cigarettes and alcohol.

By the late 1960s some New Zealand politicians, farmers, businessmen, economists, journalists and others were drawing attention to Britain's likely entry into the European Economic Community and how that could affect New Zealand's farm exports in Britain. An effort was made, somewhat belatedly, to diversify New Zealand's productive base and its markets and concurrently the British Government was lobbied intensively by New Zealand's Deputy Prime Minister Marshall to protect New Zealand's continued access to that market. In June 1971, Protocol 18 of Britain's Treaty of Accession to the EEC guaranteed New Zealand special access for butter and cheese for a transitional period. By then the 86% of New Zealand's total dairy exports which had gone to Britain in 1962–1963 had been reduced to 50%, though Britain was still taking 87% of New Zealand's butter exports.

Within New Zealand, the National Government continued, as had the second Labour Government, to encourage the restructuring of agriculture and the growth of secondary industry. Labour had held an Industrial Development Conference in 1960. National organized an Export Development Conference in 1963, an Agricultural Production Conference in 1964, and a National Development Conference in 1968 and 1969. The 1969 conference set co-ordinated targets for various sectors of the economy, particularly to encourage manufacturers to produce for export, and various councils and committees were created to promote the targets. Export incentives were introduced in 1962 and between 1961/1962 and 1971/1972 manufactured exports increased tenfold. By 1972 some 300,000 people were employed in manufacturing, twice the proportion of the work-force found in farming.

Full employment during the 1950s and most of the 1960s was accompanied by a considerable real increase in average wages and a marked rise in living standards. A shortage of skilled workers for much of the period meant effectively free wage bargaining, with the gap between minimum and market wage rates widening. That had the effect of fuelling inflation and it also ignored the fact that the expansion of both the manufacturing and service sectors of the economy had been politically determined, protected by legislation and regulation and encouraged by subsidies, at least partially to maintain full employment and not just to produce goods and services. During the recession of the late 1960s, an attempt was made to hold wage increases and in June 1968 the Arbitration Court brought down a nil wage order. That effectively killed the arbitration system and led to considerable industrial unrest and direct government intervention in the wage process. In 1971 a Remuneration Act put ceilings on awards in return for regular cost of living adjustments.

Many families' real incomes were augmented by both husbands and wives taking paid employment. One of the major socio-economic changes during the 1949–1972 period was the increasing number of women in the paid workforce, including a marked rise in the proportion of married women. One-quarter of the female labour force in 1951 were married women. By 1971 the percentage was just under half. Most returned to work after their children went to school in order to help buy a home, furniture, labour-saving home appliances, or a family car. Some undoubtedly found financial independence which enabled them to escape an unsatisfactory marriage. Others wanted to use their talents and education, or extend their interests and activities beyond housework and childcare.

Women were clearly discriminated against in occupational choice, wage levels and promotions. In 1956 Joan Parker, a public servant with five years' service, won an appeal against the reduction of her salary to the level of a newly appointed male cadet.

She challenged successfully a regulation that all men in the clerical division of the public service were automatically senior to all women. Prime Minister Holland, following discussions with various women's organizations, formed in 1957 a Council for Equal Pay and Opportunity and both the National and Labour Parties adopted equal pay in the public service as a policy plank for the 1957 election. In October 1960 the Government Service Equal Pay Bill was passed to be implemented in stages by 1963. It was hoped that the private sector would follow the example and also pay men and women the same for equal work. That hope was unrealistically optimistic.

In 1967 a National Advisory Council on the Employment of Women was established to advise the Minister of Labour and in January 1971 a Royal Commission of Inquiry into Equal Pay in New Zealand was appointed. The Commission, which had a membership of four men and only one woman, reported in September that the private sector had made insignificant movement towards the introduction of equal pay. Following considerable public debate, the National Government passed the Equal Pay Act (1972) to remove gender discrimination in the private workplace. It was possibly the most significant legislation attacking the subordination of women since they had won the vote almost eighty years before.

Many voters, both male and female, were becoming increasingly concerned about other non-economic issues. Although the National Government recognized some of them, National's inherent conservatism made moves to address the issues very tentative. The protection of New Zealand's environment was one such issue. National had a sound record in setting up National Parks, having passed a National Parks Act in 1952 and subsequently adding to the four existing national parks six new ones: Fiordland and Mount Cook (both 1953), Urewera (1956), Nelson Lakes (1956), Westland (1960) and Mount Aspiring (1964). The two million hectares included in the national parks were very important for conservation, recreation and tourism. Yet during the 1960s, growing unease, especially concerning the depletion of indigenous forests and the pollution of lakes and rivers, was not taken as seriously as it should have been because the government was eager for rapid economic development. In 1968 there was an outcry over the suggestion that the water levels in Lake Manapouri should be raised to generate hydroelectric power. The Royal New Zealand Forest and Bird Protection Society launched a nationwide campaign and a petition was signed by 265,000 people. Following an inquiry the National Government agreed not to raise Manapouri 'in the meantime'. In 1970 an Environmental Council was set up to review the environmental impact of economic development proposals but the measure failed to reassure many critics of the government. The National Government's refusal to rule out future interference with the lake's level may well have contributed to the loss at the 1972 election of three or four seats in Otago and Southland.

The social security system which National inherited in 1949, although unchanged structurally, degenerated over the following twenty years. As inflation became a constant economic reality, the real value of pensions, child allowances and medical benefits eroded in the face of the government's reluctance to raise welfare funding in line with inflation. Part of the deterioration in the availability of public hospital treatment was offset by the growth of private medical insurance schemes after the formation in 1961 of the Southern Cross Medical Care Society. But the only significant National Government innovation in the social welfare area was the Accident Compensation Act of 1972, which implemented the recommendation of the Woodhouse Commission in 1967 that there should be a no-fault accident compensation scheme to protect the victims of work-related and motor vehicle accidents. The scheme, initially funded by employers and motorists, was subsequently extended by the Kirk Labour Government to include all accidents and non-earners as well as earners.

In only one area of social expenditure, education, did the National Party in government spend more than Labour Governments. Spending on education reflected the pressure of the post-war baby boom years and the 1945 Thomas Committee Report, which moved New Zealand towards universal secondary education. With one in three of New Zealand's total population in 1971 involved directly in education as a pupil, student, teacher or educational administrator, it was not surprising that spending on education rose between 1945 and 1970 from 6% to 14% of total government expenditure. During that period primary school rolls doubled and secondary school rolls rose three and a half times. There was, particularly in the 1960s, a growing interest in pre-school education, with an increase in the number of kindergartens during that decade from 207 to 305 and an even more dramatic rise in the number of playcentres from 161 to 542. By the end of the sixties, one-third of all children under the age of five received some form of pre-school education. Day-care facilities were much less common, however, with facilities for only about 2000 of the estimated 40,000 pre-school children of working mothers.

Perhaps the most dramatic educational development during the period was in tertiary education. Following the Hughes Parry Report of 1959, the University of New Zealand was dissolved in 1961 and its four constituent colleges at Auckland, Wellington, Christchurch and Dunedin became independent universities. Expenditure on universities doubled over the following two decades and in 1964 two new universities were established at Palmerston North and Hamilton. The University of Canterbury was re-sited at Ilam and the universities of Auckland, Otago and, to a lesser extent, Wellington were rebuilt on their existing sites. A new medical school was established at Auckland and there was a rapid expansion of other professional schools such as engineering, law and commerce. Between 1945 and 1970 there was an eightfold increase in the number of sixth and seventh form students in secondary schools, a quadrupling of students in the technical institutes, and a doubling of students in universities. Many intellectually able teenagers from manual-worker families with no tradition of higher education found the universities a readily accessible doorway through which they could enter the rapidly expanding professional, technological and managerial occupations. There were still, however, relatively few women students outside the Arts faculties of the universities and even fewer Māori students of either sex anywhere in the tertiary sector.

Although during the 1950s and 1960s there was an increase from 6% to 8% in the

The Maori Women's Welfare League spearheaded the Māori renaissance during the post-war era. *NZ Herald*

proportion of the New Zealand population which claimed Māori descent, there was also considerable acceptance of the belief that the Māori would eventually become assimilated into the dominant European population and culture. Intermarriage was common, with over half the marriages of a person of Māori descent in Auckland in 1960 being to a Pākehā. By the end of the sixties, half the Māori population was aged under fifteen and three-quarters were living in the urban centres. In school young Māori learned English language and Pākehā values, goals and life-styles. Cut off, however, from their marae, tribe, whanau and kaumatua, many recently urbanized Māori suffered severe cultural alienation. The Hunn Report of 1961, adopted and implemented by the National Government, reinforced the view that integration was both an inevitable reality and a positive development which would prevent future racial conflict. The Māori and European races would fuse into New Zealanders. Education was seen as the key not only to integration but also to the future upward mobility, economically and socially, of the Māori people. A Maori Education Foundation was established to provide financial assistance to pupils of Māori descent.

Increasingly, however, throughout the 1960s some Māori publicly questioned the basic assumptions underlying the assimilationist and integrationist approaches, which many rural Māori communities and tribal authorities had never accepted anyway. The Maori Women's Welfare League formed in 1951 and the Maori Council (established by National in 1962 partly to counter Labour's dominance of the four Māori seats in Parliament and partly in belated response to a continual call for such a body since it was first publicly requested by the Māori King Tawhiao in 1886) became national forums for discussing the social, economic, spiritual and cultural problems and aspirations of the Māori.

Related to the issue of a bicultural and later a multicultural New Zealand was the issue of racially selected New Zealand rugby teams playing the South Africans. In 1960, despite widespread protests within New Zealand advocating 'No Maoris, No Tour', an All Black team from which all players of Māori descent had been excluded went ahead with a tour of South Africa. By 1966, following the formation of the pressure group CARE (Citizens Association for Racial Equality), public opinion had hardened against such a tour. Prime Minister Holyoake asked the New Zealand Rugby Union to reject an invitation to send another all-white team to South Africa. In 1970 a tour did go ahead after the South Africans agreed to the inclusion of Māori players who were classed as 'honorary whites.' But by then the issue was not simply the New Zealand Rugby Union's discrimination against Māori but the apartheid system in South Africa itself, a distinction made very plain by the organization HART (Halt All Racist Tours), established in 1969.

The growing recognition throughout the 1960s that New Zealand's own racial problems required attention involved not only New Zealanders of Māori and European descent but also immigrants from the Cook Islands, Tokelau, Niue, Fiji, Western Samoa and Tonga. The Pacific island proportion rose between 1951 and 1971 from two to fifteen in every thousand of the New Zealand population, a trend that was to accelerate in the following decades. In 1971 the government passed a Race Relations Act, which prohibited discrimination 'by reason of the colour, race or ethnic or national origins' of any person, and established a race relations conciliator with formal powers to investigate complaints.

While National governed New Zealand during the 1960s, the Labour Party gave the impression, which had considerable substance, that it had lost its sense of identity and direction. Nash finally retired in 1963 but his successor Nordmeyer found his public reputation still tarnished by memories of the 'Black Budget' and his support in the Labour movement undermined by the hostility of Nash and several other senior party and trade union figures and by the ambition of the Party president, Norman Kirk, who replaced Nordmeyer in 1965. Labour tried to compensate for its failure to rethink its policies, renew its organization, and rekindle the fervour of its electoral support, by projecting what it termed a 'New Look' at the 1963 election; by offering a 'New Leader' in 1966; and by presenting a 'New Image' in 1969. Throughout the sixties there was almost constant internal conflict within the Labour Party. Its parliamentary team was lacklustre and its organization at all levels moribund.

As New Zealand-born politicians such as Nordmeyer and Kirk took over the leadership of the Labour Party and as younger New Zealand–born activists replaced their ageing parents and immigrant predecessors in the party organization, there was a decreasing use of the rhetoric of class warfare and an increasing attempt to appeal

Many New Zealanders grew up in state housing suburbs such as this one at Tamaki. *Auckland Public Library/National Archives*

to the nation as a whole. Kirk told the Labour Party's 1968 Conference that 'the words "New Zealand" are as important as the word "Labour" '. A majority of manual-worker trade unionists continued to identify with and vote for Labour throughout the fifties and sixties but during the 1960s the party started to appeal to an increasing number of younger, well-educated men and women working particularly in the fast expanding, wage-earning, white-collar service sector of the economy. These were people whose function was to administer the welfare state and to manage the provision of education, information and social services.

The young, well-educated, white-collar workers were representative of a society very different to that of their parent's generation. Between the 1951 census and that of 1971 the population of New Zealand increased from just under two million to almost three million. The proportion living in urban areas rose from 72% to 81% in the same period, with Auckland and the Waikato-Bay of Plenty almost doubling in population. New suburbs sprawled across south and west Auckland and, after the opening of the Harbour Bridge in 1959, Auckland's North Shore; in the Hutt Valley, Porirua and Heretaunga; and on the outskirts of Christchurch. By the early 1970s almost 70% of New Zealand's housing was owner-occupied, often with a mortgage. But once the mortgage was paid off the home became a major guarantee against poverty in old age.

Part of the increase in population had come from the post-war baby boom but there was a steady stream of immigrants throughout the 1950s and 1960s. Many British and Irish migrants received assistance for a number of years after 1947, and between 1952 and 1972 some 30,000 Dutch immigrants settled in New Zealand. But although there was a trickle of Greek, Yugoslav and other European and Asian immigrants, New Zealand did not experience the post-war migration from southern and eastern Europe which transformed the demographic makeup of Australia, although a small group of European refugees who came to New Zealand in the thirties and forties, such as Fred Turnovsky, had a disproportionately beneficial influence on the business and artistic life of their adopted country. With the exception of the large and growing indigenous Māori population and the start of the influx from the Pacific Islands, New Zealand's population remained narrowly based on those of British origin.

During the prosperous 1960s social habits changed dramatically. Although the American evangelist Billy Graham drew crowds of up to 60,000 people in Auckland, Wellington and Christchurch in 1959, and there was considerable public interest in the unsuccessful attempt by fundamentalist Presbyterians in 1967 to charge Lloyd Geering, the Principal of Knox Theological College, with doctrinal error for questioning the resurrection, New Zealand became a much more secular society as church attendances declined and fewer New Zealanders even identified with any denomination. The almost universal access to motor cars, the birth control pill which removed the fear of unwanted pregnancy, and the centrality of television in entertaining and informing people, together transformed the social pattern and social attitudes.

Within ten years of the introduction of television in 1960, 83% of New Zealand households had a TV set. People who during the 1950s had frequented picture theatres and dancehalls stayed at home watching television in the 1960s or met friends in a hotel bar, after a referendum in 1967 extended the hours of closing from 6 pm to 10 pm. Television, of course, had a political as well as a social impact. From 1960 until 1972 National Government ministers had much greater access to all the news media as they determined and announced policy and commented on the day-to-day decisions of government. As a result they appeared to be more effective performers on television than did most Labour MPs with their limited exposure and of necessity more negative roles. Not until Kirk and Muldoon in the 1970s, however, did any New Zealand politician effectively harness the medium.

The politicians who did inspire young New Zealanders especially with their television images were the Americans John F. Kennedy and Martin Luther King. Their idealistic appeals to cross the 'New Frontier' and create a just, humane society had an impact throughout the world. New Zealanders watched the freedom rides to desegregate America's southern states, listened to Kennedy's rhetoric and shared King's dream. The assassinations of Kennedy and King had a profound effect on many young idealists internationally caught up in issues such as racial equality, civil liberties, the women's movement, environmentalism, anti-nuclear campaigns, and the distrust of centralized state bureaucracies. The last of these issues was one the

Television changed social habits and had a marked influence on New Zealand politics. *NZ Herald*

National Party should have been able to capitalize on in New Zealand more than it did, though in 1962 it made a gesture in that direction by establishing the office of Ombudsman to investigate complaints against government departments and report with recommendations to Parliament. The liberalism of the United States was matched by an upsurge of interest among Western intellectuals in socialist humanism, particularly the Yugoslav experiment in worker's management and the 1968 Czechoslovak reform movement.

Many of the young people who became politically active in America, Britain, Europe, Australia and New Zealand during the 1960s did not see traditional political parties or processes as attractive or effective. Some Marxist students from a variety of ideological perspectives and positions became dogmatic, intolerant and undemocratic. Other young people, often from privileged family backgrounds and with what seemed to their elders to be pretentious and impractical romanticism, saw their political protest as only part of a more general rebellion of youth against hierarchy, authority, materialism, conformity and traditional morality. They created a youth counter-culture based on a somewhat anarchic view of individual freedom, long hair and hippie dress, rock music and free sex, drugs and flower-power. Some formed communes. Inevitably but sadly the youth culture became commercialized, corrupted, politicized. The movement culminated in the 1968 student revolts in America and Europe but the issues, which young people had been socialized and motivated into supporting, remained.

Within New Zealand society generally and the Labour Party in particular there was much greater debate over non-economic issues such as Vietnam, feminism, race relations, nuclear disarmament, education, abortion, homosexuality, the freedom of the individual, and the conservation of the natural environment, not only in New Zealand but in the 'global village'. There tended to be little centre ground on most of these issues, which polarized opinions across traditional partisan lines. As the result of such issues the number of white-collar members of the Labour Party increased by almost 60% in 1965 compared to 1964 and more than doubled by 1966. In the sixties the white-collar occupational proportion of the Labour Party's financial membership changed from one in five to one in two. Some of this was as the result of upward social mobility as children of manual-workers completed higher education. But many of Labour's new converts came from wealthy, professional, business and farming families with parents who had always been anti-Labour. It was this new generation which would set the political agenda and create the economic and social patterns of the years after 1972.

12. *New Zealand*
and the other Pacific Islands

MARY BOYD

New Zealand took a long time to make up its mind that it was a Pacific country, not a European outpost. Interest in other Pacific Islands waxed and waned until Britain withdrew west of Suez and, in 1973, joined the European Community; it grew more after the ANZUS partnership with the United States foundered in 1985. These developments heightened New Zealand's awareness of its Polynesian heritage and Pacific identity. 'We . . . accept what the map tells us,' said the Prime Minister (1984–1989), David Lange, 'that we are a South Pacific nation'. New Zealand's Ambassador to the United States was even more emphatic: 'New Zealand has become, in the fullest sense, a country of the Pacific and New Zealanders take it for granted'. To an historian these confident assertions sound rather like Vogel and Seddon 'howling empire from an empty coast'.

A more sober examination of New Zealand's relationships with other Pacific Islands shows that it has still to come to terms with the realities of being a Pacific country. In Sir James Henare's words, it must 'listen to the north wind blowing from great Hawaiki', the wind that brought the Māori to Aotearoa and made it part of Polynesia over a thousand years ago. It must also listen to the prevailing winds from South Auckland, the Porirua basin and the other urban areas which are home to the third largest subsection of its total population, the people of Pacific Island Polynesian origin and descent.

The nineteenth century aspirations of European New Zealanders in the Pacific Islands were described by a Frenchman, André Siegfried who visited New Zealand in 1899, as 'the product of exclusivism and racial pride . . . characteristic of Anglo-Saxon colonials'. These were the first stirrings of nationalism but they were motivated by strategy. New Zealand was a small, distant, underpopulated British

Lord Ranfurly (centre) annexing the Cook Islands for Britain in 1900. Makea Takau Ariki is on his right, and Lt. Col. W.E. Gudgeon, who was the first Resident Commissioner of the Cook Islands, on his left. *Private Collection*

colony. It refused to accept the assurances of the British that the Royal Navy would protect it. It wanted to keep all foreign intruders out of the South Pacific. It urged Britain to adopt a more forward policy of annexations and claimed it was the country best fitted to rule Polynesians.

In 1849 Sir George Grey had tried to forestall the French in New Caledonia and Bishop Selwyn had founded the Melanesian Mission based in Auckland. Sir Julius Vogel schemed to develop island trade and plantations and subsidized transpacific shipping and mail services 1870-1877. Auckland firms slowly developed legitimate trade with the islands, but they, as well as Otago businessmen, took part in the Melanesian labour trade known as 'blackbirding'. The Bank of New Zealand speculated in Fijian land and meddled in Fijian politics. Otago Presbyterians, with Anglican support, opposed French annexation of the New Hebrides in 1886.

R. J. Seddon complained of a 'great betrayal' when Britain withdrew from Samoa leaving Germany and the United States to partition it in 1899. To convince the British that the Cook Islands desired New Zealand rule, he went on a Pacific cruise for his health which awakened his sympathy for a settler faction in Fiji who were seeking federation. After the House of Representatives adopted his resolution for the

Brigadier-General Richardson with the Fono of Faipule (advisory council of district representatives), Mulinu'u, Western Samoa. *Alexander Turnbull Library*

incorporation of the Cook Islands and had sung 'God Save the Queen', the Governor set off in HMS *Mildura* to read the annexation proclamations on each of the major islands. The Cook Islands, together with Niue, which was a British protectorate, were included within the boundaries of New Zealand, on 11 June 1901.

As the age of island-hunting drew to a close, New Zealand looked to British imperial defence for its security. As 'a great and urgent imperial service' it seized Western Samoa from the Germans in August 1914 and manned a British military administration. The Prime Minister, W. F. Massey, expected that Britain would retain control after the war. His main efforts were directed to securing a cheap, regular supply of phosphates from Nauru, which had been captured by an Australian force. But as the price of Japanese support in the war, Britain secretly agreed that Japan and the southern Dominions should keep the German islands they seized. Furthermore British officials thought — correctly — that Australian and New Zealand national pride would be affronted if they were deprived of the spoils of war.

The Paris Peace Conference ruled out annexations in favour of League of Nations mandates. Massey accepted the mandate for Western Samoa with some reluctance, preferring freehold to leasehold. After securing a guaranteed supply of phosphates for his small-farmer supporters in a phosphate-sharing agreement with Britain and Australia on a 42: 42: 16 ratio, he was content to let Australia administer the mandate for Nauru which was conferred on the British Empire. New Zealand's interests in Nauru were economic and exploitative: in Western Samoa they combined national security and national pride. In 1925, at Britain's request, New Zealand added to its burdens of governing island territories by taking over Tokelau.

A new power struggle between Britain and the United States over the islands in the central Pacific began in the mid-1930s. New Zealand adamantly refused to discuss the ownership of those it controlled, which were some of the northern Cook Islands and Tokelau. Britain kept it fully informed and New Zealand's vessels were used to survey suitable sites for airfields, establish wireless stations and prepare a base on Christmas Island. The matter lapsed during the Pacific War, 1940–1945. Tokelau was included within New Zealand's boundaries in 1948. But the United States did not formally renounce its territorial claims to Tokelau and other central Pacific Islands until 1980.

After the War in the Pacific, there was mounting suspicion that the U.S. had designs over its Pacific Island bases. This led to a restatement of the traditional Australian and New Zealand policy of keeping foreign intruders out of the Pacific. The 1944 Australian-New Zealand Agreement envisaged a regional zone of defence in the South Pacific, including the arc of islands from Papua New Guinea to the Cook Islands. But in the event it was stillborn. For post-war security New Zealand looked to the United Nations, then ANZAM (Australian, New Zealand and Malayan area, a Commonwealth defence planning arrangement) and ANZUS, not to any island bastions.

New Zealand's short-comings in governing Polynesians were more obvious than its successes. As a small, weak, developing country itself, it lacked the people, the money and the markets to develop island territories. Island affairs were bandied about in various government departments. Samoan affairs were handled by a Secretary of External Affairs in the Prime Minister's Department. Separate departments for Island Territories and External Affairs were established in 1943. New Zealand's island empire was too small to warrant a career colonial service. Officials were seconded to the Pacific for three-year terms from New Zealand's own public service. Few stayed on for a second term or learnt the local language. Little use was made of Māori experience, though three Māori ministers held responsibility for the Cook Islands and Niue: Sir James Carroll, 1909–1912, Sir Maui Pomare, 1913–1928, and Sir Apirana Ngata, 1928–1934. Island administrators and resident commissioners were often army officers or lawyers.

Like other colonial powers, New Zealand exported its own ideas and institutions. Policies vacillated between assimilation and taihoa (wait awhile), just as they did in Māori affairs. The object of assimilation was to change Pacific Islanders into New Zealanders; that of taihoa to enable them to advance slowly, and gradually from traditional to European culture, blending selected elements of both. Assimilation reflected what F. H. Corner called 'the Lower Hutt syndrome', which was the inability of European New Zealanders to recognize the validity of island cultures. Taihoa

New Zealand soldiers marching along Beach Road, Apia, Samoa, in 1914. *Alexander Turnbull Library*

combined the anthropological concept of cultural adaptation with a natural inclination to do nothing.

In the Cook Islands, Niue and Western Samoa, New Zealand rule interrupted the process of state formation that had begun in the early years after western contact. Island kingdoms had been formed and law codes and constitutions were adopted. The Cook Islands and Niue were administered by Resident Commissioners responsible to Wellington and became increasingly dependent on New Zealand officials.

The military administration in Western Samoa inherited the German colonial system which had incorporated the Samoan hierarchy of titleholders but curbed their powers. Attempts by New Zealand Administrators to adapt the German system to British law and parliamentary ways conflicted with Samoan custom and chiefly aspirations to regain the *pule* (authority).

Policies of dual development of European plantations and village agriculture began, but more money was spent on developing bureaucracies and social services than public works and agriculture. New Zealand provided small subsidies to help the Cook Islands and Niue meet the costs of local administration and social services but expected Western Samoa to pay its own way.

Lieutenant-Colonel W. E. Gudgeon, 1901–1909, introduced a land court into the Cook Islands to individualize land titles and to encourage European settlement and native production. But settlement did not eventuate and the fragmentation of land titles in the long run discouraged individual Cook Islands Māori enterprise. In the mid-1920s some effort was made to improve social services and technical services to fruit growers. The deliberate cultivation of oranges, a perishable product, for the New Zealand market and lack of facilities for handling, shipping and marketing made the territory increasingly dependent on New Zealand subsidies.

In Western Samoa Colonel R. W. Tate, 1919–1923, and Major-General G. S. Richardson, 1923–1928, attempted to restore the plantations expropriated from the Germans and handed over to the New Zealand government as war reparations. Chinese indentured labourers imported by the Germans were repatriated, preventing Western Samoa from becoming 'a little China of the Pacific'. Free Chinese labourers were recruited for three year terms. Tate commenced and Richardson pushed along programmes to encourage Samoan agriculture and to extend health, education and public works. Richardson tried to make Samoans healthy, hardworking planters by individualizing land allotments, remodelling villages, introducing a medical tax and marketing high grade Samoan copra through the New Zealand Reparation Estates. He also prohibited time-consuming customs such as *malaga* (journeys), fine mat exchange, *saofai* (ceremony for conferring titles) and village cricket. When Samoans disobeyed his edicts he banished them from their villages and took away their titles. Local banishment and title deprivation were legal sanctions based on custom but never before used so frequently. By forcing Samoans to change Richardson strengthened their resolve to hold fast to the *fa'a Samoa* (Samoan custom).

As Malama Meleisea has observed, racial discrimination was 'one of the ugliest features of colonialism'. Pre-Darwinian liberals and humanitarians believed that racial differences were cultural and would gradually vanish as Christianity, commerce and civilization spread and Europeans and native peoples were peacefully amalgamated. Social Darwinists believed that differences were physical and inborn; that whites were superior to coloureds; that half-castes inherited the worst characteristics of both. These doctrines justified their faith in white dominance and colonial rule and policies of protecting native people from European settlers and from immigrant Asian labour.

In the Cook Islands Act 1915, New Zealand distinguished natives from non-natives and Polynesians from people of mixed blood. This 'unnecessarily wounded the susceptibilities of a large number of the half-caste population' and constituted 'real hardship' to Māori wives of Europeans and their children who wished to be considered Europeans.

In Western Samoa, New Zealand continued to recognize the separate legal status of Samoans and local Europeans (who could include Chinese and mixed bloods) adopted by the Germans. This distinction was intended to protect Samoans but discriminated against local Europeans. The cohabitation of Chinese and Samoan women was prohibited and marriages between New Zealand officials and Samoans were strongly disapproved of. Local Europeans had separate political representation and were not allowed 'to meddle' in Samoan politics. They were denied access to Samoan lands and prohibited, like Samoans, from consuming alcohol.

Racial doctrine and separate legal classifications bred social discrimination and snobbery. This was much resented by local Europeans with Samoan wives, who felt ostracized. Samoans were insulted by being stereotyped as 'backward children', and part Europeans as 'half-castes' and 'the dregs of civilization'. The view that Polynesians were lazy and Chinese immoral was equally insulting. Even officials who established friendly relations with Samoans and did not practice social discrimination used such stereotypes. The prevailing belief was that to be equal, Samoans must first be civilized.

Under New Zealand rule local grievances and frustrations accumulated. A Cook Islands Progressive Association was formed in 1916 'to further the political and economic interests of residents'. Rioting and the looting of shops by returned soldiers in 1919 were attributed to depressed trade and industry and to traders' overcharging. A parliamentary delegation produced some improvements, until the great depression. Afterwards the Labour Government was approached by a Rarotongan Growers' Association seeking an export control board and by another organization asking for guaranteed prices for fruit.

Renewed unrest during the Second World War led to the formation of a more broadly based Cook Islands Progressive Association in Aitutaki and Rarotonga and an Auckland branch with Albert Henry, a forty-year old Aitutakian, as secretary. It aimed to improve wages and returns to fruitgrowers and shipping, as well as to restore self-government. From 1946 to 1948, with left-wing support from New Zealand, it took industrial action on the Rarotongan waterfront which was defeated by the intervention of the New Zealand Federation of Labour. Its attempt at co-operative trading with its own ship and a government loan collapsed.

In the forties the Fraser Government failed to recognize the seeds of Cook Islands nationalism in economic protest. Its new look policy included a citrus replanting scheme, greatly increased subsidies for works and services and some local political representation in an advisory legislative council and island councils.

Samoan opposition to alien rule erupted twice in German times and then again after the 1918 influenza epidemic, in which about one-fifth of the population died. The Samoans blamed the New Zealand authorities for failing to quarantine the *Talune* which brought the plague from Auckland. Tate had to cope with continuing disaffection. Richardson's tactless, dictatorial rule precipitated the Mau, a movement that rejected New Zealand rule and tried to get self-government under British protection.

The Mau was part of a continuing struggle to restore a Samoan government based on traditional and customary institutions. Local Europeans like the leading copra trader and Mau spokesman, O. F. Nelson, had their own grievances, and also had knowledge and understanding of Samoan custom and traditions which New Zealand lacked. New Zealand was intransigent. Police action resulted in the death of the

'Samoa for the Samoans'. A Mau parade, Beach Road, Apia. *Alexander Turnbull Library*

Samoan leader Tupua Tamasese Leolofi and ten others on 'Black Saturday'. This, followed by naval intimidation, led to an impasse which continued until Labour sympathizers in New Zealand took office and sent a goodwill mission.

The Mau, the great depression and gentle but humiliating criticism of New Zealand rule from the Permanent Mandates Commission in Geneva led to the period of taihoa which was prolonged by the second world war. A new generation of Samoan leaders consolidated their authority. Unsettled by the temporary American occupation, they renewed demands for self-government. Peter Fraser's efforts to improve living standards and education first by funding economic development and scholarships from the profits of the Reparation Estates failed to silence them.

Fraser's thinking on post-war colonial policy was influenced by his British Fabian background, by Māori experience and by regional and international discussions. Like President Roosevelt, he believed that colonies as well as captured enemy territories had the right to choose their own form of government. He espoused the principle of international accountability for all colonial powers, not just those who were administering League of Nations mandates. He appreciated that it was useless to impose change from above unless the people wanted it.

He accepted Australian proposals in the 1944 Agreement for an advisory regional

The reception for the United Nations Mission, Western Samoa, in 1947. *Alexander Turnbull Library*

commission in the South Pacific to secure a common policy in social, economic and political development with the ultimate objective of self-government in the form most suitable to local circumstances, and he made them his own. At the San Francisco Conference in 1945 he presided over the Trusteeship Committee that married and amended Anglo-American proposals on post-war colonial policy into Chapters XI–XIII of the United Nations Charter.

Chapter XI was a 'Declaration Regarding Non-Self-Governing Territories' which defined the general principles and purposes of international trusteeship. These included the development of self-government 'to take due account of the the political aspirations of the peoples'. Chapters XII and XIII made provisions for an international trusteeship system supervised by a trusteeship council. A basic objective was 'progressive development towards self-government or independence as may be appropriate to the particular circumstances of each territory and the freely expressed wishes of the people concerned'. Within this framework and in wholehearted co-operation with the United Nations, New Zealand formulated new policies of political development to decolonize its island territories in a slow, orderly, peaceful manner in consultation and co-operation with local political leaders.

Western Samoa set the pace. After New Zealand presented its leaders with a draft trusteeship agreement they petitioned the United Nations for self-government with

New Zealand as their protector and adviser, as Britain was to Tonga. Fraser responded sympathetically with a policy of political development and arrangements for a United Nations mission to investigate the background of the petition and endorse this policy. A representative Samoan Government with power of the purse was set up under a new High Commissioner, G. R. Powles (later Sir Guy). Under his guidance education in self-government commenced.

Day-to-day stresses and strains in a system that divorced political power from executive responsibility convinced Powles that without steady political advancement, he could not win the confidence of local leaders. He proposed, and New Zealand adopted, a development plan that was virtually a timetable for self-government without dates. A working party of Samoan leaders drew up constitutional recommendations which were endorsed by a constitutional convention fully representative of the Samoan people. These were largely accepted by the New Zealand Government.

Western Samoa advanced by a series of small steps rather than one big stride to responsible government with a Samoan Cabinet and Prime Minister. A second working party drafted an independence constitution with help from New Zealand's constitutional adviser and international lawyer, Professor C. C. Aikman, and the Samoans' adviser, a Pacific historian, Professor J. W. Davidson.

The constitution was partly home grown and partly imported. Its makers attempted to adapt the Westminster model to 'local circumstances', that is, Samoan custom and traditions and Christian principles. The highest titleholders, Tupua Tamasese Mea'ole and Malietoa Tanumafili II became joint heads of state and Mata'afa Faumuina Fiame Mulinu'u became Prime Minister. The *matai* (elected family heads and titleholders) elected from among themselves forty-six members of the Samoan Parliament. Two other members were elected by individual voters (local Europeans who became Samoan citizens and any Samoans who opted to enrol as individual voters.)

In the final stages both Samoan leaders and their advisers and the Nash Government realized that only 'unqualified independence', not the Tongan relationship, would satisfy Samoan aspirations. To convince the United Nations that the constitution adopted a second constitutional convention and independence fulfilled 'the freely expressed wishes of the people', a plebiscite based on universal suffrage was conducted under United Nations supervision. The Trusteeship Agreement was terminated and Western Samoa became the first independent state of Polynesia on 1 January 1962.

Economic, social and educational advancement proceeded at a slower pace, aided by profits from the Reparation Estates. These were handed back to the Samoan government in 1957 and managed as a Trust Estates Corporation. Despite a last minute crash programme, the new state lacked the educated, trained personnel it needed to localize the New Zealand type of public service it had inherited. Economically independent Western Samoa was underdeveloped and overdependent on three export staples, cocoa, copra, and bananas. As the population was increasing

The High Commissioner, G.R. Powles, meets village elders, 1949. *Alexander Turnbull Library*

by 3% a year pressure on limited resources was mounting. For higher education and better living standards, increasing numbers of Samoans migrated to New Zealand.

The Treaty of Friendship, 1 August 1962, continued the special relationship that had developed between Western Samoa and New Zealand. A three year aid programme was negotiated which provided scholarships for higher education, in-service training for public servants, plus grants and loans for agricultural development and capital works. New Zealand undertook to help Western Samoa conduct its foreign relations as long as it wished.

Decolonization of the Cook Islands and Niue started later and proceeded faster. The Cook Islands after 1945 became increasingly dependent financially and psychologically on New Zealand. Not all the far-flung Islands were represented in the Legislative Council, nor was there any real sense of a Cook Islands identity. Unofficial members criticized and opposed New Zealand officials but still let them make decisions. The citrus re-planting scheme was run by the Administration and failed to stimulate local enterprise. New Zealand did not know where the Cook Islands were going politically though Samoan progress in self-government set useful precedents. But the need to increase local revenue, and the reluctance of Cook Islanders to pay income tax, forced a change of direction.

In 1954 Professor Horace Belshaw and V. D. Stace conducted an economic survey. They stressed the need for Cook Islanders to be given more responsibility as well as

The Prime Minister, Fiame Mata'afa (right), welcoming the Joint Head of State, Tupua Mea'ole Tamasese, at the independence celebrations in Samoa in 1962. *New Zealand Herald*

aid. The Minister of Island Territories, Clifton Webb, began a move towards 'greater autonomy in local affairs through greater self-sufficiency'. Two constitutional surveys were conducted by Professor Aikman. A new course was set for representative and responsible government using the Samoan model.

Progress was slow and halting. The Resident Commissioner, G. Nevill, believed the lack of secondary education was an insurmountable difficulty. He dragged his feet in getting elected members of the new Legislative Assembly to participate in the executive. Elected members themselves were too dependent on New Zealand officials to exercise any initiatives. In 1962 New Zealand handed over budgetary control of New Zealand subsidies to the Assembly and provided these for three year periods. This unprecedented move was designed to stimulate local initiative, self-help, and planned development.

After A. O. Dare became Resident Commissioner, the transfer of power and responsibility was accelerated. The new Minister of Island Territories, Leon Gotz, met

Walter Nash, Leader of the Opposition in New Zealand, talking with Masiofo Fetaui Mata'afa at the Samoan independence celebrations. *NZ Herald*

the Legislative Assembly and outlined four constitutional alternatives: independence, internal self-government, political integration, or a Polynesian federation. In reality there was little choice. The Cook Islands had already embarked on a course for self-government. The timetable Gotz suggested was adopted. Three advisers with Samoan experience, J. B. Wright, Aikman and Davidson conferred with the Assembly and hammered out a constitution on the Westminster model. The place of the ariki (high chiefs) in it was shelved for the time being.

In Niue, years of dependence on the London Missionary Society missionaries and on New Zealand officials, and in 1953 the tension between them culminated in the murder of the Resident Commissioner, C. H. Larsen, by three prisoners. His successor, J. M. McEwen, was an able, experienced Maori Affairs officer, lawyer and Polynesian scholar. He quickly learnt Niuean and initiated a new policy of guided self-help. When Niueans said 'You decide', he refused. Subsidies and local revenue rose sharply, and education was improved by government schools which taught English.

New Zealand tagged Niue on to the Cook Islands when it passed enabling legislation for political development in 1957. A Niuean Assembly was set up in 1960 and an executive committee in 1962. Gotz offered the Assembly the same political alternatives and timetable as the Cook Islands and indicated to them that they should choose internal self-government. But the Niueans asserted their right to be different and to determine their own pace of political development.

Both the Cook Islands and Niue were decolonized in a United Nations framework. The Fraser Government had decided to treat them as if they were non-self-governing territories and to send annual reports on them to the Secretary-General. In 1960 New Zealand voted for the Declaration for the Granting of Independence to Colonial Countries and Peoples sponsored by the anticolonial bloc in the United Nations. This stated that 'Inadequacy of political, economic, social or educational preparedness should never serve as a pretext for delaying independence'.

Pressure was exerted from New Zealand representatives in New York through the Department of External Affairs on Island Territories in Wellington to get the Cook Islands and Niue off the United Nations hook. But as island territories well knew, Cook Islanders and Niueans feared that self-government would weaken their ties with New Zealand, deprive them of their rights of free entry as New Zealand citizens and of financial aid. Officials and constitutional advisers tried to alleviate their fears. As virtually all of them hoped to go to New Zealand, this was far from easy.

Plans were made to introduce a new constitution for Cook Islands self-government after the 1965 elections. These precipitated the return of Albert Henry from Auckland and the rise of the populist Cook Islands Party from the ashes of the Progressive Association. Much to everybody's surprise they swept the polls. The first responsible government was formed with Henry as Premier. The opportunity to exercise power and responsibility rapidly revived local leadership and initiative.

Niue refused to be dragged along in the wake of the Cook Islands. McEwen, now Secretary of Island Territories, understood their feelings and they were left to set their own pace. In 1963, the Assembly asked for constitutional advisers and in 1965 McEwen and Aikman were sent. The timetable approach was dropped. New Zealand accepted that no further constitutional changes would take place until Niueans felt ready and able to accept them. In 1970 Professor R.Q. Quentin-Baxter became their constitutional adviser. An international lawyer and a patient, sympathetic listener, he understood their position and persuaded them to advance to responsible government. With Robert Rex as Premier, Niue became internally self-governing in 1974.

Nearly one quarter of the Cook Islands population and about half the Niuean population were living in New Zealand when power was transferred. A special relationship was devised to preserve for all Cook Islanders and Niueans their New Zealand citizenship, and the rights of free entry and aid. The special relationship was acceptable to the United Nations because it complied with Resolution 1541 (XV) adopted by the General Assembly, 15 December 1960. This recognized alternatives to independence for smaller non-self-governing territories, namely free association or

Albert Henry's triumphant return to the Cook Islands in 1964. *Private Collection*

integration with an independent state.

While legally part of New Zealand, the Cook Islands, Niue and Tokelau had achieved a large measure of local self-government. As support for Henry and Rex demonstrated, they had no wish to lose it. Only Islanders in New Zealand had any interest in political integration. Free association matched New Zealand's own relationship with other Commonwealth countries and nationalist aspirations of the Islands. Coupled with the right of continuous self-determination, it provided a formula acceptable to the United Nations, an equal relationship 'freely entered into and freely maintained'.

A United Nations representative supervised the 1965 general election in the Cook Islands and a United Nations mission visited Niue. On the basis of their reports, the Fourth Committee of the General Assembly acknowledged that the people of both territories had exercised their rights of self-determination and would continue to do so. New Zealand's largely self-imposed obligation to report to the United Nations ended.

In Tokelau, where less than two thousand people lived on three small atolls, with the second highest population density in the region, reality prevailed. Under a resettlement scheme adopted in 1966, Tokelauans were assisted to move to New Zealand and those who remained looked to New Zealand for continuing aid. They rejected the choice of union with the Cook Islands and were placed under an administrator in Wellington. Most of his powers were delegated to an Official Secretary heading the Office for Tokelauan Affairs in Apia, set up by agreement with Western Samoa.

Each atoll had an elected *faipule* (district representative), *pulenuku* (village mayor) and a council of village elders. A General Council of representatives of all three island councils met twice a year. New Zealand's policy was to develop as much local responsibility and self-reliance as possible. But the formation of a Tokelau public service, which employed salaried teachers, nurses and casual labourers, and also New Zealand budgetary aid, prevented this. New Zealand kept the United Nations well informed about Tokelau by annual reporting. Three UN visiting missions, were received, in 1976, 1981 and 1986. Generally the United Nations respected Tokelau's wish to maintain its special relationship with New Zealand.

New Zealand blazed the trail to political decolonization of Oceania for several reasons. Nationalism was stronger in Western Samoa and the Cook Islands than elsewhere and colonial rule weaker. New Zealand had no military, naval or air bases or nuclear testing sites in the Islands. Its island trade was only about 1-1.8% of its total exports and 1-1.4% of its total imports (1967/68 percentages). Of all the administering authorities, it was the most sensitive to international criticism. The peaceful, evolutionary manner in which it transferred power followed the British model, but was more radical and innovative. At a time when Australia and Britain were still pursuing policies of balanced development, New Zealand was speeding up the final stages of decolonization. It hoped that self-government and independence would release local energies for economic, social and educational self-advancement. It believed that its national interests were better served by having friendly island neighbours than island dependencies and bastions.

New Zealand's policy of decolonization made it more willing than Australia and Britain to concede independence and control over phosphate deposits to Nauru. Indeed this seemed the best way to ensure continued access to phosphates. Under Hammer De Roburt's leadership, with Davidson as its constitutional adviser, Nauru became an independent republic in 1968 with the right to buy out the British Phosphate Commission. It later exercised the right. The Nauruan demand that the rehabilitation of land mined before independence be a charge against the three partner governments was eventually investigated by a commission of inquiry but remained unsatisfied. In the 1970s most other British and Australian island territories were decolonized. Strategic interests and integrationist policies impeded the decolonization of American and French territories.

As the process of decolonization fanned out from Western Samoa, the Cook Islands, Niue and Nauru to Fiji, Papua New Guinea, the Solomons, Tuvalu, Kiribati and Vanuatu, New Zealand's horizons widened. New relationships developed with island states that were rather like Britain's relationships with Commonwealth countries in miniature. New Zealand recognized that the island states were equal in status if not in stature. New diplomatic posts (eight by 1988) were established. Political separation created new needs for regional cooperation and consultation.

One of the first regional institutions in the South Pacific was the Suva Medical School, set up in 1928, which trained Native Medical Practitioners. The South Pacific Commission, proposed in the Australian-New Zealand Agreement of 1944, was established in 1947 by six member governments to advise them on economic and social development of their island territories. Political development was ruled out. Until the mid-1960s the South Pacific Commission 'pottered along' on a very small budget, undertaking practical research and aid projects. It produced a library of publications and a host of recommendations but cut little ice in seats of government. To provide it with a sounding board of island opinion, a South Pacific Conference of delegates from eighteen territories met trienially from 1950. At this time the South Pacific was more a geographical expression than a region. As island leaders replaced island officials as delegates, initiatives for reform came from the Conference but were impeded by conflicting views and different levels of interest and commitment of member governments.

Decolonization produced some changes. The Netherlands withdrew when it ceased to administer West Irian. Western Samoa, Fiji, Nauru and Papua New Guinea joined when they became independent and made token contributions to the budget. New Zealand and Australia were more interested in reforming the Commission and increasing their financial contributions than were France and the United States.

From 1967–8, the South Pacific Conference met annually and made recommendations on the annual work programme and budget which the Commission approved. The Conference and Commission were merging and becoming a forum for discussion and a clearing house for international aid. But leaders of new island states wanted to discuss politics. They had tried to bring up issues of French nuclear testing and local autonomy in French Polynesia under other headings, whereupon the French Senior Commissioner had walked out. The New Zealand Minister of Island Territories, Duncan McIntyre, spoke for the five metropolitan governments when he said that if the Conference discussed politics it would kill itself. In the decolonized South Pacific, the Commission was becoming a vestige of colonialism.

In 1965 Fiji and Western Samoa set up the Pacific Islands Producers' Association (PIPA) to promote closer co-operation between the Islands supplying bananas to New Zealand. Tonga, the Cook Islands, Niue and later Kiribati and Tuvalu joined. PIPA gradually broadened its activities to include production and marketing in other industries and became involved in political questions. In 1971 it asked New Zealand to host a meeting of heads of government of common interest. Out of this exploratory meeting the South Pacific Forum was born.

The Forum met annually in different capitals and as new island states emerged they joined. By 1988 it had fifteen members. Meetings were usually attended by heads of government, discussion was private and informal and communiqués were issued at the end. Methods of operation blended those of Commonwealth Prime Ministers' meetings and the Pacific way of reaching a consensus. According to the Minister of Foreign Affairs, Brian Talboys,

> We don't make a lot of noise. We put a lot of store on what we call Pacific silence . . . The tradition is you do a little talking and a lot of listening. Then after long silences . . . people on the extremes are expected to move towards the centre. I can tell you it works. Over the years we have gradually built up confidence in our part of the region. We know each other well . . . . Step by step we have moved from political cooperation to practical economic projects.

Early meetings in the 1970s focused on regional trade and economic issues; later meetings on transport and shipping. To facilitate its work the Forum established the South Pacific Bureau of Economic Co-operation in Suva with which PIPA merged. In 1977 ten Forum countries started a joint shipping venture, the Pacific Forum Line. To develop a fishing industry in the two hundred mile exclusive economic zones they set up a Forum Fisheries Agency in 1979. Duty-free access on a non-reciprocal basis to New Zealand and Australian markets for almost all products by Forum countries was permitted under the South Pacific Regional Trade and Economic Cooperation Agreement (SPARTECA) of 1980.

In the 1980s the Forum focused more on political issues. It unanimously opposed French nuclear testing at Mururoa and the dumping of nuclear waste. At Rarotonga in 1985 it adopted the South Pacific Nuclear Free Zone Treaty, which New Zealand took a leading part in promoting, and called on the four nuclear-weapons states to adhere to protocols unreservedly recognizing treaty provisions. It encouraged France to decolonize New Caledonia with the least possible violence, and supported the reinscription of New Caledonia on the United Nations list of non-self-governing territories.

New Zealand 'tended to see the Forum as primarily a regional institution — a place to address South Pacific political, economic and social problems, and to focus on shared concerns of its members'. More radical Melanesian countries wanted the Forum to expand its political character and to co-ordinate attitudes of its members to broader international issues. The Prime Minister of Vanuatu thought New Zealand and Australia were thirty years behind the times in thinking the South Pacific was no more than an insignificant part of their backyard.

Another regional institution which was oriented towards meeting the needs and problems of new island states was the University of the South Pacific (USP), set up on an old flying base site gifted by New Zealand at Laucala Bay, Suva in 1967. It provided trained personnel for government administration, the professions, agricultural

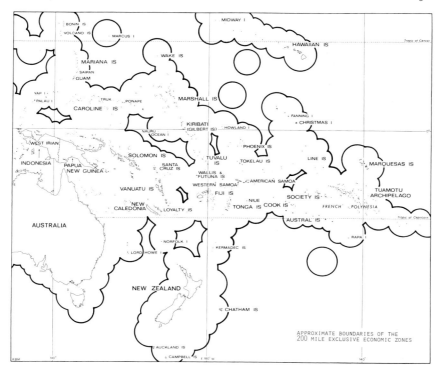

The South Pacific Exclusive Economic Zones. *Roderic Alley*

production and business. A school of agriculture was later set up at Alafua in Western Samoa and extension studies centres in Tonga, the Cook Islands, Fiji, Kiribati, the Solomons and Western Samoa. These provided pre-university, teacher-education, administration and accounting courses. New Zealand provided substantial funding and staff for the university. A number of island students attended New Zealand universities on government scholarships.

Universities in the region and a remarkable number of centres, institutes, associations and societies for Pacific studies usually attached to them created a regional intelligentsia and fostered Pacific literature and publications. A USP sociologist, Epeli Hau'ofa advanced the view that a regional society was emerging with the privileged ruling classes sharing a single dominant regional culture and the underprivileged, poorer classes maintaining local indigenous cultures. But considering the culture diversity of the region and the blend of old and new in the life-style of the privileged, this view is too sweeping. Nonetheless, decolonization fostered regional unity and integration rather than national separatism and independence.

New Zealand's special relationships with its ex-island territories ensured that trade, migration and aid continued to flow in well established channels. It also found new trading partners and sources of immigrant labour in other Forum countries and allocated some bilateral aid to them. Moral responsibility to help poorer neighbours coincided with national economic and security interests. The South Pacific was 'a much underrated market'.

By the late 1970s, New Zealand's island trade had expanded considerably. Phosphates from Nauru and sugar from Fiji accounted for nearly three-quarters of its imports from the Pacific Islands. Supplies of fruit and vegetables produced by family households in rural villages of neighbouring islands continued and diversified though the Samoan banana industry collapsed. Most of the profits went to marketing and processing firms, not to growers. Exports to the islands consisted of processed food (45% of the total in 1977) and manufactured goods (39%). New Zealand supplied about two-thirds of the Cook Islands' imports, 40% of Tonga's, 29% of Western Samoa's, and 16% of Fiji's. New Zealand had a trade surplus of nearly three to one in its favour.

Island manufacturing for export was largely limited to Raro fruit juice and canned fruit, and Samoan coconut cream. For years New Zealand manufacturers and trade unions had feared competition from more cheaply produced island goods. SPARTECA opened up the New Zealand market. In 1976 assistance was offered to New Zealand companies to invest in island industries and provide private employment in the islands under the Pacific Islands Industrial Development Scheme (PIIDS). But little or no expansion resulted, and island agriculture declined. Increasingly the smaller island countries depended on migration to New Zealand, cash remitted home by migrants and on overseas development assistance to maintain existing standards of living and welfare. Hopes and expectations that new island states would become more self-sufficient and self-reliant were not realized.

From the beginning of European penetration, the Pacific Islands had been a reservoir of cheap labour for local extractive industries and overseas mines and plantations. New Zealand's shortage of unskilled and semiskilled labour during and after the Second World War opened up its labour market to a slow, steady trickle of Pacific Island Polynesian migrants. Full employment, industrial development and affluence in the 1960s opened the floodgates. Prospects of jobs, higher incomes and living standards, higher education, trade training and 'city lights' combined with population pressures and the decline of island agriculture to pull and push Pacific Islanders to New Zealand. In the period 1945 to 1976, the total number of New Zealand residents of Polynesian origin or descent grew from 2159 to 65, 694.

Cook Islanders, Niueans and Tokelauans, being New Zealand citizens, required only a medical examination and exit permit to enter. Samoans required entry permits. These were issued for six months initially and could be renewed up to five years, after which permanent residence might be granted. After independence an annual quota of 1500 Samoans were permitted entry as residents. Under the Tokelau resettlement scheme, it was planned to bring in about half the population over a period of years. Immigration restrictions applied to other Pacific Islanders, who could only enter for

THE GANGPLANK

The *New Zealand Herald* cartoonist commented on the 'overstaying' problem in 1974. *NZ Herald*

three months on visitors' permits.

Migrants moved in stages from rural villages or outer islands to local port towns and government centres, then on to Auckland, where most resettled. Some went to Wellington, a few to Christchurch and Tokoroa. Auckland became the 'largest Polynesian city in the world', and Pacific Island Polynesians the most urbanized ethnic group in the country.

Young people came first, families and relatives followed. Migration chains linked family households in island villages and New Zealand cities. Lack of shipping impeded migration in the 1940s and 1950s; improved air services made it easier from the 1960s onwards.

As long as there was a labour shortage, migrant workers were very welcome. Liberal humanitarians felt that New Zealand, as a relatively wealthy, developed country, should open its doors to poorer, overpopulated island countries such as Tonga, Fiji, Kiribati and Tuvalu.

Encouraged by a worsening labour shortage in New Zealand in the sixties and economic pressures at home, thousands of Tongans and Samoans came on three month visitors' permits, got jobs and then overstayed. But the oil crisis and economic downturn in 1974 forced the Kirk Government to act. Immigration Department officials with police assistance sought out overstayers in their homes before they left for work, hence the allegations of 'dawn raids'. A stay of proceedings against overstayers enabled some to depart with dignity and averted more police action. New guidelines were laid down for an immigration policy. Separate rules for island countries in which New Zealand had special responsibilities were suggested. New Memoranda of Understanding were negotiated with the Tongan, Samoan and Fijian governments for six monthly work permits and for one monthly visitors' permits but overstaying delayed the adoption of work permit schemes.

Along with the worsening economic situation, nationalist talk of cutting immigration to the bone and sending lawbreakers home bred white racism and Polynesian fear in the 1975 general election campaign. The new Muldoon Government considerably reduced the flow of immigrants and dawn raids resumed. Tongan leaders called for an amnesty. Another stay of proceedings enabled 4647 to register and be considered on their merits for extended permits or permanent residence. Many failed to register and about half the applications for permanent residence were rejected. Over 200 random checks by police on Polynesians in Auckland streets, and insensitive remarks by the Ministers of Immigration and Police undid Muldoon's efforts to explain the situation to island leaders.

Amnesty Aroha was launched in Wellington and within a fortnight had recruited 380 members. Support came from Pacific Island organizations, liberal and left-wing groups, trade unions, women, social workers, churches, and university and anti-apartheid organizations. Amnesty Aroha spread to Auckland and Christchurch and through meetings, seminars, teach-ins, research and fund raising, instructed New Zealanders on the issue and confronted government policy on overstayers and immigration.

The overstayers' register was reopened for six weeks and 635 cases which had been declined for permanent residence were reviewed. Eventually nearly 70% of applications on behalf of 5381 people (2507 Tongans, 2464 Samoans, 336 Fijians and 74 from other nationalities) were provisionally accepted for permanent residence. Of the estimated 10,000 to 12,000 overstayers, some 4000 returned home voluntarily. Despite the employment of field officers to locate others and hasten their departure, there were between 3000 and 4000 overstayers in New Zealand at any one time.

Migration issues generated stress and ill-feeling in the island countries involved. Returning overstayers added to their economic and social problems. A five nation Pacific tour by the Minister of Foreign Affairs, Brian Talboys, in 1977 tried to mend bridges. Official reactions in Apia and Nuku'alofa were muted and concern about relationships with New Zealand remained.

New Zealand fears of a renewed influx were heightened by the Privy Council decision in a test appeal case, *Lesa* v *Attorney-General*, 19 July 1982, which in effect ruled that all Western Samoans born in Western Samoa between 1924 and 1948 were British subjects and therefore New Zealand citizens with rights of unrestricted entry. About 100,000 Samoans — over three-fifths of the total population — were involved. Muldoon met the Samoan Prime Minister, Va'ai Kolone at the Rotorua Forum meeting in August and they agreed to a protocol to the Treaty of Friendship. The protocol was signed in Apia on 21 August and the New Zealand Citizenship (Western Samoa) Act became law on 14 September. All Western Samoan citizens in New Zealand were given the right to become New Zealand citizens immediately on application. Western Samoans who were subsequently granted permanent residence were given the same right. Previous convictions, deportations and prohibitions from returning for overstaying were quashed. Case by case the status of Samoans in New Zealand was regularized. Meanwhile a backlog of applicants for permanent residence built up. An improved labour market enabled the government to raise the annual quota of 1100 by 200.

New arrangements for work permits for three months extendable to twelve were introduced for Tongans, Samoans and Fijians in 1983 but permits were only issued to those with skills in demand and sponsors for specific jobs. Citizens from Kiribati and Tuvalu were allowed to work for up to eleven months but few did. Permits for Fijians were suspended after the military coup in May 1987.

An abortive attempt to relax regulations from 1 December 1986 to 28 February 1987 dramatically demonstrated the mounting pressures to migrate. After Cabinet learned that 11,000 had arrived, it abruptly terminated the visa-free period on 17 February. By then visitors totalled 12,893 (3372 Fijians, 5377 Samoans, 4144 Tongans). A large number succeeded in extending their stay up to twelve months placing a severe strain on schools in the Auckland district.

Overstaying remained a chronic problem with racist overtones. A third of all overstayers in 1986 were Pacific Islanders but Pacific Islanders were 86% of those prosecuted. A three month amnesty 1987–1988 gave them another opportunity to identify themselves and legalize their stay but only a third did. When new guidelines for immigration law enforcement were introduced on 31 March 1988, overstayers were estimated to number 12,000.

From a Pacific Island perspective, existing policy is 'one of the gate-keeping systems which ensures New Zealand is predominantly white and notably this gate is opened wider for Pacific Island people during times of economic boom'. In submissions to the 1987 Royal Commission on Social Policy, they emphasized that immigration policy 'must renounce all punitive, racist and discriminating elements'. The determining factor should not be economic, but 'family reunification'. Then 'Dawn raids and witch hunts, when economic policy fails to reap a profit would be eliminated'.

Pacific Island migration to New Zealand was not a simple one or two-way movement but part of a complex interchange of population between South Pacific countries. By the 1980s the majority of arrivals and departures were New Zealand-born Polynesians and short-term Island and Australian visitors. Only a tiny percentage were long-term migrants. New Zealand gains of people born in Polynesia were heavily outweighed by losses of New Zealand-born Pacific Island Polynesians, many of whom went to Australia. Nonetheless, the number of New Zealand residents of Pacific Island Polynesian origin and descent grew from 93, 941 in 1981 to 127, 906 in 1986. Over 50% were Samoan, nearly 25% Cook Island Māori, 11% Niuean, 10%

Tongan, and 5% Tokelauan. In the dormitory suburbs of South Auckland and the Porirua basin around 15% of the residents were of Island origin or descent. Like the Māori they were a comparatively youthful population, but their birth-rate was higher.

Pacific Island migrants expected New Zealand to be 'a land of milk and honey' and 'found themselves at the bottom of the socio-economic heap'. They were over-represented in unskilled and semi-skilled jobs and lower income brackets. Their unemployment rate was double the overall rate and triple for young women. Socially they were the most disadvantaged section of the population. They had poorer standards of housing and suffered more health problems. More of their children left school without qualifications and more of them went to jail. They found themselves 'scapegoats for all sorts of evils', unemployment, lawlessness and crime. They felt 'hit by a racial backlash from both Pakeha and Maori'. Disillusionment and a sense of unfulfillment produced antisocial behaviour. New Zealand-born children grew up ignorant of their own language and culture, finding it hard to relate to what they were taught at school, feeling excluded from a predominantly monoculture trying to be become bicultural.

> Our parents' dreams are shattered
> promises of a better life broken, hopes unfulfilled.

Integration was slow and painful, mainly by self-help with some belated state assistance. Close knit ethnic communities emerged with their own leaders and organizations. Migrant churches were of central importance in providing spiritual and practical guidance and running youth clubs, mothers' clubs, social welfare programmes and other social and recreational activities. Island communities kept in touch with their homelands and enhanced the quality of life in New Zealand, in the performing, visual and practical arts, in sports and recreations, in community work and in education.

Pacific Advisory Councils were established in Auckland and Wellington to represent their views to government. PACIFICA (Pacific Allied Council Inspires Faith and Ideals Concerning All) enabled women to contribute effectively to the community and to their children's education.

A Pacific Islanders' Resource Centre within the Department of Education in Auckland helped migrants to learn English and to adapt to life in the new country. A Multicultural Centre did similar work in Wellington. The Polynesian Education Foundation provided financial assistance for education. The Maori and South Pacific Arts Council encouraged Polynesian arts. The Pacific Islands Advisory Committee of the Vocational Training Council produced bilingual booklets to promote understanding of different ethnic groups in industry. A Resettlement Unit in the Labour Department provided information, advice and assistance. Universities provided some Pacific courses and established Pacific Studies centres in Auckland and

A game of kilikiti (village cricket), in Auckland. *NZ Herald*

Christchurch. The teaching of Pacific history was pioneered by a few schools.

In 1976 a Pacific Affairs Co-ordinating Committee was formed to stimulate and monitor government activities relating to island neighbours. A real break through was the Lange Government's appointment of the first Minister of Pacific Affairs, Richard Prebble. A Pacific Island Affairs Unit in the Department of Internal Affairs provided the necessary advice, back-up, co-ordination and administration. A twelve member advisory council represented a cross-section of Pacific Island communities; a six member Pacific Island Employment Development Scheme encouraged viable, unsubsidized employment opportunities and assisted training and business initiatives. The ministry's objectives were to help accelerate the closure of existing gaps in education, employment, income, health, housing and law and order and 'foster the transmission of cultural values deemed important to the identity of various Pacific Island people . . . and of New Zealand as a whole'.

Members of the unit in submissions to the Royal Commission on Social Policy sought 'a new multicultural future based on acceptance and understanding'. They asked New Zealanders to be more sensitive to the needs of Pacific people and recognize that they had a legitimate claim to partnership with both Māori and Pākehā in Aotearoa.

Migration to New Zealand deprived small island countries of a substantial part of their labour force. This contributed to the decline of island agriculture and export earnings. Remittances from migrant workers became a major source of family income in village households enabling them to purchase imported consumer goods, contribute more generously to the church and community and pay air fares. This family support system was very unevenly spread and tended to tail off as periods of residence in New Zealand lengthened unless it was kept going by new arrivals. But not all families had members working in New Zealand.

Data on remittance 'efforts' is scattered and incomplete. Remittances financed 14% of the total imports to the Cook Islands, 1970–1983; 4% to Niue in the same period; 14% to Tokelau, 1975–1983; 52% to Tonga, 1976, and 34%, 1980; 13% to Kiribati since the exhaustion of phosphates; 20% to Tuvalu, 1979-1982, and around 15% to Western Samoa in the early 1980s. But in 1988 about 70% of Western Samoa's overseas income came from remittances, 80% of which were from New Zealand.

One way of reducing the flow of migrant workers to New Zealand and the reliance of island households on remittances was to link immigration policy with aid policy, and initiate aid projects that would create more employment in recipient countries.

On the eve of decolonization about 40% of New Zealand's total overseas aid was allocated to the South Pacific, mainly to provide budgetary support to its own island territories. The Cook Islands received about £45 per head each year and Niue £63. Western Samoa received £1. After self-government and independence, three-yearly aid programmes were negotiated and for some years aid continued to flow in well established channels.

New Zealand's aid frontiers expanded very slowly. Fiji and Tonga received independence gifts and defence support. Almost half the South Pacific Assistance Programme, started in 1968, went to the USP. Some multilateral aid was earmarked for the South Pacific Commission and other international and regional agencies in the Pacific Islands. By 1970-1971 the Cook Islands, Niue and Tokelau absorbed about $36 million, Western Samoa $400,000 and the South Pacific Assistance Programme $112,000 of New Zealand grants in aid.

A non-government agency, Volunteer Service Abroad Inc. was set up in 1962 to foster friendship and understanding between people of New Zealand and the Pacific Islands, also Asia and later Africa. Funds came from private subscriptions, contributions of service organizations and annual government grants. Volunteers were recruited to live and work with local people. In the early days many were school leavers and teachers who worked in lower forms of secondary schools and taught English. Increasingly the demand was for skilled technicians and tradesmen. The South Pacific field of operations moved out from neighbouring Polynesian Islands to Papua New Guinea, the Solomons, Kiribati and Tuvalu. Through volunteer service, growing numbers of New Zealanders learned to appreciate the need for a deeper understanding of island cultures and to give up imposing their own.

Internationally the 1960s was a development decade. A wide range of interested New Zealand organizations supported working towards the internationally accepted aid target, 0.7% of gross national product with the long-term goal of 1%. In 1967 the New Zealand Institute of International Affairs led by its president, Sir Guy Powles, sponsored an international aid conference. Out of his discussions with some twenty organisations arose the idea of South Pacific Year 1971. Conceived as an exercise in public education and international understanding, it stimulated interest in the development of South Pacific peoples and what could be done to help them; also the growing appreciation that aid was good business as well as good deeds.

The government responded to the changing climate by extending the boundaries of the Colombo Plan (its major programme) to include the South Pacific and increasing its bilateral aid vote. A special mission visited South Pacific countries to look for special projects. New initiatives of the Kirk Government in foreign policy led to a dramatic increase in overseas development assistance and the proportion channelled to the South Pacific. Its capacity to reach the 0.7% target was set back by the economic downturn. From a peak of 0.5% in 1975 the ratio fell to a nadir of 0.25% in 1984. To make better use of funds allocated an Aid Advisory Committee was set up in 1975.

The swing from Southeast Asia to the Pacific was consolidated by David Lange's Government. In 1988/89 fifteen Pacific Island states received 80% of New Zealand's bilateral overseas development assistance which was 70% of the overall aid total. But hard times and drastic cuts in government spending reduced aid to the region from $62.7 million in 1984 to $55.9 million in 1988. To cushion the blow, special efforts were made to improve the running of aid programmes and assist the smallest, most vulnerable island countries. Annual aid missions visited partner countries to help formulate aid programmes. Hurricane and disaster relief was provided as required.

The main aim of New Zealand's bilateral overseas development assistance was 'economic and social development within the recipient country'. The bulk of it was used to support a wide variety of rural projects, particularly in agriculture, forestry and fisheries. But financial support for essential government services was provided in Western Samoa, in Cook Islands, Niue and Tokelau. Multilateral assistance supported regional development and co-operation; shipping services, telecommunications, fisheries research, seabed mineral exploration, women's welfare, and environmental protection, for example. Aid funded development plans and projects were administered by island governments and public servants. One cause for concern was that aid funds helped provide relatively high salaries and New Zealand living standards for political leaders and public servants. Indeed they were 'lifeblood' to public services instead of industry and agriculture and benefitted a political and bureaucratic élite rather than poorer people.

Overseas development assistance also served New Zealand interests. Aid funds were used to buy New Zealand goods and services. Aid projects created local employment and reduced economic pressures on island people to migrate to New Zealand and compete for scarce jobs and resources. Aid to Forum partners reduced the likelihood that they would seek outside donors who might threaten New Zealand's security. 'Our prowess in the region', said Russell Marshall in 1989, 'is measured to an important degree by the quality and quantity of aid we extend.'

As a member of the Forum and an integral part of an emerging regional economy and society, New Zealand could legitimately claim to be a Pacific nation. But its social policy lagged behind foreign policy. To establish a Pacific identity and to become a Pacific people, New Zealanders still had to come to terms with the Pacific Island Polynesian communities in their midst and be genuinely multicultural.

13. *Modern Māori: The Young Maori Party to Mana Motuhake*

M.P.K. SORRENSON

The Māori have a cyclical view of history, expressed by the phrase ngā wā o mua, the old times which are in front of us. They walk backwards into the future with their gaze fixed firmly on the past. This is a useful metaphor to begin a discussion of the Māori in the twentieth century. For their attitudes in this century have been much influenced by past experiences, above all by the transformation of their lives by more than a hundred years of contact with Pākehā colonists. Having initially welcomed traders and missionaries, whom they could control, Māori found it increasingly difficult to deal with the Pākehā colonists who streamed into the country after annexation in 1840. By 1858 they were a minority in their own land. Many of the chiefs had signed the Treaty of Waitangi in the expectation that it would protect their rangatiratanga, their lands and other valuable things. They expected the colonial Governor to be a protector but found that he and the colonist politicians who took over many of his powers, enforced the law to the advantage of the settlers. The troops did not keep the peace between Māori tribes but were used to wage war against them.

Over the years Maori groups adopted various strategies to deal with the Pākehā, usually involving resistance or co-operation. Those who resisted by force of arms won numerous battles but lost the wars. Under the New Zealand Settlements Act (1863), 'rebel' tribes in Taranaki, Waikato and Bay of Plenty suffered raupatu (confiscation) of much of their land, which left an enduring legacy of bitterness. But the kupapa who co-operated, even to the extent of fighting on the Pākehā side, did little better in the long run. Under the Native Land Acts they got the opportunity of fighting in a new arena - the Native Land Court — for titles to their land. Very often they had to sell the land to pay the cost of proving that they owned it. From 1840 the Māori were steadily relieved of their land by Crown and private purchase. By 1890 the Crown and Pākehā colonists had acquired some 22 million of the 26 million hectares of New Zealand. Most of the land still in Māori possession lay in the more remote and rugged parts of

A Native Land Court sitting at Papawai as Ngati Kahungunu sign over the ownership of Lake Wairarapa to the Crown, 1906. *Alexander Turnbull Library*

the North Island.

The economic condition of the Māori was closely related to their land. Some iwi or hapū were already nearly landless and gained a precarious subsistence from cropping, food gathering and intermittent labouring for the Pākehā. Others used the proceeds from sale or lease of land to supplement — and all too often as a substitute — for such activities. But others again, especially where there was strong local leadership, were embarking on a variety of commercial enterprises, including pastoral farming, dairying, kauri gum digging, and fishing.

There was a similar variation in the Māori social condition. Some of the offspring of mixed marriages had been assimilated into the Pākehā population, although a slightly larger number, according to census returns, were assimilated into the Māori population. A few of the more prosperous lived in the Pākehā style in weather-board houses with all the trappings, but most Māori lived in makeshift quarters, and were frequently on the move. Māori health was poor and, as each census from 1874 to 1896 revealed, their numbers were slowly declining, due to high infant mortality, insanitary

Māori agricultural workers at Whangamarino, Rotoiti, 1930s. *Rotorua Museum/Auckland Institute and Museum*

living conditions, and the ravages of European epidemic diseases. Māori remedies were unavailing, indeed frequently fatal; European medicine was usually unavailable.

Nevertheless Māori society was far more resilient than many people assumed. Despite the pressures of Pākehā settlers, officials, missionaries and schoolmasters, Māori had largely resisted assimilation. Their kinship system, revolving around whanau, hapū, and iwi, remained in place. The whanau had not yet given way to the Pākehā nuclear family. Though some hapū and iwi had been decimated by warfare or depopulation, others had prospered. Some had been strengthened by Native Land Court decisions to award land to those in occupation at 1840. Māori owed loyalty to these kinship associations in ascending order, but they could also, when appropriate, trace links through intermarriage with other tribes. Such associations within and between tribes were not greatly to diminish in the twentieth century. Likewise Māori leadership, whether exercised by hereditary or ascribed chiefs, and in some tribes by women, was not to change substantially. Young people who had acquired the skills of the Pākehā, were used to deal with that world, but traditional leaders remained in command back on the marae.

In their struggle against the Pākehā in the nineteenth century, Māori had developed a number of supra-tribal organizations which were to persist into the twentieth century, each in its own way expressing a form of mana motuhake or separate authority. The King movement had survived the Waikato war and the rift between the Waikato and Ngati Maniapoto tribes which had led to the opening of the King Country in 1885. It was to continue in the twentieth century, despite occasional friction within and a gradual loss of support from outside the Tainui confederation. Even more broadly based was the Kotahitanga movement. This traced descent from those who signed Busby's Declaration of Independence in 1835 and the Treaty of Waitangi in 1840, or who attended numerous subsequent hui culminating in one at Waitangi which formed a Māori parliament in 1892. Though never formally recognized by the New Zealand Parliament, it was to continue sitting until 1907. Finally, there were the Māori prophet movements founded by Te Ua Haumene, Te Kooti Turuki, Te Whiti o Rongomai and, in the twentieth century, by Rua Kenana and T. W. Ratana, each of which had some political significance since Māori did not rigidly distinguish between politics and religion. The prophets were not usually men of traditional rangatira status but they appealed to a class of Māori who were becoming increasingly numerous, the mōrehu, the ordinary folk who were often landless and adrift from their tribes.

By the end of the nineteenth century, the Māori position in a country that was once theirs, was precarious. Their own future as a people, with their population still declining, was in doubt. Their grip on the remnants of their land was insecure. Their social structure was under threat. Their strategies, though each offering short-term satisfactions, seemed always in the end to be failing. The Pākehā juggernaut rolled on. But there was no clear-cut remedy that was acceptable to all. Many of the older leaders had their gaze fixed firmly on the past, were obsessed with old remedies for old grievances. But, as always in Māori society, a new generation was ready to break with their elders and their past.

Māori often use the expression ka pū te ruha, ka hao te rangatahi (when the old net is worn out, a new one is put into use) to signify the coming of a new generation. It was applied to the Young Maori Party, the group of zealous reformers, mostly from Te Aute College and New Zealand universities, who were gradually to remould Māori society in the first half of the twentieth century. They provided a new initiative to an old Māori problem; how to improve the social and economic conditions of the Māori people while also resisting the encroachments of the Pākehā. Though they were a Western-educated élite who knew how to operate the Pākehā system, their success also depended on the support of tribal kaumatua and that was not easily won.

Their first efforts failed. In 1889 three of the Te Aute boys spent their summer holiday touring the kāinga of Hawke's Bay, preaching a message of sobriety, godliness and cleanliness to the unresponding elders. In 1891 the senior pupils formed an Association for the Amelioration of the Condition of the Maori People, which achieved little. Then in 1897 they created a Te Aute College Students' Association which held the first of what was to become an annual conference of pupils and old boys. They presented papers dealing with Māori social, economic, cultural, moral, and political affairs. At the first conference the star performer was Apirana Ngata, the first Māori to graduate in arts and law, who presented four papers. Another who presented a paper was a pupil, Peter Buck, who was hoping to go on to Otago Medical School. Later Ngata wrote to him expressing his hopes for the young men of Te Aute:

> I am eagerly awaiting the results of the matric. & medical prelim. It is my wish that both you and Tutere [Wi Repa] will pass; it should not then be difficult to make satisfactory arrangements to see you through a five years course at Dunedin. Our circle will then be fairly complete . . . Hector, Kohere & Bennett, parsons, Hei & myself lawyers, you & Tutere doctors . . . We the parsons & lawyers will do the talking and some practical work . . . for you that come after — it is ours to remove prejudice, to argue out of existence fallacious doctrines, to lay the foundations for a healthier, more compact, more powerful social opinion among our people, that your future work may be easy. I only wish you had your M.B. or M.D. now and you could come with me . . . to begin the field-work of the association, to devote ourselves body and soul to it.

Remarkably, all of the young men listed (with the possible exception of Hector), achieved the professional goals Ngata had set out. Ngata became Travelling Secretary for the Association and in 1905 won the Eastern Maori seat. It was the beginning of an outstanding career in Parliament that was to last for 38 years. Another Te Aute old boy, Maui Pomare, who gained a medical qualification in the United States, was appointed as the first Director of Maori Hygiene in 1901. Buck, on completing his medical degree at Otago, became Pomare's assistant director. But not all of the leaders of the Young Maori Party were from Te Aute. Fred Bennett, who was to become the first Māori bishop of Aotearoa, and Hone Heke, the able member for Northern Maori from 1893 to 1909, were from St Stephen's College. Akenehi Hei, sister of lawyer Hamiora Hei, and the first Māori woman to become a registered nurse, was from Hukarere Girls' School in Hawkes Bay. For a start they called themselves Te Kotahitanga o Nga Tamariki o Te Aute, in deference to the Kotahitanga movement, but when its parliament was dissolved in 1907, they called themselves Te Ropu o te Rangatahi, the Young Maori Party.

The reforms carried out by the Young Maori Party could not have been successful without the co-operation on a local level of numerous kaumatua. Ngata always acknowledged his debt to his maternal uncle, Ropata Wahawaha, and his father, Paratene, who initiated the land reforms which he extended with conspicuous success. Pomare and Buck built on the work of recently appointed Native Sanitary Inspectors like Takarangi Metekingi of Putiki and Tamahau Mahupuku of Papawai. But such co-operation was not forthcoming everywhere. The tribes still hurt by the raupatu, regarded the reforms as tainted by Pākehā methods, and preferred to place their faith in the old Kingite or Te Whiti leadership. King Tawhiao died in 1894 and Te Whiti in 1907, but Waikato and Taranaki remained intransigent, and it was not until well after World War I that Pomare and Ngata were able to bring them into the mainstream health and land reform measures.

At the turn of the century, when the young Māori leaders were taking the initiative, Pākehā New Zealand was more receptive to measures to improve Māori conditions. The Liberal government elected in 1890 had introduced some welfare legislation, including an Old Age Pensions Act of 1898 which provided pensions for Māori, although on lower scale than for Pākehā. James Carroll, who was of Ngati Kahungunu descent, was in the Liberal cabinet and became Native Minister in 1899. Although he now represented a European seat, he remained a pivotal figure in government, forever trying to temper Pākehā demands for Māori land with the Māori need to retain the remnants of their estate. He also nurtured the Young Maori Party, his 'young colts' as he called them, using them to devise and administer important legislation, before facilitating their entry into Parliament.

On becoming Native Minister, Carroll used Ngata to assist him in drafting two important acts in 1900, the Maori Land Administration Act and the Maori Councils Act, which attempted to deal with the sickness over the land and the body. The Maori Lands Administration Act provided an alternative to the systems of private and Crown purchase of Māori land which had already caused great distress and endless litigation. It allowed Māori to sell or lease land through land boards. But, since these were to be controlled by Pākehā, Māori landowners were reluctant to co-operate. In five years no land was sold through the boards and only 68,298 hectares were leased. Carroll was condemned for taihoa, for a by-and-by policy, and in 1905 the government amended the Act, allowing Māori land to be compulsorily vested in the boards, though also requiring them to ensure that the Māori owners retained a minimum area of ten hectares per head. The boards now acted vigorously and by 1914 had approved the sale of 408,778 hectares and the lease of 1,095,246 hectares of Māori land.

In 1907 Ngata was appointed with the Chief Justice, Sir Robert Stout, to a commission to make recommendations on the reservation or further alienation of remaining Māori land. They were critical of the Crown's use of pre-emption to purchase Māori land 'below value', but conceded that it should be allowed to complete some purchases, especially in the central North Island. On the other hand they were adamant that tribes in other districts, who had retained very little land, should have that land permanently reserved. A notable example was the Ngati Whatua reserve at Orakei in Auckland, but in this instance the Crown passed special legislation to allow it a pre-emptive right of purchase. Altogether, the Crown purchased 1,416,430 hectares of Māori land in the years 1891 to 1911, leaving less than 3 million hectares still in Māori ownership. Moreover, as the Stout-Ngata commission pointed out, the state over the years had done nothing to encourage Māori to develop their own land; it had always stopped short at measures to acquire Māori land. As a consequence the Māori race was in 'a most difficult and critical position . . . . There are many of the tribes and hapus in . . . a decadent state . . . . The spectacle is presented to us of a people starving in the midst of plenty.' It was left to Māori to help themselves.

In fact Ngata and his Ngati Porou tribe were already demonstrating how this could be done. Under the shrewd guidance of Ropata Wahawaha and Paratene Ngata, Ngati Porou had retained the best of their tribal land and had begun to develop pastoral farming. By 1900 they were running more than 50,000 sheep, and had invested heavily in the improvement of pastures, buildings, and equipment. Management was controlled by informal committees of owners. After Ngata returned to the East Coast in 1897 he gradually took over the leadership of land development. The informal committees of owners were legally recognized as incorporations by the Maori Lands Administration Amendment Act in 1903. Incorporations were one way to avoid the fragmentation of Māori land titles that had resulted from the operations of the Native Land Court over the previous forty years. Instead of having their shares allocated and partitioned on the ground, the owners elected a committee of management, appointed a manager, and farmed the land as a single enterprise, providing employment and dividends for the owners. The system of incorporations proved particularly successful for pastoral farming of large blocks of land still in Māori ownership. It was gradually adopted by other tribes and, in due course, for some other economic enterprises such as timber milling.

Nevertheless, incorporation was of little use where Māori land was already fragmented into uneconomic holdings by the operations of the Native Land Court and European purchasers. Once again Ngata developed a solution: consolidation of titles, starting on the East Coast with the Waipiro block north of Tokomaru Bay in 1911. Here, through innumerable meetings of owners, he persuaded them to exchange and thus regroup their individual interests into contiguous holdings. But the task took him five years. To speed up consolidations Ngata abandoned the exchange of fragments for a valuation of the land and the apportionment of consolidated holdings according to the value of each individual's land rights. Nevertheless, the distraction of the war and the lack of government assistance meant that there could be no progress with consolidation outside Ngati Porou country until the 1920s.

Although the Ngati Porou land developments were the most spectacular in the period before 1914, other Māori were also trying to develop land or other economic enterprises, though these were frequently at risk through lack of secure tenure, capital, and expertise. But when the continuing loss of Māori land is taken into account, it is doubtful if there was any overall improvement in the Māori economic condition. Most Māori continued to eke out a precarious subsistence from land and

Māori Health Officers with the Chief Health Officer, Dr J.M. Mason (centre, front row). He is flanked by Dr Maui Pomare (his right) and Dr Peter Buck (left).

intermittent labour for the Pākehā.

Yet there was some relief for the sickness of the body. There was a slow but steady recovery of the Māori population, which rose from 45,549 in 1901 to 52,997 in 1916. (The 1916 figure does not include Māori troops overseas.) The recovery was due in varying degrees to a growing immunity to hitherto fatal European infectious diseases, and to improved medical care. Once again the initiatives came largely from Māori, although government played a part. In 1900 there was a plague scare and the government hastily established a Department of Health, adding a Maori Hygiene division the following year because of a fear that the disease could spread rapidly through unhygienic Māori kāinga. It was headed by the recently returned Maui Pomare with Peter Buck later appointed as his deputy. They embarked on a sustained campaign to improve Māori health, carrying out innoculations and operations, destroying unhygienic buildings, resiting insanitary wells and, above all, educating the Māori public in the necessities of modern Western medicine. But they were heavily dependent on the support of local Māori communities, more especially the tribal councils created by Carroll's act of 1900 and the Native Sanitary Inspectors who were appointed by the councils. And, with the aid of a Tohunga Suppression Act of 1907, they tried to combat the activities of supposedly traditional healers who were often peddlars of quack remedies. Buck informed himself on traditional Māori medicine — in 1910 he completed an M.D. on it — and did not hesitate to use his knowledge to serve the purposes of modern hygiene. The health reforms may not have reached into every Māori community, but their efficacy was demonstrated when an outbreak of smallpox in 1913 was halted by vaccination. Although the Māori councils had proved effective vehicles for carrying out the health reforms, some developed larger ambitions, setting off in the quest for tribal autonomy, or got into financial difficulties. Ngata was appointed as Organizing Secretary to sort out their problems but their funds were cut and Ngata entered Parliament in 1905. Thereafter the councils retained a shadowy existence until they were revived by Buck after the First World War to administer Māori health.

Inevitably, the gifted leaders of the Young Maori Party moved from locally-based reform to national politics. Ngata successfully challenged Wi Pere for the Eastern Maori seat in 1905. Buck, to his own great surprise, was named by Carroll to contest the Northern Maori by-election caused by the premature death of Heke in 1909. Well known for his medical work in the north, he won easily. Pomare won Western Maori in 1911. They initially supported the Liberal Government, with Ngata being appointed as Member Representing the Native Race in the Executive Council in 1909 and Buck replacing him in the short-lived Mackenzie ministry in 1912. But Pomare deserted them to take the same portfolio in Massey's Reform ministry later in 1912. Much to Ngata's and Buck's dismay and his own discomfort, he found himself having to defend the new government's quest for more Māori land. But in later years Ngata and Buck accepted Pomare's decision, realizing the importance for the Young Maori Party of having someone in government.

Before the first world war, Carroll and his 'young colts' had exercised a considerable influence in Parliament and on government. That influence was to continue over the next twenty years when first Pomare and then Ngata were important figures in cabinet.

The Māori performance in the war provided them with an opportunity to extract concessions from government. The call for Māori volunteers met a ready response from the kupapa tribes. They were grouped together in a Maori Pioneer Battalion. The commanding officer was a Pākehā, though several Māori were chosen a supernumerary officers and Buck, who went overseas initially as Medical Officer, became second in command. The Māori troops served in the Gallipoli campaign and in France. Almost half of the 2227 who served became casualties: 336 were killed or died and 734 were wounded. Although conscription was introduced for the Pākehā in 1916, it was not applied to the Māori until the dying stages of the war. Very few volunteers came from the raupatu tribes. In Waikato the resistance was led by a rising star in the King movement, Te Puea Herangi, a granddaughter of an early Pākehā magistrate, H. N. Searancke, who was assumed to have been a German. In the hysterical atmosphere of the war, Te Puea was dubbed the 'German Woman' and the government applied conscription with a vengenance to Waikato, some of whom were arrested and imprisoned just before the end of the war. There was similar hysteria towards the Tuhoe prophet, Rua Kenana, also suspected of discouraging his people from volunteering. He was arrested in 1916 on a grog selling charge following a police raid on his Maungapohatu settlement, and imprisoned after a lengthy trial in Auckland. These events were a legacy of the bitterness that still lingered from New Zealand's own wars fifty years earlier; something that would need to be resolved if the brave new world after the Great War was to see improvements in Māori-Pākehā relations.

The Massey Government did not start off very well by failing to provide Māori returned servicemen with the same aid it gave Pākehā men. Moreover, the Māori were more severely affected by the influenza pandemic that hit New Zealand at the end of the war; their death rate was seven times greater than that of the Pākehā. In desperation many Māori survivors turned to the faith-healer, Tahupotiki Wiremu Ratana, who began performing miraculous cures from his farm near Wanganui in 1919.

But there were also some grounds for hope. Despite the influenza, the 1921 census recorded a Māori population of 56,987 — an increase of some 1700 over 1916. By the mid-twenties Māori were increasing at a greater rate than the Pākehā. After the world war Buck returned to the Health Department as Director of Maori Hygiene. When he went to a Research Fellowship in Ethnology at the Bishop Museum in 1927, he was replaced by another product of Te Aute and the Otago Medical School, Edward Pohau Ellison. Pomare was Minister for Health from 1923 to the beginning of 1926. Although there were undoubtedly improvements in Māori health, including a slow decline in mortality, it was not until after the second world war, and particularly with the control of tuberculosis, that Māori mortality rates approached those of the Pākehā.

The Māori population remained overwhelmingly rural, although a few were still clinging to remnants of land on the fringes of urban areas. But, as Māori numbers increased, it became evident that they could not all find a living on their dwindling supply of land. In 1920 Native Department reported that 950,837 hectares of Māori land had been purchased since 1911 — 408,720 hectares by the Crown, the remainder by private purchasers through the Maori Land Boards. Only 1,937,549 hectares remained in Māori ownership and only 367,170 hectares of that area were considered suitable for development, less than eight hectares per head of population. The report concluded that the Māori had 'disposed of nearly all the lands that they can dispose of without leaving the bulk of them landless, and later, probably, to become a charge on the state.' The spectre of Māori paupers dependent on the state was to dampen the ardour of governments for purchasing Māori land; thereafter Māori land was acquired by the Crown or local bodies mainly in settlement for unpaid surveys or rates.

Moreover governments in the 1920s began to look more sympathetically at the resolution of long standing Māori land grievances. The change in attitude owed much to Gordon Coates, a Northland farmer with Māori sympathies, who took the Native Affairs portfolio in 1921 and retained it when he became Prime Minister after Massey's death in 1925. Though Coates failed to entice Ngata into the Cabinet, he continued to take his advice. There were official inquiries into the Ngai Tahu land claim, over the Crown purchase of the Canterbury block in 1848; the Tuwharetoa claim to the bed of Lake Taupo, and the Arawa claim to the beds of the Rotorua lakes; and, finally, the claims of the Taranaki, Waikato and Bay of Plenty tribes against the raupatu. Most of the Māori claims were upheld. Although land was not returned, compensation was paid, usually on an annual basis, to tribal trust boards. The sums awarded were hardly more then a token payment, compared with the value of land lost, and their value was greatly eroded by inflation in later years. Taranaki, for instance, received an annual payment of $10,000. Waikato were offered $6000, but refused to accept and were eventually awarded $10,000 in 1946. But some claims were dismissed so tribes like Ngai Te Rangi and Ngati Ranginui of Tauranga had to continue their struggle for many years before they succeeded.

Nevertheless, compensation for past grievances, however important in principle, did little to provide a livelihood for the tribes that received it. Their tribal trust boards usually chose to spend their annual income on cultural purposes — for instance on tribal meeting-houses, or scholarships for their children. For the Māori population at large, now increasing rapidly, it was necessary to look again at the development of their dwindled reserve of land and, increasingly, to the Pākehā economy.

Although Coates was sympathetic, the initiatives still had to come from Māori, above all from Ngata. With Carroll's defeat in 1919 and Pomare's failing health, he was the most influential Māori in the country. Despite his busy political career, Ngata remained actively involved in land reform at home and beyond. In the fertile Waiapu valley he persuaded the Ngati Porou to move into dairying, on individual units. They bought graded dairy stock, built cow sheds, installed milking machines, and supplied their cream to a co-operative dairy factory at Ruatoria. In 1926 Ngata invited Coates to the East Coast where he was so impressed with the Waiapu dairying scheme that he agreed to provide state funds for Māori land development.

Ngata never lost an opportunity to show off the progress to other tribes and to encourage them to follow Ngati Porou's example. In 1922 he persuaded Tuhoe to consolidate their lands and soon other tribes as far afield as Northland, the Wanganui river and the King Country had teams at work on consolidation. As ever, Ngata depended on the goodwill and support of local leaders like Tau Henare (who had replaced Buck as member for Northern Maori), Dick and Whina Gilbert of Hokianga, Rima Whakarua of Taranaki, Hoeroa Marumaru of Wanganui, Pei and Rotohiko Jones of the King Country, Tai Mitchell and Tiweka Anaru of Rotorua, Te Puea Herangi of Waikato. Some, including the Jones brothers, Mitchell and Anaru, had secondary education; others, like Te Puea, had little formal schooling but prestigious ancestry — she was of the kahui ariki (the King's family). Ngata 'courted' her assiduously to bring the embittered Waikato into his land reform schemes, getting Ngati Porou to provide warm hospitality and generous funds to her touring concert party in 1927 and taking a strong Ngati Porou contingent to Ngaruawahia in 1929 to open the Mahinarangi meeting-house. Later, in appreciation of her leadership, Ngata put her in charge of the Waikato land development schemes.

So far, Ngata's initiatives in land reform had been carried out while he remained in Opposition. His great opportunity to move forward came when Sir Joseph Ward's United party gained enough seats in the 1928 election to form a government. Ngata became Native Minister and, as number three in the Cabinet, was in a very influential position. He chaired important committees, sometimes took over other portfolios, even became acting Prime Minister. For several years he got virtually a free hand in Māori affairs and the opportunity to spend unprecedented sums of money on Māori land development — even though the country was slipping into the worst depression it had suffered in the century.

The details of the land development schemes were elaborately set out by Ngata himself in his annual reports to Parliament and his correspondence with Buck at the Bishop Museum. Soon after taking office Ngata switched the teams of consolidators onto land development, putting aside the question of title while the land was 'broken in' — cleared of bush or scrub, ploughed, grassed, fenced and stocked — on the assumption that the blocks would be subdivided into individual farms at a later date. Such 'schemes', as they were called, were soon underway in most parts of the country where land was still in tribal ownership. They engendered considerable enthusiasm, since they provided communal work for hitherto un- or under-employed men, women and children. Ngata saw them as a means of reviving tribal pride and culture, hoping that old marae would be revived or new ones created. Though he usually relied on local leadership, Ngata did not hesitate to use outside Māori expertise where necessary. The most spectacular case was his use of Ngati Porou and Ngati Kahungunu colonists for the Horohoro scheme on the pumice country near Rotorua, 'Ngati Pungapunga' (the tribe of the pumice lands) as they were called. Another example was his use of Tumokai Katipa, Te Puea's husband, to repair the tractors at Horohoro. In other parts of the country and particularly in Northland, where some Māori were already established on individual holdings, Ngata had to adopt different techniques, using loans, secured against the land or the cream cheques. These were seldom dishonoured. He occasionally got the opportunity to transfer Crown land or buy bankrupt Pākehā estates for Māori settlement.

Ngata administered his portfolio with great vigour, taking personal responsibility, usually on the phone, for all kinds of expenditure — on equipment, vehicles, seed, fertilizer, livestock, and labour. His beleaguered and understaffed head office was unable to keep up with the 'red tape', as Ngata called it. The Native Affairs accounts got into a mess and, although the Department was reorganized, the Auditor-General refused to pass them. The Prime Minister, George Forbes, appointed a commission of inquiry into Ngata's administration of his department and the land development schemes. In 1934 the commission reported critically on Ngata's administration,

Sir Apirana Ngata, Lord and Lady Bledisloe, and Tuhoe elders at Ruatoki, 1931. *Auckland Museum*

particularly his personal style and contempt for bureaucratic regulations, his alleged favouritism of his tribe and family, and the corruption of some of his subordinates (thought not Ngata himself). Ngata accepted responsibility for the deficiencies and immediately resigned from Cabinet. The report of the 1934 commission has a broader significance than the mere questions at issue. For it showed that the Pākehā establishment had little tolerance of Māori in positions of responsibility and Māori ways of doing things. The Labour Opposition made political capital out of the affair, though when they were in office in later years they were amply repaid in kind.

Ngata and those who worked with him were involved with far more than land development. They had embarked on a broad-ranging programme of cultural regeneration which some publicists started to call a Māori renaissance. In the 1920s a Board of Maori Ethnological Research and a Maori Purposes Fund Board were established to promote publication of Māori material and assist Māori education. Māori language became a university subject in 1925 and a university entrance subject in 1929. A Maori School of Arts and Crafts was established at Rotorua to train Māori carvers. There was a revival in the construction of carved houses, including memorial houses for Carroll at Wairoa, for Ngata's wife Arihia at Waiomatatini, and Pomare at Waitara. Te Puea was responsible for the construction of the twin houses Mahinarangi and Turongo at Turangawaewae. Another house was constructed at Waitangi for the nation's centenary. The hui which marked the opening of these houses were important events in Maoridom. They gave the tribes opportunities to

Sir Apirana Ngata leading a haka at the centennial celebrations at Waitangi, 1940. *Alexander Turnbull Library*

reciprocate hospitality and demonstrate their skills in whaikōrero, haka and poi. There were also frequent inter-tribal competitions in rugby, and, for the women, in hockey. Māori All Black teams played against visiting international sides or toured overseas, and outstanding Māori players like George Nepia and Jimmy Mill were regularly selected for the All Blacks — except when they were excluded on racial grounds from the All Black team that toured South Africa in 1928.

All of these activities were evidence of the vibrance of Māori society and culture, more especially on a tribal level. But all was not well with Maoridom. While some tribes were relatively well endowed with land, others had very little. Ngata's land development schemes could not stem the flow of Māori from these tribes into unemployment as the country entered the depression. By 1933 an estimated 40% of the Māori male workforce was unemployed, compared with 12% of the Pākehā male work-force. Ngata's land developments provided little or nothing for these mōrehu. Many had already joined the Ratana church which was gaining converts in the more depressed Māori communities in the Far North, the southern North Island and the South Island. In these communities the Ratana ministers provided a local network that supported Ratana's political mission — to capture the 'Four Quarters', the four

T. W. Ratana with the 'Four Quarters' — the candidates for the four Māori seats in Parliament, 1938. *Naitonal Museum*

Māori seats in Parliament. He tested the water in 1922 when his son Tokouru came within 800 votes of unseating Pomare in Western Maori. But in 1928 he put up candidates for all four electorates on a platform of ratification of the Treaty of Waitangi, the settlement of Māori grievances, and the achievement of Mana Māori Motuhake (the separate prestige and identity of the Māori people). All of the Ratana men ran second. They achieved the same results in 1931 but the following year E. T. Tirikatene won the Southern Maori seat for Ratana in a by-election. In Parliament Tirikatene aligned himself with the representatives of the Pākehā mōrehu, Labour. In 1935 Tokouru Ratana won Western Maori and in following elections Ratana/Labour candidates were to win and hold all four Māori seats. These political changes were symptomatic of the socio-economic transformation that was coming over Maoridom, and more especially of the failure of Ngata's land development schemes to stem the tide of proletarianization.

In the later 1930s and through the 1940s, New Zealand underwent major economic and social change, much of it engineered by the incoming Labour government and accelerated by the second world war. The country gradually recovered from the depression. Prices for agricultural exports rose, public works were expanded, local industries were protected, unemployment was virtually eliminated, and the government introduced a comprehensive range of social security measures.

On coming to office the Labour Prime Minister had promised the Māori people 'economic equality with racial individuality'. That promise was not wholly achieved, although Labour did sufficient to ensure continued Māori support at the polls. Labour increased expenditure on the land development schemes. The Native Affairs department started to construct Māori houses and some state houses were allocated to Māori tenants. But shortages of men and materials prevented any significant improvement in Māori housing until after the war. Māori were awarded the same relief rates as Pākehā unemployed, though some inequalities remained for Māori working on Māori schemes. They received the free medical services and benefits made available by the Social Security Act of 1938, though until 1945 they were usually paid lower benefits than Pākehā. Despite this, there was much Pākehā complaint at Māori 'living on Social Security' — a concern that was shared by Ngata who feared that the system would sap the self-reliance of his people.

But it was the war which brought on the most significant changes for Māori society. Once again, a Maori Battalion was recruited from volunteers. It was organized tribally into four companies, and eventually commanded in the field by Māori officers. Just after it departed overseas in May 1940, conscription was applied to the Pākehā but, on the advice of the Māori M.Ps, not to the Māori. Thereafter sufficient volunteers came forward to keep the Battalion up to strength. It fought with distinction, often being allocated difficult tasks, including covering the evacuation of Greece and Crete, the attack on the Mareth line in Tunisia, and the assault on Cassino in Italy. Not surprisingly, there were heavy casualties, with 640 killed or dying on service and 1791 wounded. Just on a hundred were decorated, including Lt. Moana-nui-a-Kiwa Ngarimu of Ngati Porou who was posthumously awarded the Victoria Cross.

At home a Maori War Effort Organisation was set up in 1942 under the chairmanship of Paraire Paikea, the member for Northern Maori, to promote recruitment, raise funds for the Battalion, and direct manpower into essential industries. The organisation established a network of 315 tribal committees and 41 executive committees. Māori recruiting officers maintained liaison between the organization's headquarters in Wellington and the tribal network on the ground. Although envisaged as a temporary body, the organization lasted through the war, took on a variety of welfare functions, and encroached on the work of the Native Department. Tirikatene, who had become chairman, wanted to use the organization as the basis for an autonomous Māori administration — for that long-sought mana motuhake — but he was outmanoeuvred by Fraser who brought the tribal committees and executives under the wing of a welfare section of the Maori Affairs Department in the Maori Social and Economic Advancement Act of 1945.

The war increased the pace of Māori social and economic change. Their high rate of unemployment was rapidly reduced as men and women were drafted into the

Sir Apirana Ngata farewelling soldiers in the Maori Battalion. *NZ Herald*

services or essential industries. Māori urbanization accelerated, with the percentage of Māori living in urban areas rising from 11.2% in 1936 to 22.9% in 1951, a process that was to continue unabated. The Māori population was now increasing rapidly — it rose from 82,326 in 1936 to 137,326 in 1956. But urbanization compounded the problems caused by the increase, especially in housing, since the new Māori migrants were herded into rental accommodation in depressed central city slums. Mostly single or newly married, and separated from the surveillance of their kaumātua, they often had problems with alcohol and the law, though the establishment of Māori community centres in the bigger cities provided some supervised entertainment. There was much fraternization and some friction with American troops stationed near the cities.

Nevertheless, it was assumed that the social problems would be resolved after the war, as the troops were rehabilitated into civilian life, the country returned to normal, and it was possible to catch up on the backlog of housing. Some of the hopes were realized in the prosperous post-war years. This time, Māori ex-servicemen were treated with the same generosity as their Pākehā comrades, and many, through trade training, higher education or loans to buy farms or businesses, got a good start.

After the war Māori integration into the national economy continued unabated.

Using a tractor on the land development schemes in the early 1930s. *National Archives*

The government speeded up the development of Māori land and housing construction, made a start on trade training, and greatly expanded Māori access to education. The raising of the school leaving age to fifteen in 1945 meant that Māori children received at least two years of secondary schooling. With the economy continuing to expand through the rapid development of farming, forestry, manufacturing, hydroelectricity, and service industries, there was ready employment for school-leavers.

Nevertheless, although the Māori standard of living was improving, their rate of improvement was not keeping pace with that of the Pākehā. The Māori were being employed largely as unskilled labour. Very few had the training, the skills, or the capital to get into the upper rungs of the civil service, or the professions, management or commerce. Their average incomes were considerably lower than those of Pākehā, and Māori had to spread their wages over larger families. Urbanization and economic development were merely converting the bulk of the Māori workforce from an under-employed proletariat rural to an urban one, few of whom had a plot of land to fall back on during hard times. Even by 1956, when it was customary to speak of 'full employment', Māori unemployment at 3.38%, was much higher than the Pākehā rate of 0.85%. Increased housing construction was insufficient to keep pace with the growing need; in 1960 it was estimated that the programme would have to be doubled or trebled to catch up with a backlog of over 6000 houses that were needed. Ominously, there was a rapid increase in Māori crime, particularly in cities like

Auckland which had received the largest influx of young Māori migrants. By the 1950s the Māori crime rate was three and a half times that of the Pākehā. That high rate was exacerbated by the fact that Māori, with their high visibility, were more likely than Pākehā to be arrested, to be unrepresented in court, and to plead guilty. Although only 7% of the total population in 1958, Māori made up 15.9% of those arrested, 17.8% of those convicted and 23.3% of those imprisoned.

Neither the Pākehā authorities nor Māori leaders were able to cope with such accumulating social problems. The revered Māori leaders of the pre-war years were at the end of their careers. Ngata and Bennett died in 1950 and Te Puea in 1952. Much was expected of the officers of the Battalion, and many of them were to attain considerable distinction in the civil service — especially, for a start, as welfare officers in the Maori Affairs Department, the professions and in tribal affairs. But several of them, including James Henare and Henare Ngata, could not reach the top politically since they stood for National in Māori electorates. It was in the cities that Māori leadership was most needed and here some younger men working in the universities as adult education lecturers, like Maharaia Winiata and Matiu Te Hau at Auckland and Bill Parker and John Rangihau at Victoria, were beginning to exert influence. Winiata, the first Māori to take a doctorate in anthropology, also took a lead in the King movement after Te Puea's death, helping to organize its centenary in 1958, but his premature death in 1959 removed one of the most promising of Maoridom's urban leaders. However, in some ways Māori women were making more progress than the men. In 1951 a Maori Women's Welfare League was founded by delegates from local welfare committees, with Whina Cooper, a veteran from the land development schemes in the North, elected as first President. It was not until 1962 that a comparable male-oriented organization, the New Zealand Maori Council, was created.

Politically, the Ratana ascendancy remained unchallenged after the war: all four seats were held by Ratana/Labour members until 1963 when Steve Watene, a Mormon, won Eastern Maori. The Ratana/Labour members twice held the balance of power in Parliament — the so-called 'Māori mandate' — when Labour held office by fewer than four seats between 1946 and 1949, and 1957 and 1960. But they were unable to extract significant concessions from the government, or provide effective Māori leadership. Three of the seats — Western, Southern and Northern — remained in the families of the original Ratana members with the second generation members being even less effective than the first. During the war Paraire Paikea was Member of the Executive Council Representing the Native Race, as was Tirikatene after him, but even when Labour returned to office in 1957, Nash kept the portfolio of Maori Affairs, merely giving Tirikatene the status of Associate Minister. Nevertheless, the Māori members could not push the 'Māori mandate' too far since they were likely to provoke a backlash of Pākehā voters at the polls. Indeed there is some evidence that this happened in 1949. Labour's success in the election for the four Māori seats, held the day before the general election, may well have contributed to Labour's defeat on that day.

THE CELTIC MANDATE

Labour's dependence on the four Māori seats, 1946-9, as depicted by the *New Zealand Herald* cartoonist, 11 August 1949. *NZ Herald*

By 1960 the future of the Māori was clouded. Although their demographic future was clearly assured, with their population still increasing more rapidly than that of the Pākehā, their relative position in other ways that could be statistically measured was deteriorating. This much was revealed in the Hunn report, commissioned by Nash, but not completed until the eve of the election. And that election saw the return of National, still bereft of Māori representation.

In its previous period of office, National had not carried out any major departures in Māori policy. It had continued Labour's social security system, expanded trade training programmes, and carried on land development schemes, though now devoting more attention to the settlement of Māori farmers on development blocks. It had begun to grapple with what was to become a recurring problem, re-fragmentation of titles. With increasing population, this was occurring at a greater rate than consolidation could be carried out. In the Maori Affairs Amendment Act (1953), the Maori Trustee was given power of compulsory acquisition of uneconomic shares in land that were valued at less than $50, on condition that the land was offered to other Māori or incorporations.

When National returned in office in 1960 their earlier policies were continued. The new Minister for Maori Affairs, Ralph Hanan, published the Hunn report. In the twelve years of National government that followed, he and his successor, Duncan

McIntyre, gradually implemented Hunn's main proposals. These included a speeding up of land development, housing and trade training; the establishment of a Maori Education Foundation to provide financial aid for Māori in higher education; changes in land tenure to arrest the further fragmentation of titles; and the elimination of discrimination in New Zealand legislation. The most controversial proposals concerned land titles, particularly Hunn's recommendation to disallow partitions or multiple successions for land valued at less than $100. These proposals were elaborated by the Prichard/Waetford committee in 1965 and incorporated in the Maori Affairs Amendment Act (1967). This laid down that Māori land owned by incorporations or by not more than four persons was to have the status of European land, and retained and strengthened the controversial provision of the 1953 Act which allowed the compulsory purchase of land not exceeding $50. In the face of determined Māori opposition, the government had abandoned Hunn's proposal to increase the sum to $100.

The Hunn report provoked much controversy which went beyond the details to the basic philosophy of government policy. Hunn had spoken out boldly on government's role in racial policy, asserting that it could accelerate or retard but not thwart or divert the process of evolution. In his view, evolution was clearly integrating Māori and Pākehā. Accordingly, integration had become the conventional expression of policy, though in the long term New Zealand, like Britain, would probably become an assimilated society. Hunn's definition of integration allowed for the continuation of some aspects of Māori culture — he specified language, arts and crafts, the institutions of the marae — though he added that only Māori themselves could keep alive these ancient arts. These bold assertions provoked widespread Māori criticism, aptly summed up in a pamphlet by the Maori Synod of the Presbyterian church, 'A Maori View of the Hunn Report', which saw Hunn's integration as merely a euphemism for the long-standing Pākehā policy of assimilation: what the shark said to the kahawai. Although the Maori Affairs Department made more attempts to define integration, the term was gradually dropped from official explanations of Māori policy. By the end of the sixties, Hanan's successor, Duncan McIntyre, was talking about 'biculturalism'.

National was also recognizing the need for a co-ordinated expression of Māori opinion, as a counterweight to the Labour/Ratana stranglehold on the four Māori seats. Hunn and Hanan therefore did what Labour had avoided in 1945 and established the New Zealand Maori Council in 1962. This completed the pyramid by placing eight (later nine) District Councils and the New Zealand Maori Council on top of the locally-based tribal and executive committees set up by the Maori Social and Economic Advancement Act (1945). The local committees often worked well, especially in rural areas where there was a strong body of kaumātua, but this sort of leadership was lacking in the cities. Some District Councils were expected to represent impossibly large areas, with a small, scattered population. Te Waipounamu, for instance, covered the South Island, Stewart Island and the Chathams. On the other hand, metropolitan District Councils like Auckland and Wellington covered a small

The first conference of the Maori Women's Welfare League, 1951. Whina Cooper is seated in the centre with Mira Petricevich standing behind her. *Alexander Turnbull Library*

area but represented a far greater proportion of Māori population than the largely rural Councils. The metropolitan Councils tended to come under the control of abrasive urban intellectuals, but the rurally-based Councils were controlled by older, more conservative men, who dominated the New Zealand Maori Council. Its three chairmen — Sir Turi Carroll, Pei te Hurinui Jones and Sir Graham Latimer — were at one time or another unsuccessful National candidates for Māori seats. But, despite the assertions of some Māori critics to the contrary, they were never mere ciphers for National governments and were indeed sometimes openly critical — as, for instance, over the proposed Maori Affairs Amendment Bill of 1967. Although there is nothing in the legislation to say so, the Council was also until the 1980s an exclusively male organization.

Nevertheless, there is an irony about the New Zealand Maori Council. Since the beginning of Pākehā colonization, Māori groups have tried to establish a national organization of their own that would express mana Māori motuhake; none has ever quite succeeded. The government-created New Zealand Maori Council has not pursued this goal, but it has not captured the imagination or fulsome support of Maoridom either. Nor, at a lower level, have its District Councils and local committees gained widespread support. In many cases they have been overshadowed by tribal trust boards and incorporations, some of which administer considerable funds from compensation, rents, and the development of lands and other resources. But here too there are difficulties since some tribes, especially smaller ones, have neither incorporations nor trust boards, and in the cities there are large numbers of Māori who have no tribal indentification and no land. They are the new morehu.

Although New Zealand as a whole enjoyed a period of almost uninterrupted prosperity in the 1960s and early 1970s, little of this rubbed off onto the Māori. There was a slight slowing of population growth, thanks to the contraceptive pill, but the lower median age of the Māori population meant that a high proportion of Māori women were in the child-bearing bracket. Those who were of half or more Māori origin increased from 167,086 (6.9% of the New Zealand population) in 1861 to 279,252, (8.8%) in 1981. Maori urbanization continued at a steady rate, rising from 38.4% in 1961 to 78.2% in 1981, when it was close to that of the the Pākehā. Yet many of the optimistic assumptions that were made about urbanization did not come about. It was assumed that in urban areas Māori would get better housing, education and social services, and thus become integrated into the economy and society, with a fair proportion of them represented in skilled trades, the professions, the bureaucracy and business. But any gains for Māori, including the slow growth of an urban élite, hardly kept pace with the progress of the Pākehā. For instance in 1951, 1.3% of employed Māori males were in professional, technical, administrative or managerial positions, compared with a New Zealand total of 7.7%. By 1981 the Māori percentage had risen to 3.1% compared with a New Zealand total of 16.5%. Employed Māori women were similarly disadvantaged. It was the same with incomes. In 1961 the average income of Māori males was 89.8% of that of non-Māori males; but by 1981 it had dropped to 83.3%. Māori women were again in a similar position. With the economic fluctuations and restructuring from the mid-1970s, Māori were to suffer a much higher rate of unemployment than Pākehā. By 1981, 14.1% of the Māori labour force was unemployed compared with only 3.7% of the non-Māori labour force. The Māori unemployment rate has continued to rise since then, particularly in the 15-19 age bracket where by 1986, 30% of Māori (compared with 15% of non-Māori) were unemployed. There was also a deterioration in Māori housing conditions from 1961, when one in four Māori households owned their own houses, to 1981, when only one in eight did so. An increase in the total number of Māori obtaining secondary and tertiary qualifications, failed to keep pace with the corresponding increase of the Pākehā. But there was one area where Māori continued to outpace the Pākehā in the statistics — in crime. Since 1979 they have been more than 50% of the prison population.

Such grim statistics, which demonstrate that in virtually every comparison with the Pākehā, Māori are in a worse and often deteriorating position, give the lie to any complacent assumption that New Zealand has achieved racial equality. Māori have paid a high price for being 'integrated' into the New Zealand economy. They have become a brown proletariat, residing for the most part in rather uneasy proximity with

Pacific Island migrants and the remnant of the Pākehā working class. Although they have been unionized, few have pushed their way into the union hierarchy. They indulge in the mores of the 'Kiwi joker' — in rugby, racing and beer. Māori youth have become addicts of pop culture and some have become successful performers. There is also a tiny but slowly increasing Māori middle class who have adopted much of the life-style of the Pākehā middle class.

But most Māori, whatever their class and Pākehā associations at work and play, have retained their Māori identity, even though they may no longer be Māori-speaking. Many urban Māori maintain contact with their rural marae, returning for tangi and unveilings, hui, or, more often these days, just for summer holidays. And they have created marae in the cities, often starting with a garage in a backyard. Recently, some of the urban marae, like Orakei in Auckland, originally set up for 'all Māori', have been reconstituted as tribal marae for the tangata whenua. The marae remains the focus for the formal use of the Māori language, for whaikōrero, but there has also been an attempt, particularly from the late 1960s, to expand the teaching of the language in the universities, the schools and, through the kōhanga reo movement since 1982, in pre-school centres. There has been a flowering of Māori literature and art, encouraged originally by the Maori Affairs journal, *Te Ao Hou*, and more recently by the Association of Maori Artists and Writers. Some writers and artists have achieved national, indeed international, acclaim. There has been revived interest in and respect for traditional Māori taonga, for instance in the 1984 Te Māori exhibition which toured the United States. Radio and television, the civil service, central and local government, the churches and the schools, have all begun to respect taha Māori, though Māori themselves often complain that this is no more than a token recognition. It is being said that there is in progress a new Māori renaissance, like that engendered by the Young Maori Party more than fifty years ago.

Yet there is also doubt whether this new renaissance is reaching down to the mass of Māoridom, and more particularly the large number of young unemployed Māori frequently at odds with their parents as well as the authorities. Many of them are into drugs, violence and larceny, and end up, with monotonous regularity, in welfare homes, borstal and prison. Since the 1960s many of the young urban Māori have lived in gangs, such as the Mongrel Mob and Black Power. These have been growing as unemployment has also increased. The gangs have local chapters and meet at national congresses. Some of them have aquired property and embarked on business enterprises or work schemes. The gang members are seldom Māori speaking, rarely attend marae functions, and have few contacts with their kaumātua or urban Māori leaders. They are a measure of the gulf between the generations in Maoridom that is probably deeper now than at any previous time. There is also considerable friction between gangs, particularly Black Power and the Mongrel Mob. But there has been little violent confrontation with the police, despite frequent stand-offs, periodic raids on gang headquarters, the removal of offensive weapons, and many arrests. The gang members form a large part of the Māori prison population.

Although the gangs are largely an urban phenomenon, they have had little

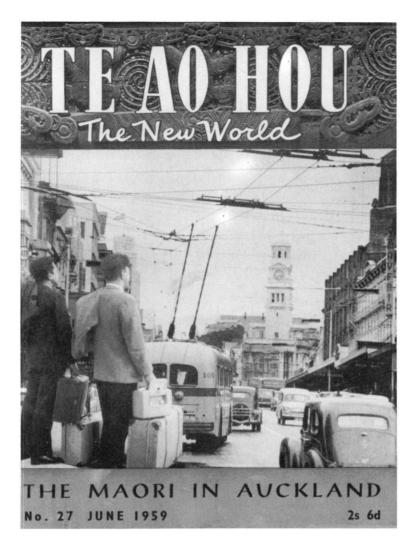

Te Ao Hou, the Department of Maori Affairs magazine, portrays the Māori urban migration, 1959.
Te Ao Hou

association with the numerous and often ephemeral urban pressure groups and protest movements that also emerged in the 1960s. These include the Maori Students Association and the Maori Graduates Association which were mainly concerned with organizing young Māori leader conferences in the mould of the Te Aute conferences of the turn of the century. But other student groups like Auckland's Nga Tamatoa, inspired by the Black Power movement in the United States, were more activist and abrasive, sometimes adopting tactics that earned them the displeasure of rural kaumātua as well as the Pākehā. However Nga Tamatoa faded out of existence as its

The Maori Land March across the Auckland Harbour Bridge, on its way from Cape Reinga to Wellington, 1975. *Auckland Star*

young men and women went on to other jobs, sometimes in the establishment. In the 1960s the radical urban groups got support from several liberal, Pākehā-led organizations such as the Citizens Association for Racial Equality (CARE) and Halt all Racist Tours (HART), both of which still exist more than twenty years after their formation. Significantly, both were formed in the mid-sixties to protest against continuing sporting contacts with apartheid based South Africa, but were forced by pressures from Māori to concern themselves also with racism at home.

In the 1970s, new Māori organizations emerged to deal with more specific grievances, especially in relation to land. To some extent this represented a new turn in the wheel, with the grievances of the past, like the running sore of the raupatu, turning up before a new generation of Māori leaders. The long-standing grievance of the Tauranga tribes was reactivated and they got compensation for their raupatu in 1977, fifty years after the original commission had denied their claim. There was also Māori concern that they were still losing their land — often now through compulsory

A police cordon rings the settlement at Bastion Point, prior to the arrest of the protestors and the removal of their buildings in 1978. *Auckland Star*

acquisition under the Public Works Act at the instigation of local bodies or government departments. It was such concerns that led to the formation of Te Matakite o Aotearoa, under the leadership of Dame Whina Cooper. In the summer of 1974/75, she led a Land March from the Far North to Parliament steps in Wellington.

Another old grievance surfaced again because of a new provocation in 1977: the Ngati Whatua claim to land at Bastion Point in the heart of Auckland's plush eastern suburbs. It was the last remnant of the Orakei reserve which the Crown had finally purchased in 1950, using compulsory powers under the Public Works Act to acquire the final shares and to remove the remnant of Ngati Whatua from their traditional marae in Okahu Bay to state houses on the adjacent ridge. In 1977, when the government proposed to sell off part of the Bastion Point land for high-class housing, Joe Hawke led Ngati Whatua and other supporters onto the land which they continued to occupy for 506 days. They were finally cleared from the site by a massive police and army operation that was reminiscent of the removal of Te Whiti from Parihaka in 1881. There was no violence but some of Hawke's supporters were prosecuted for trespass.

The Bastion Point affair was the most notable of several Māori attempts to resolve grievances by occupation of disputed land. The annual Waitangi Day ceremonies provided further opportunities. Hitherto they had been used for much complacent speechifying to the effect that Hobson's cherished wish — he iwi tahi tatou (we are now one people) — had at last been realized. Māori groups who trekked to Waitangi vigorously made the point that there was nothing for them to celebrate, and some called the treaty a fraud, much to the embarrassment of the official party and their Ngapuhi hosts.

The waxing and waning of Māori protest had much to do with the party in power. When National was in office there was rising protest. But this tended to dissipate, if not entirely disappear, when Labour took over. When Labour returned to office in 1972 two of its four Māori members, Matiu Rata and Whetu Tirikatene-Sullivan, were elected to Cabinet. Rata was the first Māori since Ngata to gain the Maori Affairs portfolio. As a trade unionist with little formal education, he lacked Ngata's ability to confront the Pākehā establishment, but he ran into trouble for much the same reason as Ngata. He repealed or amended some of the unpopular legislation of the previous National governments, used state resources to purchase land for Māori settlement, returned the symbolically important Taupiri and Taranaki mountains to Māori ownership, and in 1975 created the Waitangi Tribunal to consider Māori grievances over any future breaches of the principles of the Treaty.

Criticism of the Labour government's handling of Māori issues in general and Rata's performance in particular figured prominently in National's campaign during the 1975 election and probably contributed to their handsome victory. National finally accepted that it could not win any of the Māori seats and put up Māori candidates in winnable general electorates. Two were elected: Ben Couch for Wairarapa, and Ralph Austin for Awarua. In the 1979 election Winston Peters won a third seat for National and Couch became the Minister for Maori Affairs. Like Rata, he had some difficulty handling bureaucrats and slick media operators. A Mormon who took a very conservative stance on many social issues, and a former Māori All Black who supported rugby contacts with South Africa, Couch was anathema to many urban radicals, but he did have the support and respect of more conservatively inclined rural Māori.

In any case, all was not well in the Labour camp. Rata, who headed the Maori Policy Committee, was at odds with the Labour leader Bill Rowling. When Rowling removed Rata from the chairmanship of the committee, he resigned from Parliament, provoking a by-election for the Northern Maori in 1980. He formed a new party, Mana Motuhake, a name which encapsulated the long-standing Māori quest for identity and self-determination. Labour selected a non-Ratana candidate, Dr Bruce Gregory, who won the seat by just under a thousand votes from Rata. Mana Motuhake put up candidates in all four Māori seats in 1981; all of them came second, thereby displacing National candidates into third or fourth place. Mana Motuhake tried again in 1984, but lost ground, coming second to Labour in only two of the four electorates. These electoral results demonstrated that Labour no longer needed to depend on Ratana candidates and that it was still the party of the Māori working class, now suffering severe unemployment. With Labour's victory in 1984, two of the four Māori members were again elected to Cabinet. But Koro Wetere, the Minister for Maori Affairs, ran into a great deal of flak for his administration of the department, like Rata and Ngata before him, this time mainly from National's formidable Māori member, Winston Peters. Nevertheless, Wetere was able to get through some important legislation, notably his amendment to the Treaty of Waitangi Act in 1985, giving the Waitangi Tribunal retrospective jurisdiction back to the signing of the Treaty in 1840. It resulted in a veritable flood of Māori claims, including Ngai Tahu in the South Island and several raupatu (land confiscation) claims in the North Island, to the new Tribunal — an indication of the widespread sense of grievance within the Māori community.

The Tribunal has been unable to hear more than a tiny number of the claims though its membership has been increased to sixteen, in an effort to cope with the flood of claims. Some of its recommendations, such as the return of the disputed land at Bastion Point to Ngati Whatua, have been accepted without too much difficulty by government and the public. But others, like the finding on the Muriwhenua fishing claim — that the Treaty did guarantee the Māori 'full, exclusive and undisturbed possession' of their fisheries — has been controversial and strongly resisted by the Pākehā-controlled fishing industry. When large resources are at stake and there is any attempt by the Māori to roll back the tide of colonialism, there is bitter resistance and litigation. Since the 1970s, Māori have gained prominent positions in church and state, and one, Sir Paul Reeves, who has been successively Anglican Primate and Governor-General, in both. But they have not got real political or financial power; those commanding heights remain with the Pākehā. They have been winning before the Waitangi Tribunal and the courts and the protest movements have been quietened. Those who called the Treaty a fraud are now demanding that it be implemented. But if the Māori fail in the courts and at the hands of government, they can return to the streets and to Waitangi. For each generation advances into the future recalling the past, ngā wā o mua.

Norman Kirk, Prime Minister from 1972 until his death in 1974. *NZ Herald*

14. Hard Times
(1972-1989)

KEITH SINCLAIR

Norman Kirk was a very large man, 'Big Norm', with large, almost hypnotic eyes, and hands the size of hams. Like Holyoake, he had not received any secondary schooling. He once said, in conversation, that he would probably be the last uneducated New Zealand political leader — for, since the mid-1940s, almost every child had attended high school. Like Fraser and Nash, who were similarly unschooled, he was widely read, in an unsystematic way. He had little interest in political theories, but had a 'big heart' — a genuine concern for the welfare of 'ordinary people'. His parents were soldiers in the Salvation Army. He appeared to know little about economics, but, soon after coming to power, he revealed a surprising interest in foreign affairs, probably to the neglect of domestic problems.

Compulsory military training was abolished. The remaining troops were pulled out of Vietnam. New Zealand recognized the government of China, and over the next few years established a close and friendly relationship with the Chinese. The embassy in Moscow, which had been closed in 1950, during the 'Cold War', was reopened.

Kirk's speeches began to sound a note of international idealism rarely heard in New Zealand since the death of Michael Joseph Savage. In 1973 he said that his government was determined to 'find and hold to a firm moral basis for its foreign policy . . . I believe that to base our foreign policies on moral principles is the most enlightened form of self-interest. What is morally right is likely to be politically right.' He wanted all of New Zealand's actions abroad to reflect the qualities of decency and humanity that he believed characterized its people. Thus there was a great change in style and tone in foreign policy. This renewed idealism was a striking feature of two of the most significant government actions relating to foreign affairs.

New Zealand's voting record on apartheid in the United Nations, and its persistence in playing rugby football with South Africa, had led to widespread domestic and international criticism. Although Labour had promised not to interfere in the affairs of sporting bodies, in 1973 Kirk instructed the Rugby Union not to receive a racially-selected South African rugby team in New Zealand. This was undoubtedly politically damaging, for thousands of rugby enthusiasts were outraged.

New Zealand had repeatedly protested against the French nuclear tests at Mururoa. In 1973 Australia and New Zealand applied to the International Court of Justice to try to stop these atmospheric tests. If the devices exploded were as harmless as the French maintained, why not test them near Paris? The Court asked the French to desist while the case was being heard, but they persisted. In 1972 some small New Zealand vessels had sailed into the test area to protest. Now the government sent the frigates *Otago* and *Canterbury* into the test zone, a protest which received world-wide publicity.

Under Kirk there was a renewed stress on the humanitarian side of foreign relations, for instance in aid for poor and developing countries. In a speech in India he said: 'we believe that peace depends upon justice. That poverty and underdevelopment deny ordinary men and women justice.' He was personally very moved by the massacres in Bangladesh, a country he visited twice. New Zealand moved swiftly to recognize and help that country. Sometimes Kirk's statements sounded sentimental, but they were certainly sincere. He was a child of the New Zealand depression of the 1930s.

An important part of this new stress on aid was a growing and intense interest in the affairs and welfare of the new Pacific Island states, such as Fiji and Western Samoa. The Pacific was assuming a more central position in New Zealand policies.

Following the détente between the great powers, there was a reduced United States commitment to the Pacific and Asia: there was thus more room in which small countries could move. Kirk was much concerned to discover the possibilities for a more constructive framework of international order in the region. Labour was critical of the SEATO pact, and thought it divisive and obsolete: perhaps it could be replaced? What Kirk had in mind was perhaps something like the South Pacific Forum, in which heads of governments and ministers have discussed their problems since 1971. There was talk of an Asian-Pacific Forum, including China and Japan. But Thailand and some other South-East Asian countries were not yet ready to come to terms with China. The project had to 'lie on the table'.

A further idea, perhaps originated by Kirk, was a sub-regional grouping of Australia, Indonesia, Papua-New Guinea and New Zealand. This met with the same fate. Thus little came out of these new diplomatic initiatives.

In 1973 New Zealand was enjoying considerable prosperity. There was a — temporary — boom in world agricultural prices. Immigration, from Great Britain and the Pacific, was rising rapidly. The dollar was revalued by 10%. Then came the first oil shock, when oil prices quadrupled in a few months. There was a sharp drop in the terms of trade, that is, the relationship between the prices of imports and exports. They fell 43% in less than a year. The great surplus in the balance of trade in 1973 became a massive deficit of over a thousand million dollars by 1975.

The government had been misled about fundamental economic problems by the boom. The structures erected by the first Labour government had seemed to be working: there had been a national consensus upon the welfare state, full employment, and a manufacturing industry protected by import licensing. The government reacted to the crisis in a spirit of optimism and sought to avoid deflationary policies which would cause unemployment. It resorted to extensive overseas borrowing — by 1975 the external public debt stood at a record $863 million. The dollar was devalued again.

Inflation accelerated after the oil shock and was running at about 10% a year. The government responded with controls. It sought to introduce a Maximum Retail Price scheme whereby all retail prices were controlled, but it was too complex and did not work. In addition, the government extended the already numerous subsidies to industries: there was a wool subsidy, a sheep meat subsidy, a sugar subsidy, a milk subsidy. The Post Office and the railways were subsidized. New Zealand must have been among the most regulated — and subsidized — countries on earth.

In late 1974 Norman Kirk died tragically. He was succeeded by a small, chirpy man, Bill (later Sir Wallace) Rowling, who had been an economics tutor. In the eyes of the public he did not become a successful leader, probably because he never managed to master the art of television interviews as Kirk had and as his first two successors, Muldoon and David Lange, were to do.

Rowling and his Minister of Finance, Bob Tizard, persisted with the policies of trying to borrow their way out of recession, mainly from overseas. But one local source of funds proved politically damaging. Rowling introduced a new, actuarial government superannuation scheme whereby citizens contributed throughout their working lives to a fund from which they would eventually draw a pension. The 1938 scheme had been paid for from taxation. The Opposition, led by Robert Muldoon, promised to return to that scheme and offered a superannuation payment to married couples of 80% of the average wage, at the age of sixty, irrespective of their wealth or other income. This was the most expensive electoral bribe in the country's history, and the most successful. It was said that at the election in 1975 superannuitants were queueing up at the polling booths when they opened, to vote the government out. A clever National Party television advertisement had reinforced the message by suggesting that the Labour government intended to use its huge superannuation fund to buy up private enterprises and introduce socialism by purchase. It should be added that Muldoon's 'super' could be regarded as more radical than Rowling's.

There were other ways in which Labour's welfare measures were unpopular. In the early 1970s there had been massive immigration, almost the biggest in the country's history. This greatly increased the demand for housing. Young married Kiwis noticed and complained that numerous state houses were going to new immigrants and solo mothers. In some electorates this resentment contributed to a swing against Labour. There can be little doubt, however, that the main influence on the 1975 election was the economic crisis. The government had achieved very little in domestic and economic policy: it was, and is, difficult to see any sense of direction or purpose, except in foreign policy and racial issues.

In 1975 the Labour Government was blown away in the strongest electoral cyclone in the country's history up to that time. The number of seats held by the parties was reversed. Now National held 55 seats to Labour's 32.

The new Prime Minister, Robert Muldoon, was to become one of the most dominant, not to say domineering, leaders in New Zealand history, rivalled in that respect only by Richard Seddon and Peter Fraser. He was an accountant who, like Kirk, had been brought up in hard circumstances during the depression of the 1930s. He had, however, received a good secondary school education. A journalist, Spiro Zavos, wrote that he had a unique capacity to arouse strong emotions in the allegedly passionless New Zealand people. His supporters thought that he could do no wrong. To his enemies he was leading New Zealand towards bigotry, callousness and an uncaring society.

In foreign policy he was unadventurous, holding firmly to the Commonwealth and the American alliances, ANZUS and, until it was folded up in 1977, SEATO. This was at a time when New Zealand's position in the world was changing rapidly as Great Britain had joined the European Economic Community in 1972 and, like the USA had largely disengaged from involvement in Asia. Looking back, it is surprising that New Zealand's policies changed so little.

Some of the government's worst problems related to race relations, about which it showed little sensitivity. Many of the immigrants of the early 1970s were Pacific Islanders. People from Niue or the Cook Islands were New Zealand citizens, but many immigrants from Tonga and Samoa were not, and entered the country with visitors' or short-term work permits. The government believed that there were 10,000 'overstayers' in the country. Following the oil crisis of 1973–1974 and the rise of unemployment, the Kirk Government had tried to deal with the problem of overstayers. Immigration officials and police carried out 'dawn raids' on homes, but these were stopped by the government. In 1976 following further dawn police raids and random street checks of anyone who looked Polynesian, many of these people were deported. This was the worst example of racial tension in recent years.

The government had promised not to interfere in sport. The General Assembly of the United Nations had asked members to stop sporting contacts with South Africa, but that had no weight with the Rugby Union, which sent another All Black team to play the Springboks. The result was that African and other athletes walked out of the next Olympic Games in Montreal in 1976 and New Zealand's name was held in wide contempt.

Like Kirk, Muldoon had to change his mind. By the Gleneagle's Agreement of 1977, each Commonwealth country accepted it as a duty 'to vigorously combat the evil of apartheid . . . by taking every practical step to discourage contact or competition by their nationals with sporting organizations . . . from South Africa'.

This was not, however, the end of the matter. In 1981 the Rugby Union agreed to a tour of New Zealand by the South Africans. The government did not stop them, though accused of breaking the Gleneagles Agreement. The result was extraordinary scenes of street violence, as huge processions of demonstrators tried to disrupt or

R.D. Muldoon, Prime Minister and Minister of Finance, with his 'mini Budget' of 1980. *NZ Herald*

protest against the games. One game was disrupted when the protesters broke onto the rugby ground. Thereafter riot police, armed with long batons, guarded the fields — and sometimes protected the demonstrators from angry rugby fans. There was much violence on both sides.

Rugby football, a game played in a few small countries and by minorities in a few large ones, was a significant political issue in New Zealand from 1958 for about thirty years. It was not, however, a racial issue in New Zealand as it was in the United Nations. Large numbers of Māori and Pacific Islanders were eager to play — and beat — the Springboks. Many of them had never heard of apartheid in sport and agreed with the view that politics had nothing to do with sport.

Robert Muldoon had won an election and introduced his own superannuation system. But the country's economic problems did not go away: indeed it was only now that they became very clear to most people. Inflation was high, nearly 18% in mid-1976 and now running higher than in the country's major trading partners, which was bad news economically, because it pushed up production costs. For most New Zealanders the most startling fact was that their country had slipped from about fourth to twentieth in the list of wealthy, OECD nations. They had always prided themselves on

Anti-Springbok Tour protest in Grafton, Auckland, 3 August 1981. *NZ Herald*

their wealth, on being 'a people of plenty'.

Unemployment was rising, with 25,000 out of work in early 1979, with another 31,000 on 'job creation' schemes. Large numbers of skilled people 'voted with their feet' by migrating to Australia. This 'brain drain' was very damaging to the country's future. At the same time, as wages fell behind prices, there was a great increase in industrial disputes. There were four times as many stoppages annually in the late seventies and early eighties as there had been a decade before.

The National Party had, since 1936, presented itself to the public as a free enterprise party, but Muldoon had other ideas. In a book giving his views on the New Zealand economy, he stoutly defended the idea of a 'managed economy'. He claimed that the 'whole concept of government is based on intervention'. 'Any country which today allowed its economy to run completely free would . . . go downhill very rapidly.'

The government intervened in the economy in numerous ways. There were many consumer subsidies, not all of them new, for instance on electricity. When prices for lamb fell rapidly the government introduced Supplementary Minimum Prices. Millions of dollars of the taxpayers' money were handed out to farmers. Land prices rose as sheepmeat prices fell, as farmers competed for more SMPs. Large quantities of meat proved unsaleable and were turned into fertilizer.

When inflation continued at a record level in 1982, Muldoon introduced a wage and price 'freeze'. The government controlled rents, dividends and directors' fees. It also tried to control interest rates. Muldoon was arguably the biggest 'interventionist' in New Zealand history.

The second oil shock of 1979 pushed up inflation and the price of imports. The new high price of petrol led the government to conclude that New Zealand was, for its population, relatively energy-rich. Local sources of energy that had not previously seemed worth developing now seemed viable. This was one of the factors that led the government to formulate a growth strategy known as 'think big'.

New Zealand embarked upon an ambitious petrochemical programme. Natural gas, which the country possessed in abundance, was made into synthetic petrol. In other plants the gas was turned into urea and methanol. The use of compressed natural gas and liquid petroleum gas in motor vehicles was encouraged. Other 'think big' projects included a big expansion of the New Zealand Steel mill and a projected expansion of the aluminium industry.

The cost of these projects was staggering. By 1984 the overseas public debt stood at $8226 million. The budgetary deficit was $3100 million.

Some National Party leaders were critical of all this government intervention. They demanded a 'more market' approach, that is, that more reliance should be placed on market signals. One minister, Derek Quigley, was sacked when he criticized 'think big'. He was not, however, alone in his opinion. It was soon made clear that Muldoon's economic management was perceived by large numbers of people not to be working.

Several political movements had in recent years been undermining National support. In the early 1970s the Values Party, an idealistic environmental (or 'green') party, had arisen, preaching the 'small is beautiful' philosophy of no-growth economics. At one stage it attracted large numbers of young voters who were probably captured by Labour a decade later.

A Social Credit Party, preaching an incomprehensible credit reform message, won two National seats in the early 1980s. It was to lose both in 1987.

Much more damaging to National was the New Zealand Party formed in 1983 by Bob Jones, a rich property developer. Its policy stressed personal freedom; it advocated *laissez-faire* capitalism and denounced government inventionism in the economy. It emphasized education and opposed all defence expenditure. Like both Labour and Social Credit, it wanted to keep the country 'nuclear-free'. There had been several popular protests against visits by nuclear-powered, and possibly nuclear-armed American warships. Most people wanted to forbid such visitors.

By 1981 Robert Muldoon had only a small majority, and one at risk as one or two National MPs crossed the floor of the House to vote with Labour, for instance on anti-nuclear issues. In 1984 Muldoon called a snap election and lost, with 37 seats to Labour's 56 and Social Credit's 2. Although it won no seats, the New Zealand Party had clearly attracted many votes away from National.

The consensus which had kept National in power for twenty-nine of the past

Bob Jones, Leader of the New Zealand Party, on election night in 1984. *NZ Herald*

thirty-five years had broken down. A new generation had come to power, which had experienced neither the war nor the depression of the thirties, events which had moulded the attitudes of older people. They did not greatly admire the USA — they had been students during the Vietnam war, and many of them protested against American policies in that country.

The new Prime Minister, David Lange, was a big, ebullient man with a ready wit, a man rarely short of a quip. He was a lawyer, like his deputy, Geoffrey Palmer. The Minister of Finance, Roger Douglas, a businessman and accountant, was for a time to dominate the government in economic affairs. Few of the trade unionists who had established the party were to be seen. The new government ministers were young, mostly people in their forties and mostly professional people.

No New Zealand government had experienced such a baptism of fire as the Lange administration. During the election there had been a massive run on foreign currency. The country's overseas reserves could be exhausted within a few days. The outgoing Prime Minister agreed to the Reserve Bank's recommendation to close the foreign exchange market, but he flatly refused to carry out the incoming Prime Minister's wish to devalue, as the Reserve Bank also recommended. There was a brief

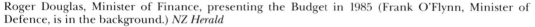
Roger Douglas, Minister of Finance, presenting the Budget in 1985 (Frank O'Flynn, Minister of Defence, is in the background.) *NZ Herald*

constitutional crisis. Sir Robert thought that there could be a quick change of government and then Labour could devalue, but the new ministers could not be sworn in until the writs were returned, about ten days after the election. In the end Sir Robert agreed to carry out the wishes of the incoming government, according to convention.

At the same time Lange had a meeting with George Schultz, the US Secretary of State, and Bill Hayden, the Australian Foreign Affairs Minister, who were in Wellington for a meeting of the ANZUS council. The incoming government's intention to ban visits by nuclear-powered or armed ships was anathema to New Zealand's two allies. Schultz announced that access for American naval vessels to New Zealand ports was essential to the validity of the ANZUS treaty. There was a clear threat that New Zealand would be expelled from the alliance if it refused to accept the USA's uncompromising policy of 'neither confirming nor denying' that a ship carried nuclear arms. Thus there was maximum pressure on the home and the international fronts.

The fact that it was a snap election brought Labour an accidental bonus: it did not have to spell out its policy proposals in detail. Very few people had any idea of Roger

Douglas's economic plans, some of which would have been very unpalatable to traditional Labour voters.

It was becoming clear to many people that the economy was in a mess. The economic structures erected by the first Labour Government, which had been tinkered with by later governments, simply no longer worked. Two events had destabilized the New Zealand economy, Great Britain joining the European Economic Community and the first oil shock. New Zealand had succeeded in diversifying its export markets. Only 9% of exports now went to the UK, in comparison with over 80% in the 1930s. In 1987 the United States, Australia, Japan and the EEC were the major export markets. But in all of those markets New Zealand exports ran into agricultural protectionism.

The country had also diversified the products exported. Meat, wool, butter and cheese now accounted for only half the export earnings. Horticultural products, forest products and fish now made a major contribution.

But New Zealand had not shared much in the fastest-growing sector of the international economy in the 1960s, that in manufactured goods. World incomes had risen while New Zealand's had stagnated. As economic growth had become slower it had become more and more difficult to pay for the desired imports.

Roger Douglas's approach to solving the country's problems, and raising its living standards, was derived partly from Treasury, but also from his own 'think tank', a discussion group of academic and other friends. He moved away from the Labour and Keynesian approach to economic growth and unemployment to a monetarist approach of which the chief aim was to beat inflation. The market, not the government, was to make economic decisions wherever possible. This attitude involved an almost complete rejection of Muldoonism as well as of Labour's economic past. The aim was to create a more efficient economy, capable of creating jobs and wealth; to restore New Zealand to what many people regarded as its rightful place, near the top of the economic tree.

Roger Douglas and his financial assistants tackled their task, the demolition of the first Labour Government's economic controls, with the evangelical fervour of born-again capitalists. The years 1984-1987 saw numerous and rapid changes which amounted to a revolution of the Right. Many people found the changes bewildering. The only comparable periods of change were the 1890s under the Liberals, and perhaps the late 1930s under Labour.

The financial market was deregulated at speed. The New Zealand dollar was allowed to float early in 1985. All controls on foreign exchange transactions were removed. New banks were permitted to enter the market or to be set up.

For many years taxation experts had advocated reforming the tax system which relied to an unusual degree on income and other direct taxes. The top income tax rate of sixty-six cents in the dollar was reached on quite modest incomes. This was a disincentive to increased effort. Douglas introduced a Goods and Services tax of 10% (later raised to 12.5%) on all sales of goods and other transactions. The marginal tax rate was reduced to forty-eight cents in the dollar, and later to thirty-three. These were

David Lange in a triumphant moment in 1985. *NZ Herald*

the biggest taxation reforms since income tax was introduced in 1891.

Agricultural subsidies, consumer subsidies on electricity, export incentives and import licences were all phased out, or, in the case of the tariffs, nearly so. State intervention in the export and internal marketing of farm and horticultural products was greatly reduced.

For years the country's labour practices had encouraged inefficiency. For instance, there was extensive 'feather-bedding' — that is, under union pressure, maintaining an unnecessarily large work force on a job — and 'moonlighting' — that is, taking two jobs and doing neither well. Good examples of the former were trains which needed only drivers carrying guards as well. The Forestry Service was greatly over-staffed.

Forestry, Lands, Coal and Electricity were turned into commercial state corporations and told to make a profit. It was planned that numerous other state agencies would follow suit. One of the most regulated economies in the world was swiftly becoming one of the most deregulated. This was a change that no one would have been likely to forecast ten years before.

There were also extensive changes in the system of welfare which, according to Douglas, had come to benefit the rich as much as the poor. The most dramatic change was a surtax on the expensive national superannuation introduced by Muldoon. The surtax meant that people on high incomes repaid their 'super' in tax. It affected about 25% of superannuitants. Because of other tax changes, the majority were slightly better off. A 'Family Care' package helped low-income families by providing tax refunds. 'Targetting' those really in need was the aim of the government's welfare policy. It was also committed to improving education, especially for low-income families, many of whom were Māori and Polynesians. But achieving those goals was not easy. In 1987 welfare, education and health took over half the government expenditure. Reconstructing the welfare state at a level the country could afford was a hard task.

Business responded to 'Rogernomics' with enthusiasm, after fifty years of being protected and timid. Several large companies expanded into Australia, Canada and South America. There was a mood of great optimism and, in 1986, a remarkable stock-market boom. The dire warnings of Sir Robert Muldoon that prices were quite unrealistic were ignored by a speculative public.

In 1987 there was another election in which, to most people's surprise, given the 'pain' that some of the government's measures had inflicted, the Lange Government increased its number of seats.

The government had appeared unusually united up to the election, but began to fall apart shortly afterwards. The rot set in with the stock-market crash of late 1987. Although this crash occurred in many other Western markets, it was unusually severe in New Zealand and its effects persisted unusually long. Many companies, major and minor, folded up; thousands of individuals lost heavily.

The other influence destabilizing the government was the rising level of unemployment. By late 1988 the unemployed numbered 137,000, just over 10% of the workforce, a rate almost as bad as during the depression of the 1930s. Many people, including some economists, began to say that 'Rogernomics' was not working or that its successes were not worth the pain since the country was no better off than before. There were loud demands that the experiment in economic purity should be abandoned.

Successes there had been. Inflation had been reduced to about 5% (and later even lower) for the first time in a decade. Douglas produced a surplus in the budget of 1987 for the first time in a generation. The trade deficit had fallen. The terms of trade had improved and the balance of payments remarkably so. But the unemployed remained to haunt the government.

The fanatical Douglas appeared determined to forge ahead with his policies regardless of immediate social consequences. Deep divisions appeared in the Cabinet and within the Labour Party, especially over the question of selling off state assets. The government proposed to sell NZ Steel, Petrocorp and some proportion of Air New Zealand. There was also talk of selling off the Post Office Bank and the Bank of New Zealand. The aim was to raise extra funds to pay off the huge government overseas debt, without raising taxes. About a fifth of government spending went to pay the interest on that debt.

A mirror-glass building in Day Street, Auckland. *NZ Herald*

Within the Labour Party and the caucus of MPs there was strong opposition to these sales from traditional Labour supporters, but the Minister for State-Owned Enterprises, Richard Prebble, seemed determined to press on with the sales whether the Party agreed or not.

The Prime Minister had indicated his wish to slow down the pace of 'Rogernomics', as he said, to have a 'breather' and to place more emphasis on social rather than economic goals. Douglas had announced a further 'package' of economic reforms, including a 'flat' tax of 23%, instead of the graduated tax on all incomes. The aim was to restore business confidence following the stock market crash. The Prime Minister unilaterally cancelled this 'package' early in 1988.

Later in the year there was a major public row between Lange and the other two ministers over the sale of public assets. The truculent Prebble publicly denounced the Prime Minister and was dismissed from office. Douglas then wrote an arrogant letter to his leader saying (italics added) that 'New Zealand is now a country led by a Government paralysed by *your* inability to work with *me*.' He publicly described the Prime Minister as 'acting irrationally'. He, too, was sacked out-of-hand and replaced by the more moderate David Caygill. Both Douglas and Prebble, who were regarded by the unemployed as the Forbes and Coates of the 1980s, had fallen, at least for the time being. It was the most spectacular Labour brawl since John A. Lee was expelled from the Party in 1940.

It was not yet over. A very old-fashioned looking New Labour Party tried to nibble at the trade union wing of the Labour Party, while a right-wing business club, inspired by Roger Douglas, campaigned for a continuance of his policies. For a time it appeared that the government might be undermined as Muldoon's had been. But further drama intervened. In early August 1989 the Labour caucus voted to replace the sacked ministers. After seven months in the political wilderness, Roger Douglas was re-elected to cabinet, though he was not be finance minister. The Prime Minister promptly resigned, saying that he had stopped 'what had seemed to be some relentless juggernaut of the New Right'. His successor was another lawyer, the rather dour Geoffrey Palmer, with Helen Clark, a former political scientist, as the first woman Deputy Prime Minister. All available political crystal balls were clouded, though public opinion polls showed the two main parties as close together.

The Lange-Douglas era was over, but it had left some spectacular legacies. The sale of state assets went ahead more or less as planned, so 'Rogernomics' was not quite abandoned. The Government sold, within a short period of time, a number of State-Owned Enterprises, including the Post Office Bank, the Development Finance Corporation, NZ Steel, Petrocorp, Air New Zealand and the Shipping Corporation and Petrocorp. This was the greatest turn-around in New Zealand's century-old tradition of stateism. An election was expected in late 1990. Whether the planned social benefits would by then be flowing from the economic restructuring remained to be seen.

Traditional New Zealand society was being shaken to its foundations, not least in education. The old Education Boards, which had run much of the education system for over a century, were abolished, and schools were to be managed by elected boards of trustees, with vastly more power than the old school committees.

Under the Lange Government there were equally dramatic changes in foreign and defence policies. Throughout 1985 there were frequent threats from American congressmen of trade sanctions against New Zealand if it persisted in banning nuclear ship visits. American admirals, too, were darkly indignant. It did not occur to many Americans that New Zealand's anti-nuclear policy was its declaration of independence.

In July the Greenpeace vessel, *Rainbow Warrior*, which was on its way to protest against French nuclear tests at Mururoa, was mined in the Waitemata harbour and a crew member was killed. A few days later two members of the French secret service were arrested and gaoled for this act of terrorism. Eventually the French government admitted that its agents were responsible.

The Greenpeace vessel *Rainbow Warrior* after its sabotage by French divers. *NZ Herald*

New Zealanders did not enjoy being bullied by the Americans and the French, their former allies in war and peace. Nor did they like being told that they had to remain under a nuclear umbrella. Public opinion polls showed that the majority of people supported the government's policy. However, over 70% of the people polled also wanted their country to remain in the ANZUS alliance. This was a package that the government could not deliver.

Parliament passed legislation banning nuclear ship visits. The Government signed the South Pacific Nuclear Free Zone Treaty, as did most member states of the Pacific Forum. The USA unilaterally pushed New Zealand out of ANZUS. This caused problems over access to intelligence, but few New Zealanders seemed to be worried. In 1985 no country seemed likely to threaten New Zealand except its friends.

A new defence strategy now came to be necessary to fit new circumstances. It seemed most unlikely that New Zealand would again send armed forces to distant wars. The servicemen stationed in Singapore were gradually brought home. So, for the first time in over thirty years, there were no New Zealand forces stationed abroad except for a few UN observers in the Middle East.

Helen Clark, Deputy Prime Minister, and Geoffrey Palmer, Prime Minister, after their appointment in August 1989. *NZ Herald*

A new 'fire brigade' army unit, the Ready Reaction Force of a battalion kept at a high state of readiness was formed. It was to be capable of rapid action, for instance against terrorists or hijackers. But the action was to be in the South Pacific, where New Zealand had responsibilities to Tokelau, Niue and the Cook Islands. The navy was to acquire two or more Australian-built frigates, capable of steaming the vast distances of the Pacific. The focus of defence planning was now to be upon the South Pacific, Australian and New Zealand region, including Papua New Guinea. There was to be much closer defence co-operation with Australia.

Recent years have been marked not only by rapid political and economic change but also by striking social changes. Probably the greatest of these has been in the position and roles of women, changes spearheaded by the women's liberation movement.

The women's franchise movement of the 1890s had been strikingly successful, but many women felt that that victory had not been followed up. They felt that there was a wide gap between the idealized roles assigned to women and the reality of their lives. A new women's movement was required. There had been other women's movements since 1893, for instance the Working Women's Movement of the 1930s.

The United Women's Convention, 1975. *NZ Herald*

The Council for Equal Pay and Opportunity was set up in 1957. Equal pay in the public service was achieved in 1960. In 1972 an Equal Pay Act forbade discrimination in wages on the basis of gender.

The 'women's libbers' appeared in the 1970s. By 1971 there were six Women's Liberation groups in the country. They held their first national conference in 1972. Many women, liberal feminists, however, could not stand the tactics of some of the early activists. De-sexing bars and burning bras were not activities to everyone's taste. The liberal feminists launched the National Organisation of Women in the same year. A year later many women's groups met at the first United Women's Convention.

Despite high ideals, women proved to be no more united by gender than men. By the mid-1970s there were deep divisions between radicals and liberals, especially radical lesbians and heterosexual feminists. Born-again Christians fiercely attacked the radical feminists over their support for abortion, which became one of the most contentious issues in the country, and one difficult to resolve.

Some of the goals of the feminists were, if not impracticable, not politically possible, in New Zealand or perhaps anywhere else. The Wellington Women's Liberation Movement demanded free, twenty-four hour community-controlled child-care centres, financed by the government, because women should not be expected to have the sole responsibility for the care of children. There was much female resentment about 'unwaged work'. In 1988 a Royal Commission on Social Policy at least raised the possibility of a 'carer's wage' for people looking after dependents at home. The Domestic Purposes Benefit already provided for solo Mums or Dads, but not for married people who do the same job.

Although the women's movement declined, it had achieved, or contributed to some significant changes. Certainly it had raised women's self-awareness; many men had become aware of male chauvinist and other attitudes towards women previously scarcely questioned. Women had achieved a new prominence in public life. For a century they had been to the forefront in literature and other arts, but now they achieved a major role in politics. In 1987 there were fourteen women MPs. Dame Cath Tizard, Marilyn Waring, Dame Anne Hercus, Margaret Wilson, Helen Clark and many others played significant leadership roles in the 1980s. Dame Cath became the first woman Governor-General in 1990, after serving as Mayor of Auckland for several years.

The biggest change of all, the greatest social change since the Māori migration to the cities thirty years before, was the importance of women in the work-force. In the 1950s women made up only 23% of the full-time work-force; by 1981 they were 46% and formed the bulk of the part-time work-force. Married women outnumbered the 'never married' in the work-force. The Commission on Social Policy observed, 'The reality is that the majority of women are now primarily members of the paid workforce, who take time out for child-bearing and rearing . . . rather than unpaid house-hold workers who take on paid work from time to time.'

Women are still concentrated in a limited number of occupations, such as clerical work, nursing, waitressing, teaching, and as shop assistants, jobs often with no training, career structures and traditionally lowly paid. As a result equal pay has not worked: on average, women earned only about 80% of male income.

The gender differences in the distribution of the work-force is not rational but traditional. Why a qualified nurse should earn less than a wharf labourer is not obvious. Women now demand 'equal pay for work of equal value', or 'equal pay for work of comparable worth'. While the determination of equality is difficult, it is not impossible.

There is evidence that many women no longer accept the roles traditionally assigned to them in the work-force. There are now numerous women studying in the university law schools and medical schools. Large numbers of older women now attend university, gaining the higher educational qualifications they have missed earlier. The social consequences of women staying in the work-force have been immense, notably in the effects on the family. For instance, often there is no mother at home to greet the returning school child. Changes in attitudes towards marriage mean that there are now large numbers of solo Mums and some solo Dads.

Another change which has affected families has been a steady decline in the fertility of women until, in the 1980s, it was not high enough, or barely high enough, to replace the existing population. The fertility of Māori women declined later than

Canoeing champions Paul MacDonald and Ian Ferguson at the Seoul Olympics in 1988. *NZ Herald*

that of Pākehā, but by the late eighties it was only a point higher than that of Pākehā.

Some other kinds of change must be noted, those in the intellectual and artistic life of the people, in what is sometimes called 'high culture' as opposed to popular culture, or their daily customs. As the colonial people became a nation, both their life-style and their mind-style became more distinct. But never quite distinct, as Māori culture was in the eighteenth century. Because of jet travel, radio, television, fax and other communications, becoming different has become more difficult. Although geographically isolated, New Zealanders live in an increasingly international world.

Probably the biggest advance in literature has been in the novel. Numerous novels are published and a number of novelists have achieved international reputations, notably Janet Frame, Keri Hulme and Sylvia Ashton-Warner, Maurice Gee, Maurice Shadbolt and C.K. Stead. Janet Frame won the Commonwealth Writers Prize for Fiction in 1989.

The poets are legion, many of them women, many of them 'modernists' or 'post-modernist', but it is difficult, at least for the present writer, to discover rivals to the poets of the 1940s and 1950s, such as James K. Baxter, or Allen Curnow and Kendrick Smithyman, both of whom have continued to write outstanding poems. Allen Curnow

Janet Frame. *NZ Herald*

won the Commonwealth Poetry Prize in 1989 and in that year became the first non-resident of the U.K. to be awarded the Queen's Gold Medal for poetry. Much of the new poetry is academic, smart, witty, chilly.

Writers are now greatly encouraged and supported by numerous prizes and sponsorships, especially the Goodman Fielder Wattie awards and the national Book Awards.

There have been brave but usually fleeting attempts at professional theatre — the population is too small to sustain a substantial permanent theatre. But there has been home-grown theatre and also playwrights, like Roger Hall and Greg McGee. There have also been very successful modern dance groups, notably Limbs.

Painting has become increasingly international, more sophisticated and professional. There are now numerous private galleries in a number of towns and cities as well as an 'up-market' art journal, *Art New Zealand*. It should be added that there has been a re-birth of traditional Māori arts, notably carving and weaving. An excellent example is the whare whakairo (carved meeting-house) at the University of

Auckland, the driving-force of which was the master carver, Paaki Harrison and his wife, Hinemoa.

There have also been notable advances in some European crafts. Pottery is very popular and the potters have established a quite excellent local tradition. Locally made glassware is also excellent.

In the late 1980s New Zealand was a country inhabited by 70 million sheep, 4.7 million cattle and 3.3 million people, a very small population for a country larger than Great Britain. Most of the people lived in the North Island. There were only 865,000 in the South Island, scarcely more than in the largest urban area, Auckland. Most people lived in towns and cities — 2.7 million people, as compared with 513,000 in the country. There were over 400,000 Māori, virtually all partly European in descent, and 97,000 Pacific Island Polynesians.

The landscape had seen great changes in the 1970s and 1980s. Deer farming for venison, and then goat farming for the production of mohair, had added variety to the rural scene. Even more so had the great expansion of horticulture. In some districts, notably the Bay of Plenty, dairy farms had been replaced by large areas of kiwifruit vines. This fruit, once called the Chinese gooseberry, was the main horticultural export.

The urban landscape was rapidly changing too. In the main cities so many glass-sided buildings had been erected that the term 'mirror city' had come into use. They were inward-looking, less human, less populated. More and more the population went shopping, not in the city centre but in great shopping malls erected in the suburbs. Thus the population could be more accurately described as suburban, not urban. It may be said that the New Zealand cities had lost their individual character and had come to look like any other cities, in a graceless international style.

Hence it might be said 'that the real' New Zealand, the distinctive New Zealand, is still rural; that it exists in the incomparably varied and beautiful land forms — forests, lakes, beaches and mountains that have existed for millions of years, when no one lived here at all.

Further Reading

General

Bassett, Judith, Keith Sinclair, and Marcia Stenson. *The Story of New Zealand*. Auckland, 1985.

Bunkle, Philida and Beryl Hughes. *Women in New Zealand Society*. Sydney, 1980.

Brookes, Barbara, Charlotte Macdonald, and Margaret Tennant. *Women in New Zealand. Essays on European Women in New Zealand*. Wellington, 1986.

Eldred-Grigg, Stevan. *A New History of Canterbury*. Dunedin, 1982.

Hawke, G.R. *The Making of New Zealand*. Cambridge, 1985.

Oliver, W.H. with B.R. Williams (eds.) *The Oxford History of New Zealand*. Wellington and Oxford, 1981.

Olssen, Erik. *A History of Otago*. Dunedin, 1984.

Sinclair, Keith. *A History of New Zealand*. Auckland, 1988 ed.

Chapter One

Bellwood, Peter. *The Polynesians: Prehistory of an Island People*. London, 1987.

Best, Elsdon. *The Maori*. Wellington, 1924.

Biggs, Bruce. 'Maori myths and traditions' in *An Encyclopaedia of New Zealand* (vol.2) pp. 447-454. Wellington, 1966.

Davidson, Janet. *The Prehistory of New Zealand*. Auckland, 1984.

Firth, Raymond. *Economics of the New Zealand Maori*. Wellington, 1929.

Hiroa, Te Rangi (Sir Peter Buck). *The Coming of the Maori*. Wellington, 1949.

Houghton, Philip. *The First New Zealanders*. Auckland, 1980.

Stevens, Graeme, Matt McGlone and Beverley McCullough, *Prehistoric New Zealand*. Auckland, 1988.

Chapter Two

Adams, Peter. *Fatal necessity: British Intervention in New Zealand, 1830-1847*. Auckland, 1977.

Binney, Judith. *The Legacy of Guilt: A Life of Thomas Kendall*. Auckland, 1968.

Colenso, William. *The Authentic and Genuine History of the Signing of the Treaty of Waitangi*. Wellington, 1890; (reprinted Christchurch, 1971).

Cook, James. *The Journals of Captain James Cook on his Voyages of Discovery*. Ed.

J.C. Beaglehole. 4 vols in 5. Cambridge, 1955-1974.

Cruise, Richard A. *Journal of a Ten Months' Residence in New Zealand*. London, 1823 (2nd ed., 1824, reprinted Christchurch, 1974).

Earle, Augustus. *A Narrative of a Nine Months'* Residence in New Zealand, in 1827 . . . London, 1832, (reissued as *Narrative of a Residence in New Zealand* . . . Ed. E.H. McCormick. Oxford, 1966).

Facsimiles of the Declaration of Independence and the Treaty of Waitangi. Wellington, 1877 (reprinted 1976).

Howe, K.R. *Race Relations: Australia and New Zealand: A Comparative Survey*. Wellington, 1977.

McNab, Robert, ed. *Historical Records of New Zealand*. 2 vols. Wellington, 1908-1914 (reprinted 1973).

McNab, Robert. *The Old Whaling Days: A History of Southern New Zealand from 1830 to 1840*. Christchurch, 1913 (reprinted Auckland, 1975).

Marsden, Samuel. *The Letters and Journals of Samuel Marsden*. Ed. J.R. Elder. Dunedin, 1932.

Nicholas, John L. *Narrative of a Voyage to New Zealand, Performed in the Years 1814 and 1815*. 2 vols. London, 1817.

Orange, Claudia. *The Treaty of Waitangi*. Wellington, 1987.

Owens, J.M.R. *Prophets in the Wilderness: The Wesleyan Mission to New Zealand, 1819-27*. Auckland, 1974.

Polack, J.S. *New Zealand: Being a Narrative of Travels and Adventures During a Residence in that Country Between the Years 1831 and 1837*. 2 vols. London, 1838 (reprinted Christchurch, 1974).

Williams, Henry. *The Early Journals of Henry Williams, 1826-40*. Ed. L.M. Rogers. Christchurch, 1961.

Wilson, Ormond. *From Hongi Hika to Hone Heke: A Quarter Century of Upheaval*, Dunedin, 1985.

Wright, Harrison. *New Zealand 1769-1840: Early Years of Western Contact*. Cambridge, Mass., 1959.

Chapter Three

Allan, Ruth. *Nelson: a History of Early Settlement*. Wellington, 1965.

Brown, Gordon H. *Visions of New Zealand: Artists in a New Land*. Auckland, 1988.

Burns, Patricia. *Fatal Success: A History of the New Zealand Company*. Auckland, 1989.

Docking, Gil. *Two Hundred Years of New Zealand Painting*. Wellington, 1971.

Drummond, Alison and L.R. Drummond. *At Home in New Zealand: An Illustrated History of Everyday Things Before 1865*. Auckland, 1967.

Easdale, Nola. *Kairuri — the Measurer of the Land*. Wellington 1988.

Ebbett, Eve. *In True Colonial Fashion: A Lively Look at what Colonials Wore*. Wellington, 1977.

Godley, John R. ed. *Letters from Early New Zealand by Charlotte Godley 1850-*

1853. Christchurch, 1951.

Hankin, Cherry. *Life in a Young Colony: Selections from Early New Zealand Writing*. Christchurch, 1981.

Knight, Hardwicke. *Photography in New Zealand: a Social and Technical History*. Dunedin, 1971.

Leys, T.W. (ed.) *Brett's Colonist's Guide and Cyclopaedia of useful Knowledge*. Auckland, 1883 (reprint, Christchurch, 1980).

Macgregor, Miriam. *Petticoat Pioneers: North Island Women of the Colonial Era*. 2 vols. Wellington 1973, 1975.

McLintock, A.H. *Crown Colony Government in New Zealand*. Wellington, 1958.

Maddock, Shirley. *A Pictorial History of New Zealand*. Auckland, 1988.

Main, William. *Wellington Through a Victorian Lens*. Wellington, 1972.

Main, William. *Auckland Through a Victorian Lens*. Wellington, 1977.

Main, William. *Maori in Focus*. Wellington, 1976.

New Zealand Historic Places Trust (Frances Porter ed.) *Historic Buildings of New Zealand: North Island*. Auckland, 1979.

Historic Buildings of New Zealand: South Island. Auckland, 1983.

Platts, Una. *The Lively Capital: Auckland 1840–1865*. Christchurch, 1971.

Richardson, Len and W.David McIntyre (eds.) *Provincial Perspectives: Essays in Honour of W.J. Gardner*. Christchurch, 1980.

Scott, Dick. *Inheritors of a Dream: A Pictorial History of New Zealand*. Auckland 1962.

Sinclair, Keith and Wendy Harrex. *Looking Back: a Photographic History of New Zealand*. Wellington, 1978.

Stacpoole, John. *Colonial Architecture in New Zealand*. Wellington, 1976.

Stone, R.C.J. *Young Logan Campbell*. Auckland, 1982.

Temple, Philip. *New Zealand Explorers: Great Journeys of Discovery*. Christchurch 1985.

Thornton, Geoffrey. *New Zealand's Industrial Heritage*. Wellington, 1982.

Woodward, Joan. *A Canterbury Album: Collodion Photography in Canterbury 1857–1880*. Lincoln, 1987.

Chapter Four

Belich, James. *The New Zealand Wars and the Victorian Interpretation of Racial Conflict*, Auckland 1986.

Belich, James. *'I Shall Not Die': Titokowaru's War*, Wellington, 1989.

Clark, Paul. *Hauhau: The Pai Marire Search for Maori Identity*, Auckland, 1975.

Cowan, James. *The New Zealand Wars: A History of the Maori Campaigns and the Pioneering Period*. 2 vols. Wellington, 1922-3.

Gorst, John. *The Maori King*, ed. Keith Sinclair, Hamilton and London, 1959.

Grover, Ray. *Cork of War: Ngati Toa and the British Mission; an Historical Narrative*, Dunedin, 1982.

Hill, Richard. *Policing the Colonial Frontier: The Theory and Practice of Coercive Social and Racial Control in New Zealand, 1767-1867* Wellington, 1986.

Mikaere, Buddy. *Te Maiharoa and the Promised Land*, Auckland, 1988.

Parsonson, Ann. 'The Pursuit of Mana', in Oliver and Williams (eds.), *The Oxford History of New Zealand*, 1981.

Rutherford, J. *Sir George Grey*, London, 1961.

Sinclair, Keith. *The Origins of the Maori Wars*, Wellington, 1957.

Sorrenson, M. P. K. 'The Maori King Movement, 1858-1885', in Chapman and Sinclair (eds.) *Studies of a Small Democracy*.

Ward, Alan. 'The Origins of the Anglo-Maori Wars: A Reconsideration', *New Zealand Journal of History*, Vol. 1, No. 2 (1967).

Ward, Alan. *A Show of Justice. Racial 'Amalgamation' in Nineteenth Century New Zealand*, Auckland 1978.

Wards, Ian. *The Shadow of the Land. A Study of British Policy and Racial Conflict in New Zealand, 1832-1852*, Wellington, 1968.

Chapter Five

Arnold, Rollo. *The Farthest Promised Land: English Villagers, New Zealand Immigrants of the 1870s*. Wellington, 1981.

Bassett, Judith. *Sir Harry Atkinson 1831-1892*. Auckland, 1975.

Brookes, Barbara, Charlotte Macdonald, and Margaret Tennant (eds.) *Women in History: Essays on European Women in New Zealand*. Wellington, 1986.

Dalziel, Raewyn. *Julius Vogel: Business Politician*. Auckland, 1975.

Eldred-Grigg, Stevan. *A Southern Gentry: New Zealanders who Inheritied the Earth*. Wellington, 1980.

Fairburn, Miles. *The Ideal Society and its Enemies: The Foundations of Modern New Zealand Society 1850-1900*. Auckland, 1989.

Grimshaw, Patricia. *Women's Suffrage in New Zealand*. Auckland, 1972.

Morrell, W.P. *The Provincial System in New Zealand 1856-76*. London, 1932.

Ross, Angus. *New Zealand Aspirations in the Pacific in the Nineteenth Century*. Oxford, 1964.

Stone, R.C.J. *Makers of Fortune: A Colonial Business Community and its Fall*. Auckland, 1973.

Chapter Six

Burdon, R.M. *King Dick: a Biography of Richard John Seddon*. Christchurch, 1955.

Hamer, D.A. *The New Zealand Liberals: The Year of Power 1891-1912*. Auckland, 1988.

Holt, J. *Compulsory Arbitration in New Zealand: the First Forty Years*. Auckland, 1987.

Siegfried, A. *Democracy in New Zealand*. Wellington, 1982.

Sinclair, K. *William Pember Reeves, New Zealand Fabian*. Oxford, 1965.

Chapter Seven

Adas, Michael. *Prophets of Rebellion. Millenarian Protest Movements against the European Colonial Order*. Cambridge, 2nd ed. 1987.

Binney, Judith, Gillian Chaplin, Craig Wallace. *Mihaia: The Prophet Rua Kenana and his Community at Maungapohatu*. Auckland, 2nd ed. 1987.

Clark, Paul. *'Hauhau': The Pai Marire Search for Maori Identity*. Auckland, 1975.

Elsmore, Bronwyn. *Like Them That Dream: The Maori and the Old Testament*. Tauranga, 1985.

Elsmore, Bronwyn. *Mana from Heaven. A Century of Maori Prophets in New Zealand*. Tauranga, 1989.

Greenwood, William. *The Upraised Hand or The Spiritual Significance of the Rise of the Ringatu Faith*. Wellington, 3rd ed. 1980.

Henderson, J. McLeod. *Ratana: The Man, the Church, the Political Movement*. Wellington, 2nd ed. 1972.

Mikaere, Buddy. *Te Maiharoa and the Promised Land*. Auckland, 1988.

Misur, Gilda. 'From Prophet Cult to Established Church: The Case of the Ringatu Movement' in I.H. Kawharu, (ed.) *Conflict and Compromise: Essays on the Maori since Colonisation*. Wellington, 1975.

Ong, Walter. *Orality and Literacy: The Technologizing of the Word*. London, 1982.

Riseborough, Hazel. *Days of Darkness: Taranaki 1878-1884*. Wellington, 1989.

Scott, Dick. *Ask That Mountain: The Story of Parihaka*. Auckland, 1975.

Walzer, Michael. *Exodus and Revolution*. New York, 1985.

Webster, Peter. *Rua and the Maori Millennium*. Wellington, 1979.

Wilson, Ormond. *War in the Tussock. Te Kooti and the Battle at Te Porere*. Wellington, 1961.

Chapter Eight

Baker, P. *King and Country Call*. Auckland, 1988.

Burdon, R. M. *The New Dominion*. Wellington, 1965.

Chapman, R. M. *The Political Scene, 1919-1931*. Auckland, 1968.

Gustafson, B. *Labour's Path to Political Independence*. Auckland, 1980.

Olssen, E. *The Red Feds*. Auckland, 1988.

Sutch, W. B. *Poverty and Progress in New Zealand*. Wellington, 1969.

Chapter Nine

Bassett, Michael. *Confrontation '51: The 1951 Waterfront Dispute.* Wellington, 1972.

Burdon, R. M. *The New Dominion: A Social and Political History of New Zealand 1918-39.* Wellington, 1965.

Gustafson, Barry. *From the Cradle to the Grave: A Biography of Michael Joseph Savage.* Auckland, 1986.

Hanson, Elizabeth. *The Politics of Social Security: The 1939 Act and Some Later Developments.* Auckland, 1988.

O'Farrell, P.J. *Harry Holland: Militant Socialist.* Canberra, 1965.

Olssen, Erik. *John A. Lee.* Dunedin, 1977.

Simpson, Tony. *The Sugar Bag Years.* Wellington, 1974.

Sinclair, Keith. *Walter Nash.* Auckland, 1976.

Taylor, Nancy. *The New Zealand People at War: The Home Front.* 2 vols. Wellington, 1986.

Wood, F. L. W. *The New Zealand People at War: Political and External Affairs.* Wellington, 1958.

Chapter Ten

Baker, Paul. *King and Country Call.* Auckland, 1988.

Bennett, Bruce. *New Zealand's Moral Foreign Policy 1935–1939* Wellington, 1988.

Burdon, R. M. *The New Dominion.* London, 1965.

Condliffe, J. B. *New Zealand in the Making.* London, 1930.

Gustafson, Barry. *Labour's Path to Political Independence.* Auckland, 1980.

McGibbon, Ian. *Blue Water Rationale.* Wellington, 1981.

McIntosh, A.D. et al (eds.) *New Zealand in World Affairs,* v.1. Wellington, 1977.

McIntyre, W. David. *New Zealand Prepares for War.* Christchurch, 1988.

O'Farrell, P. J. *Harry Holland Millitant Socialist.* Canberra, 1964.

Siegfried, André. *Democracy in New Zealand.* Wellington, 1982.

Sinclair, Keith. *Walter Nash.* Auckland, 1976.

Sinclair, Keith. *A Destiny Apart.* Wellington, 1986.

Taylor, Nancy M. *The Home Front.* Wellington, 1986.

Wood, F. L. W. *The New Zealnd People at War. Political and External Affairs.* Wellington, 1958.

Chapter Eleven

Brown, G.H. *New Zealand Painting 1940-1960, Conformity and Dissension.* Wellington, 1981.

Brown, G. H., H. Keith. *An Introduction to New Zealand Painting.* Auckland, 1982.

Chapman, R.M. 'New Zealand Since the War: Politics and Society', *Landfall*, XVI.3 (1962), pp. 252-76.

Gould, J. *The Rake's Progress? The New Zealand Economy Since 1945.* Auckland 1983.

Gustafson, B. *Social Change and Party Reorganization: The New Zealand Labour Party Since 1945.* London, 1976.

Gustafson, B. *The First Fifty Years: The New Zealand National Party 1936-86.* Auckland, 1986.

Harre, J. *Maori and Pakeha. A Study of Mixed Marriages in New Zealand.* Wellington, 1966.

Henderson, J., K. Jackson, R. Kennaway. *Beyond New Zealand: The Foreign Policy of a Small State.* Auckland, 1980.

Hunn, J.K. *Report on Department of Maori Affairs with Statistical Supplement.* (Appendices to the Journals of the House of Representatives, G10, 1961).

Ingram, R. 'The politics of patriarchy. The response of capital and organised labour to the movement of women into the paid workforce in New Zealand', unpublished M.A. thesis, University of Auckland, 1988.

Jackson, M.P. & O'Sullivan, V. *The Oxford Book of New Zealand Writing Since 1945.* Auckland, 1983.

King, M. *After the War. New Zealand Since 1945.* Auckland, 1988.

McLaren, I. A. *Education in a Small Democracy: New Zealand.* London, 1974.

Metge, A. J. *A New Maori Migration.* London, 1964.

Schwimmer, E. *The Maori People in the Nineteen-Sixties.* Auckland, 1968.

Sinclair, K. *Walter Nash.* Auckland, 1976.

Smithyman, K. *A Way of Saying: A Study of New Zealand Poetry.* Auckland, 1965.

Vaughan, G. *Racial Issues in New Zealand.* Auckland, 1972.

Winston Rhodes, H. *New Zealand Fiction Since 1945: A Critical Survey of Recent Novels and Short Stories.* Dunedin, 1968.

Chapter Twelve

Alley, R. M. (ed.) *New Zealand and the Pacific.* Boulder, Colorado, 1984.

Boyd, Mary. *New Zealand and Decolonisation in the South Pacific.* Wellington, 1987.

Brown, Bruce (ed.) *New Zealand in the Pacific.* Wellington, 1970.

Chapman, Terry M. *The Decolonisation of Niue.* Wellington, 1976.

Crocombe, Ron and Ahmed Ali (eds.) *Foreign Forces in Pacific Politics.* Suva, 1982.

Hooper, Anthony et al (eds.) *Class and Culture in the South Pacific.* Auckland, 1987.

Larkin, T. C. (ed.) *New Zealand's External Relations.* Wellington, 1962.

Macdonald, Barrie. *In Pursuit of the Sacred Trust: Trusteeship and Independence in Nauru.* Wellington, 1988.

Pitt, David and Cluny Macpherson. *Emerging Pluralism: The Samoan Community in New Zealand.* Auckland, 1974.

Ross, Angus. *New Zealand's Aspirations in the Pacific in the Nineteenth Century.* Oxford, 1964.

Ross, Angus (ed.) *New Zealand's Record in the Pacific Islands in the Twentieth Century*. Auckland, 1969.

Spoonley, P. et al (eds.) *Tauiwi: Racism and Ethnicity in New Zealand*. Palmerston North, 1984.

Chapter Thirteen

Henderson, J.M. *Ratana: The Man, the Church, the Political Movement*. 2nd ed. Wellington, 1972.

Kawharu, I.H. (ed.) *Waitangi: Māori and Pākehā Perspectives of the Treaty of Waitangi*. Auckland, 1989.

King, M. *Te Puea: a biography*. Auckland, 1977.

King, M. *Whina: A Biography of Whina Cooper*. 1983.

Metge, J. *A New Maori Migration, Rural and Urban Relations in Northern New Zealand*. London, 1964.

Metge, J. *The Maoris of New Zealand*. 2nd ed. London, 1976.

Schwimmer, E. (ed.) *The Maori People in the Nineteen-Sixties*. London, 1968.

Sorrenson, M.P.K. *Integration or Identity: Cultural Interaction in New Zealand Since 1911*. Auckland, 1977.

Sorrenson, M.P.K. (ed.) *Na To Hoa Aroha: From Your Dear Friend: The Correspondence between Sir Apirana Ngata and Sir Peter Buck 1925-50*. 3 vols. 1986, 1987, 1988.

Sutherland, I.L.G. (ed.) *The Maori People Today*, Christchurch, 1940.

Walker, R. *Nga Tau Tohetohe: Years of Anger*. Auckland, 1987.

Williams, J. *Politics of the New Zealand Maori: Protest and Co-operation, 1891-1909*. Seattle, 1969.

Chapter Fourteen

Awatere, Donna. *Maori Sovereignty*. Auckland, 1984.

Dann, Christine. *Up From Under: Women and Liberation in New Zealand, 1870-1985*. Wellington, 1985.

Douglas, Roger, Louise Callan. *Toward Prosperity*. Auckland, 1987.

Easton, Brian. *Social Policy and the Welfare State in New Zealand*. Auckland, 1980.

Gould, John. *The Rake's Progress? The New Zealand Economy Since 1945*. Auckland, 1982.

James, Colin. *The Quiet Revolution: Turbulence and Transition in Contemporary New Zealand*. Wellington, 1986.

Jesson, Bruce, Allanah Ryan, Paul Spoonley. *Revival of the Right: New Zealand Politics in the 1980s*. Auckland, 1988.

Muldoon, Robert. *Muldoon*. Wellington, 1977.

Muldoon, Robert. *My Way*. Wellington, 1981.

Muldoon, Robert. *The New Zealand Economy: A Personal View*. Auckland, 1985.

Index

accident compensation, 288
Adcock, Fleur, 271
aged, old and poor, 112, 142-3
aggressiveness, 17
agriculture, 24-26, 280
Aikman, C.C., 304, 306-8
Airey, Willis, 263
Air New Zealand, 280, 366
air-raid drill, Devonport children, 225
Albrecht, Gretchen, 273
All Black rugby team, 234, 274, 290, 336, 356
Allen, Bugler William, 79
Allen, Sir James, 189
Amon, Chris, 274
Anaru, Tiweka, 333
Anglicans, 155
Angus, Rita, 220, 273
ANZUS Treaty, 282-3, 298, 356, 361, 367
apartheid, 290, 353
Apia, Samoa, 299, 302
Arawa canoe, 153
Arbitration Court, 135-6, 197
architecture, 231, 233, 365
Ariki, Matea Takau, 296
Arikirangi, 169
Art Gallery, National, 230
artists, 187, 220, 230, 269, 273-4
    performing, 269
arts, 122-3, 219, 270, 318, 335, 372
Arts Advisory Council, 270
Ashbridge, Bryan, 269
Ashton-Warner, Sylvia, 273, 371
Atkinson, Henry (Harry), 101-2, 109-12
Auckland, 108-9, 140-2, 200, 232, 259, 273, 358, 365
Austin, Ralph, 350
Australian, New Zealand and Malayan area (ANZAM), 298

Ballance, John, 110, 112, 125, 128
ballet, 269-70
Ballet, New Zealand, 270
Bambridge, William, 59
Bank of New Zealand, 231
Barker, Lady, 123
Bastion Point, 349, 351
Batten, Jean, 216-17

Baxter, James K., 271, 371
Beaglehole, J.C., 219, 230
Begg, Campbell, 216
Bell, Francis Dillon, 101
Belshaw, Horace, 305
Bennett, Fred, 327, 341
Binney, Don, 273
birds, introduced, 62
'Black Budget', 281-2
Bledisloe, Lord and Lady, 335
boarding houses, 200
Boulcott's Farm, attack on, 79
Bracken, Thomas, 123
Braithwaite, Errol, 271
Brasch, Charles, 270
Brickell, Barry, 273
British connection, 237-8, 242
Browne, Thomas Gore, 81, 88, 90
Buck, Sir Peter, 327-8, 330-3
burial grounds, Maori, sanctity of, 33
Busby, James, 38-46
bush burns, 69-70
business, 106-7, 238
butter quota, 249

Cambridge, 75
Cameron, General Duncan, 91-3
Campbell, Alistair, 271
Campion, Edith and Richard, 270
canoes, Maori, 2, 9-12, 23, 153
Canterbury Players, 270
cargo, refrigerated, 135
Carmichael, Lieutenant-Colonel of the Salvation Army, 181
Carr, Edwin, 270
Carroll, Sir James, 298, 328, 331
Carroll, Sir Turi, 344
carvings, 12, 373
Castle, Len, 273
Catholics, 155, 192
Caxton Press, 271
Caygill, David, 366
centennial, NZ, 229, 336
Charles, Bob, 274
children, 66-71, 144-5
China, government of recognized, 353
Christchurch, 108, 147, 210
Christianity, 78, 153
Church Missionary Society (CMS), 29-35

cities, 108, 140-2, 373
Citizens Association for Racial Equality (CARE), 290, 348
Clark, Helen, 366, 368, 370
Clark, Russell, 220
class differences, 60
climate, 61
coach traffic, 104-5
Coalition Government, 213, 248
Coates, Joseph Gordon, 189, 216, 222, 232, 247-9, 333
Cobb & Co., 104-5
Cobbe, John, 247
colleges, 122
Colonial Office, 42-3
Colony system, Crown, 55-6
Communist Party, 213, 215, 249, 252
composers, 270
conferences, on development, 286
confiscation of Maori land, 94, 97, 323
conscription, 199-200, 241, 250-1, 261
contraception, 118
Cook, Captain James, 20-4
Cook Islands, 296 *passim*
Cooper, Dame Whina, 341, 344, 349
Corner, F.H., 298
cottages (cob houses), 60-1
Couch, Ben, 350
Council for Equal Pay and Opportunity, 369
Cowley, Joy, 273
Cross, Ian, 272
Crump, Barry, 272
culture, 35, 122-3, 146, 230, 268-74
Curnow, Allen, 219-20, 228, 270-1, 371

dancers, 269
Dare, A.O., 306
Davidson, J.W., 304, 307
Davin, Dan, 271
Declaration of Independence of New Zealand, 40-3
defence policy, 223, 238, 366
Democratic Labour Party, 224
democratic society, 132-3
Department of Maori Affairs, *see* Maori Affairs Department

depression, 111, 130-1
Despard, Colonel Henry, 86
development, conferences on, 286
Development Finance
     Corporation, 366
diseases, 6-7, 31-2, 72-3
Doidge, Fred N., 262, 276
Douglas, Norman, 224
Douglas, Roger, 360-6
Downstage Theatre, Wellington,
     270
Duckworth, Marilyn, 273
du Fresne, Marion, 23
Duggan, Maurice, 271
Dunedin, 99, 106, 108, 133, 206
dwellings, weatherboard, 60

earthquakes, 61, 63
economic controls, 362
economic development and
     growth, 280-1
economic problems, 354-5
economic relations, external, 248-9
economy, performance of, 187
education, 67, 121-3, 205-7, 288,
     318, 335, 366
Edwards, Jim, 214-15
Eketahuna, 107
Elizabeth affair, 38
Elliott, Howard, 193-4, 201-3
Ellis, Robert, 273
Ellison, Edward Pohau, 332
Empire connection, 237-8, 240
Empire Games, 274
employees, government, 130
employers, organizations of, 137
employment, full, 232
Equal Pay Act 1972, 287
estates, 132-4
Europeans, 15, 52, 59-60, 78, 99-
     100, 144, 166, 300
Evans, Charlotte, 123
explorers, 59
export, 108-9, 246, 280, 285-6

Fairburn, A.R.D., 219, 270-1
family life, 111
farmers, 138-9, 185-6, 188, 190, 209
farm incomes, inequality of, 199
farm products, 108-9
farms, 'rehab.', 205
Federation of Labour (FOL), 197,
     276, 301
feminists, 369
Ferguson, Ian, 371
fiction, 371-2
Fiji, 1, 243, 296 *passim*
Film Unit, National, 230
financial market, 362
Finlay, Martyn, 231
fires, in towns, 73
FitzRoy, Robert, 77, 84-5
flax, 24, 27-8, 56, 137-8

flooding, 57
Fono of Faipule, 297
Forbes, George, 334
foreign policy, 263, 282, 366
foreign relations, 238, 259
'Four Quarters', 336-7
Fox, William, 102, 123
Frame, Janet, 270-2, 371-2
France, Ruth, 273
Fraser, Peter, 194, 231, 256-7, 261-
     3, 273-4, 302-4, 353
Freyberg, Sir Bernard, 273

galleries, art, 273
Gallipoli, 239-40, 331
gas, 281
Gee, Maurice, 272, 371
Geering, Lloyd, 292
General Assembly, bicameral, 54
Gilbert, Ruth, 271
Gilbert of Hokianga, Dick and
     Whina, 333
glassware, 373
Gleneagles Agreement, 356
Glover, Denis, 219, 232, 270
Gnatt, Poul, 270
gold, 56, 137
Goldie, Charles F., 123, 146
golf, 274
Gorst, John, 87
Gotz, Leon, 306
government, expansion of, 130
governors of New South Wales,
     37-9
Grafton, Auckland, 358
Grand Orange Lodge, 192
Grant, Alexander, 269
Greenpeace *Rainbow Warrior,*
     366-7
Gregory, Bruce, 350
Grey, Sir George, 55, 77, 84, 88,
     90, 94, 101, 110, 296
Gudgeon, Lieutenant-Colonel
     W.E., 300
gum, *see* kauri gum

Haahi o Te Wairua Tapu (Church
     of the Holy Ghost), 180
haka, 17
Halberg, Murray, 274
Hall, David, 230
Hall, John, 101-2, 111
Hall, Roger, 372
Halt All Racist Tours (HART),
     290, 348
Hanan, Ralph, 282, 342-3
Hanly, Patrick, 273
hapu, 76, 226-7, 324
Harris, Emily, 123
Harrison, Paaki and Hinemoa, 373
Hauhau faith (Pai Marire), 159
Hau'ofa, Epeli, 313
Hawke, Joe, 349

Hayden, Bill, 361
healers, 157
health, 72-3, 143-4, 330-1
Hei, Akenehi and Hamiora, 327
Heke, Hone, 82, 85, 156, 327, 331
Henare, James, 341
Henare, Tau, 333
Henry, Albert, 301, 308-9
Hepetipa, 179
Hercus, Dame Anne, 370
Hill, Alfred, 146
Hilliard, Noel, 271
historians, 230
Hobson, William, 42-8, 77
Hodgkins, Frances, 146, 187
Hokianga, 154, 174-5
Holcroft, Monte, 229
Holland, 287
Holland, Harry, 242, 247, 263
Holland, H.E., 196
Holland, Sidney, 232, 257, 275-9
Holloway, Phillip, 280
Holyoake, Keith Jacka, 267, 279-
     84, 290, 353
Home Guard, 228-9
home ownership, 205-9
horticulture, 373
hostility, 17
hotels, local, 65-6
Hotere, Ralph, 273
houses and housing, 222-3, 291,
     338, 340, 355
Hoyte, John, 123
Hulme, Denis, 274
Hulme, Keri, 371
Hunn Report, 342-3
Hursthouse, Charles, 172
Hyde, Robin, 219
hydroelectric power, 281, 287
hygiene, 72-3

Ihimaera, Witi, 272
illness, 72-3
immigrants and immigration, 98-9,
     104, 143-4, 196, 235, 243-4,
     290, 292, 314-18, 354-5
Imperial Conference, 245
imports, 238
income tax, 279
industries, 109, 137
inflation, 287-8, 357
Ingiki Potatau (King Potatau), 160
integration, racial, 289
intellectuals, 270
international relations, 250-1
intervention, government based on,
     358-9
investors, British, 238
Israelites, 167; *see also* Jews
iwi, land of, 324

Jackson, Rowena, 269
Japan in Pacific, 244-5

Jerusalem, Maungapohatu, 178-9
Jews (Tiu), 159-60, 162, 171, 184;
    see also Israelites
Johnson, Louis, 270-1
Jones, Bob, 359
Jones of the King Country, Pei Te
    Hurinui and Rotohiko, 333,
    344
Jordan, William, 223
Joseph, M.K., 271-2

Kaaro, Ani, 173-4
Kaikohe, 173
Kakahi, Tohu, 163
Kau, Paru, 172
kauri gum, 137-8
Kenana, Rua, 326, 332
Kennedy, John F., 292
Kereopa Te Rau, 162
kilikiti (village cricket), 319
King, Truby, 150
King Country, 93, 96, 326, 333
Kingitangi, 159, 163, 170, 173
Kingites, 91-3, 328
King Movement, 88, 90, 93, 96,
    326, 341
Kiribati, 310, 313
Kirk, Norman, 285, 290, 292, 352-5
Kohukohu, Hokianga, 28
Kolone, Va'ai, 316
Kotahitanga movement, 326-7; *see
    also* Treaty of Waitangi
kumara, 3-4
Kupe, captain of canoe, 2

labour, 134-8, 203
Labour Government
    (1935-1949) 220, 232-3, 247,
        250, 274-5, 337-8
    (1957-1960) 280-1, 341
    (1972-1975) 315, 321, 350
    (1984-1990) 319, 359
Labour Party, 136-7, 200-1, 203-5,
    231-3, 241-2, 244-5, 247,
    249-52, 259, 275-6, 281-2,
    285, 290-1, 294, 365
Lake, Harry, 282
Lake Manapouri, 287
Lake Wairarapa, 324
land, 108, 112, 132-4, 205, 207, 231
Land Court
Cook Islands, 300
    Native, 94, 96-7, 324
Land Girls, 227
Lange, David, 295, 355, 360
Larsen, C.H., 307
Latimer, Sir Graham, 344
law, 81-3
League of Nations, 250-1
Lee, John A., 219, 222-4
Legislative Council, 276
Leolofi, Tupua Tamasese, 302
Liberals, 125-31, 135-7, 151, 209,
    241

Lib-Labs, 136-7
Lilburn, Douglas, 270
Lindauer, Gottfried, 146
Liston, Bishop, 244
literacy, 34
Literary Fund, State, 230, 270
literature, 145-7, 270, 371
Lloyd, Thomas, 162
lock-out, Wellington waterside,
    198-9
looting, 212

Macandrew, James, 101, 110
MacDonald, Paul, 371
Mackay, Jessie, 146
Mackenzie, Thomas, 151-2
Mahupuku of Papawai, Tamahau,
    328
mana, 17, 34
Mander, Jane, 187
Maniapoto, Rewi, 87, 96, 170
Maning, Judge Frederick, 75-6
Mansfield, Katherine, 146, 187
manufacturing, 226, 232
Maori
    agricultural workers, 325
    ancestry and descent, 6, 11-14
    arts, 372
    Battalion, 226, 338-9
    candidates in electorates, 350
    carving, 373
    chiefs, 7, 10
    Council, 289-90, 343-4
    crime, 340-1
    culture, 35, 343
    descent, 289
    education, 335
    fieldwork at Paterangi, 92
    gangs, 346
    grievances, 348-9
    health, 330-2
    housing, 338, 340
    identity, 346
    independence, 97
    land, 80, 87-8, 94, 103, 165,
        323-4, 328, 332-4, 340, 343,
        348-9
    Land March, 348
    leadership, 341
    marriages, 289, 324
    mythology, 7
    painters, 274
    Pioneer Battalion, 331
    population, 289, 345
    protest, 350
    renaissance, 335, 346
    retailers, 80
    School of Arts and Crafts, 335
    seats in Parliament, 342, 350
    social condition, 324-6
    social security and, 338
    society, 24
    standard of living, 340

tribes, commercialized, 80-1
    Ngai Tahu, 96, 167, 351
    Ngai Te Rangi, 162, 333
    Ngapuhi, 76, 82-3, 85-6,
        155-6, 350
    Ngati Hao, 173-4
    Ngati Haua, 75, 90
    Ngati Kahungunu, 84, 177,
        324, 328-9
    Ngati Kinohaku, 13, 171
    Ngati Mahuta, 76
    Ngati Maniapoto, 12, 75,
        85, 170-2, 326
    Ngati Maru, 14, 168
    Ngati Matakore, 13
    Ngati Porou, 163, 329, 333
    Ngati Ranginui of
        Tauranga, 333
    Ngati Raukawa, 12, 180
    Ngati Raunui, 75, 164, 166
    Ngati Rereahu, 13, 173
    Ngati Toa, 82-4
    Ngati Tumata-kokiri, 21-3
    Ngati Whatua, 85, 349, 351
    Rangihoua, 155
    recruiting and, 226-7
    Tainui, 11, 326
    Taranaki, 159, 166, 180, 328
    Tuhoe, 335
    Waikato, 326, 328
    unemployed, 212
    unemployment, 340, 345
    urbanization of, 339
    urban migration, 347
    visionary leaders, 157
    women, 341
    Women's Welfare League, 289,
        344
    Young Maori Party, 326-8
    zone, 97
Maori Affairs Department, 338,
    341, 343, 347
Maori-Pakeha relations, 84-7
maps, 20, 22, 53-
markets, 280
Marquesas, 1-2
marriage, 66-74, 114-16, 118, 226,
    289, 324
Marsden, Ernest, 261
Marsh, Ngaio, 270
Marshall, John, 282
Marshall, Russell, 322
Marshall Plan aid, 260
Marumaru of Wanganui, Hoeroa,
    333
Mason, Bruce, 270
Mason, J.M., 330
Mason, R.A.K., 187-8, 219, 270
Massey, W.F., 151, 187-8, 195, 201-
    3, 205, 209, 241, 297
Massey House, Wellington, 233
Mata'afa, Fiame, 306
Mata'afa, Masiofo Fetaui, 307

Mata-hourua, 2
Matchitt, Para, 274
maternity, 143-4
Matete, Anaru, 163
Mauger, Ivan, 174
Mau in Samoa, 301-2
McCahon, Colin, 220, 273
McCormick, Eric, 229
McEwen, J.M., 307-8
McGee, Greg, 372
McIntyre, Donald, 269
McIntyre, Duncan, 343
McIntyre, Peter, 273
McLaren, Bruce, 274
McLaren, David, 136
McLean, Donald, 101
McLeod, Jenny, 270
Mea'ole, Tupua Tamasese, 304
meeting-house on Waipapa marae,
    12
Meleisea, Malama, 300
men, society dominated by, 114
Mercury Theatre, Auckland, 270
Mete, Hone, 175
Metekingi of Putiki, Takarangi,
    328
Middleton, O.E., 271
migrants and migration, South
    Pacific, 314-18; *see also*
    immigrants
militarism, 247
military action, 62, 64; *see also*
    warfare
military base, British, at Taranaki,
    97
military collaboration, 94-6
military involvement, 283
milking, 191
Milner, Ian, 219
miners, gold, 197; *see also* gold
miners and mining, coal, 57, 109,
    137, 197
misery, riots and, 215
mismanagement, economic, 190
missionaries, 19, 29-35, 78, 155, 307
Mitchell of Rotorua, Tai, 333
Morrieson, R.H., 272
motor-car and motor-cycle, 148-9,
    274
Motuhake, Mana, 350
Mrkusich, Milan, 273
Muldoon, Sir Robert, 355-61, 364
Mulgan, John, 219
Mulinu'u, Faumuina Fiame, 304
Munro, Donald, 270
muru, 17
Mururoa, French nuclear tests, 354
music, 146, 270

Nakahi (biblical serpent), 155
Nash, Walter, 221, 231, 251, 258,
    278-81, 290, 307
National Government

(1949-1957) 233-4, 262, 278
(1960-1972) 267, 282-3, 285-6,
    342
(1975-1984) 316, 350
National Parks, 287
National Party, 209, 252, 259, 275-
    6, 279, 358
Native Land Court, *see* Land
    Court, Native
Natzke, Oscar, 269
Nauru, 242, 297 *passim*
Naval Conference, Washington,
    245
naval vessels, American, 361
Nelson, O.F., 301
Nevill, G., 306
New Caledonia, 312
New Labour Party, 366
New Zealand
    as democratic society, 132-3
    Division, 227-8, 231
    flag of, 40
    flora of, 4
    forces (1941), 254-6
    international personality of,
        264
    island trade, 314
    Labour Party, *see* Labour
        Party
    land mass, 5
    Legion, 216
    map of, Cook's, 20
    overseas aid to Pacific Islands,
        320
    plant life of, 4
    Polynesian heritage, 295
    society, small scale, 203
New Zealand Forest Products, 281
New Zealand Party, 359-60
New Zealand Steel, 366
Ngata, Henare, 341
Ngata, Sir Apirana, 298, 327-37,
    341, 350
Ngatapa defeat, 96
Ngatoro-i-rangi, 153
Niue, 298 *passim*
niu poles, 159
Nordmeyer, Arnold, 280-1, 285,
    290
novelists and novels, 219, 270-1,
    371
nuclear ships, visits, 367
nuclear tests, French at Mururoa,
    354

Oceania, political decolonization
    of, 310
oil, 281
Oliver, W.H., 271
Olympic Games, 274, 356
Ombudsman, 293
Opera Company, New Zealand,
    270

Orakau, fieldworks at, 93
Orangemen, 192
Ormond, John, 101
Otahuhu, 253
Ottawa Economic Conference, 247
overseas market, Britain as, 238
overseas representation, 123
'overstayers', 315-17, 356

Pacific, *see* South Pacific
Pacific Advisory Councils, 318
Pacific Allied Council Inspires
    Faith and Ideals
    Concerning All
    (PACIFICA), 318
Pacific Islands, 295 *passim*
    aid from New Zealand, 320
    assimilation in, 298
    immigrants, 290
    Industrial Development
        Scheme (PIIDS), 314
    population, 290
    Producers' Association (PIPA),
        311
    remittances to households, 320
    states of, 354
Page, Evelyn, 273
Paikea, Paraire, 226, 341
Pai Marire or Hauhau faith, 159,
    162-3, 167-8, 172-3
painters and painting, 123, 270,
    272-4
Palmer, Geoffrey, 360, 366, 368
Pangari, Aporo (Apostle), Maria
    (Miriam) and Remana, 173-
    5
Papahurihia (Te Atua Wera), 154,
    158, 163, 175, 181
Papawai, 324
Papua New Guinea, 310-11
Paretahi, Mete Kingi, 95
Parewanui, 180
Parihaka community, 164-7, 172,
    180
Parker, Bill, 341
Parliament House, 106
party politics, 125-31
Pascoe, John, 230
Patara Te Raukatauri, 162
Paterangi, fieldworks at, 92
Pay As You Earn (PAYE), 279-80
peacemakers, prophets, 96
Pearson, Bill, 232, 272
Peebles, Donald, 273
pensions, old age, 142-3
Pere, Wi, 331
periodicals, 270
Perkins, Christopher, 220
Peters, Winston, 350
Petrocorp, 366
phosphates, 297-8, 310
photographers and photography,
    49-51, 54, 56, 58, 67-9, 107,
    230

pigs, 15, 17
pioneers, life of, 49-54, 69-74
Players, New Zealand, 270
Plishke, E.A., 231, 233
Plunket Society, 145, 150
poetry and poets, 123, 219, 229-30, 271, 371-2
police, riots and, 213-14
politics, 54-6, 65-6, 100-4, 112, 125-31, 187-91, 294
polling station, 151
polygamy, 33
Polynesians, 1 *passim*, 296 *passim*, 314-18
Pomare, Sir Maui, 298, 327-8, 330-1, 337
populations, 139-42, 289-92, 345
portraiture, 49-51, 54, 67-9
Post Office Bank, 366
post offices, 148
Potatau, King (Ingiki Potatau), 160
potatoes, 15-16
potters and pottery, 273, 373
Powles, Sir Guy R., 304-5
Prebble, Richard, 319, 365
Presbyterians, 292
Princes Street, Auckland, 141
privation, 56
profits, inequality of, 199
prohibitions, ritual, 17
prophets, 96, 159-65, 175
prosperity, 131
Protectors of Aborigines, 81
Protestant Political Association (PPA), 96, 192-5
Protestants, 155
protest movements, 191, 349
public works, 138, 143
publishing, 270
pubs, 117
Puketutu, battle at, 156
Pyke, Vincent, 123

Queen Elizabeth Arts Council, 270
Queen Street riot, 214
Quentin-Baxter, R.Q., 308
Quigley, Derek, 359

rabbit infestation, 62
race relations, 24, 289-90, 356
railways, 103-5
Rainbow Warrior, 366-7
Rakiriki, Mere, 180
Ranfurly, Lord, 296
rangatiratanga, 40-3
Rangawhenua, 173
Rangihau, John, 341
Rarotonga, 3
Rata, Matiu, 350
Ratana, 341
Ratana, Tahupotiki Wiremu, 180-1, 183-4, 326, 332
Ratana, (Haami) Tokouru, 337

Ratana church, 182, 221, 336
Ratana pa, 181
rating laws, 175
Raukura, Eria, 168, 179
raupatu (confiscation of land), 323
Rawlinson, Gloria, 271
rearmament, 261
Recruiting Office, Auckland, 236
Reed, A.H., 230
Reed, William J., 220
Reeves, Sir Paul, 351
Reeves, William Pember, 123, 128-9, 135-6, 145
Reform Party, 130, 151-2, 187-90, 194, 197, 201-3, 209, 241, 245 refrigeration, 131, 135
relief, camps and depots, 213, 218
religion and the church, 120
remittances, Pacific Islands, 320
Reserve Bank, 221, 360
Resident Magistrates, 81-2
resistance, non-violent and violent, 94, 96-7
Rex, Robert, 308-9
Richardson, John, 116-17
Richardson, Major-General G.S., 297, 300
Richmond, James, 123
rights, civil, 186-7, 202
Ringatu religion, 96, 168-73
riots, 213-15, 234
roads, 104, 148
'Rogernomics', 364, 366
Rolleston, William, 54-5, 101-2, 112
Romana Te Paehangi, 175
Rotoiti, 325
Rowling, Sir Wallace (Bill), 355
Rua Kenana Hepetipa, 177-82
Ruakura State Farm, Waikato, 227
Ruanui, Te Karakia o, 2
Ruatoki, 335
rugby football, 119, 353
Rugby Union, 290, 354, 356
rural areas, 108
rural scene, 373
Russell, Thomas, 102

sailors, Maori, 26
Samoa, *see* Western Samoa
Sargeson, Frank, 219, 270-2
Satchell, William, 146
Savage, Michael J. (Micky), 183, 197, 220-1, 250, 252-3, 353
schooling, 121-3, 204
Shultz, George, 361
seals, 24-5
Searancke, H.N., 332
SEATO, 283, 354, 356
security treaty with USA, 265
Seddon, Richard John (King Dick), 126-7, 136, 148, 150, 296

Selwyn, Bishop, 296
Semple, Robert (Bob), 151, 197, 221
servants, 115
settlers, 36, 59-60
Shadbolt, Maurice, 271, 371
Shand, Tom, 277, 282
Shelton, Norman, 282
Sheppard, Kate, 112-13
shipping and ships, 23, 25, 37-8, 123, 277
Shipping Corporation, 366
short stories, 271
Siegfried, André, 295
Sinclair, Keith, 271
singers, 269
slavery, 33
Smith, Kingsford, 216
Smither, Michael, 273
Smithyman, Kendrick, 271, 371
Snell, Peter, 274-5
social conflict, 209
Social Credit, 217, 278, 359
Social Democratic Party (SDP), 197
social hierarchy, 132
social realism, 219
social security, 223-5, 274, 338
Solomons, 310, 313
South Africa, 353, 356
South Pacific, 148
    Bureau of Economic Co-operation, 312
    Commission, 311
    Exclusive Economic Zones, 313
    Forum, 311 *passim*, 354
    market, 314
    naval powers, 244-5
    Nuclear Free Zone Treaty, 367
    Regional Trade and Economic Cooperation Agreement (SPARTECA), 312
    United States and security, 262, 265
    University of the (USP), 312
Soviet Union, 256, 260
sport, 274, 356
Springboks, 274, 356, 358
Stace, V.D., 305
State-Owned Enterprises, 365-6
Statute of Westminster, 262
Stead, C.K., 271-2, 371
Stevens, Edward, 102
St Heliers, The Parade, 268
Stitchbury, Peter, 273
Stout, Sir Robert, 111-12, 328
strife, civil, 191
strikes, 150-1, 198, 200, 277-8
Suda Bay, Crete, 255
Sullivan, Bill, 277
Sullivan, Timothy, 75, 97
superannuation, 355
Supplementary Minimum Prices (SMPs), 358

surburban sprawl, 268
surveyors, 59
Sutch, W.B., 229
Symonds Street, Auckland, 140
Symphony Orchestra, National,
    230, 270

taihoa (wait awhile), 298
Talboys, Brian, 282, 312
Tamaki, 291
Tamasese, Tupua Mea'ole, 306
Tamehana, Wiremu, 87
Tanumafili, Malietoa, 304
Taonui, Aperahama, 180-1
tapu, 17, 33
Taranaki, British military base, 97
Tasman, Abel Janszoon, 21-3
Tasman Empire Airways Ltd.
    (TEAL), 280
Tasman Pulp and Paper Company,
    281
Tate, Colonel R.W., 300
Tawhiao, King, 89, 164, 170-3, 181,
    183, 290, 300, 328
taxation, on dogs, 175
    income tax, 281, 363-4
    single (land), 112
Te Atua Wera (Papahurihia) (the
    Fiery God), 154-5
Te Aute, 326-7
Te Hau, Matiu, 341
Te Hikutu, 155
Te Hura, 157
Te Kanawa, Kiri, 269
Tekaumarua (the Twelve), 172
Te Kani a Takirau, Hirini, 163
Te Kohititanga o Te Marama (The
    Rising of the New Moon),
    177
Te Kooti Arikirangi Te Turuki, 96,
    168-73, 176-7, 179, 181, 183
Te Kotahitanga o Nga Tamariki o
    Te Aute, 327
Te Kumi, 181
television, 292-3
Te Mahuki Manukura, 171-2
Te Maiharoa, Hipa, 167
Te Makara, Wiremu, 175
Te Matakite o Aotearoa, 349
Te Matenga Tamati, 177
Te Miringa Te Kakara (house of
    learning), 173-4
tennis, 115
Te Popoto, 180-1
Te Puea, 332-4, 335, 341
Te Puna, 155
Te Ra Karepe, 173
Te Rangihaeata, 83-4
Te Rangitake, Wiremu Kingi
    (William King), 85, 88
Te Rauparaha, 83-4, 86
Te Ropu o te Rangatahu (the
    Young Maori Party), 327

Te Tiu (Jew) Tamihana, 162
Te Toiroa, 153
Te Ua Haumene Tuwhakararo,
    159-65, 167, 181, 184, 326
Te Whetu Marama, 181
Te Whiti o Rongomai, 165, 167,
    171-73, 175-76, 180-81, 183,
    326, 328
Te Wiata, Inia, 269
theatre, 146, 270, 372
thermal springs, 146
Thorn, James, 235
Tikaokao, Tawhana, 87
timber, 24, 27-9, 56, 138, 281
Tirikatene, E.T., 337, 341
Tirikatene-Sullivan, Whetu, 350
Titokowaru, Riwhe, 96, 164, 167
Tiu, *see* Israelites, Jews
Tizard, Dame Cath, 370
Tohu, 167, 175
tohunga, 33
Toia, Hone, 175-6
Tokanganui a Noho, 170
Tokelau, 298
Tombs, Harry, 230
Tomory, Peter, 273
Tongariro, 153
tourist industry, 146
towns, 107-8, 110
trade, 36
Trade Union Congress, 276
trade unions, *see* unions
transport, 71-2
travel, by air and by sea, 71-2, 280-
    1
Treaty of Waitangi, 43-8, 166, 323,
    326, 351
Treaty of Waitangi Kotahitanga
    (Unity) Movement, 174,
    181-2, 184
tribes; *see* Maori
Tuhoe, 177, 335
Tupaea, Hori, 162
Turanganui, 179
Turongo, 12
Tuvalu, 310
Tuwhare, Hone, 271
Twelve, the, 172

Unemployed Workers Movement
    (UWM), 213, 215, 217
unemployment, 111, 142, 210-18,
    222, 318, 340, 345, 358, 364
unions, 130, 135-8, 197-201, 215,
    232-3, 249, 276-7
United Federation of Labour, 197-
    9
United Kingdom, sphere of
    influence, 260
United Nations Organization, 257-
    8, 303 *passim*, 353
United Party, 190
United States, in the Pacific, 244-5,
    262

sphere of influence, 260
universities, 122, 288, 318, 341
University of the South Pacific
    (USP), 312
urban landscape, 373
utu (compensation), 17

Values Party, 359
Vanuatu, 310
vegetation of Pacific islands, 4
Victoria Street, Christchurch, 110
villages, 14-15, 107
violence, 23, 54-5, 94, 96-7, 356-8
V.J. Day celebrations, Auckland,
    259
Vogel, Sir Julius, 101-3, 109-11,
    296
Volkner, Carl, 162
Volunteer Service Abroad Inc.,
    320-1

wages, 286
Wahawaha, Paratene and Ropata,
    328
Waihi strike, 198
Waihou river, 173
Waikato, 12
Waima, Hokianga, 154, 175
Waitahuna, Otago, flax mill, 138
Waitangi, 45, 336
Waitangi, Treaty of, *see* Treaty of
    Waitangi
Waitangi Day ceremonies, 349-50
Waitangi Tribunal, 351
Walsh, Fintan Patrick, 260, 276
Walters, Gordon, 273
Ward, Sir Joseph, 129, 150-1, 190,
    192, 201, 209, 241
warfare, 17, 31, 61, 64; *see also*
    military action
    futility of, 247
    Korean War, 262
    Maori wars, 323
    Pacific campaign, 254-5
    Poverty Bay wars, 153, 168
    South African War, 147-8
    Taranaki War, 89-93
    Turanganui, civil war at, 163
    Vietnam War, 283-5, 353
    Waikato Wars, 90-1, 326
    war dance (hari), 17, 154
    Whanganui War, 162
    World War, First, 238-9
    World War, Second, 252-6,
        338-9
Waring, Marilyn, 370
waterfront dispute, 277-8
Waterhouse, George, 102
waterside disputes, 198-9
Waterside Worker's Union, 276-8
Watts, Jack, 279
Webb, Clifton, 306
Webb, Paddy, 197

Weeks, John, 273
Wellington, 106, 142, 198-9, 200
Westbrook, Eric, 273
Western Samoa, acquired by New
    Zealand, 242-3
    marines deployed in, 246
    Mulinu'u of, 297
Wetere, Koro, 351
Whaitiri, 177
Whakarua of Taranaki, Rima, 333
whales and whaling, 24-7
Whangamarino, Rotoiti, 325
Whanganui, 162
Whatihua, 12
wheat, 56
Whitaker, Frederick, 102, 111
White, A. Lois, 220
White, Robin, 273
Williams, Henry, 30, 43, 154
Williams, Yvette, 274
Wilson, Guthrie, 271
Wilson, Margaret, 370
Wilson, Ormond, 231
Winiata, Maharaia, 341
women
    in armed forces, 226
    athletes, 274
    in the church, 120
    contraception and, 118
    discriminated against, 286
    in domestic work, 118, 207
    educated, 121
    employment of, 116-17
    equal pay for, 287, 369
    exploitation of, 117
    in factories, 111, 116-18
    in family, 191
    farm training, 227
    fertility of, 370
    groups for, 369
    in home production, 115
    leisure of, 108
    Maori, 289, 341
    Maori Women's Welfare
        League, 344
    marrying, 118
    as matriarchs, 119
    as migrants, 114-20
    milking cows, 191
    moral changes and, 120
    movements, 368-71
    occupations of, 208
    organizations of, 287
    Pacific Islanders, 318
    pioneers, 59, 62, 64-74
    poets, 271
    as prophets, 173
    and pub life, 117
    as servants, 115
    and the sewing machine, 119
    unemployed, 211-12
    the vote and, 112-13, 149-51
    vote for, 149-51
    wages of, 116
    in Western Samoa, 300-1
    in the work force, 370
    writers, 272-3
Women's Christian Temperance
    Union, 112-13
Wong, Brent, 273
Wood, F.L.W., 230
wool, 56
Woollaston, Toss, 220, 273
workers, white-collar, 291
Wright, J.B., 307
writers and writing, 187, 219, 270,
    272, 372

Young Maori Party, 326-8